Childhood in Modern Europe

This invaluable introduction to the history of childhood in both Western and Eastern Europe between c.1700 and 2000 seeks to give a voice to children as well as adults. The work is divided into three parts, covering childhood in rural village societies during the eighteenth and nineteenth centuries; in the towns during the Industrial Revolution period (c.1750–1870); and in society generally during the late nineteenth and twentieth centuries. Each part has a succinct introduction to a number of key topics, such as conceptions of childhood, infant and child mortality, the material conditions of children, their cultural life, the welfare facilities available to them from charities and the state, and the balance of work and schooling. Combining a chronological with a thematic approach, this book will be of particular interest to students and academics in a number of disciplines, including History, Sociology, Anthropology, Geography, Literature and Education.

Colin Heywood is Professor Emeritus of Modern French History at the University of Nottingham and is currently the honorary president of the Children's History Society. He is a fellow of the Royal Historical Society and has served on the Committee of the Society for the History of Childhood and Youth. His previous books include *Childhood in Nineteenth-Century France: Work, Health and Education* (1988), and *Growing Up in France: From the Ancien Régime to the Third Republic* (2007).

New Approaches to European History

Series Editors

T. C. W. Blanning, *Sidney Sussex College, Cambridge*

Brendan Simms, *Peterhouse, Cambridge*

New Approaches to European History is an important textbook series, which provides concise but authoritative surveys of major themes and problems in European history since the Renaissance. Written at a level and length accessible to advanced school students and undergraduates, each book in the series addresses topics or themes that students of European history encounter daily: the series embraces both some of the more 'traditional' subjects of study and those cultural and social issues to which increasing numbers of school and college courses are devoted. A particular effort is made to consider the wider international implications of the subject under scrutiny.

To aid the student reader, scholarly apparatus and annotation is light, but each work has full supplementary bibliographies and notes for further reading: where appropriate, chronologies, maps, diagrams, and other illustrative material are also provided.

For a complete list of titles published in the series, please see: www.cambridge.org/newapproaches

Childhood in Modern Europe

Colin Heywood

University of Nottingham

CAMBRIDGE
UNIVERSITY PRESS

University Printing House, Cambridge CB2 8BS, United Kingdom

One Liberty Plaza, 20th Floor, New York, NY 10006, USA

477 Williamstown Road, Port Melbourne, VIC 3207, Australia

314–321, 3rd Floor, Plot 3, Splendor Forum, Jasola District Centre, New Delhi – 110025, India

79 Anson Road, #06–04/06, Singapore 079906

Cambridge University Press is part of the University of Cambridge.

It furthers the University's mission by disseminating knowledge in the pursuit of education, learning, and research at the highest international levels of excellence.

www.cambridge.org
Information on this title: www.cambridge.org/9780521866231
DOI: 10.1017/9781139046756

First published 2018

Printed in the United Kingdom by TJ International Ltd. Padstow Cornwall

A catalogue record for this publication is available from the British Library.

Library of Congress Cataloging-in-Publication Data
Names: Heywood, Colin, author.
Title: Childhood in Modern Europe / Colin Heywood, University of Nottingham.
Description: Cambridge ; New York : Cambridge University Press, 2018. | Series: New approaches to european history ; 56 | Includes bibliographical references and index.
Identifiers: LCCN 2018009865 | ISBN 9780521866231 (hardback) | ISBN 9780521685252 (paperback)
Subjects: LCSH: Children–Europe–History.
Classification: LCC HQ792.E8 H49 2018 | DDC 305.23094–dc23
LC record available at https://lccn.loc.gov/2018009865

ISBN 978-0-521-86623-1 Hardback
ISBN 978-0-521-68525-2 Paperback

Contents

Figures

Acknowledgements

I have acquired numerous debts while writing this book. First, to the staff at the University of Nottingham's library service, and in particular to the interlibrary loans section. Second, to the scholars who have given me advice on various points, especially Rosaria Franco, Louise Jackson, Nicola Pitchford (from Psychology), Liudmyla Sharipova and Catherine Davies; members of the seminar organised by Oxford University's Centre for the History of Childhood; and also to those who have read draft chapters: Sarah Badcock, Nick Baron, Harry Cocks, Sophie Heywood, Matthew Thomson and two very helpful anonymous readers. Third, I must thank my editor at Cambridge University Press, Michael Watson, for his unstinting support and patience in seeing the work through. Finally, I have appreciated the forbearance of my wife, Dr Olena Heywood, who commented on the whole script and encouraged a proper work–life balance with a warm and loving family.

Introduction

It was a long time before historians deigned to take an interest in children. If they were slow to pay much attention to the role of women in past societies, they were even more reluctant to pursue research on the young. As late as 1960, a general history of childhood had yet to be written. Historians were for long open to the jibe that they were only interested in kings and battles. They certainly devoted most of their resources to the study of a very adult and very masculine world, centred on such areas as high politics, diplomacy, warfare, major intellectual movements and trade union struggles. Children were largely invisible in the historical record. At best, they might manage a bit part as threats to law and order on the streets or as victims of exploitation and neglect by adults.

Studies of Childhood in the Social Sciences

From the late nineteenth until the middle of the twentieth century, the study of childhood was left largely in the hands of psychologists. They brought a wealth of new knowledge to the area, above all in the form of developmental psychology. A string of luminaries, including G. Stanley Hall, Alfred Binet, Arnold Gesell and Jean Piaget, contributed to the emergence of the 'developmental paradigm', a set of ideas that continues to exert an influence on society in Europe during the twenty-first century.[1] Parents, teachers and others involved with children have become familiar with the idea of the 'normal' child, and the numerous charts, record forms and IQ tests that scientists use to measure and classify children. The seemingly intuitive notion of 'development', in which a child passes through a sequence of stages, predictable from their age, is also deeply embedded in institutions such as the justice and welfare

---

[1] See, for example, Dennis Thompson, John D. Hogan and Philip M. Clark, *Developmental Psychology in Historical Perspective* (Oxford: Wiley-Blackwell, 2012).

systems as well as the schools.[2] Other social sciences joined history in generally ignoring children during this period.[3] According to a division of labour established during the 1880s and 1890s, 'The child belonged to Psychology, the family to Sociology, the tribe to Anthropology, and the school to Education'.[4] The Child Study Movement of the late nineteenth and early twentieth centuries, with its concern to understand the development of the child from birth to adolescence, gave psychologists the initial lead in this area. In so far as other disciplines took any interest in children it was to study their socialisation – that is to say, the process by which individuals acquire the knowledge, skills and values they need for integration into their society.

All this began to change during the 1960s and 1970s among academics, which brought an enormous upheaval in the study of children and childhood. The social and intellectual climate of the period favoured a questioning of established values. Rebellious youth, up in arms about such issues as the Vietnam War or the rigidities of the French educational system, helped to undermine respect for the existing authorities. Postmodernists posed a challenge to accepted ways of thinking in both the natural and the social sciences.[5] Historians played their part in rethinking approaches to the study of childhood: indeed, according to the sociologists Alan Prout and Allison James, 'it was perhaps from history that the opening moves were made' during this period.[6] The work of Philippe Ariès stood out during the early stages because of the huge impact it had on social scientists and historians. With his famous contention that 'in medieval society the idea of childhood did not exist', Ariès gave an early hint that other societies might think differently about childhood from the way we do in the West today.[7]

It was during these years in the late twentieth century that a number of developmental psychologists began to ask whether their efforts in

---

[2] This section is indebted to André Turmel, *A Historical Sociology of Childhood: Developmental Thinking, Categorization and Graphic Visualization* (Cambridge: Cambridge University Press, 2008).

[3] Heather Montgomery, *An Introduction to Childhood: Anthropological Perspectives on Children's Lives* (Oxford: Wiley-Blackwell, 2009), p. 5.

[4] Lloyd J. Borstelmann, 'Children before Psychology: Ideas about Children from Antiquity to the late 1800s', in Paul Mussen (ed.), *Handbook of Child Psychology* (New York, NY: Wiley, 1983), pp. 1–40 (p. 2).

[5] R. Murray Thomas, *Recent Theories of Human Development* (London: Sage, 2004), pp. 23–4, 195–205.

[6] Alan Prout and Allison James, 'A New Paradigm for the Sociology of Childhood? Provenance, Promise and Problems', in Allison James and Alan Prout (eds.), *Constructing and Reconstructing Childhood: Contemporary Issues in the Sociological Study of Childhood* (London: Falmer Press, 1990), pp. 7–34 (pp. 16–17).

[7] Philippe Ariès, *Centuries of Childhood* (Harmondsworth: Penguin, 1962), p. 125.

'sorting, grading and straightening children out' were not having the perverse effect of helping to prop up the *status quo*, with all its social, ethnic and gender inequalities.[8] There was the context of a general reaction against the tendency of behaviourism and psychoanalysis to reduce children to a passive role in their own upbringing. The 'cognitive revolution' of the 1960s saw the theories of Jean Piaget and Lev Vygotsky come to prominence. Although still concerned with identifying the stages of growth at the heart of developmentalism, they at least envisaged children engaging with their social and cultural environment as they matured.[9] No less importantly, there were calls to abandon any notion that a child would grow according to the same set of stages or sequences wherever it was raised. Cross-cultural studies of childrearing practices across the globe revealed considerable variation in the abilities and competencies expected of the child.[10] As the psychologist Rex Stainton Rogers put it in a critical essay, the maturation of a child had all too often appeared as 'a process that is "wired in" to the human organism, and which inexorably unfolds just as, say, green leaves turn to red and gold in the autumn, or tadpoles turn to frogs in the spring'.[11] A number of influential works insisted that developmental theories were firmly rooted in modern Western civilisation, and might not apply to other societies, particularly non-literate ones.[12] In the case of Piaget, for example, for all of his awareness of the influence of the social context on the child's development, he stands accused of taking as his ideal of adult cognitive competence a peculiarly Western philosophical one.[13]

[8] David Ingleby, 'Development in Social Context', in Martin Richards and Paul Light (eds.), *Children of Social Worlds: Development in a Social Context* (Cambridge: Polity Press, 1986), pp. 297–317 (pp. 298–9).

[9] Alan Slater, Ian Hocking and Jon Loose, 'Theories and Issues in Child Development', in Alan Slater and Gavin Bremner (eds.), *An Introduction to Developmental Psychology* (Malden, MA and Oxford: Blackwell, 2003), pp. 34–63 (p. 42).

[10] Allison James, 'From the Child's Point of View: Issues in the Social Construction of Childhood', and Robert A. LeVine, 'Child Psychology and Anthropology: An Environmental View', in Catherine Panter-Brick (ed.), *Biosocial Perspectives on Children* (Cambridge: Cambridge University Press, 1998), pp. 45–65 and 102–30, respectively.

[11] R. W. Stainton Rogers, 'World Children', in Karin Lesnik-Oberstein (ed.), *Children in Culture* (London, 1998), as cited by Turmel, *Historical Sociology*, p. 280.

[12] See, for example, Glenn H. Elder Jr., John Modell and Ross D. Parke (eds.), *Children in Time and Place: Developmental and Historical Insights* (Cambridge: Cambridge University Press, 1993); and Martin Woodhead, 'Child Development and the Development of Childhood', in Jens Qvortrup et al. (eds.), *The Palgrave Handbook of Childhood Studies* (Basingstoke: Palgrave Macmillan, 2009), pp. 46–61.

[13] David Archard, *Children: Rights and Childhood* (London: Routledge, 1993), p. 93, as cited in Chris Jenks, *Childhood* (2nd edn., London and New York: Routledge, 2005), pp. 21–2.

Anthropologists and sociologists were in their turn moved by these same upheavals to rethink their approach to the study of childhood. They began to adopt a child-centred approach in their research, recognising that children possessed agency and that children's understandings of their own lives and what was happening around them were to be taken seriously. There was therefore a call to 'give children a voice', granting that they should be treated as reliable informants. Thus anthropology experienced a 'noticeable shift' in this field during the 1970s, moving from relative neglect of children to a greater interest in their roles in society.[14] With a 'new paradigm', the sociology of childhood underwent an even fiercer reaction against its earlier preoccupation with 'developmentalism' and socialisation theory.[15] What this had amounted to, critics alleged, was finding ways to turn the child, an incomplete being variously described as immature, irrational and incompetent, into an adult, that is to say the complete article, mature, rational and competent.[16] This simple binary division both demeaned the child and flattered the adult. It suggested, according to revisionists, that children were a different order of beings to adults – 'human becomings' rather than full 'human beings'. It also implied that adults had a 'natural' right to exercise power over children.[17]

Historians and the 'New' Social Studies of Childhood

This revisionist approach, sometimes known from the 1990s as the 'new' social studies of childhood, affected both the cultural and social history of children. Following the usual convention among historians, the former involves a study of changing ideas about childhood in the past, the latter a focus on the lives of young people themselves. (This is not to lose sight of links between the two.) The history of childhood started in 1960 with *L'Enfant et la vie familial*, by Philippe Ariès. Ariès doubtless took his argument to its logical extreme, to the point of absurdity even, in asserting that medieval society had no idea of

[14] Montgomery, *Anthropological Perspectives*, pp. 43–8.
[15] Prout and James, 'New Paradigm'. For a European perspective, see Manuela du Bois-Reymond, Heinz Sünker and Heinz-Hermann Krüger, *Childhood in Europe: Approaches-Trends-Findings* (New York, NY: Peter Lang, 2001); and *Current Sociology*, 58 (2010), special issue on the Sociology of Childhood.
[16] Robert MacKay, 'Conceptions of Children and Models of Socialization', in Hans Peter Dreitzel (ed.), *Childhood and Socialization* (New York, NY: Macmillan, 1973), pp. 27–43 (pp. 27–8).
[17] Jens Qvortrup, 'Childhood Matters: An Introduction', in Jens Qvortrup et al. (eds.), *Childhood Matters: Social Theory, Practice and Politics* (Aldershot: Avebury, 1994), pp. 1–23 (pp. 3–4).

childhood. The work soon provoked a fierce counterblast from historians of the period, indignant that people from 'their' period were
considered incapable of recognising this stage of life. It also encouraged
researchers to explore representations of childhood in different periods
and places. It is now generally accepted that every culture has some
notion of infancy and childhood as stages in the life cycle, though how
they are subdivided according to age and the meanings attached to
them vary considerably.[18]

There exists a wealth of texts and images for researchers to consult in
this area, including works by famous philosophers, paintings depicting
the young, poems and novels conveying thoughts about them, and eventually photographs and films. There is also support in finding and interpreting these sources from studies in related disciplines such as art
history, theology and literary criticism.[19] The upshot is a varied and
well-documented array of conceptions, including the idealisation of a
'sweet and sacred childhood' during the later Middle Ages in Western
Europe; the 'filthy bundles of original sin' perceived by the more extreme
Puritans in sixteenth- and seventeenth-century England and the American colonies; the innocent child of nature associated with Jean-Jacques
Rousseau during the Enlightenment and the 'sexually knowing child' of
the late twentieth century.

In this respect, historians have often joined social scientists in considering childhood as a social construction. This involves grasping that,
in the words of social psychologist Arlene Skolnick, 'much of what we
tend to think of as obvious, natural, and universal about childhood may
actually be problematic, arbitrary, and shaped by historical and cultural
conditions'.[20] It has become clear that, as in the case of race and gender,
very different ideas can be constructed from the same biological starting
point. In the case of childhood, Nicholas Tucker argues that the small
size, early dependency on adults and constant growth of the young
provide the foundations. This biological immaturity of children is universal. From birth, however, the young have to adapt to the demands of
the society in which they live, creating the potential for as many variations
on childhood as there are societies.[21]

---

[18] LeVine, 'Child Psychology and Anthropology', p. 113.
[19] One might cite Anne Higonnet, *Pictures of Innocence*; Marcia Bunge, ed., *The Child in
   Christian Thought*; and Marilyn Brown, ed., *Picturing Children*.
[20] Arlene Skolnick, 'Introduction: Rethinking Childhood', in Arlene Skolnick (ed.),
   Rethinking Childhood: Perspectives on Development and Society (Boston, MA: Little,
   Brown, 1976), pp. 1–15 (p. 1).
[21] Nicholas Tucker, *What Is a Child?* (London: Fontana, 1977), p. 13.

This approach, for all its insights, leaves open awkward questions on the relationship between the biological and the social. A 'new wave' among sociologists in the twenty-first century has called for a reconsideration of some of the basic assumptions of the new social studies of childhood, suggesting that it is reaching its 'intellectual limits'. This includes cautioning against the dangers of 'social constructionism'. The tendency, according to Alan Prout, is 'to make the territory of the social as large as possible by winning as much as possible from biology, conceding to it, if at all possible, only a residue'. Rather than positing an opposition between culture and nature, he argues that they are 'mutually implicated with each other at every level'.[22] More specifically, playing down the material dimension to the study of the young risks ignoring the bodies of children, much in evidence when considering, for example, the history of their diet or their work in industry.[23] Finally, in stressing the vast potential for diversity in childhoods, the social constructionist approach obscures what is common to all children. For some purposes, it is useful to think of children as an age group in any society, with common interests that need to be considered in relation to those of adults and the elderly. Government policies, for example, may hinder or advance the welfare of children in a particular period.[24]

New Approaches to the History of Children

Researching the history of childhood has always been a relatively straightforward exercise, in so far as it can rely on material produced by adults. By contrast, writing a history of children, concerned with the experiences of the young in the past, has proved more challenging. Children have always found themselves excluded from positions of power: for all their numerical weight in society, they can be classified as a 'minority' group for this reason. And they have not left much in the way of written evidence behind them in archives and libraries. Hence it is all too easy to write a 'history of childhood' that leaves out the children. To move on, historians have had to join their colleagues from the social sciences in

[22] Alan Prout, *The Future of Childhood* (London: Routledge/Falmer, 2005), pp. 2–3, 54.
[23] Alan Prout, 'Childhood Bodies: Construction, Agency and Hybridity', in Alan Prout (ed.), *The Body, Childhood and Society* (New York, NY: Palgrave, 1999), pp. 1–18 (p. 1); idem, *Future of Childhood*, pp. 54–7; Martin Richards, 'The Meeting of Nature and Nurture and the Development of Children: Some Conclusions', in Panter-Brick, *Biosocial Perspectives*, pp. 130–46.
[24] This is a perspective adopted by Jens Qvortrup in *Childhood Matters*; see also Adrian L. James, 'Competition or Integration? The Next Step in Childhood Studies?', *Childhood*, 17 (2010), 485–99.

shaking off the legacy of the past, above all by questioning the emphasis among earlier generations of scholars on the development and socialisation of children. The crucial change in approach has required researchers to consider children worth studying in their own right, rather than merely as adults-in-the-making.[25] The 'new paradigm' has played down the differences and accentuated the similarities between children and adults, seeing them all as 'beings'. It has insisted that childhood and old age are essential components of 'personhood', breaking the monopoly of adulthood as a focus of scholarly interest. Moreover, it has encouraged scholars to question the legitimacy of the existing distribution of power and authority between adults and children. They have begun to ask whether adults did always act 'in the best interests of the child', as was so often claimed, and whether they sometimes took advantage of their position to exploit, abuse or silence the young.[26] Again, it should be added sociologists will now admit that some of the arguments put forward in the first flush of enthusiasm for the new social studies over-reached themselves. They have conceded that they underestimated the diversity of approaches within developmental psychology during its early stages and the way its ideas have evolved since. And they have reined back on the refusal to see children as 'becomings'. Nick Lee, for example, argues that from the seventeenth century onwards nation states began to take an interest in the size and quality of their population, encouraging them to invest in the future of their children. Efforts to preserve the lives of the young left them dependent on adults, creating the conditions for the 'becoming view of childhood': conditions that remained in place until the 'age of uncertainty' loomed during the 1970s. Indeed, children are surely best considered as both beings and becomings. As the anthropologist Heather Montgomery observes, 'Childhood is a time of transition and change, and despite the enormous variation in the ways in which childhood is understood, there is no society that does not acknowledge that children (however they are defined) are very different from adults, have different needs, and have different roles and expectations placed on them'.[27]

---

[25] Note that Patrick J. Ryan, in 'How New is the "New" Social Study of Childhood? The Myth of a Paradigm Shift', *Journal of Interdisciplinary History*, 38 (2008), 553–76, argues that the ideas touted as new by sociologists have deep roots in developmental psychology and historical studies.

[26] Prout and James, 'A New Paradigm'; and Turmel, *Historical Sociology*, ch. 1.

[27] Prout, *Future of Childhood*, p. 2; Nick Lee, *Childhood and Society: Growing Up in an Age of Uncertainty* (Buckingham: Open University Press, 2001), p. 7; Montgomery, *Anthropological Perspectives*, p. 9.

Historians have caught the *zeitgeist* in their own way by re-orientating their research in various directions. Firstly, they have widened the range of topics that interest them, beyond the experiences of the young in the family and the school. They have therefore considered the young in other roles, for example, as workers, as gang members, as hospital patients and as consumers. Some have also investigated the emotional life of children, reflecting current interest in the history of emotions generally, throwing light on such topics as parent–child relations and the way children learned how to express their feelings through their reading.[28] Secondly, historians have sought to avoid simple generalisations about children in the past, exploring the impact of such influences as class, gender and ethnicity in different historical contexts. Thirdly, historians have followed the mantra associated with the sociologist Leena Alanen that children should be seen as 'social actors in their own right'. This stems from the realisation among psychologists and sociologists that even young children can manage their social relations with considerable competence. Alanen in 2001 added the important gloss that 'children's powers (or lack of them)' need to be seen in their generational context; that is to say, their relationships with parents, schoolteachers, employers and fellow workers, among others.[29] In some circumstances, children have influence; in others, notably any level of government, virtually none. Moreover, as anthropologists have noted, one needs to recognise both agency and vulnerability when discussing children.[30] Overall, instead of depicting children solely as passive creatures, historians have brought the young to life by showing how they negotiate their role in such contexts as the family or the streets.

Attempting to give a voice to a 'muted group' such as children has proved particularly challenging for historians, because of the scarcity of

---

[28] Susan Broomhall (ed.), *Emotions in the Household, 1200–1900* (Basingstoke: Macmillan, 2008); Joanne Bailey, *Parenting in England 1760–1830: Emotion, Identity, and Generation* (Oxford: Oxford University Press, 2012); and Stephanie Olsen, *Juvenile Nation: Youth, Emotions and the Making of the Modern British Citizen* (London: Bloomsbury, 2014).

[29] Leena Alanen, 'Rethinking Childhood', *Acta Sociologica*, 31(1988), 53–67 (59–60); eadem, 'Explorations in Generational Analysis', in Leena Alanen and Berry Mayall (eds.), *Conceptualizing Child-Adult Relations* (London and New York: Routledge-Falmer, 2001), pp. 11–32 (p. 31); Allison James, 'Agency', in Qvortrup et al., *Handbook*, pp. 34–45.

[30] E. Kay, M. Tisdall and Samantha Punch, 'Not So New? Looking Critically at Childhood Studies', *Children's Geographies*, 10 (2012), 249–64 (255–6); Myra Bluebond-Langner and Jill E. Korbin, 'Challenges and Opportunities in the Anthropology of Childhoods', *American Anthropologist*, 109 (2007), 241–6 (242).

documentary evidence available.[31] However, they have exercised their ingenuity to look from the bottom up as well as from the top down. They have managed to glean information from conventional sources such as official reports and newspaper articles. They have also resorted to 'ego documents', defined as texts in which authors write about their own 'acts, thoughts and feelings'.[32] Letters and diaries written by children are rare, and often heavily influenced by adult expectations, but revealing when written by older children in particular.[33] More abundant are childhood reminiscences and autobiographies written by adults, and oral history projects tapping people's memories. This type of material was often scorned by historians in the past as the least reliable of the sources available to them, but if treated with the same caution as others, can yield interesting insights. There are certain well-rehearsed drawbacks to autobiographies as a source for the history of children. They are vulnerable to lapses in memory or deliberate distortion. They are in effect a literary form, requiring a creative effort to reconstruct the early years in a life. And those who write their own life stories are likely to be exceptional individuals. Nonetheless, they serve to put some flesh and blood on the bare bones of a historical narrative. Fortunately for present purposes, those written from around 1800 onwards tend to pay more attention to the childhood years of the author than their predecessors. They are also more likely to explore in some detail the author's private life, including its seamier side, following in the footsteps of Jean-Jacques Rousseau and his *Confessions* (1781). No less importantly, as a pioneer of the use of working-class autobiographies, the historian David Vincent observed, 'if we wish to understand the meaning of the past, we must first discover the meaning the past had for those who made it and were made by it'.[34]

---

[31] Charlotte Hardman, 'Can There Be an Anthropology of Children?', *Journal of the Anthropology Society of Oxford*, 4 (1973), 85–99 (85); Harry Hendrick, 'The Child as a Social Actor in Historical Sources: Problems of Identification and Interpretation', in Pia Christensen and Allison James (eds.), *Research with Children: Perspectives and Practices* (New York and London: Routledge, 2008), pp. 40–65.

[32] Rudolf Dekker, *Autobiography in Holland*, p. 12.

[33] See, for example, Emily C. Bruce, '"Every Word Shows How You Love Me": The Social Literacy Practice of Children's Letter Writing (1780–1860)', *Paedagogica Historica*, 50 (2014), 247–64; and Philippe Lejeune, *Le Moi des demoiselles: enquête sur le journal de jeune fille* (Paris: Seuil, 1993).

[34] David Vincent, *Bread, Knowledge and Freedom: A Study of Nineteenth-Century Working Class Autobiography* (London: Europa, 1981), p. 6. See also Richard N. Coe, *When the Grass Was Taller: Autobiography and the Experience of Childhood* (New Haven, CT: Yale University Press, 1984); Mary Jo Maynes, *Taking the Hard Road*; Dekker, *Autobiography in Holland*.

The Argument

This study takes issue with a tendency among historians of childhood to adopt a 'Whiggish' approach to their subject. That is to say, the end of the story is what is variously described as our 'modern', 'middle-class', 'privileged' or 'protected' childhood and adolescence, associated in Europe with the welfare state as it emerged in the twentieth century. Contemporary childhood does of course have much to recommend it, given the material progress and concern for children's rights evident in contemporary Europe. At the same time, it is common currency to perceive some sort of crisis among the young.[35] Critics of a long, protected childhood and adolescence have pointed to the risk of 'infantilising' young people by treating them as innocents. They doubt the benefits of excluding them from the world of work and politics, and the unreasonable expectation that they should be 'purer' than adults in their personal lives.[36] Already one can see, for example, a reluctant acceptance that children cannot remain 'innocent' in a highly sexualised society. It is clear, then, that change continues apace in Western society. There is also the growing awareness of the diversity of experiences among the young in the past. There were numerous paths through the early years, ranging from the aristocratic to the proletarian. Most have diverged to a greater or lesser extent from the protected childhood generally accepted today, in theory if not always in practice.[37] The challenge for the historian is to understand these paths in their own particular context and ponder what we may have lost as well as gained. The challenge, also, is to reconnect histories of childhood to wider histories of social, cultural, economic and political development, so that these latter are no longer 'merely' context.[38] To quote Martha Sexton, 'Our understandings of individual identity formation, the structure of the family, the relationship between the household and the state, as well

---

[35] See, for example, Barry Goldson, '"Childhood": An Introduction to Historical and Theoretical Analyses', in Phil Scraton (ed.), *Childhood' in Crisis?* (London: UCL Press, 1997), pp. 1–27 (pp. 19–20); and Sue Palmer, *Toxic Childhood: How the Modern World Is Damaging Our Children and What We Can Do About It* (London: Orion, 2006).

[36] Martin Hoyles, 'History and Politics', in Martin Hoyles (ed.), *Changing Childhood* (London: Writers and Readers Publishing Cooperative, 1979), pp. 1–14; Martin Killias, 'The Emergence of a New Taboo: The Desexualisation of Youth in Western Societies since 1800', *European Journal on Criminal Policy and Research*, 8 (2000), 459–77.

[37] Paula Fass 'Is There a Story in the History of Childhood?', in Paula Fass, *Childhood in the Western World*, pp. 1–14.

[38] I owe this point to Dr Nick Baron, of Nottingham University.

as a wealth of cultural and social institutions are significantly altered once we focus on the experiences of childhood and youth'.[39]

The Scope and Organisation of the Book

The work is framed by existing studies of childhood in the West, but its narrower focus in terms of period and place allows more detail on the social and cultural context for childhood and, of course, on modern Europe.[40] It takes a comparative approach, to bring out national and regional differences (as well as common features) across Europe, in a field dominated by studies of individual countries or of particular themes in the history of childhood. It therefore extends its geographical coverage south and east, to include the Mediterranean regions, Russia as far as the Urals, Western Europe and the Nordic countries. However, it must be admitted that the north-western part of Europe receives the most detailed coverage, partly because the historical literature is more abundant, and partly because it was countries such as Britain, France, Germany and Sweden that made much of the running in the changes that occurred.[41] What follows is also mainly concerned with developments within Europe, rather than with the place of European childhood in a global perspective. However, it would be unwise to ignore entirely interaction with the rest of the world, given the importance of such phenomena as the exchange of ideas with the United States, the imperial conquests of the European powers and mass migrationary movements (see Figure I.1).

As should be evident by now, modern definitions of childhood, heavily influenced by the school system, do not necessarily make much sense in the past. Adopting the current convention of describing those of primary-school age and below as children, and those of secondary-school age and above as young people, bears no relation to reality until the mass schooling of the late twentieth century came into existence. What is a child if it is not understood as an age category? One possibility is to follow people in pre-industrial Europe in ascribing status to a child according to its functions and experience: what he or she could manage when, say, helping their

---

[39] Martha Sexton, 'Introduction', to launch the *Journal of the History of Childhood and Youth*, 1 (2008), 1–3.
[40] Cf John Sommerville, *The Rise and Fall of Childhood* (Beverly Hills: Sage, 1982); Colin Heywood (ed.), *A Cultural History of Childhood and Family in the Age of Empire* (Oxford: Berg, 2010); Hugh Cunningham, *Children and Childhood in the West since 1500* (2nd edn., Harlow: Pearson Longman, 2005); Elizabeth Foyster and James Marten (eds.), *A Cultural History of Childhood and Family* (6 vols., Oxford and New York: Berg, 2010); Paula Fass (ed.), *The Routledge History of Childhood in the Western World* (Abingdon: Routledge, 2013).
[41] Peter N. Stearns, *Childhood in World History* (New York, NY: Routledge, 2016), p.14.

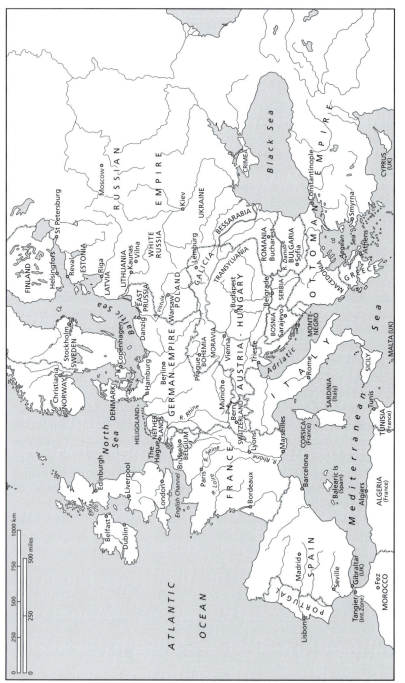

Figure I.1 Map of Europe in 1900.

parents around their farm or workshop. Moving on from what was thought of as child's work, for example, depended on the strength and skill of the individual rather than their age. Alternatively, one can focus on the relations between generations, and particularly the extent of dependence of children on their parents and other adults, where again age was not a significant marker.[42] Hence, there is no point in attempting to set down parameters for this study according to age. The focus of the work is on childhood and the transitionary period to youth/adolescence, with the generous (or aspirational) United Nations definition of a child from 1989 as anyone under eighteen years of age as a rough guide.

The main focus of the book runs from the early eighteenth century to the turn of the twenty-first century, following through its various themes according to their importance at particular periods. Part I considers village society, still predominant across Europe during the eighteenth and much of the nineteenth centuries. It provides the essential point of departure for all that follows. Part II shifts the focus to towns during this period, and the impact on the young from intellectual movements such as the Enlightenment and Romanticism, and of developments in the material world, notably the Industrial Revolution and the early phase of urbanisation. Finally, Part III begins around 1870 and considers childhood in an increasingly affluent society, concerned to protect its young people from some of the rigours of adult society, though falling short of its ideal for many of them.

A few key questions run like red threads through the work. In particular: How have ideas about childhood changed over the past three centuries in Europe? What have been the elements of continuity and of change in the experiences of young people during this period? How did notions of childhood and children's experiences diverge according to such influences as class, gender, religious belief and rural or urban location? And which influences from the surrounding societies have made the most impact on them? The overall aim in this survey is not to provide a comprehensive survey across Europe, hardly possible in the space available, but rather to give students of history a feel for the various approaches that have bubbled up from among the growing ranks of researchers in the area since the 1960s. Beyond that, the hope is that specialists in other disciplines will gain some insight into the type of evidence mustered by historians and the controversies that arise among them when they set about interpreting it.

---

[42] Virginia Morrow, 'What's in a Number? Unsettling the Boundaries of Age', *Childhood*, 20 (2013) 151–5; Alanen, 'Explorations in Generational Analysis', passim.

Part I

Childhood in Villages, Eighteenth and Nineteenth Centuries

Most children born in Europe at the beginning of the eighteenth century came from a peasant background. Around three-quarters of the male population was still employed in agriculture, though with variations across the continent: perhaps no more than 60 per cent in Britain, but up to 90 per cent in Russia.[1] Not all of those living in the countryside were employed full time in agriculture, but only a small minority were entirely detached from working the land. Moreover, although sooner or later trade and industry increased in importance, the agrarian sector continued to play a significant role in the various national economies during the nineteenth and early twentieth centuries. This was especially the case as one moved towards the southern and eastern parts of the continent. In 1910, for example, whereas in Western Europe agriculture accounted for only 30 per cent of the working population, in Eastern Europe the equivalent figure was still 80 per cent.[2] Yet historians of modern Europe have paid far less attention to young people in villages than to their urban counterparts: the tail has wagged the dog. An obvious starting point for this study therefore is an investigation of childhood in the farming communities of Europe.

[1] N. F. R. Crafts, *British Economic Growth during the Industrial Revolution* (Oxford: Clarendon Press, 1985), pp. 62–3, table 3.6; David Moon, *The Russian Peasantry, 1600–1930: The World the Peasants Made* (London: Longman, 1999), p. 21.
[2] Gerald Ambrosius and William H. Hubbard, *A Social and Economic History of Twentieth-Century Europe* (Cambridge, MA: Harvard University Press, 2003), p. 56.

1 Conceptions of Childhood in Rural Society

This chapter establishes the inheritance from early modern Europe concerning childhood, and its development in rural communities during the eighteenth and nineteenth centuries. More specifically, it investigates how villagers understood this early stage of life: the boundaries they established between age groups, their views on the nature of childhood and the significance they attached to it. It seeks to answer questions on how rural communities supported their members through the early stages of life, the influences on their ideas about young people and the diversity of experience across the continent.

Boundaries of Childhood in Villages

From Infancy to Childhood

By the age of two or three, when children were big enough to be able to play together, they no longer needed constant attention from their families, and could form a group of their own in society. From then until somewhere around the age of six or seven, children in the countryside enjoyed a relatively carefree existence. They played with others of their own age for much of the time, watched over by slightly older children and any adults who happened to be around. Once this early phase of early childhood was over, whether a boy or a girl, the young had to start helping around the home, the farm and the workshop. An official enquiry in Spain during the 1840s found that in response to a question on when children started work on the farms, the peasantry rarely gave an age. Instead, they replied with such expressions as at a 'tender age' or 'when they can manage'.[1] This important milestone in life was often marked for

[1] José María Borrás Llop, 'El Trabajo infantile en el mundo rural español (1849–1936). Género, edades y ocupaciones', in J. M. Martínez Carrión (ed.), *El Nivel de vida en la España rural, siglos XVII–XX* (Alicante: Universidad de Alicante, 2002), pp. 497–547 (p. 504).

17

a boy with a breeching ceremony, when he gave up the little gown worn by both sexes in infancy for a pair of breeches. Pierre-Jakez Hélias recalled in some detail his *fête du pantalonnage* in a peasant household in Brittany at the end of World War I. His parents laid on a special meal for a number of his close relatives, where he was paraded in his new brown trousers. 'They called me young man. And someone said: "Now he can go to school."' Hélias admitted having listened with a mixture of pride and anxiety. In the Netherlands, 'going into trousers' was celebrated as a symbol of the intellectual awakening and assumption of a masculine role by a son and heir.[2]

In fact, the majority of children from the families of peasants and agricultural labourers spent very little time in school until well into the nineteenth century, especially where girls were concerned. They might spend a year or two in class, but it was often during the winter months only, and subject to frequent interruption when the child was needed at home. Instead they went through a system of on-the-job training among adults, 'the school of life', in which they acquired the skills that they would need to run a home or cultivate the soil.[3] On family farms, parents gradually stepped up the intensity of the work as the strength and experience of the individual child increased. This pattern of watching, helping and eventually working independently during childhood appears in many parts of Europe (see Figure 1.1).[4] Johann Baptist Schad, son of a peasant-cum-innkeeper in Germany, recalled early in the nineteenth century that his father classified tasks for his children according to age. Each year, as the children moved up the scale, they considered it an 'honourable distinction', and looked forward to the next advance. Ephraïm Grenadou, born in the Beauce region of France in 1897, recalled starting at the age of three or four by watching his father plough the fields. At ten his father gave him a flock of a hundred geese to raise, and by fourteen he was able to plough fields himself.[5]

[2] Pierre-Jakez Hélias, *The Horse of Pride: Life in a Breton Village* (New Haven, CT: Yale University Press, 1978), pp. 50–1; Pieter R. D. Stokvis, 'From Child to Adult: Transition Rites in the Netherlands ca. 1800–1914', *Paedagogica Historica*, 24 (1993), 77–92 (81).
[3] See, for example, Loftur Guttormsson, 'Parent-Child Relations', in David Kertzer and Marzio Barbagli (eds.), *The History of the European Family* (New Haven, CT: Yale University Press, c. 2001–3), vol. 2, pp. 251–81 (pp. 256–8).
[4] Colin Heywood, *Childhood in Nineteenth-Century France*, ch. 2; Boris B. Gorshkov, *Russia's Factory Children*, ch. 1; Elisabeth Engberg, 'Useful and Industrious: Fostering and Rural Child Labour in Nineteenth-Century Sweden', in Lieten and van Nederveen-Meerkerk (eds.), *Child Labour's Global Past, 1650–2000* (Bern: Peter Lang, 2011), pp. 331–61.
[5] Johann Baptist Schad, *Lebensgeschichte* (1828), as cited by Jürgen Schlumbohm, 'The School of Life: Reflections on Socialization in Preindustrial Germany', in Andrea Immel and Michael Witmore (eds.), *Childhood and Children's Books*, pp. 305–27 (p. 324, n. 14);

BIRD-BOY TENTING THE CORN,

Figure 1.1 Engraving from 1850 of a boy protecting a field of corn from
the birds.
Getty Images, 184393327.

From Childhood to Youth

Life on family farms gives a hint that the boundaries between childhood,
youth and adulthood were fluid and vaguely defined in rural communities. The elaborate initiation rites that marked the transition from
childhood to adulthood around the time of puberty in many non-
European societies were unknown. Even the idea that there was a relatively short period of transition, championed by Philippe Ariès with his
denial of an awareness of both childhood and adolescence during the
Middle Ages (and allegedly continuing among the working classes up to
the twentieth century), is now generally considered unsustainable by
historians.[6] Instead they envisage a long, drawn-out phase of increasing
independence in various spheres of life between infancy and adulthood.
In this way, the young could gradually ease themselves into the adult
world. The historian Michael Mitterauer is surely right to argue that
within the western Christian tradition 'youth cannot be seen as a period
of time between clearly defined starting and finishing point, but rather as
a phase of many partial transitions'.[7]

Ephraïm Grenadou and Alain Prévost, *Grenadou: paysan français* (Paris: Editions du
    Seuil, 1966), pp. 11, 19 and 25.
[6] Philippe Ariès, *Centuries of Childhood* (Harmondsworth: Penguin, 1960), ch. 2.
[7] Michael Mitterauer, *A History of Youth* (Oxford: Blackwell, 1992), p. 39.

Leaving Home

Moving away from the parental home stands out as one potentially important marker of transition in the life of a young person. John Gillis, in his pioneering book, *A History of Youth* (1974), proposed the age of seven or eight as the end of childhood in pre-industrial society. He reasoned that this was when the child often became 'somewhat independent' of its family through leaving home. By the age of fourteen, he asserted, the great majority of young people would be living in a state of 'semi dependence', either as servants in a household, apprentices living with their master or students boarding away from home.[8] There is a grain of truth in this, but research since the 1970s has modified the picture considerably.

In the first place, there were parts of Europe, particularly in the south and east, where the young rarely left home before marriage. In Mediterranean culture, for example, it was not considered appropriate for a young, single woman to work outside her own household. Fathers saw it as their duty to protect and care for their children, which in this context meant not entrusting them to others until they married and left the family.[9] This type of arrangement was often associated with a complex family structure, where working away from home as a servant was comparatively rare. Here the logic for the families was to assemble a large number of unpaid workers from their own ranks, for example to exploit a serf tenure in Russia, or a sharecropping system in parts of central France and central and northern Italy.[10] An early and much-quoted case study from Russia investigated an estate in the central Black Earth province of Riazan between 1814 and 1858. Its agricultural serf families almost invariably formed large, multi-generational families, and in the words of Peter Czap, 'it seems reasonable to speculate that as many as half of the male peasants living in Mishino in the first decades of the nineteenth century could expect to pass their entire lives not only within their village of origin, but also within their household of birth'. Females married early, usually under the age of twenty, and it was generally the bride who left the parental household at this point to live with the groom. Slightly different was the case of sharecropping families in a village in

---

[8] John R. Gillis, *Youth and History: Tradition and Change in European Age Relations 1770–Present* (New York, NY: Academic Press, 1974), pp. 1–3.
[9] Giovanna Da Molin, 'Family Forms and Domestic Service in Southern Italy from the Seventeenth to the Nineteenth Centuries', *Journal of Family History*, 15 (1990), 503–27 (518).
[10] André Burguière and François Lebrun, 'The One Hundred and One Families of Europe', in André Burguière et al. (eds.), *The History of the Family*, vol. 2, The Impact of Modernity (Cambridge: Polity Press, 1996), pp. 11–94 (p. 47).

the Grand Duchy of Tuscany, between 1819 and 1859. Here it was not uncommon for males in their teens to leave home temporarily to become a farm servant or to take up an apprenticeship, but as in the Russian example they would later remain in the household with their new brides. Females, by contrast, usually left home definitively upon marriage during their twenties or early thirties.[11]

Secondly, it is now clear that leaving home as early as the age of seven or eight would have been very much the exception in northern Europe, rather than the rule. Instead of some 'universal early exodus' from the family home, the movement was a very gradual one.[12] Studies in a number of regions suggest that only the very poorest children left home this early. Fritz Pauk, born in northern Germany in 1888, was a case in point. He first left home at the age of eight to work on a neighbouring farm over the summer months, to help his impoverished single mother.[13] Although many parents might have been eager to have one less mouth to feed, they had to contend with the general reluctance of farmers to hire puny youngsters unsuited to most of the work on the land. The movement away from home therefore did not start in earnest until the young reached their early or even mid-teens.

During the eighteenth and nineteenth centuries, live-in servants in the Nordic countries were generally aged between fifteen and thirty, with a minority (known as 'half servants') in the age-group twelve to fifteen. Moreover, it was customary for the eldest son or daughter of a farm family to remain at home.[14] In the English case, a sample of settlement examinations in three villages, dating from 1599, 1790 and 1796, indicated that thirteen or fourteen was the most common age to leave home

---

[11] Peter Czap, 'A Large Family: The Peasant's Greatest Wealth, Serf Households in Mishino, Russia. 1814–1858', in R. Wall, J. Robin and P. Laslett (eds.), *Family Forms in Historic Europe* (Cambridge: Cambridge University Press, 1983), pp. 105–51; Marco Bresci and Matteo Manfredini, 'Leaving the Family: Departures from the Household in an Italian Rural Context during the Nineteenth Century', in Frans van Poppel, Michel Oris and James Lee (eds.), *The Road to Independence: Leaving Home in Western and Eastern Societies, 16th–20th Centuries* (Bern: Peter Lang, 2004), pp. 221–41.

[12] Richard Wall, 'The Age at Leaving Home', *Journal of Family History*, 3 (1978), 181–202; idem., 'Leaving Home and the Process of Household Formation in Pre-Industrial England', *Continuity and Change*, 2 (1987), 77–101; Frans van Poppel and Michel Oris, 'Introduction' in van Poppel et al., *Road to Independence*, pp. 1–29 (p. 5).

[13] 'Fritz Pauk, Cigar Maker', in Alfred Kelly (ed.), *The German Worker: Working-Class Autobiographies from the Age of Industrialization* (Berkeley, CA: University of California Press, 1987), pp. 399–427 (p. 401).

[14] Beatrice Moring, 'Nordic Family Patterns and the North-West European Household System', *Continuity and Change*, 18 (2003), 77–109; Christer Lundh, 'The Social Mobility of Servants in Rural Sweden, 1740–1894', *Continuity and Change*, 14 (1999), 57–89.

for service. Nearly as many followed suit at the ages of fifteen and sixteen.[15] In the Dutch province of Zeeland, leaving school around the age of twelve meant leaving home at the same time, in the case of boys to find work as resident farmhands, and girls as maids.[16] Overall, in rural areas of northwestern Europe, notably in Scandinavia, the British Isles and northern France, Linda Pollock estimates that somewhere between 25 and 50 per cent of young people normally left home to become servants.[17] This involved productive work on farms and in craft workshops as well as domestic duties. Able to make some savings, move from employer to employer and meet others of their own age, these young 'life-cycle servants' awaiting marriage and the establishment of a household of their own were partially independent of parents. Leaving home was for them assuredly of major significance in the transition from childhood to youth.[18]

Thirdly, this 'semi independence' of young people who left home mentioned by Gillis is now better documented than before. Above all, it is clear that it was often a protracted process, rather than the clean break with the family that the term might suggest. Children who went off to another village or to a town usually remained in contact with their parents, sometimes sent their wages home and often made more than one move before finally setting up their own household upon marriage. This was possible because of the short distance and temporary nature of most migrationary movements, including those of young males and females in their teens and early twenties. The outstanding exception was the big cities of Europe, which could attract migrants over long distances. Recent research reveals that during the nineteenth century, nearly as many migrants left towns as entered them.[19] Migration to the city, to quote Lesley Page Moch, looks more like a 'pulsing two-way

---

[15] Ann Kussmaul, *Servants in Husbandry in Early Modern England* (Cambridge: Cambridge University Press, 1981), pp. 70–8.

[16] Stokvis, 'From Child to Adult', 82.

[17] Linda Pollock, 'Parent–Child Relations', in Kertzer and Barbagli, *European Family*, vol. 1, pp. 191–220 (p. 208).

[18] Deborah Simonton, 'Bringing Up Girls: Work in Preindustrial Europe', in Mary Jo Maynes et al. (eds.), *Secret Gardens, Satanic Mills: Placing Girls in European History, 1750–1960* (Bloomington, IN: Indiana University Press, 2005), pp. 23–37 (pp. 28–31).

[19] Steve Hochstadt, 'Migration and Industrialization in Germany, 1815–1977', *Social Science History*, 5 (1981), 445–68 (448); James H. Jackson, *Migration and Urbanization in the Ruhr Valley, 1821–1914* (Boston, MA: Humanities Press, 1997), pp. 16–18; Colin Pooley and Jean Turnbull, *Migration and Mobility in Britain since the 18th Century* (London: University College London Press, 1998).

current between town and country' than the attraction to a magnet.[20] This meant that for those young people who struck out from their home in the village there was the possibility of an emotional break from parents and some personal autonomy. Such a step from childhood to youth, and ultimately to adulthood, could prove a huge wrench, but it was evidently tempered in most cases by the maintenance of close family ties.

Hierarchies at Work

The world of work provided another dimension to the transition.[21] Like the children working beside their parents, farm servants and day-labourers could gain increasing status as they acquired new skills and greater physical strength during their teens and early twenties. Although difficult to measure precisely, the usual assumption is that the young peasants only began to produce more than they consumed somewhere around their mid-teens.[22] Farm work did not require a great deal of skill, though during the 1890s in Britain a Royal Commission on Labour reported that tasks such as managing horses, ploughing and sowing called for 'a certain amount of judgement, dexterity, and practice'. Joyce Burnette calculates that approximately half of the rapid rise in the wages of male farm labourers typically achieved during their teen years could be attributed to an increase in skills, the other half to an increase in strength. It should be added that females working for wages on the land put in fewer days per year than their male counterparts, and so acquired very little skill during their youth, and had lower wage increases as they grew up.[23]

For both males and females, progress depended on individual cir-cumstances rather than puberty or a fixed age. Sooner or later, and ideally around the age of twelve or thirteen, the young peasant would hope to move on from such tasks as bird scaring and the herding of farm animals typically associated with children. At this point, the two sexes went their separate ways for much of the time, following the gendered division of labour among adults on the land. But on the larger

---

[20] Leslie Page Moch, *Moving Europeans: Migration in Western Europe since 1650* (Bloomington, IN: Indiana University Press, 1992), p. 103.
[21] For details on the experiences of working on the land as a young person, see below, Chapter 3.
[22] Marjatta Rahikainen, *Centuries of Child Labour: European Experiences from the Seventeenth to the Twentieth Century* (Aldershot: Ashgate, 2004), p. 53.
[23] Joyce Burnette, 'How Skilled Were English Agricultural Labourers in the Early Nineteenth Century?', *Economic History Review*, 59 (2006), 688–716.

Figure 1.2 Engraving of a milking maid by Harold Copping, 1894.
Getty Images, 545440590.

farms in particular, both could climb a hierarchy of status and pay.
In nineteenth-century France, for example, the young male began as a
petit domestique, a general dogsbody (*vaque-à-tout*) who worked in the
farm yard, under the supervision of the mistress, doing little jobs for the
other servants. At the top of the hierarchy were the older servants, the
maîtres valets, responsible for the horses and ploughing the fields, acting
in effect as the foremen of the farm workers. On the female side, in
Bavaria at the beginning of the twentieth century, a contemporary
observer reported that girls were usually taken on at around the age of
thirteen or fourteen to help the peasant's wife with the household chores
and looking after the children. As they grew older they were gradually
promoted through the ranks of servants involved with farm work (see
Figure 1.2).[24]

[24] Jean-Claude Farcy, 'Jeunesse rurale et travail', in Ludivine Bantigny and Ivan Jablonka
(eds.), *Jeunesse oblige: Histoire des jeunes en France XIXe-XXIe siècle* (Paris: Presses
Universitaires de France, 2009), pp. 51–65 (p. 60); Regina Schulte, 'Peasants and
Farmers' Maids: Female Farm Servants in Bavaria at the End of the Nineteenth
Century', in Richard Evans and W. R. Lee (eds.), *The German Peasantry: Conflict and
Community in Rural Society from the Eighteenth to the Twentieth Centuries* (London: Croom
Helm, 1986), pp. 158–73 (p. 163).

Confirmation and First Communion

Confirmation for Protestants, First Communion for Catholics and the Bar Mitzvah for Jews were the closest that villagers in Western Europe came to initiation rites helping individuals make the transition from childhood to youth. (The Eastern churches continued the custom of the early church of administering the sacraments of Baptism, Confirmation and the Eucharist to infants immediately after birth.) After Confirmation, a special ceremony for First Communion was common in many Catholic countries, following decisions made by the Council of Trent during the sixteenth century. In the French case, for example, it was near universal by the eighteenth century.[25] In this latter period, children usually took their First Communion at the age of twelve to fourteen, but it could be as early as ten or eleven, or even as late as fifteen or sixteen.[26] Jewish girls celebrated their Bat Mitzvah at twelve, admitting them to full membership of the community, in principle if not in practice. For Jewish boys, the Bar Mitzvah came when they reached thirteen, in their case with a religious ceremony. It should be added that Jews were rare in villages, outside a few areas such as Alsace and the Polish lands.[27]

Catholics in France often remembered their First Communion as *le plus beau jour de la vie* ('the most beautiful day in one's life'), though it was generally valued more highly by women than by men.[28] They might also note its role as an important turning point in life. The ceremony was impressive, even in villages, with the boys dressed in blue or black, the girls in white, decorations in the church and a procession. On a more profane note, there was also a family reunion and a feast. Afterwards boys often wore their first long trousers and girls put their hair up. As full members of the community, they could now become godparents, enter a religious community and marry. First communion might also be the time when a boy or a girl left school and started to work full time. Henri Pitaud, brought up in a family of poor peasants in the Vendée at the beginning of the twentieth century, recalled that his First Communion at

---

[25] Richard L. DeMolen, 'Childhood and the Sacraments in the Sixteenth Century', *Archiv für Reformations geschichte*, 65 (1974), 49–71.

[26] Odile Robert, 'Fonctionnement et enjeux d'une institution chrétienne au XVIIIe siècle', in Jean Delumeau (ed.), *La Première Communion: quatre siècles d'histoire* (Paris: Desclée de Brouwer, 1987), pp. 77–113 (pp. 93–5).

[27] See Jay R. Berkovitz, 'Judaism', in Paula Fass (ed.), *Encyclopedia of Children and Childhood in History and Society* (New York, NY: Thomson Gale, 2003), vol. 2, pp. 508–11.

[28] Martine Sonnet, 'Education et première Communion au XVIIIe siècle', in Delumeau, *La Première Communion*, pp. 115–32.

the age of eleven meant his childhood was over. With the end of his catechism classes, he was free to leave school and work full time in the fields.[29] However, the ethnologist Arnold Van Gennep argued in his *Manuel de folklore français* that popular customs in France put back the start of adolescence to the age of sixteen. An ethnographic study of a village in Burgundy during the nineteenth and twentieth centuries concluded that girls waited two or three years after First Communion, until about the age of fifteen, before starting their new life among local youth. At this point their bodies were ready to cope with their new rights and duties, such as learning a trade, as well as going out to dances and courting.[30] Similarly, in nineteenth-century Spain there were various rituals to mark the shift from childhood to youth. In the Leon region, for example, boys paid a fee, usually in the form of a large pitcher of wine, to join the local youth; girls bought a candle for the Virgin.[31]

Protestant reformers diverged from Catholics by associating spiritual maturity with physical maturity. Hence, they expected Confirmation to take place a little later, though there was no set age, and in practice the age varied considerably.[32] In Finland, for example, fifteen or sixteen was the usual age to start preparing for Confirmation. According to Beatrice Moring, 'When persons had mastered the central articles of the Christian faith, had some ability to read the Bible and had been admitted to Holy Communion, they had become an adult in the eyes of the church.' In the Swiss canton of Neuchatel, sixteen for girls and seventeen for boys was the norm for Confirmation, partly because the population wanted to ensure that the candidates could read well and had a firm grasp of the catechism. Gunnar Benediktsson (b. 1892), raised on a farm in Iceland, recalled that:

My conscious being transformed at this moment. I was no longer a child. I had reached manhood, with the right to self-rule and I became responsible for myself and my actions. This change took place right after the confirmation.[33]

---

[29] Jean Delumeau, 'Présentation', in Delumeau, *La Première communion*, pp. 7–13; Robert, 'Institution chrétienne'; Henri Pitaud, *Le Pain de la terre: mémoires d'un paysan vendéen du début du siècle* (Paris: J.-C. Lattès, 1982), p. 140.

[30] Arnold Van Gennep, *Manuel de folklore français contemporain* (Paris: Picard, 1943), vol. I.1, p. 147; Yvonne Verdier, *Façons de dire, façons de faire: la laveuse, la couturière, la cuisinière* (Paris: Gallimard, 1979), pp. 160, 190–3.

[31] Josette Borderies-Guereña, 'Niños y niñas en familia', in José María Borrás Llop (ed.), *Historia de la infancia en la España contemporánea, 1834–1936* (Madrid: Ministerio de Trabajo y Asuntos Sociales, 1996), p. 50.

[32] Christina de Ballaigue, 'Faith and Religion', in Colin Heywood (ed.), *A Cultural History of Childhood and Family in the Age of Empire* (Oxford: Berg, 2010), pp. 149–66 (p. 162).

[33] Moring, 'Nordic Family Patterns', p. 84; Sigurður Gylfi Magnússon, 'From Children's Point of View: Childhood in Nineteenth-Century Iceland', *Journal of Social History*, 29

As among Catholics, this religious ceremony was often a necessary prelude to other changes, in clothing, in civic status and in the move from school to the labour market.

There was also the opportunity to join local youths in their leisure activities. In great swathes of continental Europe, in such countries as France, Germany, Switzerland, Austria and Romania, organisations of young, unmarried men in villages had existed during the medieval and early modern periods. These were variously known as, for example, *bachelleries* (bachelors) and Abbeys of Youth in parts of France, *Knabenschaften* (boys' societies) in Switzerland, and *Burschenschaften* (fraternities) in Germany. Some survived into the twentieth century, though they were declining in importance well before then in many areas.[34] According to a detailed study of the *bachelleries* in the Centre West of France, for example, they barely survived 1789. Yet in Upper Bavaria, Regina Schulte notes that, even in the late nineteenth century, single young men were regarded by villagers as a special, closed group, with their *Burschenschaften* and *Zechen* (drinking clubs). Similarly, in southwest Germany, *Lichstuben* ('light rooms') for male youth to meet in continued to flourish right into the twentieth century.[35] Admission to such a group from the age of sixteen or so granted rights to male youths to go to dances, visit girls or to start smoking and drinking.[36]

From Youth to Adulthood

To round off, we might note that the final step in the long transition from childhood to adulthood was marriage. There was considerable variation across Europe in the age of marriage. At one end of the spectrum, couples in England and the Nordic countries generally married late, towards the end of their twenties. At the other end, early marriage was

(1995), 313; Pierre Caspard, 'Les Trois âges de la première communion en Suisse', in Jean-Pierre Bardet et al. (eds.), *Lorsque l'enfant grandit: entre dépendance et autonomie* (Paris: Presses de l'Université de Paris-Sorbonne 2003), pp. 173–81.

[34] Natalie Zemon Davis, 'The Reasons of Misrule: Youth Groups and Charivaris in Sixteenth-Century France', *Past and Present*, 50 (1971), 41–75, reprinted in eadem, *Society and Culture in Early Modern France* (London: Duckworth, 1975), pp. 97–123; Mitterauer, *History of Youth*, pp. 155–82.

[35] Nicole Pellegrin, *Les Bachelleries: organisations et fêtes de la Jeunesse dans le Centre-Ouest XVe–XVIIIe siècles* (Poitiers: Societe des Antiquaires de l'Ouest, 1982), p. 315; Regina Schulte, *The Village in Court: Arson, Infanticide and Poaching in the Court Records of Upper Bavaria, 1848–1910*, transl. Barrie Selman (Cambridge: Cambridge University Press, 1994), pp. 142–4; Andreas Gestrich, 'Protestant Religion, the State and the Suppression of Traditional Youth Culture in Southwest Germany', *History of European Ideas*, 11 (1989), 629–36 (632).

[36] Mitterauer, *History of Youth*, p. 67.

much in evidence in large parts of eastern and southern Europe. As the former serf Savva Dmitrievich Purlevskii helpfully observed, on his experience in Central Russia during the early nineteenth century: 'According to our local customs, marriage at the age of eighteen was nothing unusual.'[37] It follows that in some regions marriage soon followed the end of childhood, while in others the young faced an extended period of youth, lasting somewhere between their mid-teens and late twenties. In the latter case, they had more independence than when they were considered children, but still faced constraints of their own, notably in their sexual lives.

Change on the Land

Agricultural society was far from immune to the changes wrought by industrialisation and social reform in the modern period, which had implications for the boundaries around childhood and youth. In England, though apparently not in continental Europe, farmers gradually gave up the practice of employing young, unmarried people as live-in farm servants from the late eighteenth century onwards. Moving away from home in this case became associated with the end rather than the beginning of youth.[38] The increasing importance of formal education in the lives of peasant children during the nineteenth century, either by choice or by the imposition of compulsory schooling, meant that leaving elementary school largely supplanted First Communion as a marker for the end of childhood. This was in the context of 'dechristianisation' eventually reaching villages, and a reversion in 1910 to an earlier practice of Catholics taking First Communion at the age of seven, while the minimum school-leaving age gradually rose to around twelve, thirteen or fourteen. The upshot was that by the end of the nineteenth century there had emerged a relatively abrupt end to childhood for most of the population during their early teens. This was when they left school and moved straight into full-time work, instead of undergoing a long period with a fluid boundary between the two.[39] Nonetheless, the forces of inertia were evident in certain parts of Europe where the school system and the urban culture were particularly slow to make an impact. The

---

[37] Lundh, 'Servants in Rural Sweden', 71; Boris B. Gorshkov transl. and ed. *A Life under Russian Serfdom: The Memoirs of Savva Dmitrievich Purlevskii 1800–1868* (Budapest: Central European University Press, 2005), p. 73.
[38] Simonton, 'Bringing Up Girls', p. 31.
[39] Mary Jo Maynes, *Taking the Hard Road: Life Course in German and French Workers' Autobiographies in the Era of Industrialization* (Chapel Hill, NC and London: University of North Carolina Press, 1995), pp. 103–4.

ethnologist Yvonne Verdier, for example, traced through to the 1950s the traditional pattern for educating girls in her Burgundian village of Minot. That is to say, they spent more time in *champ-les-vaches* herding farm animals than in school between the ages of seven and twelve, or even later, when they received First Communion, and then moved on to a period of youth that ran from the age of fifteen or so until marriage. Similarly, Floyd Martinson asserts that not until the 1950s and 1960s was there a serious reduction in the work of children on the farms in Norway, when mechanisation eliminated their tasks and made farming a profession like any other.[40]

Conceptions of Childhood among the Peasantry

Childhood

To understand peasant thinking about childhood, one must in the first instance look to religious influences. Christianity has always conveyed diverse and even contradictory messages on the nature of the child, evident from the outset in the scriptures.[41] On the one hand, there was a tradition dating back to the early Middle Ages of emphasising the purity, humility and innocence of children. On the other, there was the equally long-standing tradition that highlighted the stain of Original Sin on the newborn infant, inherited from Adam and Eve after the Fall. This pointed to the capacity of the child to do evil.[42] It is hard to avoid the conclusion that the Christian churches have generally veered towards the pessimistic view.

For the Catholic Church, the sacrament of baptism cleansed the child of this Original Sin, though it was felt that young children remained vulnerable to the temptations of evil. The Protestant sects that emerged in Europe during the sixteenth and seventeenth centuries brought a renewed emphasis on Original Sin. This was partly because Protestants did not believe that the sacrament of baptism cleansed the child. They held that there was a more direct and unmediated relationship between the soul and God: the individual had from an early age to struggle to achieve an awareness of their own sinfulness and to conquer it through

[40] Verdier, *Façons de dire*, p. 160; Floyd M. Martinson, *Growing Up in Norway, 800 to 1990* (Carbondale, IL: Southern Illinois University Press, 1992), p. 87.
[41] Marcia Bunge, 'Introduction', in Marcia Bunge (ed.), *The Child in Christian Thought* (Grand Rapids, MI: William B. Erdmans, 2001), pp. 1–28 (p. 11).
[42] Daniel Herlihy, 'Medieval Children', in Bede Karl Lackner and Kenneth Roy Philp (eds.), *Essays on Medieval Civilization: The Walter Prescott Webb Memorial Lectures* (Austin, TX: University of Texas Press, 1978), pp. 109–41.

faith. This led to striking images of stubbornness, lewdness and savagery left by the evangelical wing of Protestantism when discussing infancy.[43]

It follows that villagers in early modern Europe would have gained a very mixed view of childhood from their priests and pastors, with the good side jostling forever with the bad. Of course, the beliefs of the *hoi polloi* frequently diverged from those of the religious elites in the various churches, particularly when it came to matters affecting their private lives.[44] And it is regrettably the case that villagers rarely left any record of their thoughts on the abstract notion of childhood. In this area, the historian must grasp at straws, making it difficult to document similarities and differences across the regions. What evidence there is suggests that the popular tradition generally followed the orthodox discourse in holding an unsentimental view of childhood. Proverbs may give a hint of the collective values of rural communities in this area. A common image across Europe was of children as carriers of wisdom and truth, with the familiar 'out of the mouth of babes come words of wisdom'. However, proverbs often included the insane or the drunk with the babes and sucklings mentioned in the Bible, to produce less a flattering depiction, as in the 'children and drunkards speak truth' from Denmark. An even harsher view of children was not hard to find in the proverbs, notably the Russian 'children are a torment and nothing more'. They also illustrate the well-known peasant preference for a boy over a girl. For the Irish, it was 'an inch of lad is better than a foot of a girl'; for the Spanish, the rather desperate 'male child, even if a thief'.[45]

Ethnographic studies provide further evidence of peasant thinking. On the positive side, they suggest that the peasantry was prepared to accept children as in some sense messengers from another world. The ethnographer André Varagnac asserted that in the 'traditional civilization' of France, children had a role to play in blessing and sanctifying villagers' homes. He cited as most characteristic the custom in Champagne and Lorraine of the May Queen dancing in front of each house to a song that invoked a good cereal crop. 'Modern civilization', in the form of newspapers, schools and railways, ensured that such rituals barely survived the nineteenth century.[46] Conversely, a more down-to-earth assessment

---

[43] Bunge, 'Introduction', pp. 13–16.

[44] Åke Sander, 'Images of the Child', in C. Philip Hwang et al. (eds.), *Images of Childhood* (Mahwah, NJ: Lawrence Erlbaum, 1996), p. 15.

[45] Jesús Palacios, 'Proverbs as Images of Children and Childrearing', in Hwang, *Images of Childhood*, pp. 75–98.

[46] André Varagnac, *Civilisation traditionnelle et genres de vie* (Paris: Albin Michel, 1948), pp. 23 and 122–3.

surely prevailed in everyday life. An American observer of village life in France, from the mid-twentieth century, recorded that:

People in Peyrane do not believe that man is naturally good, because it is obvious to them that children are not naturally good. They are more like little animals which must be domesticated at home and in the school. They obey the rules imposed on them because they are forced to obey them, not because they want to.[47]

The custom in villages had always been to discourage infants from crawling on all fours, as this was too close for comfort to the behaviour of an animal. There was a high priority to instilling obedience and respect for elders, typical of the emotional life in agricultural societies, as well as moral and religious values. This required a strict disciplinary regime – principally because it was running against the grain of wilfulness in the young.[48]

The Significance of Childhood in Rural Society

Childhood in a village was generally short and not particularly important, by twenty-first century standards, insofar as work on the land or around the farm started early. Some of the pressures faced by modern children were also absent, above all the feeling that failure to do well at school could ruin career prospects. Young peasants and agricultural labourers often followed in the footsteps of their parents in a farming community, enjoyed the support of other villagers and went through a succession of rites of passage to help them through life. All the same, children set out at an early age on a long odyssey, beginning around the age of seven, with a view to marrying and starting a family of their own, sometime during their twenties.[49] During the early stages, varying in some respects according to their gender and family background, they needed to earn a reputation as a good worker, fulfil their duties as a Christian and scrape together some savings. In this way, childhood in villages shaded gradually – and in some ways unobtrusively – into youth and eventually adulthood.

---

[47] Laurence Wylie, *Village in the Vaucluse* (2nd edn., Cambridge, MA: Harvard University Press, 1964), p. 121.
[48] See Peter N. Stearns, 'Obedience and Emotion: A Challenge in the Emotional History of Childhood', *Journal of Social History*, 47 (2014), 593–611.
[49] See, for example, Olwen H. Hufton, 'Women, Work and Marriage in Eighteenth-Century France', in R. B. Outhwaite (ed.), *Marriage and Society* (London: Europa, 1981), pp. 186–203.

Conclusion

In sum, farming communities laid out a path for their young to follow, with key turning points such as breeching, starting to earn their keep, and Confirmation. The peasantry has left little evidence on how they felt about childhood, but an informed guess would be that they shared the ambiguous attitudes of their more educated contemporaries: seeing a combination of good and evil, virtue and vice. One suspects they valued maturity and experience more than youth and had some tendency to view their offspring as potential sources of labour and carers in old age. It follows that age relations were conceived of in uneven terms: the young were subordinate to the head of a household, as children or servants. The Fourth Commandment buttressed the authority of parents over children, and both church and state supported it during the eighteenth and nineteenth centuries – though historians are generally agreed that subsequently various forces gradually undermined patriarchal power.

That said, there are limits to how far one can generalise on these conceptions of childhood in villages. There is a wealth of evidence now available on the way such variables as the age of leaving home or starting work were affected by socio-economic background, gender, ecological conditions and cultural norms. Rural society was highly stratified, as we have seen, with landownership the key to prosperity, affecting when the young started work. Gender was a major influence, most evidently with the concern in Mediterranean society to defend the reputation of young females in a family. And contrasts between Catholic and Protestant areas were important in a number of ways, notably for our purposes here in determining the age when people were confirmed.

2   Growing Up in Villages

The question inevitably arises of whether growing up in a village would be a pleasant experience, a neat counterpoint to the grim conditions for the young in the new industrial centres of the nineteenth century or a matter of languishing in a rural backwater. Contrasting the rude health and simple virtues of the peasantry with the corruption of the city dwellers has a long history in Western civilisation. There is a case to be made, hinted at by Philippe Ariès, that young people in early modern Europe enjoyed an intense sociability in their local communities, and were spared the heavy hand of the schools, reformatories and barracks of the 'disciplinary society' that would follow. Against that, there is the suggestion that agricultural societies tended to lean heavily on children for work on the farms and in the workshops.[1] They were fiercely patriarchal in their gender relations, often wary of formal education in the schools, and a majority of those employed on the land remained desperately poor. It need hardly be said that much depended on the position of the family in the social hierarchy, principally determined by how much land it owned or rented. Being brought up as a serf in eastern Europe, a sharecropper in the Mediterranean region or a rural labourer anywhere was generally to draw a short straw in life. It was far better to be among the offspring of peasants owning or renting a large farm in areas such as northern Italy and north-eastern France, enjoying a measure of status and material prosperity.

Historians have found it difficult to come to terms with many of the child-rearing customs still prevalent in villages at the beginning of the modern era. Some of the pioneers in the history of the family were notorious for their unsympathetic attitude to parents from the 'popular classes'. Lawrence Stone gave them short shrift in the English case, with parenting among the poor during the early modern period described as 'often indifferent, cruel, erratic and unpredictable'. In a similar vein,

---

[1] Peter N. Stearns, *Childhood in World History* (New York, NY: Routledge, 2016), ch. 1.

Edward Shorter argued that the 'traditional indifference' of mothers to their infants lasted until the end of the eighteenth century in the European villages, and well beyond that in certain regions. 'Good mothering', as he famously put it, 'is an invention of modernization'.[2] This line of argument was not without its critics. The historian E. P. Thompson, for example, rounded on Stone and Shorter for accusing the poor of indifference to their children when they had so little supporting evidence to support their case.[3]

The obvious alternative, following in the footsteps of anthropologists, is to take a more sympathetic look at child-rearing practices among the villagers in the light of their material conditions and the popular culture. This does not deny that a number of practices current in villages will make the modern observer shudder, such as binding an infant tightly in long strips of cloth or plunging a feverish child into cold water. But the argument is that villagers believed they were doing the best they could for their children: as Catriona Kelly observes in the Russian context, peasant parents often 'killed with kindness'.[4] One needs to move beyond the easy criticisms of peasant 'superstitions' made by eighteenth-century elites, not to mention our contemporary sensibility, to understand parental behaviour in villages. The historian Françoise Loux emphasises the internal coherence of peasant beliefs, involving a constant interplay between the symbolic and the empirical. She considered them less a matter of irrationality than of a different order of rationality to our own. The assumption made here is therefore that parents were far from indifferent to the well-being of their children, making strenuous efforts to look after them in difficult circumstances.

This chapter therefore falls into two parts. The first part analyses the social context for a village childhood, beginning at the macro level with the salient features of an agricultural society influencing this stage of life, and continuing at the micro level, considering two important institutions for children with a peasant background: the local community and the family. The second part focuses directly on the process of growing up in villages, with particular emphasis on family life and relationships with other children.

---

[2] Lawrence Stone, *The Family, Sex and Marriage in England, 1500–1800* (London: Weidenfeld and Nicolson, 1977), p. 470; Edward Shorter, *The Making of the Modern Family* (London: Fontana, 1977), pp. 170–90.

[3] E. P. Thompson, 'Happy Families', *New Society*, 8 September 1977, 499–501.

[4] Catriona Kelly, *Children's World: Growing Up in Russia, 1890–1981* (New Haven, CT: Yale University Press), p. 294.

The Social Context

Agricultural Society

High fertility rates meant that children were numerous in eighteenth- and nineteenth-century Europe, accounting for approximately one-third of the population. To take the well-documented English example, in 1701 historians estimate the share of those aged 0–14 in the total population to have been 32.1 per cent. (The equivalent proportion at the 2011 census for England and Wales was 17.6 per cent, a little under one-sixth.) This meant that villages teemed with children. To quote Peter Laslett:

In the pre-industrial world there were children everywhere; playing in the village street and fields when they were very small, hanging round the farmyards and getting in the way, until they had grown enough to be given child-sized jobs to do; thronging the churches; forever clinging to the skirts of women in the house and wherever they went and above all crowding round the cottage fires.[5]

Feeding the large number of mouths was always difficult, given the low productivity of both land and labour. The increase in population, which gathered momentum from the late eighteenth and early nineteenth century onwards, compounded the problem. The increase was particularly rapid in England, Ireland and the German states but more modest in the 'Latin' countries of France, Spain, Portugal and Italy. The total population in Europe (including Russia) rose from an estimated 146 million in 1750 to 288 million in 1850. Most of this growth occurred in rural areas, and, perversely, among families with little or no property. There were hints of improved agricultural techniques during the seventeenth and eighteenth centuries, leading to increased farm yields, but they were largely confined to parts of north-western Europe, and in particular England and the Dutch Republic. Conversely, techniques that had changed little since the medieval period held sway over much of the continent. The typical peasant farm could barely lift a family beyond subsistence level, and with recurrent harvest failures, not even that during a crisis period. For families dependent on the earnings of a rural labourer, the position was even more precarious. In much of central and eastern Europe, serfdom guaranteed landowners a labour force, but did little to encourage innovation. For all but a small minority of the population across Europe, hunger and the deficiency diseases that

---

[5] Peter Laslett, *The World We Have Lost, Further Explored* (3rd edn., London: Methuen, 1983), p. 119.

went with it were a constant concern. Not surprisingly, as we shall see, empty stomachs during childhood featured prominently in peasant autobiographies.

Generally of shorter stature than those higher up the social scale, the young peasants soon learned that townsfolk were contemptuous of their whole way of life: notably their clothes, their dialects and their 'old wives' tales'. Pierre-Jakez Hélias discovered during the 1920s that when he left his Breton village for a *lycée* in the town of Quimper, 'the seediest bourgeois considered himself far above the most subtle peasant'.[6] Nonetheless, if poverty, insecurity and scorn from those higher up the social scale were generally all-too-familiar to peasants of all ages, there were compensations within their local communities. Village children were often illiterate, and hence isolated from the print culture, but they had the oral culture of their region to help them make sense of the world around them. In the words of David Cressy, 'The oral culture ... with its traditions and tales, its proverbs and jokes, customs and ceremonies, offered enough in the way of entertainment and enrichment to sustain a satisfactory alternative'.[7] They needed to start earning their keep at a tender age, by modern standards, but their long 'apprenticeship' as a farmer or an artisan was evidently useful for their future working lives (in a way that school might not have been).

The Rural Community

In a peasant society, the young could learn all they needed to know from those around them in their household and the local community, at least until industrialisation and urbanisation began to make an impact. This was their universe, and by taking part in its daily life they gradually acquired the values, ways of behaving and occupational skills they needed.[8] The schools and the churches were in some ways alien institutions, importing urban influences that threatened the popular culture of villages. The schoolteacher in a nineteenth-century village was, in the words of Barnett Singer, 'akin to a foreigner', conspicuous in his black clothing, bow tie and polished shoes, or sombre long dress and neat bun

---

[6] Pierre-Jakez Hélias, *The Horse of Pride: Life in a Breton Village*, transl. June Guichenard (New Haven and London: Yale University Press, 1978), p. 305.

[7] David Cressy, *Literacy and the Social Order: Reading and Writing in Tudor and Stuart England* (Cambridge: Cambridge University Press, 1980), p. 13.

[8] Michael Mitterauer and Reinhard Sieder, *The European Family: Patriarchy to Partnership from the Middle Ages to the Present* (Oxford: Basil Blackwell, 1982), p. 94.

if a female.[9] In the long run, of course, the school system, not to mention increasing contacts with towns during the nineteenth and twentieth centuries, would integrate the villagers into their national culture. Yet a language barrier well into the nineteenth century was a daily reminder in many regions that the teacher and the priest were outsiders. As the son of a peasant in north Germany, Friedrich Paulsen had to contend with High German in his school, Low German in the homes of some of his friends and Frisian in his own family. Jürgen Schlumbohm writes that for children among the peasantry, 'print media, writing, and verbal communication in general had a rather limited impact'. They remained closely in touch with the daily routines of adults, sometimes joining them at work, listening to their gossip and observing their struggles with paperwork.[10]

There was most likely some feeling among villagers that the rural community into which they were born would provide support throughout their life. Peasant families helped each other out with little services, such as exchanging children as farm servants or giving food to the very poor. An annual round of festivals brought the popular culture to life, as did the French *veillées* or German *spinnstuben* (spinning bees) during the long winter evenings. Children listened to stories passed down the generations, learned about supernatural forces at work around them and went through an informal 'apprenticeship' working beside others on the land. The intense sociability and firm sense of identity encouraged in villages was certainly appreciated by peasants as they witnessed its decline during the twentieth century. Pierre-Jakez Hélias, for example, missed the constant visits from neighbours in his Breton village of Plozévet once he had moved on to a town.[11]

Most importantly for children, they spent a good deal of their time in the company of other young folk of various ages in their village. Out on their own in the countryside, it is conceivable that they learned more from them than from adults. They played numerous games together, made toys such as little windmills and whistles, bartered with each other and learned about the flora and fauna around them. In northern Europe, this included a certain amount of horseplay of a sexual nature, especially among the adolescents, such as a game from eighteenth-century Burgundy where a blindfolded male 'wolf' would try to grab and 'eat' his female prey.[12] Girls,

---

[9] Barnett Singer, *Village Notables in Nineteenth-Century France: Priests, Mayors, Schoolmasters* (Albany, NY: State University of New York Press, 1985), pp. 109, 121–2.

[10] Jürgen Schlumbohm, 'The School of Life: Reflections on Socialization in Preindustrial Germany', in Andrea Immel and Michael Witmore (eds.), *Childhood and Children's Books in Early Modern Europe, 1550–1800* (London: Routledge, 2006), pp. 305–27 (pp. 306, 315).

[11] Hélias, *Horse of Pride*, p. 318.

[12] Colin Heywood, 'Innocence and Experience: Sexuality among Young People in Modern France, c. 1750–1950', *French History*, 21 (2007), 44–64 (58).

expected to help their mothers around the home, had less opportunity to play than boys, and they tended to mingle in twos and threes. Boys meanwhile formed little gangs, with their own territory and rules. Pierre-Jakez Hélias provides a rare account of a village *société enfantine*, perhaps one tinged with a certain nostalgia for his own childhood. He rose up the gang's hierarchy to become a 'man' (aged ten). To do so he had to undergo a series of tests of his courage under the watchful eye of the older 'lad from Pouloupri', such as crawling along a stream as it passed through a dark, narrow tunnel, and climbing to the top of a tree as it swayed in the wind to try to bring down a bird's nest. There were also battles between gangs of children from the upper and lower parts of his village, reminiscent of Louis Pergaud's fictional account in *La Guerre des boutons* (1912).[13]

Yet for all of its benefits, there were strict limits to what these communities could do for their members in the face of rising numbers and inadequate food supplies.[14] As Olwen Hufton shows in the case of eighteenth-century France, children from indigent families often had to resort to desperate measures such as begging, thieving with a gang of other children or smuggling salt and tobacco.[15] There was also a potentially oppressive side to the formal and informal institutions that imposed their discipline on villagers, such as the civil parish in England and the *obschina* in Russia. Rural Württemberg provides an example of exceptionally tight control of people's lives. Institutions such as the rural guild and the Lutheran congregation often intervened to ensure, for example, that children were brought up in a particularly disciplined fashion.[16] No less importantly, an informal education in the village was fine for those remaining on the land, but of little use to those opting to migrate to towns – an increasing stream during the nineteenth and twentieth centuries. In the depths of Brittany, Pierre-Jakez Hélias had his grandfather urging him to go to school to learn French: 'With French, you can go everywhere. With only Breton, you're tied on a short rope, like a cow to his [sic] post.'[17]

---

[13] Pierre-Jakez Hélias, *Le cheval d'orgeuil* (Paris: Plon, 1972), pp. 259–63 (abbreviated in the English translation); Louis Pergaud, *La Guerre des boutons* (Paris: Mercure de France, 1963).

[14] See below, 'Orphaned and Impoverished Children in Villages'.

[15] Olwen Hufton, *The Poor of Eighteenth-Century France, 1750–1789* (Oxford: Clarendon Press, 1974), pp. 108, 176, 268–9, 287–8.

[16] Sheilagh C. Ogilvie, 'Coming of Age in a Corporate Society: Capitalism, Pietism and Family Authority in Rural Württemberg, 1590–1740', *Continuity and Change*, 1 (1986), 279–331.

[17] Hélias, *Horse of Pride*, p. 193.

The Peasant Family

The most immediate influence on the young villagers from infancy was their family. It was tempting for conservatives in particular to romanticise the peasant family as the bedrock of a stable, hierarchical society. The French economist Frédéric Le Play (1806–82) famously idealised the *famille-souche* (stem family), which he was aware of in certain parts of central and southern France, as a source of both stability and enterprise. The custom was for one child to marry and remain with the parents, ensuring the continuity of the family tradition, while the others could either remain as unmarried members of the original family, or strike out on their own elsewhere. What Le Play liked most of all was the way it reinforced paternal authority, and hence in his view the whole social order.[18]

The pleasing image of children in villages basking in the attention of parents, numerous siblings, grandparents, aunts, uncles and other kin can only be taken so far: the reality is more complex. For a long time, scholars assumed that large, complex families were the norm in pre-industrial Europe, until the onset of industrialisation brought a funda-mental shift to small, nuclear families. It is now clear from the research of demographic historians that in parts of western Europe, from as far back as the sixteenth century at least, nuclear families were the norm, with a mean household size of 4.75 emerging for a large sample of English villages before 1900 (see Figure 2.1).[19] It should be added that examples of what Nicola Tadmor calls the 'household-family' of the early modern period, German historians the *ganzes Haus* (whole household), their Spanish counterparts the *hogar*, were something more than the modern nuclear family. They also included the servants, apprentices, lodgers and others who resided in a house under the authority of its head – and who in common usage at the period of were described as part of the family.[20] This picture needs to be balanced by consideration of southern and eastern Europe, for long neglected in general surveys. There were plenty of examples from across the continent of what Peter Czap described,

[18] Frédéric Le Play, *L'Organisation de la famille* (Tours: A. Mame et fils, 1884), ch. 2.
[19] Peter Laslett, 'Mean Household Size in England since the Sixteenth Century', in Peter Laslett and Richard Wall (eds.), *Household and Family in Past Time* (Cambridge: Cambridge University Press, 1972), pp. 125–58 (pp. 126–7, 139).
[20] Nicola Tadmor, *Family and Friends in Eighteenth-Century England: Household, Kinship, and Patronage* (Cambridge: Cambridge University Press, 2001); Sheilagh Ogilvie (ed.), *Germany: A New Social and Economic History*, vol. 2, '1630–1800' (London: Arnold, 1996), pp. 4, 156–7; Josette Borderies-Guereña, 'Niños y niñas en familia', in José María Borrás Llop (ed.), *Historia de la infancia en la España contemporánea, 1834–1936* (Madrid: Ministerio de Trabajo y Asuntos Sociales, 1996), pp. 23–4.

"Home, Sweet Home."

Figure 2.1 Sentimentalised view of a Victorian family returning home after a day's work in the fields.
Getty Images, 544795396.

from a nineteenth-century Russian example, as the child brought up 'in crowded proximity with kin other than members of his biological family'.[21]

Peasant autobiographies reveal childhood memories of spending time with relatives, especially cousins, uncles, aunts and grandparents, even when they did not live under the same roof. From a sample of three villages in nineteenth-century Essex, Barry Reay shows that although the nuclear family predominated, kinship relations were important: no less than 60 per cent of households in the village of Hernhill were related to other households.[22] Grandparents everywhere might have more time to spend with young children than parents who were preoccupied with work

---

[21] Peter Czap, 'A Large Family: The Peasant's Greatest Wealth, Serf Households in Mishino, Russia. 1814–1858', in R. Wall, J. Robin, and P. Laslett (eds.), *Family Forms in Historic Europe* (Cambridge: Cambridge University Press, 1983), pp. 105–151 (p. 144).

[22] Barry Reay, 'Kinship and the Neighbourhood in Nineteenth-Century Rural England: The Myth of the Autonomous Nuclear Family', *Journal of Family History*, 21 (1996), 87–104 (93).

on a farm. In Russia, Savva Dmitrievich Purlevskii stated that 'I loved my grandmother more than anyone else' and was devastated when she died. Later in the nineteenth century, Antoine Sylvère started life in the Auvergne living with his grandparents while his mother worked as a wet nurse in Lyon. He also recalled the 'incomparable' time he spent as a young boy with his grandfather, learning the ways of farming.[23]

Finally, peasant families, complex or not, were not necessarily as stable or harmonious as Le Play fondly imagined. Like all families, they were rendered unstable by the high mortality prevailing among both children and adults. Families broke up with the death of a husband or wife, reconstituted quite quickly in many cases, and so produced blended families bringing together children from one or even two earlier marriages. For a stem family this type of evolution meant sliding in and out of its characteristic mingling of three generations: there were periods when, for example, it might take the form of a nuclear family in the absence of any grandparents. There was also plenty of scope for friction in a complex family. Doubtless most young people more or less willingly accepted the authority of their father and rubbed along with their parents as best they could while learning the routines of life on a farm. But there were potential conflicts of interest with parents as they grew older, such as the choice of a marriage partner or deciding who would inherit the property.[24]

Life and Death during Infancy

Surviving Infancy

The first consideration in a peasant household was to try to keep the newborn baby alive. Death hovered ominously over infants in villages during the eighteenth and nineteenth centuries. Semën Ivanovich Kanatchikov, born in a village near Moscow in 1879, remarked that there were no outstanding events during his early childhood as a peasant, 'unless one counts the fact that I survived'.[25] Attempts to measure infant mortality during this period are hampered by a lack of raw data, but as a

---

[23] Savva Dmitrievich Purlevskii, *A Life under Russian Serfdom: The Memoirs of Savva Dmitrievich Purlevskii 1800–1868*, transl. and ed. Boris B. Gorshkov (Budapest: Central European University Press, 2005), p. 53; Antoine Sylvère, *Toinou: le cri d'un enfant auvergnat* (Paris: Plon, 1980), pp. 2, 78–81.

[24] Elizabeth Claverie and Pierre Lamaison, *L'Impossible mariage: violence et parenté en Gévaudan, 17e, 18e et 19e siècles* (Paris: Hachette, 1982), chs. 3–4.

[25] *A Radical Worker in Tsarist Russia: The Autobiography of Semën Ivanovich Kanatchikov*, transl. and ed. Reginald E. Zelnik (Stanford: Stanford University Press, 1986), p. 1.

general indication, historians estimate that during the seventeenth century between 20 and 40 per cent of those born alive would not survive their first year.[26] The late eighteenth century brought some improvement, but during the years 1800–9 the infant mortality rate in rural France still stood at an estimated 198 per thousand live births, and in a sample of English villages (in 1800–24) at the relatively low level of 144 per thousand. A sustained decline did not set in until the late nineteenth or early twentieth centuries in most parts of Europe. At the national level, around 1900 a few countries such as Norway, Sweden and the Netherlands veered towards the lower end of the spectrum, with around 100 infant deaths per thousand live births, while others, notably Russia at around 250 per thousand, were up at the higher end. It might be noted here that life remained precarious for children who survived their first year: before 1750, in the most extreme cases, only around half of those born survived to the age of ten. By the early nineteenth century, approximately 40 per cent in rural France still died before their tenth birthday, and 25 per cent in the English villages sampled.[27] Even in the mid-nineteenth century, while growing up in Iceland, Indriði Einarsson had to face the experience of diphtheria wiping out nine of his siblings: later in life, he wrote that 'There was a time during my childhood when I was certain that the diphtheria would kill me before the age of 14'.[28]

National averages everywhere masked considerable regional variation, often attributable to different feeding practices.[29] There were a few areas in central and northern Europe that had a long tradition of not breastfeeding their young, including northern Sweden, southern Bavaria and parts of Württemberg, Baden, Saxony, Bohemia and the Austrian Tyrol.[30] Parents in southern Germany fed their children sugared water and 'meal pap': a concoction of milk and barley flour. John Knodel and Etienne Van de Walle cite a report from Oberbayern, in 1888, which described how:

[26] Michael W. Flinn, *The European Demographic System, 1500–1820* (Brighton: Harvester Press, 1981), p. 17.

[27] Robert Woods, *Children Remembered: Responses to Untimely Death in the Past* (Liverpool: Liverpool University Press, 2006), ch. 3; B. R. Mitchell, *International Historical Statistics: Europe, 1750–2005* (Basingstoke: Palgrave Macmillan, 2007), pp. 121–9.

[28] Sigurður Gylfi Magnússon, 'From Children's Point of View: Childhood in Nineteenth-Century Iceland', *Journal of Social History*, 29 (1995), 301.

[29] See below, 'Caring for Infants'.

[30] Loftur Guttormsson, 'Parent–Child Relations', in David I. Kertzer and Marzio Barbagli, *The History of the European Family* (New Haven, CT: Yale University Press, 2001), vol. 2, pp. 251–81 (pp. 254–6); John Knodel, 'Breast-Feeding and Population Growth', *Science*, 198 (1977), 111–15.

A woman who came from northern Germany and wanted according to the customs of her homeland to nurse her infant herself was openly called swinish and filthy by the local women. Her husband threatened he would no longer eat anything she prepared, if she did not give up this disgusting habit.[31]

Such areas often had disastrous infant mortality rates before the development of safe artificial feeding methods in the late nineteenth century. In rural communities in northern Sweden, infant mortality rates in the early nineteenth century hovered around the 400 per thousand mark, as infants were fed cow's milk and various solids.[32] It should be added that rural areas rarely matched the heavy toll taken on infant lives in towns, notably during the nineteenth century. Nonetheless, children during their first year or so succumbed in droves to digestive diseases, notably a catastrophic loss of weight with summer diarrhoea, and to respiratory diseases, such as bronchitis and pneumonia, that most often struck them down in winter. They were also particularly vulnerable to the epidemics that periodically swept through villages, such as smallpox and diphtheria.[33]

Caring for Infants

During their early years, children in villages were largely in the hands of their mother and other female relatives. Fathers were not so much indifferent to the well-being of their offspring at this stage of life as inclined to see it as the responsibility of the mother in the then-customary division of labour between the sexes. To begin with, the mother concentrated on the food, clothing and spiritual welfare of her newborn baby. Peasant women in most of Europe always breastfed their infants if they were capable of doing so, with the exceptions noted earlier. Breastfeeding was after all the natural way to feed a baby, costing nothing, and it was thought to be pleasurable for both mother and child.[34] Only a small minority of gentry

---

[31] John Knodel and Etienne Van de Walle, 'Breast Feeding, Fertility and Infant Mortality: An Analysis of Some Early German Data', *Population Studies*, 21 (1967), 109–31 (119–20).

[32] Anders Brändström, 'The Impact of Female Labour Conditions on Infant Mortality: A Case Study of the Parishes of Nedertorneå and Jokkmokk, 1800–96', *Social History of Medicine*, 1 (1988), 329–58.

[33] Carlo Corsini and Pier Paolo Viazzo, 'The Historical Decline of Infant Mortality: An Overview', in Carlo Corsini and Pier Paolo Viazzo (eds.), *The Decline of Infant Mortality in Europe, 1800–1950* (Florence: UNICEF, 1993), pp. 9–17; Naomi Williams, 'Urban-Rural Differentials in Infant Mortality in Victorian England', *Population Studies*, 49 (1995), 401–20 (413).

[34] Jacques Gélis, Mireille Laget and Marie-France Morel, *Entrer dans la vie: naissances et enfances dans la France traditionnelle* (Paris: Gallimard/Julliard, 1978), p. 110.

and wealthy farming families in the countryside could afford the expense of a wet nurse.[35] Peasant families had some tendency to overfeed children, by supplementing breast milk with various broths after a few days or weeks: explicable, perhaps, by their obsession with food shortages. Their assumption was that breast milk on its own was insufficient for the baby to develop its strength. Olga Semyonova, for example, noted that food for infants among peasants in her Black Earth region of Russia consisted of 'breast milk, the *soska* or rag pacifier, kasha [porridge], bread, potatoes, and cow's milk'.[36] Weaning in Europe took place anywhere between six months and two years of age, according to the circumstances of the mother and the size of the baby. This could come as a particularly unpleasant shock for the infant if the mother followed the custom in parts of Europe of smearing a substance such as mustard, pepper or garlic over her nipples.[37]

Swaddling was also universal among the peasantry. They might even persist with it into the twentieth century in isolated areas, long after it came under attack in elite circles. Immediately after birth, the baby was tightly wrapped in long strips of cloth over its swaddling clothes, because the villagers believed this would ensure a strong, upright body. Given the threat of deficiency diseases such as rickets, which left the victim permanently bow-legged, this was readily understandable (if unscientific). Swaddling kept the baby warm, made it easy to carry, and encouraged it to sleep. After a month or so the head and arms were left free, and eventually both boys and girls moved on to the little gown worn during early childhood. Swaddling was evidently convenient for peasant families – especially the alleged practice of hanging the child on a hook while its parents went about their work. But it was also a time-consuming task to wind and unwind the strips a few times a day, and evidently country folk believed it to be important for the health of the child, even though constraining a child's limbs in this way flew in the face of medical advice.

Trying to ward off disease and the various evil forces that the villagers feared were waiting to harm the vulnerable baby was a grim prospect, but one they did not shirk. They made every effort to avoid a baby dying before baptism. Most Catholics believed that the soul of such unfortunates went into limbo: an intermediary position between heaven and hell. Protestant doctrine rejected this position, yet in rural Lincolnshire, in

---

[35] Valerie A. Fildes, *Breasts, Bottles and Babies* (Edinburgh: Edinburgh University Press, 1986), ch. 3.
[36] Olga Semyonova Tian-Shanskaia, *Village Life in Late Tsarist Russia*, ed. David L. Ransel (Bloomington and Indianapolis: Indiana University Press, 1993), p. 24.
[37] Gélis et al., *Entrer dans la vie*, p. 125.

England, the popular view during the nineteenth century was still that the souls of the unbaptised wandered for eternity as wild geese.[38] Both the Catholic and Protestant Churches were prepared to sanction emergency baptisms by midwives and other members of the laity in cases where a newborn child looked as though it might die at any moment. To protect the unbaptised infant from a 'string of elves, devils and evil spirits', there were various rituals available. Across Europe, the baby was kept indoors, protected with the magical power of salt, and watched over with a lighted candle. Under the Catholic influence, the nineteenth century saw the resort to such devices as consecrated rosaries and amulets placed near the child.[39] It follows that baptism was for the villagers, even in Protestant areas, a 'quasi-magical rite essential to the child's welfare', as the historian Ralph Houlbrooke puts it.[40] Catholics in villages usually tried to baptise their newborns on the day of its birth or the day after; Protestants were prepared to wait until the following Sunday or saint's day.

When a baby died, the peasantry everywhere appeared resigned to their loss. It is tempting to accuse parents of indifference to children by drawing attention to the terse recordings of their losses. A study of peasant diaries in nineteenth-century Sweden opens with an entry from one such that mentioned the death of his twelve-year-old daughter with 'Drove manure until noon, Hädda dead'. It is of course quite conceivable that high infant death rates meant that parents were reluctant to make much of an emotional investment in their youngest children. However, the general tenor of the diaries in question works against any such interpretation. There were plenty of heartfelt laments, such as that from Gustaf Persson of Värmland, who wrote in 1826: 'And daily I cry over my boy who has passed away, because I miss him daily with sorrow.' Doubtless villagers needed to develop ways to grieve over their losses, and their Christian faith was on hand to help with a reassuring message. Jonas Olsson, another Swedish peasant, in this case from the Hälsingland in 1865, comforted himself with the thought:

As I write these words I come to think of little passed-away Brita and it is sad and very regretful that she was taken away from us but on the other hand it is joyful to

---

[38] James Obelkevich, *Religion and Society: South Lindsey 1825–1875* (Oxford: Clarendon Press, 1976), p. 272.

[39] Jacques Gélis, *History of Childbirth: Fertility, Pregnancy and Birth in Early Modern Europe*, transl. Rosemary Roberts (Cambridge: Polity Press, 1991), pp. 194–6.

[40] Ralph Houlbrooke, *The English Family, 1450–1700* (London: Longman, 1984), p. 130.

think that blessed are those who sleep well. She will inherit the crown of salvation which is intended by the almighty Lord for those children of innocence.[41]

In general, however, the peasantry kept their thoughts to themselves on this matter.

The Murder of Newborn Infants

Villagers were long familiar with the sight of tiny corpses, still bloody from the birthing process, lying in ditches or hastily stuffed into chests in the mother's room.[42] By the eighteenth and nineteenth centuries, infanticide in Europe had become associated with unmarried women trying desperately to rid themselves of an illegitimate child. Doubtless married women quietly disposed of unwanted babies, possibly including puny or defective ones, in numbers impossible to know. It was difficult to prove that deaths in the home by, say, overlaying (the smothering of a child in bed with its parents) or extreme neglect, were not accidental or due to natural causes. As a result, married women, as well as those from the middle classes, rarely appeared in court. Those who did, which was still not very often, were female farm labourers, domestic industrial workers, the daughters of small farmers and tradesmen, and above all, servants. They were closely watched by their neighbours – in fact, most court cases the accused came from a village or small town, where everybody knew everybody else's business: 80 per cent of them in nineteenth-century French courts.[43]

Mark Jackson uses evidence from northern England to draw attention to the hostility to single mothers among villagers, resentful of the financial burden on the poor rates of illegitimate children. Fear was what motivated the young women to commit murder.[44] The stigma of having spawned a bastard meant that single mothers everywhere risked being

---

[41] Bo Larsson, 'Deaths of Children as Reflected in Peasant Diaries', in Bo Larsson and Janken Myrdal (eds.), *Peasant Diaries as a Source for the History of Mentality* (Stockholm: Nordiska Museet, 1995), pp. 141–7 (pp. 141–2).

[42] Hufton, *The Poor*, pp. 349–51.

[43] R. W. Malcolmson, 'Infanticide in the Eighteenth Century', in J. S. Cockburn (ed.), *Crime in England, 1550–1800* (London: Methuen, 1977), pp. 187–209; Deborah Symonds, *Weep Not for Me: Women, Ballads, and Infanticide in Early Modern Scotland* (University Park, PA: Penn State University Press, 1997), ch. 3; James M. Donovan, 'Infanticide and the Juries in France, 1825–1913', *Journal of Family History*, 16 (1991), 157–76; Regina Schulte, 'Infanticide in Rural Bavaria in the Nineteenth Century', in Hans Medick and David Warren Sabean (eds.), *Interest and Emotion: Essays on the Study of Family and Kinship* (Cambridge: Cambridge University Press, 1984), pp. 77–102.

[44] Mark Jackson, *New-Born Child Murder: Women, Illegitimacy and the Courts in Eighteenth-Century England* (Manchester: Manchester University Press, 1996), passim.

disowned by their families (particularly in southern Europe, where notions of honour were taken very seriously[45]), losing status in the village, poor prospects in finding a husband and, in the case of farm servants, dismissal from their job. They also faced the near-impossible task of raising a child on their own. A study of infanticide in Imperial Germany finds that 'poverty, not illegitimacy, drove infanticide', for in this case it was most common in poor regions such as East Prussia and Mecklenburg.[46] Moreover, Regina Schulte argues from evidence drawn from rural Bavaria that mothers accused of infanticide in effect faced two trials. In the first, the local community decided on her reputation: if it was good, they shielded her from the law, but if she was considered 'dissolute', they informed on her.[47] What emerges from this seemingly 'unnatural' killing by a mother is the pressure of poverty on poor families with too many children, and the multitude of difficulties faced by single mothers and illegitimate children.

Childhood among the Peasantry

Following infancy, childhood in villages was generally a sociable affair, unless the family lived in an isolated farm or hamlet. The younger children might form small groups to explore the fields and woods around them, and play with rudimentary toys they or their parents made themselves, such as balls, whistles, rag dolls, little wooden carts, toy domestic animals and the like. Dmitrii Ivanovich Rostislavov (1809–77), son of a priest, recalled that in his Russian village during the early nineteenth century, 'Until we were six, sometimes even seven, we were permitted only to eat, sleep, run around, and frolic in all sorts of ways.'[48] Boys generally enjoyed more freedom to roam than girls. In Upper Brittany, for example, the folklorist Paul Sébillot stated that little girls stayed at home, while boys wandered around in stables, cracked whips and played at being horses.[49] Live animals also acted as faithful 'playthings and

---

[45] Stephen Wilson, 'Infanticide, Child Abandonment, and Female Honour in Nineteenth-Century Corsica', *Comparative Studies in Society and History*, 30 (1988), 762–83.

[46] Jeffrey S. Richter, 'Infanticide, Child Abandonment, and Abortion in Imperial Germany', *Journal of Interdisciplinary History*, 28 (1998), 511–51 (534).

[47] Schulte, 'Infanticide', pp. 94–8; eadem, *The Village in Court: Arson, Infanticide, and Poaching in the Court Records of Upper Bavaria, 1848–1910* (Cambridge: Cambridge University Press, 1994), ch. 4.

[48] Dmitrii Ivanovich Rostislavov, *Provincial Russia in the Age of Enlightenment: The Memoir of a Priest's Son*, transl. and ed. Alexander M. Martin (De Kalb, IL: Northern Illinois University Press, 2002), p. 38.

[49] Paul Sébillot, *Coutumes populaires de la Haute-Bretagne* (Paris: Maisonneuve, 1886), p. 31.

playmates' for farm children.[50] Later, when working as shepherds in the pastures, they were sometimes able to meet up with others and pass the time agreeably, unsupervised by adults. Doubtless brothers and sisters played together more in the past than today, given the larger families and closer spacing of births.[51] Relations between parents and children partly depended on individual personalities, but as we have seen, historians have generally retreated from the bleak view current during the 1970s. Jacques Gélis and his colleagues asserted that country folk in France had a 'spontaneous and lively' way of loving children that remained independent of thinking among other social groups. In a similar vein, Boris Gorshkov wrote that their Russian counterparts 'provided children with love and care, as well as tolerating some of their mischief'.[52]

Orphaned and Impoverished Children in Villages

To begin with, it is worth bearing in mind that an estimated one in three children in agricultural society would lose at least one parent while they were growing up. Thus, a study of the Nottinghamshire village of Clayworth found that in 1688 approximately one-third of the children were living with a widowed parent, or were step-children with a parent who had remarried.[53] How this affected children is difficult to say, for want of evidence. Certainly, the stereotype of the 'wicked step-mother' of folk tales was a tempting figure for some who wrote their autobiographies. Jelle Sipkes (b. 1738), a Dutch cattle-farmer and Mennonite minister, described his step-mother as 'mean', and concluded on a vengeful note with 'I say that orphaned children are unhappy in this world, but such step-mothers will be unhappy when the Lord will judge them'. Capitaine Coignet, 'soldier of the empire', recorded his unfortunate experience during the 1780s when his mother died and his father married their eighteen-year-old servant. He depicted the step-mother beating him and his siblings mercilessly, and skimping on their food. Aged eight, he

---

[50] Floyd M. Martinson, *Growing Up in Norway, 800 to 1990* (Carbondale, IL: Southern Illinois University Press, 1992), p. 147.

[51] Jane Humphries, *Childhood and Child Labour in the British Industrial Revolution* (Cambridge: Cambridge University Press, 2010), pp. 126–8.

[52] Gélis et al., *Entrer dans la vie*, p. 44; Boris B. Gorshkov, *Russia's Factory Children: State, Society, and Law, 1800–1917* (Pittsburgh, PA: University of Pittsburgh Press, 2009), p. 17.

[53] Peter Laslett, 'Parental Deprivation in the Past: A Note on the History of Orphans in England', *Local Population Studies*, 13 (1974), 11–18.

ran away from home with his older brother and hired himself out as a farm servant.[54] All the same, we should keep in mind that cruel step-mothers and step-fathers are more interesting to write about than dutiful ones.

More precarious still was the position of those children who had lost both parents or whose family was unable to support them.[55] They had scant hope of finding support from charities or the state. The approach to poor relief varied across the continent, but what was common to all regions was the concentration of what meagre resources there were in towns rather than the countryside. In the Catholic countries of Italy, Spain and France, the poor had to rely on the Church and voluntary donations from the faithful. Although reinvigorated by the Catholic Reformation, during the eighteenth century this system was struggling to cope with a rising tide of poor, especially as the first stirrings of 'dechristianisation' were discouraging donors. In France, for example, the poor in villages could turn to the odd monastery for help in cash or kind, a special fund for them available in some villages, or the more a formal *bureau de charité*. Although these sources were likely to look favourably on children in distress, beyond a very small community they were pitifully inadequate for the scale of the problems they faced.[56]

In parts of the Protestant north of Europe, notably in England and Germany, the state tended to play more of a role in poor relief. Even so, institutions such as the Poor Law in England also struggled to cope with rising costs during the late eighteenth and early nineteenth centuries. A common measure to deal with impoverished children was to board them out with a local family. Paying a subsidy to encourage families to take them on as pauper apprentices was often considered a cost-effective solution. Such was the case in the Devonshire village of Colyton, under the old Poor Law system (before 1834). The fostering family undertook to feed and lodge the child for around thirteen years, usually starting at the age of ten. In return, the paupers were expected to work without being paid, as 'servants in husbandry' if a boy and in 'housewifery' if a girl. In the Nordic countries, poor children in villages were often boarded out to foster parents by auction. A case study from northern Sweden shows destitute children being regularly put up for auction during the nineteenth century. The youngest were often taken by childless couples,

---

[54] Rudolf Dekker, *Childhood, Memory and Autobiography in Holland: From the Golden Age to Romanticism* (Basingstoke: Macmillan, 2000), p. 112; Coignet, *Les Cahiers*, pp. 1–2.

[55] See above, 'The Rural Community'.

[56] Olwen Hufton, *The Poor of Eighteenth-Century France, 1750–1789* (Oxford: Oxford University Press, 1974), ch. v.

the older ones by farmers seeking cheap labour. Sometimes the system of boarding out worked well, with foster children treated as a son or a daughter; in other cases it failed, as they were ruthlessly exploited. Autobiographies from Finns who had been boarded out ranged from memories of being a twelve-year-old boy happy to have enough to eat for the first time in his life, despite the arduous labour on a farm, to another who recalled being fed an inadequate diet and being beaten all too often. Everywhere, the austere upbringing of the foster children was not far removed from that of others around them in villages, but there was always the risk that the pecuniary interest of foster parents would prevail in the relationship.[57]

Parents and Children

Among those with two parents, autobiographies provide plenty of examples of imperious patriarchal figures (particularly where there was land to be inherited), or of fathers who drank heavily and viciously beat their wife and children. Mothers and fathers too preoccupied with their work routines to fuss over their children were also common. It was hard for many authors to avoid some feelings of resentment towards their parents, sometimes depicting them as petty tyrants, doubtless aware that by the time many of them were writing, in the twentieth century, warmer relationships were more common.[58] Yet children generally recognised, or grasped with hindsight, that parents tried their best, and often had to make difficult decisions, such as whether to pull them out of school or send them away to relatives when times were hard. Outward shows of affection, such as hugging and kissing, were certainly rare.[59] Much in evidence was a respectful attitude to fathers, and a closer relationship with mothers. 'There is no other friend like your mother', according to a Russian proverb, and the young there were typical in considering a

---

[57] Pamela Sharpe, 'Poor Children as Apprentices in Colyton, 1598–1830', *Continuity and Change*, 6 (1991), 253–70; Elisabeth Engberg, 'Boarded Out by Auction: Poor Children and their Families in Nineteenth-Century Northern Sweden', *Continuity and Change*, 19 (2004), 431–57; Marjatta Rahikainen, 'Compulsory Child Labour: Parish Paupers in Finland, c. 1810–1920', *Rural History*, 13 (2002), 163–78.

[58] Mary Jo Maynes, *Taking the Hard Road: Life Course in German and French Workers' Autobiographies in the Era of Industrialization* (Chapel Hill, NC: University of North Carolina Press, 1995), pp. 78–9.

[59] John Burnett (ed.), *Destiny Obscure: Autobiographies of Childhood, Education and Family from the 1820s to the 1920s* (London and New York: Routledge, 1994), pp. 37–8; Martinson, *Growing Up in Norway*, pp. 47–8.

mother's love 'gentler and purer' than a father's.[60] Among French life-writers, for example, Antoine Sylvère, from a hard-pressed family in the Auvergne, had a troubled relationship with his mother, while the poet Frédéric Mistral, brought up in the more comfortable circumstances of well-off landowning peasants in Provence, remembered a loving relationship with his mother, as did Pierre-Jakez Hélias in his Breton village.[61] Fathers were often out in the fields rather than in the home for much of the day, and as head of the household, authoritative and even punitive figures. Peasants were quite prepared to use fear as a method of disciplining children: they saw themselves attempting to break the will of a 'little animal'.[62] Hence they threatened the young with an assortment of 'bogeymen' and routinely resorted to corporal punishment.[63] The Russian *Domostroi*, originally a medieval manual, advised, 'Do not spare your child any beating, for the stick will not kill him, but will make him healthier; when you strike the body, you save the soul from death'.[64] Children generally accepted this when they felt they had deserved it, and only became indignant when convinced they had not. Jane Humphries is persuasive in arguing that an abusive father was usually one who was failing as a breadwinner and whose family as a consequence was falling apart.[65] A far more common practice was to apply corporal punishment in moderation. Savva Dmitrievich Purlevskii, from Central Russia, stated that his father beat him 'only on rare occasions'. Ephraïm Grenadou in France recorded that his father did so with a bunch of nettles three or four times a year when he neglected his work on the farm after school.[66]

Material Conditions for Children in Villages

The material circumstances of village children were more or less Spartan, depending on where they stood in the village hierarchy. Their clothing was simple, described in the case of the Russian peasantry observed by Olga Semyonova as consisting of a homespun or linen shirt, which fitted loosely or could be gathered at the waist with a belt. Gradually, the boys

[60] Christine Worobec, *Peasant Russia: Family and Community in the Post-Emancipation Period* (Princeton, NJ: Princeton University Press, 1991), pp. 209–12.
[61] Colin Heywood, *Growing Up in France: From the Ancien Régime to the Third Republic* (Cambridge: Cambridge University Press, 2007), pp. 125–6.
[62] See Chapter 1, 'Childhood'.
[63] On the role of fear in childrearing during the early modern period, see Peter N. Stearns, 'Childhood Emotions in Modern Western History', in Paula Fass, *The Routledge History of Childhood in the Western World* (Abingdon: Routledge, 2013), pp. 158–73 (pp. 160–1).
[64] Worobec, *Peasant Russia*, p. 211.   [65] Humphries, *Childhood and Child Labour*, p. 135.
[66] Purlevskii, *Life under Russian Serfdom*, p. 53; Ephraïm Grenadou and Alain Prévost, *Grenadou: paysan français* (Paris: Seuil, 1966), p. 15.

moved on to trousers, the girls to homespun skirts. Both sexes normally went barefoot, though occasionally they had woollen stockings and shoes.[67] Poorer children everywhere often had to put up with ill-fitting hand-me-downs from older siblings.

Village children also faced crowded living conditions, although the early modern period had brought improvements to farm houses in many parts of Europe, with more spacious, two-story buildings, partitioned rooms and stoves for cooking and heating.[68] However, housing remained rudimentary for the village poor until well into the twentieth century. Henri Pitaud (b. 1899) recalling bitterly his 'trou de maison' (hole of a house) in the Vendée: a house with one bedroom, a kitchen and attached stables. In addition, personal hygiene was almost entirely neglected in the peasant household. The example of the peasantry in the Nivernais region of France reveals that even during the early twentieth century they rarely washed, merely splashing some water on their face from time to time, wore the same clothes for days on end and never cleaned their teeth. For children this led to chronic problems with skin infections, head lice and intestinal parasites. Jean-Roche Coignet remembered three years infested with vermin while employed as a young shepherd in the Morvan during the 1780s and expected to sleep rough in a barn every night.[69]

The most pressing concern for poor children in villages was getting enough to eat. Young people whose parents owned or rented the bigger farms could take for granted a well-stocked table. Rétif de la Bretonne, in *Monsieur Nicolas* (1797), mentioned eating white bread (as opposed to the 'grey', wholemeal bread of the peasantry) as a sign that his family was comfortable. Similarly, Savva Dmitrievich Purlevskii, from a family of successful traders among the serf population of Central Russia, remembered eating well as a child: 'on meat days we would have cold jellied meat, boiled ham, then Russian cabbage or noodle soup, grilled lamb or chicken.' However, he was aware that the 'common folk', particularly hard-pressed in eastern Europe, had to make do with a diet revolving around rye bread and grey vegetable soup. All the meat, dairy products and eggs produced by these peasants had of necessity to be sold.[70] Even in England, during the

[67] Semyonova, *Village Life*, pp. 29–30.
[68] Raffaella Sarti, *Europe at Home: Family and Material Culture, 1500–1800* (New Haven, CT: Yale University Press, 2002), p. 98.
[69] Guy Thuillier, 'Pour une histoire de l'hygiène corporelle.Un exemple régional: le Nivernais', *Revue d'histoire économique et sociale*, 46 (1968), 232–53; Jean-Roche Coignet, *Les Cahiers du Capitaine Coignet, 1799–1815* (Paris, 1883), p. 5.
[70] Rétif de la Bretonne, *Monsieur Nicolas* (Paris: Gallimard, 1989), p. 38; Purlevskii, *Life under Russian Serfdom*, pp. 59–60.

late nineteenth century, fresh milk was in short supply in villages, as most of it was sent to towns, and skimmed milk was fed to pigs.[71]

A common theme in peasant memoirs was that of always feeling hungry. In the words of the future trade union leader Joseph Arch, born the son of an agricultural labourer in Warwickshire in 1826, the 'wolf of hunger' prowled around the poor man's home night and day, 'a ravenous, profane beast ... always snapping, and snarling, and growling round the corner'.[72] Bread, and later potatoes or rice, was the basis of the popular diet, with variations according to local conditions. A staple for many mothers and children in Victorian England was bread with weak, milkless tea.[73] Bread was supplemented by vegetables, and any produce that the family could obtain from keeping poultry, a pig or a cow. This starchy diet was barely adequate for healthy growth, but some families always struggled to provide a basic subsistence level for their members. In Sweden, there is evidence of deteriorating nutrition and a rise in mortality for children in villages of the western part of the country during the mid-nineteenth century. It seems that when food was scarce poor families had to prioritise the needs of working adults, at the expense of children who were weaned but too young for serious labour.[74] Food shortages reduced a child to desperate measures such as begging from neighbours or for-aging for berries and edible plants in the hedgerows. Jean-Marie Deguignet (1834–1905) remembered trailing round his Breton village at the age of six on his daily task of begging dinner from local farmers: 'often, when they had stuffed my little stomach with oatmeal mush, they would also give me chunks of black bread and moldy crêpes to take home.' Even in England, George Mockford, born in 1826 in Sussex, recalled relief from a monotonous diet of potatoes with a little bacon fat on them by cooking and enjoying rats he had caught after cleaning out a barn.[75]

Conclusion

In sum, children grew up in villages with a set of conventions on what was appropriate for child-rearing. These began with a framework for

[71] Pamela Horn, *The Victorian Country Child* (Stroud: Sutton Publishing, 1997), p. 12.
[72] Joseph Arch, *The Autobiography of Joseph Arch*, ed. Gerard O'Leary (London: Macgibbon & Kee, 1966), pp. 31–2.
[73] Horn, *Victorian Country Child*, p. 11.
[74] Lars G. Sandberg and Richard H. Steckel, 'Overpopulation and Malnutrition Rediscovered: Hard Times in 19th-Century Sweden, *Explorations in Economic History*, 25 (1988), 1–19.
[75] Jean-Marie Déguignet, *Memoirs of a Breton Peasant*, transl. Linda Asher (New York: Seven Stories Press, 2004), p. 29; George Mockford, *Wilderness Journeyings and Gracious Deliverances* (1901), as cited in Humphries, *Childhood and Child Labour*, p. 99.

preserving the life of newborn babies, attentive to their spiritual as well as their physical welfare. And they influenced parent–child relations, with the absolute rule of the father taken as a starting point – though historians now generally agree that this did not prevent a loving relationship prevailing with both the mother and the father. The weight of community disapproval doubtless went some way to shield children from abusive parents and employers, though there was always some reluctance to interfere with the authority of fathers. Moreover, all the efforts to protect children from the rigours of peasant life could only go so far: the realities of high infant and child mortality, recurrent food shortages and a pessimistic view of childhood loomed large well into the nineteenth and even twentieth centuries. The peasantry was far from immune to various forces of change in society at large during this period, but they were generally among the last to be affected. They struggled to afford the expense of doctors, for example, and had to put up with very basic housing. Above all, they were slow to embrace wholeheartedly one of the major influences on childhood in the modern world: the school system.

3   Work, Education and Religion for Children in the Countryside

Children's Work on the Land

With many families in villages struggling to put enough food on the table, it is hardly surprising that children were called on from an early age to help with the numerous tasks that needed to be done on the farms. If they were not helping their parents, they could try to hire themselves out for work on a big commercial farm. There was a well-established view that an early start was necessary to acquire the skills and the discipline required later in life. Floyd Martinson notes in the Norwegian case that a 'mentality of work' dominated peasant life, including the assumption that work was part of a proper upbringing.[1] Child work in agriculture was therefore a matter of learning on-the-job as well as earning or producing. A farmer in Somerset stated during the 1840s that 'All the best labourers, who, consequently, get employment, are those that were taken young into the fields'.[2] Even the children of prosperous farmers might become involved with the work going on around them – though they had more time available for their schooling.

Tasks for Children

Much of the work on a farm was too heavy for children to manage, but there were numerous little tasks in the home or out in the fields that they could do to relieve the burden on adults. Across Europe, children were to be seen minding younger siblings, bird scaring, picking stones from fields, hoeing in the vegetable plots, collecting firewood, fetching water from a well, minding the family's livestock, and (boys especially) leading a plough team. During the late spring and summer, when the demand for labour on the land reached its peak, children worked in the fields beside

[1] Floyd M. Martinson, *Growing Up in Norway, 800 to 1990.* (Carbondale, IL: Southern Illinois University Press, 1992), pp. 83–4.
[2] Joyce Burnette, 'Child Day-Labourers in Agriculture: Evidence from Farm Accounts, 1740–1850', *Economic History Review*, 65 (2012), pp. 1077–99 (1089).

Figure 3.1 Italian shepherd-girl alone with her flock.
Getty Images, 666961084.

the haymakers and reapers, taking out food, binding sheaves and so forth. Many of their jobs were seasonal, or easy enough to leave plenty of time for play. Olga Semyonova described small boys aged seven to eleven who were sent out to watch over the family's horse as it grazed around the village getting together and foraging for food. Besides gathering nuts, berries and mushrooms from neighbours' woods, the young lads organised expeditions to steal apples or even ducks for roasting. Meanwhile, the girls observed by Semyonova grazed their family's calves, and gathered together for harmless pursuits such as playing games of jacks or singing (see Figure 3.1).[3]

Attitudes of Children to Working

The meagre wages that children earned if they hired themselves out as day labourers showed that they remained partly dependent on their parents for subsistence. Children took it for granted that they would help their parents, without any obvious resentment if the autobiographies they wrote later in life are to be believed. Rather, they were proud of contributing to the family budget, and gained in confidence as they worked. From Iceland, Hallgrímur Jónsson (b. 1902) wrote that:

[3] Olga Semyonova Tian-Shanskaia, *Village Life in Late Tsarist Russia*, ed. David L. Ransel (Bloomington, IN: Indiana University Press, 1993), pp. 36–7.

I have often listened to people who have felt pity for the shepherds and some actually have argued that it was not appropriate to expect children to do this job. But I am certain that a lot of boys developed enormously during their shepherd years, exactly because this task came with great responsibility and increased both strength and courage.

Agricol Perdiguier (1805–75) remembered his feelings of pride as he gradually mastered an assortment of skills on the family holding near Avignon. Together with his brothers and sisters, he tended vines, hoed the soil, harvested grapes, picked olives and collected mulberry leaves for silkworms.[4] However, the autobiographies also give a hint of the long hours out in the fields, the cold and wet of northern climates, and the sheer drudgery of much of the work. Roger Langdon (1825–94) wrote of his experience on a farm in England, 'For the princely sum of one shilling a week I had to mind sheep and pull up turnips in all winds and weathers, starting at six o'clock in the morning … After this, until I was thirteen years of age, my life was not worth living.' If left out on their own as shepherds, loneliness, boredom and a fear of strangers or wolves could make life miserable, not to mention the difficulty of keeping control of the animals. Emile Guillaumin wrote in *La Vie d'un simple* (1905), a novel based on the experiences of his grandfather:

Sometimes fear and sadness overtook me, and I started to cry, to cry without reason, for hours on end. A sudden rustling in the woods, the scampering of a mouse in the grass, the unfamiliar shriek of a bird, that was enough during these hours of anxiety to make me burst into tears.

Where the young worked beside adults, they had to keep up with the stiff pace of work. Writing in the 1850s, Joseph Ricketts recalled work as a plough boy during his Wiltshire childhood 'with a very ill-tempered carter … and being a little lame could not keep up with the horses without holding the traces – and very frequently was knocked down with a large lump of hard dirt'.[5] For farm servants, male as well as female, there was the risk of sexual harassment by employers or fellow-workers. Ulrich Bräker (1735–98) lost his innocence among ribald fellow goat-herds in Switzerland; Angélina Bardin (b. 1901), brought up under the

---

[4] Sigurður Gylfi Magnússon, 'From Children's Point of View: Childhood in Nineteenth-Century Iceland', *Journal of Social History*, 29 (1995), 310; Agricol Perdiguier, *Mémoires d'un compagnon* (Paris: Maspero, 1977), pp. 50–5.

[5] Roger Langdon, 'The Life of Roger Langdon, Told by Himself (1909)', as cited in John Burnett (ed.), *Destiny Obscure: Autobiographies of Childhood, Education and Family from the 1820s to the 1920s* (London: Routledge, 1994), p. 46; Emile Guillaumin, *La Vie d'un simple* (Paris: 1905), p. 11; Joseph Ricketts, 'Notes on the Life of Joseph Rickets' (1858), as cited by Jane Humphries, *Childhood and Child Labour in the British Industrial Revolution* (Cambridge: Cambridge University Press, 2010), p. 219.

supervision of the Assistance Publique, faced an attempted assault by one of her employers when working as a farm servant in the west of France.[6]

Working Conditions

Conditions naturally varied according to local circumstances: life was harder in the mountains than on the plains, and children on small family farms were under more pressure to start work early than those on the big commercial ones. In Russia, anthropological studies revealed that small nuclear families, and those with no adult males present, worked their children harder than extended families.[7] It may be that the 'industrious revolution' of the late-eighteenth and early nineteenth centuries, as envisaged by historian Jan de Vries, increased the scale of child labour on the farms. The model proposes that families devoted more time to money-earning activities so that they could consume more goods on the market. However, evidence from the English case indicates that the increased workload that families of farm labourers shouldered during this period enabled them to afford basic necessities rather than to expand into little luxuries.[8] In general, child labour does not feature in the story of the agricultural revolution in Europe. There was no particular link between the employment of child workers and the introduction of machinery on the farms. And certainly there was a general reluctance on the part of states to regulate the employment of children in the agricultural sector: if anything, the inclination was to idealise work on the land. England passed an Agricultural Children Act in 1873, banning children under eight years of age from working in agriculture (though with an exemption for children employed by their father or guardian), and requiring some attendance at school up to the age of twelve. With numerous exemptions, and no inspection service, it was a complete failure. More typically in Italy, a predominantly agricultural country during the 1880s, child labour legislation ignored farm workers altogether.[9]

---

[6] Mary Jo Maynes, *Taking the Hard Road: Life Course in German and French Workers' Autobiographies in the Era of Industrialization* (Chapel Hill, NC: University of North Carolina Press, 1995), pp. 76–7.

[7] Gorshkov, *Russia's Factory Children*, pp. 24–5.

[8] R. C. Allen and J. L. Weisdorf, 'Was There an "Industrious Revolution" before the Industrial Revolution? An Empirical Exercise for England, c. 1300–1830,' *Economic History Review*, 64 (2011), 715–29 (722).

[9] Pamela Horn, *The Victorian Country Child* (Stroud: Sutton Publishing, 1997), pp. 67–9; Carl Ipsen, *Italy in the Age of Pinocchio: Children and Danger in the Liberal Era* (New York, NY: Palgrave Macmillan, 2006), p. 87.

What did disturb contemporaries in some areas was the practice of employing children in agricultural gangs. Europe had a long tradition of temporary and seasonal migrations, notably with groups of workers moving around to take on harvest or construction work. During the second half of the nineteenth century, gangs of rural women and children became increasingly involved with work on large-scale farms.[10] In nineteenth-century Piedmont and Lombardy, for example, groups of women and children moved around to work in the rice fields. This involved toiling with their feet immersed in water, sowing in the spring and weeding during the summer.[11] In Norfolk, gangs consisted for the most part of young people aged between seven and eighteen, employed at tasks thought fit for women and children, such as cleaning fields of weeds and stones, and harvesting root crops. Gang masters in this case were accused of exploiting the children and their parents, and there is no doubting the system involved an arduous work regime, plus long walks to and from work. During the 1850s, the future Mrs Burrows recalled a fourteen-hour day in a Lincolnshire gang, accompanied all the time by an old man with a whip. All the same, according to Nicola Verdon, the numbers involved were much exaggerated at the time, and families seized the opportunity for work in an area where there were few alternatives.[12]

The Expansion of Rural Industry

The massive expansion of rural industry during the seventeenth, eighteenth and early nineteenth centuries shifted the overall balance within the industrial labour force from urban workers towards the villagers for a while. It particularly took hold in the textile industries, but it was also to be found in others such as metalworking, leather goods and straw-plaiting. Since the workers were usually employed in domestic work-shops, the young among them played their part as members of a family unit of production. Indeed, there is general agreement that the burden of extra work that came with the spread of cottage industries fell particularly heavily on women and children. Data from a sample of household

[10] Leslie Page Moch, *Moving Europeans: Migration in Western Europe since 1650* (Bloomington, IN: Indiana University Press, 1992), pp. 120–3.

[11] Simonetta Ortaggi Cammarosano, 'Labouring Women in Northern and Central Italy in the Nineteenth Century', in John Davis and Paul Ginsborg (eds.), *Society and Politics in the Age of Risorgimento* (Cambridge: Cambridge University Press, 1991), pp. 152–83 (p. 171).

[12] Mrs Burrows, 'A Childhood in the Fens about 1850–60, in Margaret Llewelyn Davies (ed.), *Life As We Have Known It* (London: Virago, 1977), p. 111; Nicola Verdon, 'The Employment of Women and Children in Agriculture: A Reassessment of Agricultural Gangs in Nineteenth-Century Norfolk', *Agricultural History Review*, 49 (2001), 41–55.

budgets in England shows that among families of outworkers (such as handloom weavers and stockingers) children contributed around a third of the total, well above the twelfth among farming families.[13]

Proto-Industrialisation

'Proto-industrialisation' theory, as it emerged during the 1970s, sought to bring some rigour to the study of rural industry. It concentrated on those peasant workers who tapped into inter-regional and international markets, as opposed to the reliance on local outlets of other rural crafts.[14] How did this development affect children? In the first place, it is now clear that 'proto-industries' and their child workers were much more widely dispersed across the continent than was once thought. The original focus was on proto-industrialisation in western Europe, starting with influential case studies of Flanders and the countryside around Zurich, then moving on to numerous examples in Britain, the Low Countries, France and Germany. 'Peripheral' regions then came into the frame, such as northern Italy, Catalonia, Scandinavia and Russia. Take the Italian case. A growing demand on the international market for raw and semi-manufactured silk led to rapid expansion of the industry during the early nineteenth century, and a new source of income for rural communities. A segmented labour market meant that it was left almost entirely to children and unmarried women, working for part of the year in industry, the rest on the land. In the province of Como, in 1873, two-thirds of silk workers over the age of twelve were women, and 22.6 per cent of the total were children under this age.[15] The Italian silk industry was for most of the nineteenth century carried out both by hand in small village workshops and in mills. The work involved softening the cocoons. In the small workshops, a young peasant girl plunged them into a basin of hot water and wound the filament around a stick; in the mills, the workers had steam heating and mechanical brushes in the basins.[16]

---

[13] Sara Horrell and Jane Humphries, '"The Exploitation of Little Children": Child Labor and the Family Economy in the Industrial Revolution', *Explorations in Economic History*, 32 (1995), 491, table 1.

[14] Sheilagh C. Ogilvie and Markus Cerman (eds.), *European Proto-Industrialization* (Cambridge: Cambridge University Press, 1996).

[15] Anna Cento Bull, 'I filatori di seta lombardi nel XIX secolo: una forza lavoro industriale in un ambiente rurale', *Storia in Lombardia*, 3 (1989), 3–32 (15).

[16] Alain Dewerpe, *L'Industrie aux champs: essai sur la proto-industrialisation en Italie du Nord (1800–1880)* (Rome: Ecole française de Rome, 1985), pp. 95–9, 342–50; Carlo Marco Belfanti, 'Rural Manufactures and Rural Proto-Industries in the "Italy of the Cities" from the Sixteenth through the Eighteenth Century', *Continuity and Change*, 8 (1993), 253–80 (269–71).

Secondly, proto-industrialisation theory suggests that there was a reorganisation of work roles within the peasant household, undermining or even erasing the traditional division of labour according to gender and age group. Among handloom weavers, in a number of regions, females and adolescents made inroads into this adult male territory. In the Pays de Caux, in Normandy, the period 1780–1850 saw a golden age for cottage weaving, with the number of looms increasing from around 20,000 to 110,000. Competition from agriculture and the artisan trades made it hard to recruit enough men, encouraging women, many of whom had been made redundant as spinners by the mills, to take over most of the work. Young children wound yarn on to bobbins for the weavers, and then, from the age of ten or eleven, both boys and girls learned how to weave, the former to produce the heavier fabrics, the latter to concentrate on the lighter calicoes and kerchiefs. Similarly, in England a parliamentary enquiry into the condition of framework knitters during the 1840s observed an erosion of the traditional monopoly of adult males:

Vast numbers of women and children are working side by side with men, often employed in the same description of frames, making the same fabrics, and at the same rate of wages; the only advantage over them which the man possesses being his superior strength, whereby he can undergo the fatigues of labour for longer hours than the weaker physical energy of women and children enable them to bear; and therefore he earns more money, but turning off more work.[17]

Finally, historians have pointed to the greater intensity of effort expected from child workers in the domestic workshops, as in the factories, when compared to work on the land. An oft-cited passage from Hans Medick asserts that children often fared poorly in proto-industrial families:

For the children of weavers, spinners, and knitters, the work within their family of origin frequently took the place of work as servants in other households. But this alternative was not the result of free choice. Child labour, which both in its intensity and its duration went far beyond the corresponding labour of peasant households, was a vital necessity for the rural cottage workers' families.[18]

---

[17] Gay L. Gullickson, *Spinners and Weavers of Auffay: Rural Industry and the Sexual Division of Labor in a French Village, 1750–1850* (Cambridge: Cambridge University Press, 1986), pp. 108–9; David Levine, 'The Demographic Implications of Rural Industrialization: A Family Reconstitution Study of Shepshed, Leicestershire, 1600–1851', *Social History*, 1 (1976), 177–96 (182).

[18] Hans Medick, 'The Proto-Industrial Family Economy: The Structural Function of Household and Family during the Transition from Peasant Society to Industrial Capitalism', *Social History*, 1 (1976), 291–315 (301–2, 310–11).

There is some support for Medick's view among other historians. The 'sweating' of various trades during the nineteenth century, with domestic workshops relying on the contribution of wives and children to remain competitive, is well known. In the Pays de Mauges, in western France, Tessa Liu writes that, among rural handloom weaving families, the importance of unpaid labour for the survival of the enterprise meant that the 'disciplining of bodies and habits was the first lesson the child learnt from weaver parents'. A good weaver needed both speed and endurance, with constant attention to such tasks as counting threads and keeping the cloth taut. Children had these qualities drummed into them, by example and by constant correction. Parents even devised little games and sang songs to make the training more palatable.[19]

Becoming a Proto-Industrial Worker

The frequent association of proto-industrialisation with impoverishment hardly suggests that combining agricultural and industrial work, or specialising exclusively on the latter while remaining in a village, was a particularly desirable path for the young to follow.[20] This may partly be because of the long, losing battle against factories fought by peasant workers during the nineteenth century. Yet the fierce desire of such men and women workers to maintain their links with the land despite all the hardships might also indicate some advantages. There was the potential satisfaction of working as part of a team with the rest of the family – with the father, it must be said, firmly in position at its head. During the years of prosperity enjoyed by most of these industries, up to the early nineteenth century, there was the security of having a plot of land or even the appeal of having a variety of jobs. For most young people, it was doubtless a matter of escaping poverty rather than achieving a comfortable standard of living. A fortunate minority, however, among the better-off farming families, or among those with adolescent children working at home, could treat it as a useful additional source of income during the winter months.[21]

---

[19] Tessa P. Liu, *The Weaver's Knot: The Contradictions of Class Struggle and Family Solidarity in Western France, 1750–1914* (Ithaca, NY: Cornell University Press, 1994), pp. 224–5.
[20] Medick, 'Family Economy', pp. 54–8.
[21] See, for example, Didier Terrier, *Les Deux âges de la proto-industrie: les tisserands du Cambrésis et du Saint-Quentinois, 1730–1880* (Paris: Ecole des Hautes Etudes en Sciences Sociales, 1996), p. 104.

'Civilising' the Masses: Churches and Schools

As the young grew up in villages, within the firm embrace of their family and their local community, they could not escape the influence of outside agencies. The educated elites in Europe generally considered the labouring classes of villages as a 'lower order of beings':[22] delightful in certain respects, but for the most part wallowing disgracefully in their own backwardness. Church and state made determined efforts to bring what they considered a superior civilisation to villagers, assisted by the generally corrosive effects of industrialisation and urbanisation on the popular culture. For children, the most extensive contacts they had in these campaigns were with the clergy and schoolteachers. Both groups resided in the local community, and often had a similar background to their charges, but their training and missions meant that, to a greater or lesser extent, they stood apart from the peasantry. They might also be in conflict with each other where ideologies clashed. 'Civilising' the rural masses proved an uphill struggle, one that started well before the modern period. Nonetheless, these institutions had some success in imposing a more orthodox version of Christianity on the villagers, and in bringing literacy and an awareness of a national identity to them.

Children and Religious Reform

The Christian churches worked hard in the wake of the Reformation and Counter-Reformation to assert their influence in everyday life. These efforts naturally ebbed and flowed over the decades, and varied in their intensity according to local conditions, whether in a Protestant or Catholic region, or in southern or northern Europe. The glaring exception was the Russian Orthodox Church, which delayed any such moves until the nineteenth century, and even then they were 'greeted with scepticism'.[23] But in general the churches improved the training of their clergy, put the organisation of their parishes on a sounder footing and expected the laity to follow their teaching more conscientiously. They paid particular attention to the young, on the reasonable assumption that children and youths would be less set in their ways than adults. They encouraged priests to run catechism classes in their parish and sought

---

[22] The quotation is from George Sturt, *Change in the Village* (1912), as cited in K. D. M. Snell, *Annals of the Labouring Poor: Social Change and Agrarian England, 1660–1900* (Cambridge: Cambridge University Press, 1985), p. 8.

[23] Valerie A. Kivelson and Robert H. Greene (eds.), *Orthodox Russia: Belief and Practice under the Tsars* (University Park, PA: Pennsylvania State University Press, 2003), Introduction, p. 18.

to ensure that teaching in the schools was suffused with their version of Protestantism or Catholicism. They also produced teaching materials that would be accessible to children, such as catechisms and ABC primers.[24]

These campaigns needed time to take effect, but they were certainly making headway by the late seventeenth and eighteenth centuries in western Europe. There was a renewed burst of activity to 'rechristianise' the population during the first half of the nineteenth century. In Ireland, the Catholic Church flourished, once freed from the repressive regime of the Penal Laws (1697–1703 through to 1782), while in France it organised missionary work to try to make up ground lost during the 1789 Revolution. Meanwhile in England, Scotland and Scandinavia there were revivalist movements to extend the influence of Protestant churches.[25] Reaction in villages was mixed. In some ways, the clergy were pushing against an open door, as the peasantry were generally willing to make sacrifices to ensure that their offspring were prepared for Confirmation or First Communion. At the same time, the influence of the churches was uneven, being notably weak in areas of outstanding social inequality such as the Paris region or southern Spain. Moreover, especially in Catholic Europe, the orthodoxy of pastors and priests had to compete with the decidedly unorthodox beliefs of the villagers. As Hugh McLeod emphasises, the rural population lived in a dangerous world, its livelihood constantly threatened by the forces of nature. In the absence of natural defences, it turned to the supernatural: 'Prayers, pilgrimages, spells, rituals of all kinds were called in aid by the individual or by the community as a whole.' Hence the clergy met some resistance to their teaching, or at least an interesting coexistence of Christian doctrine and magic in the rural community.[26]

Children and the Schools in Rural Society

Persuading the peasantry to send their children to school for an extended period was a long, drawn-out process that began in the Middle Ages and ended only in the mid-twentieth century. It was notably slow in much of

---

[24] Jean Delumeau, *Catholicism between Luther and Voltaire* (London: Burns and Oates, 1977); John Bossy, *Christianity in the West, 1400–1700* (Oxford: Oxford University Press, 1985); and Silvia Evangelisti, 'Faith and Religion', in Sandra Cavallo and Silvia Evangelisti (eds.), *A Cultural History of Childhood and the Family in the Early Modern Age* (Oxford: Berg, 2010), pp. 153–70.

[25] Hugh McLeod, *Religion and the People of Western Europe 1789–1989* (Oxford: Oxford University Press, 1997), p. 67.

[26] McLeod, *Religion*, pp. 55–6.

southern and eastern Europe. In Russia, for example, under Catherine II (r. 1762–96), a statute of 1786 promised the spread of primary education to the provinces but in practice remained a dead letter, as Catherine preferred to devote funds to elite institutions rather than public schools.[27] Elsewhere, the spur of competition between Protestants and Catholics to capture souls for their faith gave the movement some impetus from the sixteenth century onwards.[28] The modern era therefore inherited a range of elementary schools, which concentrated on teaching religion and morality to their pupils. They also taught reading, and later on writing for those who could afford it. Dedicated school buildings were not unknown in villages of Europe: a study of northern Baden reveals that many villages had a schoolhouse, with classroom space and accommodation for the teacher and his family. Otherwise, teaching took place in makeshift premises set up in premises such as a church, a priest's house, a cottage or a barn (see Figure 3.2).[29] Indeed, in the poorest areas, villages during the eighteenth century had nothing that could be described as a school: all the children could expect were catechism classes with the local priest in the parish church.

The founding of these early schools relied heavily on philanthropy. A local landowner with an interest in education might provide funds to subsidise a schoolteacher. In Catholic countries, the parish priest was often the inspiration, supported by a confraternity dedicated to this task, such as the Companies of Christian Doctrine that flourished in northern Italy. Religious orders were also active in bringing religious education to the populace, as in the case of the Jesuits and the Capuchins.[30] Alternatively, it was possible for a village community to support a school, in association with the local priest, as in the case of the *petites écoles* in France. A study of the diocese of Lyon found that schools were 'relatively common' in the countryside during the eighteenth century, appearing in approximately a third of parishes.[31] In England, the plundering of

[27] Ben Eklof, *Russian Peasant Schools: Officialdom, Village Culture, and Popular Pedagogy, 1861–1914* (Berkeley, CA: University of California Press, 1986), pp. 20–2.
[28] James Bowen, *A History of Western Education* (London: Methuen, 1981), vol. 3, chs. 4 and 14.
[29] Mary Jo Maynes, *Schooling for the People: Comparative Local Studies of Schooling History in France and Germany, 1750–1850* (London: Holmes & Meier, 1985), pp. 37–9; Roger Sellman, 'The Country School', in G. E. Mingay (ed.), *The Victorian Countryside* (London: Routledge & Kegan Paul, 1981), pp. 542–53 (p. 543).
[30] Christopher F. Black, *Church, Religion and Society in Early Modern Italy* (Basingstoke: Palgrave Macmillan, 2004), ch. 6.
[31] Karen E. Carter, *Creating Catholics: Catechism and Primary Education in Early Modern France* (Notre Dame, Indiana: University of Notre Dame Press, 2011), passim; Philip T. Hoffman, *Church and Community in the Diocese of Lyon, 1500–1789* (New Haven, CT: Yale University Press, 1984), pp. 114–16.

THE VILLAGE SCHOOL.

Figure 3.2 Children learning to read in a Victorian village school, 1870. Getty Images, 838955460.

Church properties during the Reformation deprived the clergy of resources so that private schools set up by a teacher featured more prominently. These included the notorious 'dame schools', which as the name implies involved a local woman in the village giving some basic instruction in her home.

All of these schools attempted, with varying degrees of success, to teach the basics of Christian doctrine and morality. The assumption among the ruling elites was that they should reinforce the existing social hierarchy rather than encourage social mobility. Teachers relied heavily on rote learning methods – now disparaged as tedious and uninspiring, but the accepted way of learning at all levels in the eighteenth century. An observer in the Russian province of Tula reported that during the 1860s, after a day spent memorising verse, 'the pupils left the school dull and in a stupor, walked a few yards as if stepping out of the grave, and only then, when they had gained some distance from the school ... began to liven up'.[32] Similarly, the teaching of reading involved what David Cressy calls a 'grim regime' of learning the letters of the alphabet, and then being drilled in the combinations of letters and syllables before starting to read from books. It was a method likely to fail with many children, in spite of all the scolding and beatings they had to endure.[33] In addition, the Church hierarchy was insistent that boys and girls be taught separately, for fear of encouraging immorality, though in practice this was impossible in the smaller village schools. In rural Germany, for example, 'teaching in the trivia' was always delivered to boys and girls together.[34]

Everywhere, historians agree, rural areas lagged well behind urban ones in the provision of schools. Local elites were often hostile to primary education for the masses, seeing it as a threat to their labour supply. They themselves, of course, took seriously the education of their own children. Johann Friedrich Töllner (1804–91) was a wealthy farmer from the Weser marshland of Oldenburg, who described his own progress in some detail in a journal he kept. At the age of six he began at the local village school, learning his letters and his catechism from 'Luther's kleinem Katechismus'. At the age of eight he began to learn to write, and at ten he was studying the Bible, arithmetic and singing. Reaching his teens, he moved on to geography, biblical history and a little bit of Latin and French with a local pastor. At fourteen he took lodgings in a nearby town, enabling him to take lessons in English, German, essay-writing, geography and history with another pastor, and in mental and written arithmetic during the evenings with a head teacher. Finally, further religious instruction from one of the pastors led to Confirmation around the age of fifteen in 1819.[35]

Meanwhile, the peasants expected very little from schoolteachers, being content with some preparation for confirmation and basic literacy: a short period at school was generally thought sufficient. They had no compunction in pulling their children out of class when they needed them for work around the home or on the farm, and they were particularly indifferent where the schooling of their daughters was concerned.

---

[32] As cited in Eklof, *Russian Peasant Schools*, p. 43.

[33] David Cressy, *Literacy and the Social Order: Reading and Writing in Tudor and Stuart England* (Cambridge: Cambridge University Press, 1980), pp. 20–1 and 28.

[34] Ernst Schubert, 'Daily Life, Consumption, and Material Culture', in Sheilagh Ogilvie (ed.), *Germany: A New Social and Economic History*, vol. 2, '1630–1800' (London: Arnold, 1996), pp. 350–76 (p. 369).

[35] Helmut Ottenjann, 'Private Written Sources relating to Everyday History and Popular Culture in Rural Environments', in Bo Larsson and Janken Myrdal (eds.), *Peasant Diaries as a Source for the History of Mentality* (Stockholm: Nordiska Museet, 1995), pp. 18–24 (p. 21).

Hence, they tended to see small private schools, such as the dame schools in England, closer attuned to their needs than those of the teaching orders or charities. The fees were low, the content suitably limited and the teachers relaxed about irregular attendance.[36] Adam Rushton (b. 1821), who later became a preacher, revealed (possibly in retrospect) the bitterness of someone determined to escape from this milieu when describing his early impressions of one such school in a village:

On my first visit, I found the room full of children, some at play, some in mischief, and some repeating lessons in the broadest and roughest dialect of Cheshire. In the midst of this village babel was Nanny Clarke, a thin, tall, gaunt, infirm old dame, with spectacles on nose, and birch-rod in hand. At frequent intervals the rod was heard going swish, swish, all round the school, when a little temporary order would ensue. Here it was my long pursuit of knowledge, under difficulties, began.[37]

Across the Channel, Agricol Perdiguier (b. 1805) started school in his village with a M. Madon, who was a doctor as well as a teacher – and pretty hopeless at both jobs in his view. Armed with a series of straps, whips and rulers, Madon struck his pupils for any mistake or sign of disobedience. Fortunately, a better teacher soon followed, and Perdiguier left school after two or three years able to read, write and cipher, though not very well.[38]

Conditions in rural schools in central Europe were generally far worse, both materially and intellectually. Robert Köhler, attending school in Bohemia around 1850, noted that there were about 100 pupils in his class, with no teaching aids and nothing beyond the 3 Rs on offer.[39] To the north, in rural Norway, the so-called ambulatory school (*omgangsskolen*) involved teachers moving around various farmhouses large enough to hold their classes, receiving board and lunch equivalent to the school tax payable by the families involved. The training these teachers received from the clergy was very limited, concentrating on the catechism and hymn singing. During the eighteenth and nineteenth centuries, village children usually spent no more than eight to twelve weeks a year in their classes. The school term was always in the winter,

---

[36] Laura S. Strumingher, *What Were Little Girls and Boys Made Of? Primary Education in Rural France* (Albany, NY: State University of New York, 1983); Phil Gardner, *The Lost Elementary Schools of Victorian England: The People's Education* (London: Croom Helm, 1984), ch. 3.

[37] Adam Rushton, *My Life as Farmer's Boy, Factory Lad, Teacher and Preacher* (Manchester: S. Clarke, 1909), p. 17.

[38] Agricol Perdiguier, *Mémoires d'un compagnon* (Paris: Denoel, 1943), pp. 5–7.

[39] Robert Köhler, *Erinnerungenaus dem Lebeneines Proletariers* (1913), as cited by Maynes, *Taking the Hard Road*, p. 88.

the agricultural 'dead season'.[40] In much of Scandinavia, through to the twentieth century, the authorities bowed to popular pressure and only required schooling every second day.[41]

Efforts by the various states in Europe to establish a national system of education during the nineteenth century had a considerable impact on in villages. Governments made funds available to provide schools in the more remote areas of the countryside, to improve the quality of teachers, and, sooner or later, to establish a system of free, compulsory elementary schooling.[42] These initiatives were matched by a growing demand for schooling among the peasantry themselves. A number of influences came into play here, including the recognition that education could be useful to the villagers as agriculture became increasingly commercialised, and the desire for the social status associated with education. A classic study by Roger Thabault from the 1940s showed how in his native village of Mazières-en-Gatine, in western France, the fortunes of the local school were linked to changing social circumstances. As the semi-closed economy that survived up to the mid-nineteenth century opened up to towns during the 1860s, and as national politics began to impinge on daily life during the Third Republic, so the number of pupils in the local school finally increased sharply from the 1870s onwards.[43] By 1900, school enrolment rates for boys aged six to fourteen in primary schools were at the level of 90 per cent or more in Prussia, Bavaria, France, Sweden and England and Wales – though, indicative of southern Europe, still at 57 per cent in Italy.[44]

These figures mask considerable differences in the types of school to be found across Europe during the late nineteenth century, and hence in the experience of school pupils. In Prussia the state had a firm grip on the school system, installing conservative, monarchist teachers as far as possible. In France, by contrast, the school system was dominated by a long-running battle between Catholic and Republican forces. During the 1850s and 1860s, under the Second Empire, Catholic schools had made the running among the peasantry, but under the Third Republic the tables were turned, and village children faced the loyal 'black Hussars

---

[40] Martinson, *Growing Up in Norway*, pp. 113–17.

[41] Loftor Guttormsson, 'Parent–Child Relations', in David I. Kertzer and Marzio Barbagli, *The History of the European Family* (New Haven, CT: Yale University Press, 2001), vol. 2, pp. 251–81 (p. 259).

[42] For more detail, see Chapter 7, 'Towards Mass Schooling'.

[43] Roger Thabault, *Education and Change in a Village Community: Mazières-en-Gâtine, 1848–1914*, transl. Peter Tregear (New York, NY: Schocken, 1971).

[44] Mary Jo Maynes, *Schooling in Western Europe: A Social History* (Albany, NY: State University of New York, 1985), p. 134, table 8.

of the Republic', as their teachers were known. In England, a heavy reliance on voluntary provision by charitable societies meant that most country schools were run by the Church of England's National Society.[45] It is important not to exaggerate the quality of what was on offer in the countryside. Even in Imperial Germany, for example, teachers in single-class rural schools would have to cope with between 120 and 200 pupils aged between six and fourteen.[46] Not surprisingly, Fritz Pauk (b. 1888) recalled from his childhood in the Principality of Lippe that 'There wasn't really much to learn in the little village school. Most of the time was devoted to the catechism and innumerable Bible passages'.[47] The appetite for formal education among parents and children in villages also had its limits, with irregular attendance a persistent problem into the twentieth century in more backward areas. A study of schooling in Spain revealed that as late as 1933, with compulsory schooling well-established in the legal system, around half of the school age population was still not receiving any primary education. Educators were consistent in denouncing child labour on the farms as the main cause for absenteeism from class.[48] In this way, the tendency of modern societies to segregate children from the world of adults, principally in schools, was well under way in the rural areas of Europe by the late nineteenth century, but far from complete.

The Impact of Reforms in Villages

For all the obstacles they faced, this army of post-reformation clergy and school teachers doubtless had some success in mobilising the masses in villages for their cause. An older view that there was a division between an 'elite' and a 'popular' culture, and that the two were growing apart during the early modern period, is now discredited among historians. The binary division now looks simplistic, a finer grading of society being

[45] Bowen, *History of Western Education*, vol. 3, p. 322; Maynes, *Schooling in Western Europe*, p. 150; Sarah A. Curtis, *Educating the Faithful: Religion, Schooling, and Society in Nineteenth-Century France* (Dekalb: Northern Illinois University Press, 2000); Horn, *Country Child*, p. 31.

[46] Gunilla Budde, 'From the Zwergschule (One-Room Schoolhouse) to the Comprehensive School: German Elementary Schools in Imperial Germany and the Weimar Republic, 1870–1930', in Laurence Brockliss and Nicola Sheldon (eds.), *Mass Education and the Limits of State Building, c. 1870–1930* (Basingstoke: Palgrave Macmillan, 2012), pp. 95–116 (p. 97).

[47] 'Fritz Pauk, Cigar Maker', in David Kelly, *The German Worker: Working-Class Autobiographies from the Age of Industrialization* (Berkeley, CA: University of California Press, 1987), pp. 399–427 (p. 402).

[48] José M. Borrás Llop, 'Schooling and Child Farm Labour in Spain, circa 1880–1930', *Continuity and Change*, 20 (2005), 385–406.

more realistic. There was interaction as well as divergence between the various levels.[49] By the eighteenth century, peasant families were slowly coming around to the idea that their children should have some instruction from their priest or pastor and from a schoolteacher.

The Spread of Literacy

The link between the growth of the school system and the rise of mass literacy in the various European nations was by no means straightforward. Children might learn to read and write at home or with the help of other members of the local community – or spend several years in class without making much headway in either. However, during the nineteenth century the schools gradually came to dominate the teaching of the 3Rs in villages. The spread of literacy was particularly evident in north-western Europe; in the southern and eastern parts of the continent, great swathes of the countryside remained cut off from the urban, literate world well into the nineteenth century. It was also the case that while literacy rates were relatively high among these in villages involved in trading activities, including many of the bigger farmers, they generally remained modest among the smaller peasants and rural labourers.[50] In a sample of English parishes, the marriage registers for the period 1815–44 reveal that only 17 per cent of yeomen and farmers were unable to sign their name, whereas a little over half of husbandmen could not do so, and two-thirds of labourers and servants. Across the Channel, in the Eure-et-Loire Department, during the 1830s, agricultural wage earners once again stand out as the least literate group in society. Military conscription records (for males aged twenty) show that 22 per cent of independent farmers were illiterate, compared to 56 per cent of shepherds and agricultural labourers. Most disadvantaged of all were farm servants, with 70 per cent classified as unable to read or to read and write, presumably because they came from modest backgrounds, left home relatively early and undertook work that did not need a formal education.[51]

---

[49] Bob Scribner, 'Is a History of Popular Culture Possible?', *History of European Ideas*, 10 (1989), 175–91; Martin Ingram, 'From Reformation to Toleration: Popular Religious Cultures in England, 1540–1690', in Tim Harris (ed.), *Popular Culture in England, c. 1500–1850* (Basingstoke: Macmillan, 1995), pp. 95–123 (pp. 95–7).

[50] R. A. Houston, *Literacy in Early Modern Europe: Culture and Education 1500–1800* (Harlow: Longman, 2002), and David Vincent, *The Rise of Mass Literacy: Reading and Writing in Modern Europe* (Cambridge: Polity, 2000).

[51] R. S. Schofield, 'Dimensions of Illiteracy, 1750–1850', *Explorations in Economic History*, 10 (1972–3), 437–54 (449–50, table 1); Alain Corbin, 'Pour une étude sociologique de la croissance de l'alphabétisation au XIXe siècle: l'instruction des conscrits du Cher at

At the national level, Sweden stood out with a high level of literacy among most of the population, girls as well as boys, the outcome of a religiously inspired campaign during the seventeenth century insisting that parents teach their offspring 'to read in a book'. By the end of the eighteenth century, besides Sweden, mass literacy had arrived in Denmark, Finland, Iceland, Scotland and Geneva. In parts of England, France and Germany, the ability to read was becoming widespread.[52] In France, where the Maggiolo survey of literacy (1877–9) between the late seventeenth and late nineteenth centuries gave a solid platform for later research, there was a clear distinction between regions separated by the famous Saint Malo to Geneva line. 'Broadly speaking, northern and north-eastern France was able to read and write by the end of the 18th century, at a time when the other France was only just embarking on the process of catching up.'[53] Thus in Provence, deep in the 'other France', Michel Vovelle talks in terms of a 'rural cultural ghetto', with peasants largely illiterate and their wives completely so. In Spain, the peasantry was an even more formidable obstacle, holding back the tide of literacy for decades: in 1860, for example, 65 per cent of males and 87 per cent of females were illiterate. And in southern Italy, the peasants remained almost completely so during the nineteenth century. In the province of Naples, for example, the 1861 census revealed that 85.3 per cent of males and 96.6 per cent of females in rural areas were unable to read or write.[54]

Religious and Moral Education

More important to the peasantry than literacy during the eighteenth and even nineteenth centuries was religious and moral instruction. Nearly all children in villages spent up to three or four years memorising the long passages of text, with their teachers using the question-and-answer format of the catechism (see Figure 3.3). Failure to master the exercise would lead to the humiliating experience of being refused First

de l'Eure-et-Loir, (1833–1883), *Revue d'histoire économique et sociale*, 153 (1975), 99–120 (107, 117, table 1).

[52] Vincent, *Mass Literacy*, p. 8.

[53] François Furet and Jacques Ozouf, *Reading and Writing: Literacy in France from Calvin to Jules Ferry* (Cambridge: Cambridge University Press, 1982), p. 45.

[54] Michel Vovelle, 'Y a-t-il eu une révolution culturelle au XVIIIe siècle? A propos de l'éducation populaire en Provence', *Revue d'histoire moderne et contemporaine*, 22 (1975), 89–141 (108–9, 113–14, 140); Jean Louis Guereña, 'Infancia y escolarización', in José María Borrás Llop (ed.), *Historia de la infancia en la España contemporánea, 1834–1936* (Madrid: Ministerio de Trabajo y Asuntos Sociales, 1996), pp. 349–458 (pp. 352–3); Jean-Michel Sallmann, 'Les Niveau d'alphabétisation en Italie au XIXe siècle', in *Mélanges de l'Ecole française de Rome. Italie et Méditerranée*, 101 (1989), 183–337 (247).

CATECHISING AFTER SERVICE IN A COUNTRY CHURCH IN NORWAY.

Figure 3.3 Engraving of catechising after a service in a country church in Norway, 1862.
Getty Images, 180748246.

Communion. In Catholic Europe, most children by the eighteenth century were 'learning their catechism'. In Southwest Germany, for example, the Catholic population gradually came around to such classes during the seventeenth century, the *Kinderlehr* being held on Sundays in church after the services.[55] In Protestant Iceland, the pastor held only a supervisory role, leaving to the parents the task of teaching Luther's Minor Catechism. Around the age of fourteen, the child faced the ordeal of answering questions in front of the whole parish, providing ample motivation to prepare thoroughly.[56] Unfortunately for the churches, all too often once the individual had overcome this hurdle they soon forgot

---

[55] John Bossy, 'The Counter-Reformation and the People of Catholic Europe', *Past and Present*, 47 (1970), 51–70 (66); Marc R. Forster, *Catholic Revival in the Age of the Baroque: Religious Identity in Southwest Germany, 1550–1750* (Cambridge: Cambridge University Press, 2001), pp. 126–7.
[56] Magnússon, 'Childhood in Nineteenth-Century Iceland', p. 312.

much of what they had learned. Nonetheless, they had acquired a basic knowledge of Jesus Christ and God, the sacraments and prayer.[57]

Most of the peasantry probably took a down-to-earth, even instrumental view of religion. In the Swiss case, around Zurich, Rudolph Braun wrote that 'Under the terms of popular piety, the peasant struck a bargain with God: "I go to church for you and you preserve my harvest from hail."'[58] Villagers were generally diligent in observing the sacraments of baptism, marriage (a sacrament for Catholics) and burial. Social conformity may well have been as important as inner conviction. Autobiographies indicate that children in their turn 'took religion more or less in their stride', as John Burnett suggests from British evidence, 'something mainly reserved for Sundays and solemn occasions but not of great import in everyday life'.[59] The Russian peasant children followed by Olga Semyonova during the 1890s imitated adults by crossing themselves in front of the icons in their homes, realising that they were in the presence of 'God'. In the Orthodox Church they also learned to repeat prayers such as 'Our Father' and 'Hail Mary', and went to confession – though Semyonova noted that they soon picked up 'free thinking' from other children, doubting the dire threats of punishment by God emphasised by their priests.[60] However, a minority of children in Europe took a deeper interest in spiritual matters. English Protestant dissenters were exceptionally communicative about their early years, following their tradition of confessional literature. Adam Rushton (b. 1821) wrote that when he was eight years old, he followed the advice of a Sunday school teacher who told him to go home and find a quiet place to pray, so that he could hear God. At the foot of a large pear tree on the family farm, hidden by some saplings, 'I seemed inspired and transfigured. The sunlight playing around me was not so bright as the inner light irradiating the soul. Outward voices there were none, but inward voices many. If God ever did speak to a child, He spoke then'.[61] On the Catholic side, there were those who claimed to have had Visions of the Virgin Mary, in this case often poorly educated young girls. Best known were those of the young shepherdess Bernadette Soubirous at Lourdes in 1858, and of some girls at Palmar de Troya, in Seville province, during the mid-

---

[57] For example, Ralph Gibson, *A Social History of French Catholicism, 1789–1914* (London: Routledge, 1989), pp. 165–6.
[58] Rudolph Braun, *Industrialisation and Everyday Life*, transl. Sarah Hanbury Tenison (Cambridge: Cambridge University Press, 1990), p. 94.
[59] Burnett, *Destiny Obscure*, p. 23.   [60] Semyonova, *Village Life*, pp. 33–4.
[61] Rushton, *My Life as a Farmer's Boy*, p. 26.

twentieth century. They were generally viewed as unreliable by the clergy, but they inspired popular cults among the masses.[62]

The School in the Village

Such acquiescence in the authority of the church hierarchy and schoolteachers should not be allowed to mask an ambiguity in peasant attitudes towards efforts to 'civilise' them. One cannot ignore entirely a 'clash of cultures', as the essentially oral, communal and tradition-bound culture of villagers came up against the more literate, national and forward-looking culture of elites. Efforts to reform villagers had mixed success. As far as children were concerned, the main battleground was the primary school system. This was increasingly the case as the various states of Europe made education compulsory during the nineteenth century. Many peasant families undoubtedly saw the schools as a way out of rural poverty, with a school certificate a ticket to an easier and more secure existence in towns. During the 1890s, those in the Black Earth region of Russia felt the lure of higher wages in Moscow, conditional on being able to read and write. Similarly, those in the impoverished villages close to Besançon sent their children to school regularly because many of them would later have to migrate to towns. In Sicily, by the early twentieth century, the incentive for a male was the chance of making enough money with a spell working in the United States to escape the life of a sharecropper or agricultural labourer. Sicilian wives and daughters also took up formal education in the schools with enthusiasm, as their part of the migrant's dream of moving up the social scale.[63] Others who remained on the land were unimpressed with the 'book learning' that the schools increasingly emphasised from the eighteenth century onwards. They did not wish to be seen as 'donkeys', unable to read or write, but they had little time for much of the additional knowledge that their teachers were eager to impart, in the realms of national history, geography, music and the like. Robert Hayward, son of a farm labourer, recalled the efforts of the headmaster of his village school in

---

[62] Gibson, *French Catholicism*, pp. 145–51; Frances Lannon, *Privilege, Persecution, and Prophecy: The Catholic Church in Spain 1875–1975* (Oxford: Clarendon Press, 1987), p. 29.
[63] Semyonova, *Village Life*, pp. 44–5; Jacques Gavoille, 'Les Types de scolarité: plaidoyer pour la synthèse en histoire de l'éducation', *Annales ESC*, 41 (1986), 923–45 (939–40); Linda Reeder, 'Women in the Classroom: Mass Migration, Literacy and the Nationalization of Sicilian Women at the Turn of the Century', *Journal of Social History*, 32 (1998), 101–24.

Wiltshire to broaden the curriculum early in the twentieth century, admitting that they were frustrated by the pupils themselves:

> It must be confessed that we were an untalented lot (with just one or two exceptions) and trying to teach us to sing melodiously offered as much prospect of success as trying to teach the subject to a flock of geese ... Even now, after 60 years, I feel sad for him when I think of the daunting prospect confronting him each Monday morning; rows of unwilling, untidy, unruly, grubby ignorant kids facing him with a surly expression, hating the prospect of five days of confinement; a prospect to deter any but the most dedicated.[64]

Emilie Carles, raised in an Alpine village during the 1900s, stated that people there had a 'morbid distrust' of the school, because it took away their farmhands.[65] Like many others on small peasant farms during the nineteenth and early twentieth centuries, Carles had to work when she was not in school. During her lunch break, she joined her brother looking after sheep, carrying water to them and removing basketfuls of their dung; in the evenings, this all started again. Above all, peasants were sceptical of advice on agriculture from schoolteachers. In Russia, for example, Ben Eklof argues that families among all strata of the peasantry regarded it as their task to teach their children such skills. Hence during the nineteenth century parents almost invariably pulled their children out of school before the three statutory years of attendance were up, setting them to work on the farm so that they learned the job, and in addition, settled into the family hierarchy of authority, rather than that of the school system.[66]

Time in class was often a bruising and humiliating experience for village children, convinced that anything of interest was happening outside the school, and, boys in particular, as victims of harsh corporal punishments for mistakes in their work as well as for indiscipline. Some adults were able to look back on inspirational teachers in villages; others seethed at the memory of (among German autobiographies) 'authoritarian, conservative and vindictive' examples. Among the former, Fred Kitchen, brought up in Yorkshire during the late Victorian period, acknowledged that his village schoolmistress had taught him to appreciate good literature: 'Although have never made much of a success of life – which was no fault of her teaching – life has been made rich because

---

[64] Jonathan Rose, *The Intellectual Life of the British Working Classes* (New Haven, CT: Yale University Press, 2002), p. 167.

[65] Emilie Carles, *A Wild Herb Soup: The Life of a French Countrywoman*, transl. Avriel H. Goldberger (London: Victor Gollancz, 1992), p. 37.

[66] Ben Eklof, *Russian Peasant Schools: Officialdom, Village Culture, and Popular Pedagogy, 1861–1914* (Berkeley, CA: University of California Press, 1986), p. 275.

when ploughing up a nest of field-mice I could recite Robert Burns's *Ode to a Field-mouse*.'[67] Among the latter, Ephraïm Grenadou (b. 1879) remembered M. Houdard, who he felt never explained things properly and quickly resorted to the switch.[68] The upshot was widespread truancy in villages. Children stayed at home and worked, or simply defied all authority and cleared off into the fields. Above all, it was the sons and daughters of small farmers, sharecroppers and farm labourers who often fared poorly in class from an early age, at least until the mid-twentieth century. A survey of schooling in Norway, admittedly a country that was relatively slow to develop its economy, concluded that 'In farm society, work continued to be the main content in socialization; education and the school did not play a special role before the end of the 1800s'.[69]

Popular Religion in Villages

Finally, villagers managed to combine conventional (or not so conventional) Christian beliefs with apparently contradictory non-Christian ones.[70] Spanish Catholicism was typical of an official religion coexisting with 'alternative cosmologies, private scepticism, and garbled versions of itself'.[71] This doubtless started at an early age, as it was accepted that the family was responsible for the first stage of the religious education of children. Mothers in particular taught their offspring the rudiments of religious belief. James Obelkevich argues that the labourers in the Lincolnshire he studied, but also some of the craftsmen, traders and even farmers, might attend church and at the same time believe in 'ghosts, witches, warning dreams, miracles and the like'. For them, 'nature was alive' with magical forces.[72] Pierre-Jakez Hélias grew up in rural Brittany during the early twentieth century, a world of healing saints, magic springs, folk remedies and ghosts – as well as of the parish church, the *Life of the Saints* and the processions of the village *Pardons*. Thus during his infancy, he drank holy water from a nearby chapel to protect him from stomach upsets and trembled as a child at *l'Ankou*, the ghostly harbinger of death, but also claimed to have fulfilled his duties as a Christian.[73] In the Roman Catholic

---

[67] Fred Kitchen, *Brother to the Ox* (1963), as cited by Horn, *Country Child*, pp. 32–3.
[68] Maynes, *Taking the Hard Road*, p. 88; Ephraïm Grenadou and Alain Prévost, *Grenadou: Paysan Français* (Paris: Seuil, 1966), pp. 13–14.
[69] Martinson, *Growing Up in Norway*, p. 117.   [70] Burnett, *Destiny Obscure*, p. 12.
[71] Lannon, *Catholic Church in Spain*, p. 9.
[72] James Obelkevich, *Religion and Society: South Lindsey 1825-1875* (Oxford: Clarendon Press, 1976), ch. 6.
[73] Pierre-Jakez Hélias, *Horse of Pride: Life in a Breton Village*, transl. June Guicharnaud (New Haven, CT: Yale University Press, 1978), ch. 3.

and Eastern Orthodox parts of Europe the population took part in a series of great feasts running through the year, involving a celebration of the mass, and numerous ceremonies comprising processions, incense and asperging with holy waters. In early modern Russia, according to Daniel Kaiser, 'the celebrations of Orthodox Christianity provided the sensory backdrop to daily life in Muscovy, where the smell, sound, and color of the liturgy contrasted with the world outside the church door'. In Catholic Germany, R. W. Scribner emphasises the lavish nature of this liturgy, with 'the varied coloured vestments, the dress of the choristers, the large quantities of candles, the display of monstrances, crosses and reliquaries and flags, the aroma of incense and the frequent tolling of bells'.[74] These undoubtedly appealed to young and old alike, given their mingling of spirituality with entertainment in promoting the cause of the Church.[75] This did not prevent the peasantry holding tenaciously during the eighteenth and nineteenth centuries to their alternative beliefs.

Conclusion

Outsiders liked to describe peasants as 'savages', contrasting the 'civilisation' of towns with the 'superstition' of villagers. There is no doubting the differences in the upbringing of a child born to the urban middle classes and that of one born to the ranks of peasants, cottagers, sharecroppers, serfs and labourers. The assorted local beliefs of the latter had little purchase in towns, but they may well have helped sustain the rural population in their particular way of life. This is not to idealise a rural childhood. The alternative beliefs of villagers could bring real anguish, leaving people at the mercy of occult forces. There were elements of convergence between town and countryside, as the reforming zeal of the clergy and increasingly professionalised schoolteachers curbed some of the violence, indiscipline and parochialism of the popular culture. The schools also taught at least the basics of literacy and some awareness of a wider world beyond the village. In time, science and technical progress, mediated through the education systems and adopted with enthusiasm by some in villages, would narrow the difference between rural and urban culture, but it would be a slow process.

---

[74] Daniel H. Kaiser, 'Quotidian Orthodoxy: Domestic Life in Early Modern Russia', in Kivelson and Greene, *Orthodox Russia*, pp. 179–92 (p. 180); R. W. Scribner, 'Ritual and Popular Religion in Catholic Germany at the Time of the Reformation', *Journal of Ecclesiastical History*, 35 (1984), 47–77 (52).

[75] Black, *Church, Religion and Society*, p. 217; Gibson, *French Catholicism*, pp. 162–3.

Part II

Childhood in Towns, c. 1700–1870

If the rural population was numerically predominant throughout the Industrial Revolution period, its position was slipping. Indeed, the nineteenth century was pivotal in the population history of Europe, because with industrialisation, 'where for centuries living in a town had been the exception, it now became the rule'.[1] Throughout the eighteenth century, the distribution of population between town and country had hardly changed at all, with the urban population hovering at a little over 12 per cent of the total. But by 1850, it had increased to 18.9 per cent, and in 1910 it was around 40 per cent, anticipating the highly urbanised society of present-day Europe.[2] Big cities became more important. London grew from a population of around 900,000 in 1800 to 2,363,000 in 1850; Paris from 550,000 to a little over one million at the same period. People also became far more mobile than in the past, including children migrating from villages to towns with their families.

Shifting the perspective from the countryside to towns, the pace of change for young people quickened. Although the material and cultural forces associated with modernisation by no means bypassed villages, they flourished more readily in an urban environment. This was where many of the innovations that affected the young were most in evidence, stemming from such developments as the Enlightenment, social reform movements and new technologies in industry.

---

[1] Paul Bairoch, *Cities and Economic Development: From the Dawn of History to the Present* (Chicago, IL: University of Chicago Press, 1988), p. 213.

[2] Bairoch, *Cities*, p. 216, table 13.2, and p. 221, table 13.4. Note that the figures cited exclude Russia, and take 5,000 as the minimum population for a town.

4   Enlightenment and Romanticism

This chapter considers the conceptions of childhood that emerged in towns during the eighteenth and nineteenth centuries, comparing them to the equivalents in villages in the same period. It is largely concerned with the impact of Enlightenment and Romantic thinkers in this sphere. Their ideas on the nature of the child encouraged people in Europe to take this stage of life more seriously, and challenged existing methods of child-rearing. What follows also picks up on two other issues discussed in the opening chapter to this work, by tracing the boundaries of childhood in towns, and the significance people attached to the early years of an individual.

Boundaries of Childhood in Towns

From the middle of the eighteenth century, elites in the nation-states of Europe became concerned with the survival and education of their young. They were shocked by evidence of high infant and child mortality rates, and worried that their rivals would steal a march on them in the size and quality of their population, with serious implications for their military strength and wealth creation. This gave impetus to the study of childhood, particularly among medical men, pedagogues and philosophers. By this period there was already a long tradition, going back to Antiquity, of dividing people's lives into a series of 'ages', each with its own characteristics. Still influential in medical circles during the early nineteenth century, was the identification of successive stages in multiples of seven. It began with infancy from 0 to 7 years, moved on to childhood from 7 to 14, and then to adolescence from 14 to 21.[1] As Jean-Noël Luc demonstrates from a survey of 270 medical publications in France between the mid-eighteenth and late nineteenth centuries, the subsequent trend was towards a more detailed division of the early years.

---

[1] J. A. Burrow, *The Ages of Man: A Study in Medieval Writing and Thought* (Oxford: Clarendon Press, 1988), pp. 38–9.

Doctors in particular separated the infant of 0 to 2 from children aged 3 to 6 or 7 years, with weaning or the coming of milk teeth marking the transition.[2]

In towns, much as in the countryside, growing up during the Industrial Revolution period involved a series of 'partial transitions' between early childhood and adulthood. Most importantly, with hindsight one can see that the school system, and the systematic age-grading of its classes, was beginning to take a grip on the population. In countries such as Prussia and Denmark, where the state imposed compulsory elementary education quite early in the nineteenth century, it would have been possible to begin associating childhood with the school years. In 1810, all Prussians were obliged to spend three years attending a *Volkschule;* in 1868 this was extended to eight years.[3] However, over much of Europe, although school attendance was generally better in towns than in villages, there were substantial sections of the urban population whose children appeared in class for short spells only, or not at all. Secondary schooling was even more restricted in its reach during the Industrial Revolution period: only a small minority drawn from the middle and upper classes pursued their education to this level.

Starting work was either a sign of independence or, for those forced to start at a particularly early age, a sign of having to grow up very quickly. Among manual workers, with little or no property to support them, there was the familiar drift into work from an early age, as on the farms. The poorest in towns often sent their children out to work before the age of ten, eager for a contribution to the family income. Such children were all too aware that it was the 'cold, gray force of poverty' that was taking them out of school and forcing them to help earn their keep.[4] These youngsters risked ending up in dead-end jobs that would condemn them to a life of casual labour or low-paid, insecure work. There were in this category the numerous jobs on the city streets, such as hawking, running errands, sweeping crossings for pedestrians, entertaining passers-by with acrobatics or music, not to mention the notorious chimney sweeping.[5] In an interview on the streets of London during the 1850s, much quoted by British historians of childhood, the very middle-class social investigator

[2] Jean-Noël Luc, *L'Invention du jeune enfant au XIXe siècle: de la salle d'asile à l'école maternelle* (Paris: Belin, 1997), ch. 4.

[3] James Bowen, *A History of Western Education* (London: Methuen, 1981), vol. 3, p. 322.

[4] Jane Humphries, *Childhood and Child Labour in the British Industrial Revolution* (Cambridge: Cambridge University Press, 2010), p. 179.

[5] Heather Shore, 'Street Children and Street Trades in the United Kingdom', in Hugh Hindman, *The World of Child Labor: An Historical and Regional Survey* (Armonk, NY: M. E. Sharpe, 2009), pp. 563–66.

Henry Mayhew started by asking a young watercress seller about her toys and games. He soon found that her life revolved around her trade: she told him, 'I ain't a child, and I shan't be a woman till I'm twenty, but I'm past eight I am'.[6] Trades with branches requiring little in the way of strength or skill, common in metal working and straw-plaiting among others, also offered jobs for young children, and so too did the new textile mills. In the domestic workshops, children could watch and help parents with their work or chores around the house. The more skilled workers, together with the numerous shopkeepers and masters at the lower end of the middle classes, could delay the entry of their children into the workforce, or set them up with an apprenticeship. This latter might be after some years of schooling, from the age of eleven or twelve, or closer to adolescence, after confirmation for example. At the top of the scale, the period of secondary schooling that wealthy families could afford produced the long period of childhood and adolescence, quarantined from the adult world, which is now commonplace in the West.

Otherwise, there were various thresholds to be crossed that were common to urban and rural upbringings. Boys went through a breeching ceremony with family and friends at an early age, typically around the age of seven (but with wide variations), when it was thought they were ready for transfer from the world of women to that of men. Mothers often resisted this move, reluctant to let their infant go, while fathers and sons were impatient for it to happen. The five-year-old son of Lady Lincoln took the initiative himself, cutting up his frock and declaring that 'he will be a girl no longer'.[7] Further down the line, confirmation or the bar mitzvah, were pointers to adulthood. However, the young tended to leave home later in towns than villages, given the decline of live-in apprentice-ships with a master, and the possibility of earning good wages in the local labour market.[8]

The Impact of the Enlightenment

People in Europe had from the medieval period adopted a religiously-inspired conception of childhood, with God and Satan perceived as the main influences on its nature. The prevailing view from the Christian churches was a pessimistic one, asserting that after Adam's Fall children

---

[6] Henry Mayhew, *London Labour and the London Poor* (4 vols., New York, NY: Dover Publications, 1968 [1861–2]), vol. 1, pp. 151–2.

[7] Randolph Trumbach, *The Rise of the Egalitarian Family: Aristocratic Kinship and Domestic Relations in Eighteenth-Century England* (New York, NY: Academic Press, 1978), p. 251.

[8] A point first made by Michael Anderson, in *Family Structure in Nineteenth-Century Lancashire* (Cambridge: Cambridge University Press, 1971).

were born with the taint of Original Sin.[9] With the eighteenth century, a growing number of cultured men and women across the continent began to shift to a more secular perspective. The first signs of change can be linked to the intellectual world of the Enlightenment, as the educated minority concerned took their lead from its philosopher-educators. Although this movement was not exclusively an urban phenomenon, it was largely driven by the academies, salons and learned societies of towns, not to mention their less formal gatherings in cafes and private houses. According to the *Encyclopédie* produced by Diderot and d'Alembert, a *philosophe* was one who 'trampling on prejudice, tradition, universal consent, authority, in a word, all that enslaves most minds, dares to think for himself'.[10] French *philosophes* were exceptional in their fervent anticlerical and even anti-Christian attitudes, in contrast to their counterparts in England and the Netherlands.[11] But there was a general tendency among Enlightenment thinkers to reject the authority of the Church Fathers, and with it the traditional belief in the depravity of man.

It is also important to note the international context for the new ideas about childhood emerging in Europe during the eighteenth century. Enlightenment thinkers had access to a growing body of travel accounts from across the globe. These they seized upon to buttress their case for change, arguing that one could draw lessons from the way other cultures had very different ways of thinking about childhood and child-rearing. Diderot, for example, used an account of a voyage to Tahiti by Louis Bougainville as the basis for a critical view of European beliefs and values from a non-European perspective.[12]

'A scholar who wants to think, speak, and write about children has no choice but to come to terms with the Enlightenment', according to the psychologist Willem Koops.[13] In drawing up schemes for educational reform, its authors were in some cases drawn to reflect on the nature of the child. The two that historians have invariably homed in on are the English philosopher John Locke (1632–1704) and the Genevan

[9] See Chapter 3 in this volume.
[10] Cited in Roy Porter, *The Enlightenment* (Basingstoke: Macmillan, 1990), pp. 3–4.
[11] Norman Hampson, 'The Enlightenment in France', in Roy Porter and Mikuláš Teich (eds.), *The Enlightenment in National Context* (Cambridge: Cambridge University Press, 1981), pp. 41–53 (p. 46); Dorinda Outram, *The Enlightenment* (3rd edn., Cambridge: Cambridge University Press, 2013), ch. 9.
[12] Adriana Silvia Benzaquén, 'World Contexts', in Elizabeth Foyster and James Marten, eds. *A Cultural History of Childhood and Family in the Age of Enlightenment*, (Oxford: Berg, 2010), pp. 185–204 (pp. 188–94).
[13] Willem Koops, 'The Historical Reframing of Childhood', in Peter K. Smith and Craig H. Hart (eds.), *Blackwell Handbook of Childhood Social Development* (Oxford: Blackwell, 2008), pp. 82–99 (p. 83).

philosophe Jean-Jacques Rousseau. Both Locke's *Some Thoughts Concerning Education* (1693) and Rousseau's *Emile, ou de l'éducation* (1762) made decisive contributions to the shift in attention away from the effects of Original Sin, and both were widely read in literate circles across Europe.[14] A dozen editions of *Some Thoughts* had appeared by the mid-eighteenth century, and it was soon translated into French, German, Italian, Dutch and Swedish. *Emile* was an immediate *succès de scandale:* it, and the accompanying novel *La Nouvelle Héloïse*(1761), in the words of psychologist William Kessen, 'were translated, pirated, quoted, imitated, praised, and attacked in sufficiency to suggest that every literate European had read the books'.[15] Their ideas also circulated widely, in urban, middle-class circles at least, in magazines, periodicals and books produced specifically for children. In Germany, where the links between the Enlightenment and education were particularly close, the Philanthropinist movement took on the challenge of putting Rousseau's ideas into practice. Joachim Heinrich Campe (1746–1818) edited a German translation of *Emile*, with extensive footnotes to guide the reader towards their pragmatic approach, and wrote the hugely successful *Robinson der Jüngere* (1779–80), a children's version of *Robinson Crusoe* inspired by Rousseau's work.[16] Neither Locke or Rousseau was entirely original, as they expressed ideas that were widely circulating in England and France (Rousseau was even accused of plagiarism on a massive scale by one of his critics), but it was their authority that carried the day. Their ideas on the nature and education of children continue to influence teachers and psychologists down to the present.[17]

[14] John Locke, *Some Thoughts Concerning Education*, ed. John W. Yolton and Jean S. Yolton (Oxford: Clarendon Press, 1989); Jean-Jacques Rousseau, *Emile, or On Education*, transl. Allan Bloom (London: Penguin, 1991), pp. 33–4.

[15] Margaret J. M. Ezell, 'John Locke's Images of Childhood', in Richard Ashcraft (ed.), *John Locke: Critical Assessments* (4 vols., London: Routledge, 1991), vol. 2, pp. 231–45 (pp. 237–8); William Kessen, 'Rousseau's Children', *Daedalus*, 107 (1978), 155–66 (161).

[16] Hans-Heino Ewers, 'German Children's Literature from the Eighteenth to the Twentieth Century', in Peter Hunt and Sheila Ray (eds.), *International Companion Encyclopedia of Children's Literature* (London and New York: Routledge, 1996), pp. 1055–62 (pp. 1055–7); Arianne Baggerman and Rudolf Dekker, *Child of the Enlightenment: Revolutionary Europe Reflected in a Boyhood Diary*, transl. Diane Webb (Leiden: Brill, 2009), pp. 56–60; Elizabeth Foyster and James Marten, 'Introduction,' in Foyster and Marten, *Age of Enlightenment*, pp. 1–13.

[17] Lloyd J. Borstelmann, 'Children before Psychology: Ideas about Children from Antiquity to the late 1800s', in Paul Mussen (ed.), *Handbook of Child Psychology* (New York, NY: Wiley, 1983), pp. 1–40 (p. 18).

John Locke on Childhood

Locke, writing at the very beginning of the Enlightenment, is generally thought to have given a first impetus to the movement for educational reform with *Some Thoughts*. The work was written in response to a request from friends for recommendations on how to bring up their young son. Although a bachelor and childless himself, he had long experience as a tutor in upper-class families. Historians have noted that the work is full of references to his observations of the behaviour of children and of parental attitudes to them.[18] He was well aware of the developmental changes in the child, and in particular highlighted the development of the child's powers of reasoning. He asserted that children 'love to be treated as Rational Creatures sooner than is imagined'.[19] He chided parents for allowing their fondness for their offspring to override their duty of forming the character while it was still receptive to change, so 'that the Mind has not been made obedient to Discipline, and pliant to Reason, when at first it was most tender, most easy to be bowed'.[20] His concern with the development of reason is readily explained. With reformers during the seventeenth and eighteenth centuries in England opposing the absolute monarchy by asserting that political authority rested on the consent of the people, Holly Brewer draws attention to exclusion of the young from political power until they had reached the full use of their reason. Locke in his treatises on government was particularly influential in distinguishing adults from children on the basis of the former's experience and capacity for reasoning. Hence, Locke's writings defined childhood by an inability to exercise judgement, bequeathing to the generations that followed a huge emphasis on the difference between a child and an adult.[21] Locke also emphasised more than most that children were individuals with their own particular needs and abilities. He therefore advised parents to adapt their methods of child-rearing accordingly. His aim was to design a programme that would develop a moral character in the young gentleman.[22]

How far Locke went in distancing himself from the traditional Christian emphasis on Original Sin is a matter of some controversy. The usual

---

[18] Locke, *Some Thoughts*, editors' Introduction, pp. 5–8; W. M. Spellman, *John Locke* (Basingstoke: Macmillan, 1997), p. 80.

[19] Locke, *Some Thoughts*, p. 142.   [20] Locke, *Some Thoughts*, p. 103.

[21] Holly Brewer, *By Birth or Consent: Children, Law, and the Anglo-American Revolution in Authority* (Chapel Hill, NC: University of North Carolina Press, 2005), p. 97; see also pp. 1–8, 87–98, and 351.

[22] J. A. Passmore, 'The Malleability of Man in Eighteenth-Century Thought', in Earl R. Wasserman (ed.), *Aspects of the Eighteenth Century* (Baltimore, MD: Johns Hopkins Press, 1965), pp. 21–46 (pp. 37–8).

line among historians is that Locke's view of childhood focused on its malleability: he concluded *Some Thoughts* with the oft-cited assertion that the pupil was to be 'considered only as white Paper, or Wax, to be moulded and fashioned as one pleases'.[23] In other words, he 'despiritualised' the child, assuming that it was neither virtuous nor evil by nature, but a *'tabula rasa'* or blank slate (as he wrote elsewhere), that could be taught to be virtuous.[24] The opening page of the work makes the striking assertion that 'of all the Men we meet with, Nine parts of Ten are what they are, Good or Evil, useful or not, by their Education'. However, dissenting voices warn that, even though Locke had no truck with the notion of human depravity, so essential for justifying the absolutism he detested, he could not entirely escape his Protestant background. His opening page also had the line that 'Men's Happiness or Misery is most part of their own making', rather contradicting his emphasis on education, and implying that human beings bear some responsibility as individuals for whether they turn out good or evil. In other words, he did not see humans as infinitely malleable, nor did he adopt wholeheartedly the environmentalism associated with the later Enlightenment.[25] Moreover, he was clear that achieving virtue required a long and hard struggle to teach the child 'to get a Mastery of his Inclinations and submit his Appetite to Reason'. Most of the population, he felt, would never manage this mastery, and so as W. M. Spellman put it, 'would remain sinners by choice'.[26]

Jean-Jacques Rousseau Creates a Storm

There is no disputing the enduring influence of John Locke's ideas on childhood in Europe, but many historians would consider the publication of Rousseau's *Emile* as the decisive turning point in this sphere.[27] Rousseau consciously followed in Locke's footsteps in certain respects, such as in his empiricist belief that 'everything which enters into the

---

[23] Locke, *Some Thoughts*, p. 265.
[24] Passmore, 'Malleability of Man', passim.; and idem., *The Perfectability of Man* (London: Duckworth, 1970), pp. 159–64; Ezell, 'John Locke's Images', passim.
[25] Spellman, *John Locke*, pp. 84–5.
[26] Peter A. Schouls, *Reasoned Freedom: John Locke and Enlightenment* (Ithaca, NY: Cornell University Press, 1992), chs. 7–8; Spellman, *Locke*, chs. 3–4. This section is also indebted to the Introduction to *Some Thoughts*, by Yolton and Yolton.
[27] For commentries on *Emile*, this section relies on Peter Jimack, *Rousseau, Emile* (London: Grant and Cutler, 1983); Maurice Cranston, *The Noble Savage: Jean-Jacques Rousseau, 1754–1762* (Chicago, IL: University of Chicago Press, 1991), ch. 7; Tanguy l'Aminot, '"Introduction" to Emile', in Jean-Jacques Rousseau, *Oeuvres complètes*, ed. R. Trousson and F. S. Eigeldinger (24 vols., Geneva; Editions Slatkine, 2012), vol. 7, pp. 273–301.

human understanding comes there through the senses'.[28] But he also diverged in others, notably with his highly original vision of rationality in the child. Rousseau began *Emile* with the memorable opening line 'Everything is good as it leaves the hands of the Author of things; everything degenerates in the hands of man'.[29] He was therefore insistent that Emile be brought up by a tutor in the countryside, shielded from the corrupting influence of towns and the 'rabble of valets'.

At the heart of his scheme was an unshakeable belief in the underlying natural goodness of humanity: 'Let us set down as an incontestable maxim that the first movements of nature are always right. There is no original perversity in the human heart.'[30] He explicitly disagreed with 'Locke's great maxim' that it was important to reason with children from an early stage, on the grounds that the child was not ready for this. Reason was a faculty that developed late, he argued, and so there was no point in talking to a child in a language that it did not understand. What mattered was to treat pupils according to their age: 'Childhood has its ways of seeing, thinking, and feeling which are proper to it.'[31] His typically provocative assertion that 'the greatest, the most important, the most useful rule of all education' was not to gain time but to lose it, led to his call for a 'negative education' during the first twelve years of a child's life.[32] This meant allowing the child to learn by experience, 'responding to what nature asks', rather than by teaching from the tutor. Rousseau assumed that the child, moved by natural impulses, would explore the environment and gradually adapt to the realities it faced. The restructuring necessary would proceed by stages. *Emile* took its eponymous hero through infancy until the age of four, childhood until twelve, a third stage of childhood (pre-adolescence in modern terminology) until fifteen, adolescence until twenty, and finally the 'age of love' introducing him to his companion Sophie until twenty-five.[33]

Emile provoked a storm of protest in late eighteenth-century Europe.[34] The *Parlement* of Paris, the Sorbonne, the authorities in Geneva and the Pope all condemned the book without hesitation. Catholic commentators were outraged by the denial of the Fall, and the suggestion that children were born innocent, a complete contradiction of their doctrine, and even more so by the absence of any religious teaching for children.

---

[28] Rousseau, *Emile*, p. 125.   [29] Rousseau, *Emile*, p. 37.   [30] Rousseau, *Emile*, p. 92.
[31] Rousseau, *Emile*, pp. 88–9.   [32] Rousseau, *Emile*, p. 93.
[33] Cranston, *Noble Savage*, pp. 176–84.
[34] For what follows, see Gilbert Py, *Rousseau et les éducateurs: etude sur la fortune des idées pédagogiques de Jean-Jacques Rousseau en France et en Europe au XVIIIe siècle*, in *Studies on Voltaire and the Eighteenth Century*, 356 (Oxford: Voltaire Foundation, 1997), pp. 17–74, 'Scandales et polémiques'.

Fellow *philosophes* in the Enlightenment were also often hostile. The thesis of natural goodness was incompatible with their emphasis on the perfectibility of man, and they criticised his depiction of the child as an abstraction, unrelated to its social and cultural environment. A German newspaper article late in 1762 thought that the educational plan 'is born at once new, highly paradoxical, impossible to apply in practice, most instructive in certain parts and in others, much more important, very irritating and harmful'. It should be added that later feminist commentators were indignant at the treatment of Sophie, Emile's future wife, since here Rousseau followed the traditional line in preparing her for a life of submission to her husband.

Nonetheless, Rousseau had set the tone for debates on education in this period; or as the psychologist Maurice Debesse neatly put it, 'if Rousseau has perhaps invented nothing, he has inflamed everything'.[35] *Emile* was certainly not a practical manual. Attempts by parents to bring up a real Emile often produced dire results. Richard Edgeworth (b. 1764) achieved notoriety as one such 'child of nature', who was allowed by his father to run around as he pleased during his childhood. This produced a fit and healthy body, but an obstreperous character. The ungovernable youngster eventually went off to sea at the age of fifteen and had a strained relationship with his family, As for education, Norman Hampson points out that revolutionaries in France during the 1790s could hardly produce a national programme on the basis of a teacher-pupil ratio of 1:1.[36] All the same, the work made the case for a complete system of education, with each stage appropriate to the level of development of the child. No less importantly, it insisted on the need to treat the child as a child, and not as an adult-in-the-making. 'Love childhood', Rousseau urged the reader, 'promote its games, its pleasures, its amiable instinct'. (As critics pointed out, this was a bit rich from someone who gave up his five children to a foundling hospital.) It even talked in terms of the 'maturity of childhood' when the 'negative' phase of education was finished around the age of twelve.[37] As the psychologist Lloyd Borstelmann puts it, 'The associated propositions of childhood as natural and worthwhile in its own right, and the child as actively engaging

---

[35] Maurice Debesse, 'L'enfance dans l'histoire de la psychologie', as cited in Agnès Thiercé, *Histoire de l'adolescence, 1850–1914* (Paris: Belin, 1999), p. 30.

[36] Julia V. Douthwaite, *The Wild Girl, Natural Man, and the Monster: Dangerous Experiments in the Age of Enlightenment* (Chicago, IL: University of Chicago Press, 2002), pp. 136–8; Hampson, 'Enlightenment in France', p. 50.

[37] Rousseau, *Emile*, pp. 79 and 162.

the world to his [sic] own purposes and understanding, revolutionised thinking about the child and have been continuing issues of debate'.[38]

The 'Romantic Child'

Jean-Jacques Rousseau is often seen as a transitionary figure between the Enlightenment and the Romantic era, given his interest in feelings.[39] Luminaries such as William Wordsworth (1770–1850), Victor Hugo (1802–85) and Jean Paul Richter (1763–1825) added a subtle twist to the vision of the child outlined in *Emile*. If Rousseau was convinced that humans were naturally good, he did not think of them as naturally virtuous: virtue required an effort of will.[40] Hence children were different from adults, and were to be loved and respected as such, but they were not necessarily better. Some of the Romantics who followed him during the early nineteenth century went further than this: their understanding of the original innocence of childhood involved a sense of wonder, an intensity of experience and a spiritual wisdom lacking in adults. Typically, for German speakers, Richter's *Levana* (1811) asserted that children had a 'native innocence' and also a divinely-generated spirit.[41] The Romantics looked back on their early years as a lost realm that was nonetheless fundamental in shaping the adult self: the 'seed time' of the 'soul' for Wordsworth. Childhood was also, as David Grylls puts it, 'a reservoir of imagination to be drawn on in later life'.[42] Charles Baudelaire (1821–67) went as far as to assert that 'genius is merely *childhood regained*'.[43]

These views were always contested: the Evangelical movement in Britain, for example, vigorously aired traditional views on infant depravity. The Evangelicals pumped out a huge amount of reading matter during the nineteenth century for schools and Sunday schools, aimed at the children of the lower-middle and working classes.[44] Also, the Romantic view of the child was slow to make an impact in Eastern Europe, childhood autobiographies not appearing in Russia until at least

---

[38] Borstelmann, 'Children before Psychology', p. 24.   [39] Py, *Rousseau*, p. 571.

[40] Jimack, *Rousseau, Émile*, p. 30.

[41] Jean-Paul Richter, *Levana, or, the Doctrine of Education* (London: Bell, 1891), pp. 75 and 139.

[42] David Grylls, *Guardians and Angels: Parents and Children in Nineteenth-Century Literature* (London: Faber and Faber, 1978), pp. 35–6; Judith Plotz, *Romanticism and the Vocation of Childhood* (Basingstoke: Palgrave, 2001), p. 13.

[43] As cited in Rosemary Lloyd, *The Land of Lost Content: Children and Childhood in Nineteenth-Century French Literature* (Oxford: Clarendon Press, 1992), p. 102.

[44] Margaret Nancy Cutt, *Ministering Angels: A Study of Nineteenth-Century Evangelical Writing for Children* (Wormsley: Five Owls Press, 1979) p. xi.

half a century after those in the West.[45] Many thinkers were also incon-
sistent in their views, suggesting a certain ambivalence in their attitude to
children. Wordsworth, as Alan Richardson points out, ran through most
of the constructions of childhood of his age, depicting them 'sometimes
as natural innocents, sometimes as preternaturally wise or holy, and
sometimes as foolish or innately sinful'. Likewise, Samuel Wesley veered
between emphasising the ignorance and sinfulness of children, as might
be expected of the founder of Methodism, and pointing to the 'innocence
of that tender age'.[46]

All the same, poets, novelists and painters took inspiration from Rous-
seauist and Romantic notions of the child, and diffused what George
Boas describes as a 'cult of childhood', an anti-intellectual reaction to the
claims of science and reason.[47] British portraitists took a lead during the
late eighteenth century, bringing out the 'childlike' nature of children in
an unprecedented manner. Artists such as Thomas Gainsborough
(1727–88) and Sir Joshua Reynolds (1723–92), as James Steward argues,
successfully entered the world of the child, following contemporary
thinking in conveying its innocence and vulnerability. Reynolds in particular reputedly appreciated their childish behaviour (see Figure 4.1).[48]

Other artists on the continent followed suit, notably in the cases of
Delacroix, Goya and Philipp Otto Runge.[49] The portrait of his son Otto
Sigismund that Runge painted in 1805 was perhaps the first time in
history that an artist had confronted the viewer with a real baby. As art
historian Dorothy Johnson comments, borrowing in part from folk art

---

[45] Kelly, *Children's World*, p. 55.
[46] Alan Richardson, *Literature, Education, and Romanticism: Reading as Social Practice,
1780–1832* (Cambridge: Cambridge University Press, 1994), pp. 14–17; Richard P.
Heitzenrater, 'John Wesley and Children', in Marcia Bunge (ed.), *The Child in
Christian Thought* (Grand Rapids, MI: William B. Erdmans, 2001), pp. 279–99
(p. 296). See also Roderick McGillis, 'Irony and Performance: The Romantic Child',
in Adrienne E. Gavin (ed.), *The Child in British Literature: Literary Constructions of
Childhood, Medieval to Contemporary* (Basingstoke: Palgrave Macmillan, 2012),
pp. 87–115.
[47] George Boas, *The Cult of Childhood* (London: The Warburg Institute, University of
London, 1966).
[48] Marcia Pointon, *Hanging the Head: Portraiture and Social Formation in Eighteenth-Century
England* (New Haven and London: Yale University Press, 1993), ch. 7; James Christen
Steward, *The New Child: British Art and the Origins of Modern Childhood, 1730–1830*
(University Art Museum and Pacific Film Archive, University of California, Berkeley,
1995), chs. 1–2; Anne Higonnet, *Pictures of Innocence: The History and Crisis of Ideal
Childhood* (London: Thames and Hudson, 1998), introduction and ch. 1.
[49] Dorothy Johnson, 'Engaging Identity: Portraits of Children in Late Eighteenth-Century
European Art', in Anja Müller (ed.), *Fashioning Childhood in the Eighteenth Century: Age
and Identity* (Aldershot: Ashgate, 2006), pp. 101–15.

Figure 4.1 *Childhood* by Joshua Reynolds.
Getty Images, 155144643.

style, Runge managed to express 'the primitive energy and life force of the child' (see Figure 4.2).[50]

In a similar vein, Wordsworth wrote in his *Ode: Intimations of Immortality from Recollections of Childhood* (1807) that we are born 'trailing clouds of glory' and that 'Heaven lies about us in our infancy!', lines that were quoted, plagiarised and adapted by numerous writers during the nineteenth century.[51] Charles Dickens (1812–70) was doubtless the author who deployed the child figure most effectively to air his dissatisfaction with the Machine Age emerging around him. He and other Victorian novelists shifted the context for childhood from nature to towns and the social conflicts of their age. As Peter Coveney puts it, 'the child became for him the symbol of sensitive feelings anywhere in a society maddened with the pursuit of material progress'.[52] One thinks of

[50] Robert Rosenblum, *The Romantic Child* (London: Thames and Hudson, 1988), p. 23; Johnson, 'Portraits of Children', p. 112.

[51] Barbara Garlitz, 'The Immortality Ode: Its Cultural Legacy', in *Studies in English Literature, 1500–1900*, 6 (1966), 639–49.

[52] Mark Spilka, 'On the Enrichment of Poor Monkeys by Myth and Dream; or, How Dickens Rousseauisticized and Pre-Freudianized Victorian Views of Childhood', in Don Richard Cox (ed.), *Sexuality and Victorian England* (Knoxville, TN: University of Tennessee Press, 1984), pp. 161–79 (p. 165); Peter Coveney, *The Image of Childhood* (Harmondsworth: Penguin, 1967), p. 115; Naomi Wood, 'Angelic, Atavistic, Human: The Child of the Victorian Period', in Gavin, *British Literature*, pp. 116–30.

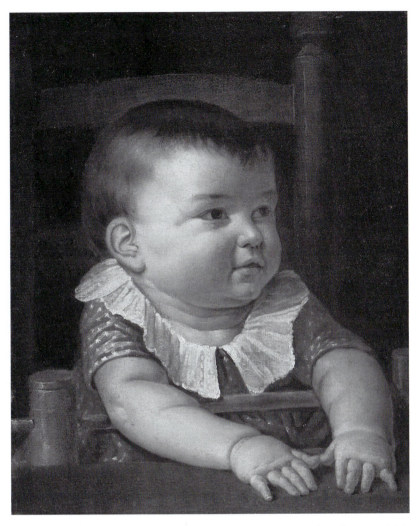

Figure 4.2 *Otto Sigismund, der Sohn des Künstlers* by Otto Runge, 1805.
© bpk / Hamburger Kunsthalle.

his 'child redeemers' such as Little Nell in *The Old Curiosity Shop* (1841)
or Sissy Jupe in *Hard Times* (1854).

The sociologist Chris Jenks is persuasive, given the analysis here, in
suggesting that both historical and cross-cultural studies reveal two
dominant ways of thinking about children. There is the belief that they
begin life in an evil or corrupted state, causing them to be wilful and

interested only in their own self-gratification. Alternatively, one can believe that they are born innocent and harbour a natural goodness and purity.[53] Both were in circulation during the eighteenth and nineteenth centuries, and indeed they continue to influence our thinking today: they are evidently 'good to think'. However, the challenge from Enlightenment thinkers to the generally dismal view of life on earth promoted by religious authorities dealt a serious blow to the notion of infant depravity.

The Changing Significance of Childhood

When in 1781 Jean-Jacques Rousseau published the first six books of his autobiography, *The Confessions*, covering the early part of his life up to the age of thirty, he provoked a hostile reaction from critics. There were a handful of precedents for such writing about one's own childhood and youth, going back to St Augustine (354–430) and his *Confessions*, but they were few and far between. Where Rousseau innovated was in writing about the intimate details of his private life rather than a religious conversion. 'I have displayed myself as I was, as vile and despicable when my behaviour was such, as good, generous, and noble when I was so.'[54] He described a series of events that he felt were turning points in his life, including the death of his mother while giving birth to him, the 'false turn' as a child when he discovered that he rather enjoyed a spanking from Mlle Lambercier, and his decision at sixteen to leave his native Geneva and the simple life of a tradesman for wider horizons. Critics were put off by the 'disconcerting frankness' of the content, and there was a long pause before others followed suit.[55] However, eventually in the nineteenth century numerous authors took up the genre of *souvenirs d'enfance* (childhood reminiscences), including Chateaubriand, Stendhal, Goethe and Gorky.[56]

Thus, in the wake of the Enlightenment, and the stress of many of its authors on the importance of early sensory perceptions in the forming of ideas, the established tendency to ignore the childhood of an individual in memoirs and biographies was frequently abandoned. And as Peter Coveney points out, 'Until the last decades of the eighteenth century the

---

[53] Chris Jenks, *Childhood* (2nd edn., London: Routledge, 2005), pp. 60–70.
[54] Jean-Jacques Rousseau, *The Confessions of Jean-Jacques Rousseau*, transl. J. M. Cohen (London: Penguin, 1953 [1781]), p. 17.
[55] Cohen, 'Introduction' to Rousseau, *Confessions*, pp. 7–14 (p. 8).
[56] Richard N. Coe, *When the Grass Was Taller: Autobiography and the Experience of Childhood* (New Haven, CT: Yale University Press, 1984).

child did not exist as an important and continuous theme in English literature'.[57] Henceforth, the idea that childhood should be considered important in its own right was at least in the air. And the gradual shift over the centuries to emphasising nurture rather than nature gained considerable momentum. During the medieval period, according to Doris Desclais Berkvam, people believed that the nature one was born with was the most important influence on life, the raw material without which the finest nurturing would be wasted.[58] The hereditary aristocracy understandably adopted this line on lineage. However, from the Renaissance onwards, the balance shifted towards nurture. By the eighteenth century, some of the wealthier members of European society were looking to Locke and Rousseau for advice on such matters as diet, clothing, discipline and teaching methods.[59]

Conclusion

There was an obvious contradiction during the nineteenth century between the belief that children were vulnerable creatures in need of protection and the harsh experiences of many on the farms and in the workshops. It seems likely that among the urban masses, no less than among their rural counterparts, decidedly 'unenlightened' views prevailed, following the churches line on the sinfulness of children. Nonetheless, historians have generally assumed that the image of the innocent child, descending from the lofty heights of philosophical treatises and Romantic poetry to the more popular level of genre paintings, prints and advertisements, encouraged the emergence of the modern 'protected' childhood. In particular, as we shall see, it is routinely advanced as part of the explanation for a growing movement to improve the lot of poor children. It is indeed hard to avoid the conclusion that it had some bearing on the way philanthropists and state officials took an interest in the conditions of such disadvantaged groups as child workers in industry, juvenile delinquents and street children. We might note here that an influential work by Viviana Zelizer, based on evidence from the United States but often cited in the European context, asserts that the conception of children as 'sacred' beings eventually swept all before it during the

---

[57] Coveney, *Image of Childhood*, p. 29.
[58] Doris Desclais Berkvam, 'Nature and Norreture: A Notion of Medieval Childhood and Education', *Medievalia*, 9 (1983), 165–80.
[59] For a well-documented example, a Protestant merchant in La Rochelle who devoured the works of Rousseau and named a son Emile, see Robert Darnton, 'Readers Respond to Rousseau: The Fabrication of Romantic Sensibility', in Robert Darnton (ed.), *The Great Cat Massacre* (Harmondsworth: Penguin, 1984), pp. 209–49.

nineteenth and twentieth centuries. She depicts a long struggle between the middle classes, opposing child labour on these grounds, and working-class families, clinging on to the older notion that children should be out earning a wage. This eventually produced the modern phenomenon of what she famously called the 'economically 'worthless' but emotionally 'priceless' child.[60]

---

[60] Viviana Zelizer, *Pricing the Priceless Child: The Changing Social Value of Children* (New York, NY: Basic Books, 1985), p. 3.

5   Middle- and Upper-Class Childhoods in Towns, c. 1700–1870

There is a case to be made that the eighteenth century brought significant improvements in family life for children brought up in towns. Early historians of childhood during the 1970s highlighted this period as an important turning point in a long-term shift towards affectionate parenting.[1] Lawrence Stone was influential in contrasting the remote parent–child relations of the early seventeenth century in England with the 'time, energy, money and love' devoted to child rearing by the end of the eighteenth. In his view, it was the middle ranks of society that first made the running: neither too high up the social scale to be diverted by politics and their own pleasures, nor too low to be struggling with keeping body and soul together. Edward Shorter also identified the middle classes as the first to take up 'good mothering' in Europe, understood in his case as the willingness to put the interests of their infants above all others.[2] Since then, with more or less generous acknowledgements of the debt they owe to these pioneers, historians have lined up to dispute such conclusions. They have downplayed the importance of the eighteenth century, casting doubt on the likelihood of such sweeping change in the emotional life of families.[3] They cite the extensive evidence of affection for children in earlier periods, going back even to the medieval period. They have also emphasised the diversity of approaches to childrearing, among the working classes as well as among the upper and middle classes, rejecting the model of a diffusion of new ideas downwards from the elites.[4]

---

[1] See the Introduction chapter.

[2] Lawrence Stone, *The Family, Sex and Marriage in England, 1500–1800* (London: Weidenfeld and Nicolson, 1977), pp. 4–8, 105, 222, 405–8; Edward Shorter, *The Making of the Modern Family* (London: Fontana/Collins, 1977), ch. 5.

[3] See Peter N. Stearns and Carol Z. Stearns, 'Emotionology: Clarifying the History of Emotions and Emotional Standards', *American Historical Review*, 90 (1985), 813–36 (821–5).

[4] Summarized in Joanne Bailey, 'Family Relationships', in Elizabeth Foyster and James Marten, *A Cultural History of Childhood and Family in the Age of Enlightenment* (Oxford: Berg, 2010), pp. 15–31.

A number of historians have therefore emphasised the long-term continuities in parent–child relations in modern Europe more than any changes. Linda Pollock and Anthony Fletcher, drawing on evidence from middle- and upper-class families in England, argue that no fundamental change occurred in this sphere during the early modern period, and beyond to 1900. According to Fletcher, parents were consistent in lavishing care and attention on their children during the period 1600 to 1914, in an intimate family circle.[5] The obvious risk here is of replacing one massive generalisation with another in the search for a strong argument. As Pollock herself soon came to realise, both continuity and change need to be taken into account. It is surely helpful to follow Joanne Bailey in thinking of social histories bringing out continuities in parenting, while more culturally-orientated studies home in on short-term changes, such as the eighteenth-century cult of motherhood.[6]

This chapter begins the exploration of childhood during the period of early industrialisation by focusing on the more privileged sections of society, in the middle and upper classes. Firstly, it examines the way new ideas on childrearing from prominent intellectuals such as John Locke and Jean-Jacques Rousseau filtered down to parents in the numerous advice manuals published during the eighteenth and nineteenth centuries. It then considers childhood experiences in the rarified atmosphere of the European aristocracy, a small but influential (and well documented) group in society. Finally, it moves on to the middling classes in towns, a diverse group that in the final analysis did much to pioneer a 'modern', protected childhood.

Advice to Parents Following the Enlightenment

There is general agreement among historians that the eighteenth and early nineteenth centuries did at the very least bring a significant change in the advice given to parents. Although most of the ideas originated in western Europe, they quickly spread across the rest of the continent.[7] In

---

[5] Linda Pollock, *Forgotten Children: Parent-Child Relations from 1500 to 1900* (Cambridge: Cambridge University Press, 1983); Anthony Fletcher, *Growing Up in England: The Experience of Childhood, 1600–1914* (New Haven, CT: Yale University Press, 2008), pp. xx–xxi and 55.

[6] Linda Pollock, 'Introduction', in *A Lasting Relationship: Parents and Children over Three Centuries* (Lebanon, NH: University Press of New England, 1987), pp. 11–15 (pp. 12–13); Joanne Bailey, *Parenting in England, 1760–1830* (Oxford: Oxford University Press, 2012), p. 11.

[7] Loftur Guttormsson, 'Parent-Child Relations', in David I. Kertzer and Marzio Barbagli, *The History of the European Family* (New Haven, CT: Yale University Press, c. 2001–3), vol. 2, pp. 251–81 (p. 252).

Russia, for example, by the 1830s and 1840s Enlightenment ideas on childrearing were spreading from a small elite of aristocrats to a wider educated public. The advice manuals delivering the message counselled less formality and more affection between husband and wife, and between parents and children. This was neatly summed up by the cosy image of *Monsieur, madame et bébé*: the title of a popular work first published in 1866 by the French journalist Gustave Droz. Affectionate parents were thought of less as following Biblical examples, and more in down-to-earth terms of intimacy and closeness.[8] They were urged to renounce existing practices such as hiring wet nurses to breastfeed their infants, swaddling newborn babies, and beating their offspring to break their will. Jean-Jacques Rousseau waxed indignant over the 'extravagant and barbarous practice' of swaddling, citing as examples of places where it was unknown from travel accounts from Siam and Canada. He added 'twenty pages with citations' to hammer home his point. Various authors recommended instead a 'rational dress' for infants, such as the little waistcoat, petticoat and light gown suggested by William Cadogan.[9] Parents were also to be flexible over feeding times, keeping in mind the hunger of the infant, and relaxed about toilet training.[10] The *Moralische Wochenschriften* (Moral Weeklies) that circulated among the upper middle classes in eighteenth-century Germany, following the British example, were typical in exhorting parents to devote a huge amount of time and effort to child-rearing. Under the supervision of the father, the mother was to keep a close eye on children below the age of five, breastfeeding them herself, and after weaning, in the words of a weekly from Königsberg, make sure that 'they are never without their mother'.[11] The 'culture of sensibility' that flourished during the eighteenth century encouraged fathers to be more caring, always with the proviso that they avoid becoming effeminate.[12] In the longer term,

---

[8] Bailey, *Parenting in England*, pp. 26–7.

[9] Jean-Jacques Rousseau, *Emile, or on Education*, transl. Allan Bloom (London: Penguin, 1991), note on p. 60; Christina Hardyment, *Dream Babies: Childcare Advice from John Locke to Gina Ford* (London: Frances Lincoln, 2007), p. 22.

[10] Reinhard Spree, 'Shaping the Child's Personality: Medical Advice on Child-Rearing from the Late Eighteenth to the Early Twentieth Century in Germany', *Social History of Medicine*, 5 (1992), 317–35.

[11] Jürgen Schlumbohm, '"Traditional" Collectivity and "Modern" Individuality: Some Questions for the Historical Study of Socialization. The Examples of the German Lower and Upper Bourgeoisies around 1800', *Social History*, 5 (1980), 71–103 (89–91).

[12] G. J. Barker-Benfield, *The Culture of Sensibility: Sex and Society in Eighteenth-Century Britain* (Chicago, IL: University of Chicago Press, 1992), pp. 101–3 and 148–5; Philip Carter, *Men and the Emergence of Polite Society, Britain 1660–1800* (Harlow: Longman, 2001), ch. 3.

though, the emphasis in child-rearing models shifted from the father to the mother. She was to devote herself to caring for her offspring during the early childhood years, as emphasised by numerous authors including Locke, Rousseau, Basedow, Pestalozzi and Maria Edgeworth, developing internal discipline and self-control by such methods as setting a good example and gentle persuasion.[13]

Underpinning the new approach to parenting in the manuals was the emphasis from the late eighteenth century on 'separate spheres' for men and women: the all-too-familiar notion that that men's sphere was the public one of commerce and politics, woman's the private one of the home.[14] The idea that mothers would shoulder much of the burden of childrearing and creating a home was hardly novel in the eighteenth century, but there was an unprecedented idealisation and sentimentalisation of the role.[15] Besides a 'cult of motherhood', the idea of separate spheres also spawned a related 'cult of domesticity'. This rested on the mother's ability to create a home that was a comfortable retreat from the rough-and-tumble world of work: a physical space but also a spiritual atmosphere. What better place could there be for a child, now deemed an innocent and vulnerable creature, than safely cocooned in a loving, family home? That was the ideal anyway.[16] Historians have for long recognised that prescriptions for parenting can only provide a starting point for understanding parent–child relations.[17] How then did families respond to the challenge of these new ideals?

---

[13] Jean-Noel Luc, *L'Invention du jeune enfant au XIXe siècle: de la salle d'asile à l'école maternelle* (Paris: Belin, 1997), p. 81. Advice manuals are well documented in Part I of Fletcher, *Growing Up in England.*

[14] See, for example, Robert B. Shoemaker, *Gender in English Society: The Emergence of Separate Spheres?* (Harlow: Pearson, 1998).

[15] Ruth Perry, 'Colonizing the Breast: Sexuality and Maternity in Eighteenth-Century England', *Journal of the History of Sexuality*, 2, Special Issue, Part 1, 'The State, Society, and the Regulation of Sexuality in Modern Europe' (1991), 204–34 (213); Hazel Mills, 'Negotiating the Divide: Women, Philanthropy and the "Public Sphere" in Nineteenth-Century France', in Frank Tallett and Nicholas Atkin (eds.), *Religion, Society and Politics in France since 1789* (London: Hambledon Press, 1991), pp. 29–54 (pp. 32–40); Rebekka Habermas, 'Parent-Child Relations in the Nineteenth Century', *German History*, 16 (1998), 43–55 (52–3).

[16] Catherine Hall, 'The Sweet Delights of Home', in P. Ariès and G. Duby (eds.), *A History of Private Life* (Cambridge, MA: Harvard University Press, 1990), vol. 4, pp. 47–93; Michael McKeon, *The Secret History of Domesticity* (Baltimore: Johns Hopkins University Press, 2005); and Colin Heywood, 'The Child and the Home: A Historical Survey', *Home Cultures*, 10 (2013), 227–44.

[17] The most influential is Jay Mechling, 'Advice to Historians on Advice to Mothers', *Journal of Social History*, 9 (1975), 44–63.

Childhood among the Aristocracy

Child Rearing among the Aristocracy

The European aristocracy was for centuries the continent's hereditary ruling elite, composed of a core of magnates plus the wealthier provincial gentry. Although under assault from the time of the Enlightenment, and haunted by its first 'martyrs' during the French Revolution, it retained considerable influence in political life and dominated high society during the nineteenth century.[18] Its small numbers, perhaps only a few hundred important landed families in each country, did not prevent the emergence of various approaches to child rearing.

Domesticity was in some ways barely compatible with the aristocratic way of life. Firstly, during the eighteenth century in particular, noblewomen as well as noblemen saw the royal court rather than the household as their sphere of activity. Being a courtier was a time-consuming business, jostling for influence with potential patrons or clients, and attending the numerous entertainments laid on at grand palaces such as Versailles. For the favoured few among high-born women, attending Catherine the Great in Russia, say, or Marie Antoinette in France, there were rich rewards to be had, in the form of land and titles. Chateaubriand (1768–1848) wrote in his memoirs, 'my mother besides, full of spirit and virtue, was preoccupied with the cares of society and the duties of religion ... she liked politics, bustle, people'. Under these circumstances, such mothers did not feel the need to involve themselves on a daily basis in the upbringing of their children – though this did not mean that they took no interest at all.[19] Secondly, the big town houses of the aristocracy, much in evidence in London, Paris and St. Petersburg, were public as well as a private places. They were sites more suited to lavish hospitality and the employment of numerous servants than to family life. Shelburne House, the London residence of the Earl and Countess of Shelburne during their brief marriage between 1765 and 1771, was one of their three houses, described by Amanda Vickery as 'great political engine rooms thronging with flunkies and dignitaries, built for public life'. The Shelburne family was compelled to snatch brief periods of 'tender domesticity' alone with their young son in the midst of their hectic social

---

[18] Dominic Lieven, *The Aristocracy in Europe, 1815–1914* (Basingstoke: Macmillan, 1992), pp. xiii–xvi, and ch. 1.

[19] Margaret H. Darrow, 'French Noblewomen and the New Domesticity, 1750–1850', *Feminist Studies*, 5 (1979), 41–65 (44); Bonnie S. Anderson and Judith P. Zinsser, *A History of Their Own: Women in Europe from Prehistory to the Present* (2 vols., London: Penguin, 1990), vol. 2, ch. 2.

whirl.[20] And thirdly, in the words of Dominic Lieven, 'the pursuit of luxury and pleasure consumed more aristocratic time and energy than any other aspect of life'.[21]

To make all this possible, aristocrats had for centuries delegated responsibility for childrearing to an assortment of servants. Typical of the continent as a whole, in Germany children of the nobility had their own 'royal household', as Ute Frevert puts it, consisting of 'servants, governesses, private teachers and tutors'.[22] Included among these servants were almost invariably wet-nurses, as for centuries breastfeeding had been considered vulgar by members of the nobility and the upper bourgeoisie in Europe.[23] This is not to say that the European aristocracy remained entirely aloof from the new ideals of domesticity and companionate relations between parents and children. As Mary Abbott describes the case among English landed families, if some mothers 'were little more than jewelled apparitions wafting through their children's lives', others involved themselves wholeheartedly in their role as carers.[24] Two of the daughters of the second Duke of Richmond, for example, had evidently read their *Emile*. Lady Caroline (b. 1723) described the book as impossible to follow to the letter, although 'immensely pretty'. During the 1760s she wrote that her son Harry was following Rousseau's system, departing from it at night to include the reading of fairy tales and the study of maps (see Figure 5.1).[25] Similarly, during the late eighteenth century, a handful of French aristocrats raised their infants *à la Jean-Jacques*, as in the case of the Comtesse de Boigne, whose mother breast-fed her at court in Versailles.[26]

Moreover, the shock of the revolutionary upheavals during the 1790s made itself felt in the private as well as the public lives of the aristocracy. In France, according to Margaret Darrow, the generation of aristocrats that experienced the Revolution was the first to engage seriously with domesticity, changing their ways as part of a power struggle with the

---

[20] Amanda Vickery, *Behind Closed Doors: At Home in Georgian England* (New Haven, CT: Yale University Press, 2009), pp. 145–7.

[21] Lieven, *Aristocracy in Europe*, p. 134.

[22] Ute Frevert, *Women in German History: From Bourgeois Emancipation to Sexual Liberation* (Oxford: Berg, 1989), p. 28.

[23] Valerie Fildes, *Wet Nursing: A History from Antiquity to the Present* (Oxford: Basil Blackwell, 1988).

[24] Mary Abbott, *Family Ties: English Families, 1540–1920* (London: Routledge, 1993), p. 63.

[25] Randolph Trumbach, *The Rise of the Egalitarian Family: Aristocratic Kinship and Domestic Relations in Eighteenth-Century England* (New York, NY: Academic Press, 1978), pp. 208–17.

[26] Colin Heywood, *Growing Up in France: From the Ancien Régime to the Third Republic* (Cambridge: Cambridge University Press, 2007), p. 124.

Figure 5.1 *The Duchess of Devonshire* by Joshua Reynolds. Georgiana, Duchess of Devonshire, and her daughter Lady Georgiana Cavendish, 1786.
Getty Images, 136550159.

middle classes.[27] Across the Channel, the English aristocracy was not immune to a general movement at this period emphasising 'domestic morality, appearances of sobriety and earnestness, and serious religiosity'.[28] England was indeed where this shift to more intimate parenting was most in evidence among the aristocracy, perhaps because of their extensive links with wealthy business and professional circles.[29] Yet old habits died hard among conservatives. Coldness and indifference were considered good form among French aristocrats surviving into the nineteenth and twentieth centuries, exemplified by increasingly archaic

---

[27] Darrow, 'French Noblewomen', 43.

[28] Dror Wahrman, '"Middle-Class" Domesticity Goes Public: Gender, Class, and Politics from Queen Caroline to Queen Victoria', *Journal of British Studies*, 32 (1993), 396–432 (401–2).

[29] Leonore Davidoff, 'The Family in Britain', in F. M. L. Thompson (ed.), *The Cambridge Social History of Britain, 1750–1950* (3 vols., Cambridge: Cambridge University Press, 1990), vol. 2, pp. 71–129 (pp. 75–6).

usages such as expecting children to stand in the presence of their parents or to use the formal *vous* when addressing them.[30] Anna de Noailles (1876–1933) wrote from her experiences in Paris that parents did not speak to their children very often, leaving them in the hands of maids and governesses.[31] Even in England, a study of autobiographies found that remoteness was a key characteristic of fathers of the 'governing classes' during the early Victorian period.[32]

Becoming an Aristocrat

The path to adulthood for a young aristocrat was undoubtedly a privileged one, even in the nineteenth century, with all the advantages of material wealth and an assured set of values. Yet it was not necessarily easy to follow. There was often the need to find a substitute (or substitutes) for the mother as a secure attachment figure. This could be achieved satisfactorily with a wet-nurse or other servants. Girls among the Russian aristocracy often remembered the tender care of their peasant nurses; Chateaubriand latched on to *la Villeneuve*, a housekeeper who carried him around and treated him affectionately.[33] There was nonetheless the risk of uncaring servants as well as of uncaring mothers. Nannies, nurses, tutors and governesses were sometimes hard on their charges: 'We were educated strictly and punished often', as one Russian woman put it.[34] The English Lord Curzon (1859–1925) and his siblings found themselves at the mercy of a Miss Perelman:

She spanked us with the sole of her slipper on the bare back, beat us with her brushes, tied us for long hours to chairs in uncomfortable positions with our hands holding poles or a blackboard behind our backs, shut us up in dark places, practised every kind of petty persecution.

---

[30] David Higgs, *Nobles in Nineteenth-Century France* (Baltimore, MD: Johns Hopkins University Press, 1987), pp. 177–83; Eric Mension-Rigau, *L'Enfance au château: l'éducation familiale des élites françaises au vingtième siècle* (Paris: Rivages, 1990), p. 251; Gabrielle Houbre, *La Discipline de l'amour: l'éducation sentimentale des filles et des garçons à l'âge du romantisme* (Paris: Plon, 1997), p. 40.

[31] Anna de Noailles, *Le Livre de ma vie* (Paris: Mercure de France, 1976), p.26.

[32] David Roberts, 'The Paterfamilias of the Victorian Governing Class', in Anthony S. Wohl (ed.), *The Victorian Family: Structure and Stresses* (London: Croom Helm, 1978), pp. 59–81 (pp. 59–62).

[33] Heywood, *Growing Up in France*, pp. 124–5, 141.

[34] Barbara Alpern Engel, 'Mothers and Daughters: Family Patterns and the Female Intelligentsia', in David L. Ransel (ed.), *The Family in Imperial Russia* (Urbana, IL: University of Illinois Press, 1978), pp. 44–59 (pp. 45–6).

Such victims were reluctant to complain if mothers were rarely seen in the schoolroom, and in any case, the children grasped that sneaking on a governess who ruled their daily lives was a risky business.[35] The formality of the aristocratic life could also prove daunting for a child. Those with haughty, distant parents recalled a tense atmosphere in the home. Vera Figner (b. 1852) remembered her fear of her father, a provincial Russian noble: 'One glance, cold and penetrating, was enough to set us trembling.' Aristocratic mothers were less forbidding, but they could still be remote. Charles de Rémusat (1797–1875) acknowledged that his mother took care of his early education, but 'despite her tenderness, she intimidated me'.[36] Acquiring the distinctive 'art of living' was a long and potentially wearing process in school and above all in the family. French aristocrats recalled learning 'how to walk, how to cross a *salon*, sit, put on gloves, fan oneself, descend from a carriage, sneeze', and, of course, behave at table.[37] In short, some sections of the European aristocracy, notably in Britain, adopted some or all of the child-rearing practices promoted by Jean-Jacques Rousseau and his followers, including maternal breastfeeding, close attention from the mother, and a concern with education. Yet tradition weighed heavily in this milieu, keeping children at arm's length from their parents, most evidently according to the existing historiography in France and Imperial Russia.

Childhood among the Middle Ranks

The 'middling ranks' in eighteenth- and nineteenth-century urban society were an amorphous and highly disparate group.[38] Across much of Europe, they were still a very small minority: in Italy in 1881, 'proprietors, industrialists, the professions, private and public employees, teachers and shopkeepers' accounted for only 6.7 per cent of the total population. In France the equivalent figure was 14 per cent, though in Britain, it was perhaps 15–20 per cent.[39] Historians have abandoned

---

[35] Kathryn Hughes, *The Victorian Governess* (London: Hambledon Press, 1993), pp. 68–70.

[36] Engel, 'Mothers and daughters', pp. 46–9; Luc, *L'Invention*, pp. 119–20.

[37] Houbre, *La Discipline de l'amour*, pp. 52–9 and 109; Mension-Rigau, *L'Enfance au château*, pp. 50–1, 75–6, 160–80, 253.

[38] Pamela M. Pilbeam, *The Middle Classes in Europe, 1789–1814: France, Germany, Italy and Russia* (Basingstoke: Macmillan, 1990), ch.1.

[39] Adrian Lyttleton, 'The Middle Classes in Liberal Italy', in John A. Davis and Paul Ginsborg (eds.), *Society and Politics in the Age of Risorgimento* (Cambridge: Cambridge University Press, 1991), pp. 217–50 (p. 224); John Seed, 'From "Middling Sort" to Middle Class in Late Eighteenth- and Early Nineteenth-Century England', in M. L. Bush (ed.), *Social Orders and Social Classes in Europe since 1500* (London: Longman, 1992), pp. 114–35 (p. 115); Amanda Vickery, *The Gentleman's Daughter: Women's Lives*

the habit of associating affectionate parenting, during any period, exclusively with the bourgeoisie, and one small section in particular: the reasonably affluent professional and commercial classes. Peasants and workers had their own ways of loving children; and the middle classes had their share of good, bad and indifferent parents. The fact remains that the urban bourgeoisie played a prominent role down the centuries in creating a suitable environment for close relationships with their young.

Child Rearing among the Middling Group: Mothers and Fathers

Given the varied socio-economic backgrounds of the middling group, and no less importantly, its cultural diversity, considerable differences in family life was only to be expected.[40] However, there were certain unifying themes underpinning these differences that were important for the young. Here we highlight three: the expectation that mothers and children would be provided for by the male head of the household; the priority given to making the home a comfortable place for the family; and the commitment to the education and training, in their different ways, of sons and daughters.

For married women in the middle classes, not having to work for a living became an important marker of their status. How much time the mothers among them devoted to their offspring was partly a matter of the amount of help they could muster. Wealthy families among the liberal professions and business people could afford to leave most of the drudgery involved in housework and child-rearing to servants. As with the aristocracy, despite what the advice literature had to say, this might include resorting to wet-nurses. Mothers were then left free, if they so wished, to concentrate on entertaining the children, and on their moral and religious education. Families in this milieu also increasingly favoured separating children from adults in the home. From the 1850s especially, the better-off families frequently kept children and servants apart from adult members of the family, most obviously in the case of the young by setting up a nursery. Whether mothers visited the nursery frequently, or restricted children to an hour or so with parents in the drawing room, was

in Georgian England (New Haven, CT: Yale University Press, 1998), Appendix 1, pp. 352–3.

[40] Eleanor Gordon and Gwyneth Nair, *Public Lives: Women, Family and Society in Victorian Britain* (New Haven, CT: Yale University Press, 2003), ch. 5; Julia Grant, 'Parent-Child Relations in Western Europe and North America, 1500-Present', in Paula Fass, *The Routledge History of Childhood in the Western World* (Abingdon: Routledge, 2013), pp. 103–24 (pp. 109–10).

up to the adults.[41] This left open the possibility that the servant in the nursery, often in England a young and untrained nanny-cum-house-maid, was more important for the children than their parents.[42] Even in these circles, being a mother was still a gruelling and nerve-wracking business, given the hazards of childbirth and the fragility of child life. Mothers worried about serious illnesses and death among their children, sinking into 'abysmal depths of misery' when they lost a child.[43] Yet the comparison in Glasgow between the life of Helen MacFie, wealthy wife of a sugar manufacturer, and Mollie Macewan, from the lower middle classes, is instructive. The former's diary during the 1870s shows a daily routine largely free of child care, while letters written by the latter give the impression that every minute of the day was taken up with it.[44]

Divergent approaches to mothering were not purely a matter of material circumstances: differences in culture also came into play.[45] If some mothers decided to treat mothering as a vocation, many others combined it with an active life outside the home. A case study from Lancashire reveals those among the gentry enjoying 'cards, tea, assemblies and oratorios'. Or one could point to the wives of industrialists in the northern textile industry in France, who began the nineteenth century with an active role in family businesses, and ended it heavily committed to charitable work. These pious women handed over most of the work of child-rearing, apart from early education, to wet nurses, servants, and boarding schools. According to Bonnie Smith, they thought themselves too refined to touch a soiled child, but could kiss it goodnight – adding that 'One of my informants, Mme S., suggested that many women were lax in this, as in most matters of child care'. Jeanne Peterson emphasises in her study of Victorian women from urban professional families that they were actively involved in the lives of their children, yet doubts that mothering was the 'central focus' of their lives. They picked favourites,

---

[41] Ingeborg Weber-Kellerman, '*Die Kinderstube*: A Cultural History of the Children's Room' in Alexander von Vegesak, Jutta Oldiges and Lucy Bullivant (eds.), *Kid Size: The Material World of Childhood* (Milan: Skira and Vitra Design Museum, 1997), pp. 25–39; Jane Hamlett, *Material Relations: Domestic Interiors and Middle-Class Families in England, 1850–1910* (Manchester: Manchester University Press, 2010), ch. 3; Michel Manson, 'La Chambre d'enfant dans la littérature de jeunesse: représentations et histoire d'une émergence en France de 1780 à 1880', *Strenae*, 7 (2014).

[42] Jane Hamlett, '"Tiresome Trips Downstairs": Middle-Class Domestic Space and Family Relationships in England, 1850–1910', in Lucy Delap, Ben Griffin and Abigail Wills (eds.), *The Politics of Domestic Authority in Britain since 1800* (Aldershot: Palgrave Macmillan, 2009), pp. 111–31.

[43] Bonnie Smith, *Ladies of the Leisure Class: The Bourgeoises of Northern France in the Nineteenth Century* (Princeton, NJ: Princeton University Press, 1981), pp. 86–7; Vickery, *Gentleman's Daughter*, pp. 110–25, 286.

[44] Gordon and Nair, *Public Lives*, pp. 140–7.   [45] Gordon and Nair, *Public Lives*, p. 147.

stayed away from their children for long periods when it suited them, and of course handed them over to servants.[46]

It should be added that fathers by no means confined themselves to the role of breadwinner for the family, often being active beside mothers in the private sphere.[47] The stereotype of the stern patriarchal father during the Victorian era has long been discredited, as many of them adopted the Enlightenment ideal of a peaceable, family-orientated figure. As John Tosh has noted in the case of Victorian England, what he calls 'tyrannical fathers' had not entirely disappeared, but they were in a minority. The best known example is the odious clergyman father, Theodore, depicted in Samuel Butler's autobiographical novel *The Way of All Flesh* (1903). However, a number of studies have revealed some middle-class men revelling in their role as fathers, particularly entertaining and teaching older children. James Ransome, prominent in the civic affairs of Ipswich as well as his family's iron foundry, 'was a much loved father of ten children who found time to take them for walks on Sundays and weekday evenings to the shipping docks and occasionally to the works'.[48] But the relationship was often made difficult by the amount of time fathers spent away from home, at work, or in the company of friends. In Glasgow, Madeleine Smith perceived her father to be entirely wrapped up in his work as an architect: 'Appearing in low spirits has no effect with Papa, he never notices me, I see very little of him, only in the evenings.'[49] Letters and diaries written by young girls in France presented fathers as peripheral figures, veering between bouts of shouting at their offspring, and efforts to take them out for treats at weekends.[50] Other fathers found it difficult to form a close relationship with their offspring, fearing that it was unmanly.[51]

[46] Vickery, *Gentleman's Daughter*, p. 116; Smith, *Ladies of the Leisure Class*, pp. 63–4, 74–6, 81, n. 50, p. 246; M. Jeanne Peterson, *Family, Love, and Work in the Lives of Victorian Gentlewomen* (Bloomington, IN: Indiana University Press, 1989), pp. 103–8.

[47] Leonore Davidoff and Catherine Hall, *Family Fortunes: Men and Women of the English Middle Class, 1780–1850* (London: Hutchinson, 1987), pp. 329–35; Yvonne Knibiehler, *Les Pères aussi ont une histoire* (Paris: Hachette, 1987); Jean Delumeau and Daniel Roche (eds.), *Histoire des pères et de la paternité* (Paris: Larousse, 1990); John Tosh, *A Man's Place: Masculinity and the Middle-Class Home in Victorian England* (New Haven, CT: Yale University Press, 1999); Trev Lynn Broughton and Helen Rogers (eds.), *Gender and Fatherhood in the Nineteenth Century* (Basingstoke: Palgrave Macmillan, 2007).

[48] Davidoff and Hall, *Family Fortunes*, p. 331.

[49] Eleanor Gordon and Gwyneth Nair, 'Domestic Fathers and the Victorian Parental Role', *Women's History Review*, 15 (2006), 551–9 (554).

[50] Heywood, *Growing Up in France*, p. 149.   [51] Tosh, *Man's Place*, pp. 93–100.

Home as a Nest: Material and Cultural Environment

The middling ranks of society had a long history of domesticity, as far back as the fourteenth century among the English 'burgeiserie'. The older version involved a 'household-family', including all those living in the same house under the authority of its master, with a routine of working as well as living together in the home.[52] Hence, the ideal was that of a household where the male head worked at his craft or his trade, assisted by his wife, children, apprentices, journeymen and servants.[53] The late eighteenth and early nineteenth centuries ushered in the modern ideal of domesticity, which centred on the nuclear family alone, and its children in particular. Middle-class families were henceforth inclined to retreat from the wider world into their homes. As John Gillis has shown in the English case, during the second half of the nineteenth century, they created their own festivals, to replace the traditional ones organised by the local community. Children were central to these: their baptism became for the first time centred on the home; their birthdays were celebrated every year; and their confirmation was a further occasion for a family gathering. Christmas also took on increasing importance as a holiday with an emphasis on children, particularly in Germany, involving decorations for the home, a family celebration and the exchange of gifts. The market for toys peaked at this season (see Figure 5.2).[54]

To account for this new form of domesticity, historians often start with the increasing separation of work and home in towns. In Germany, this was under way by 1800, encouraged by the development of large state bureaucracies. Among the 'new' middle classes, including professors, doctors, lawyers and civil servants, families were dependent on the salary of the man alone.[55] More generally in western Europe, historians usually point to the influence of industrialisation. The suggestion is that with the

---

[52] See Chapter 3.

[53] Felicity Riddy, '"Burgeis" Domesticity in Late-Medieval England', in M. Kowaleski and P. J. P. Goldberg (eds.), *Medieval Domesticity: Home, Housing and Household in Medieval England* (Cambridge: Cambridge University Press, 2008), pp. 14–36; Cordelia Beattie, 'Economy', in Sandra Cavallo and Silvia Evangelisti (eds.), *A Cultural History of Childhood and the Family in the Early Modern Age* (Oxford: Berg, 2010), pp. 49–67 (p. 56).

[54] John Gillis, *A World of Their Own Making: A History of Myth and Ritual in Family Life* (Oxford: Oxford University Press, 1997), p. 72; David D. Hamlin, *Work and Play: The Production and Consumption of Toys in Germany, 1870–1914* (Ann Arbor, MI: University of Michigan Press, 2007), pp. 28–37.

[55] Karin Hausen, 'Family and Role Division: The Polarisation of Sexual Stereotypes in the Nineteenth Century – An Aspect of the Dissociation of Work and Family Life', in Richard J. Evans and W. R. Lee (eds.), *The German Family* (London: Croom Helm, 1981), pp. 51–83 (pp. 68–9).

Figure 5.2 Parents playing with a newborn child, from an engraving for Rousseau's *Emile*, 1848.
Getty Images, 475565940.

rise of the factory system, and eventually white-collar jobs in offices, there was less likelihood of workshops and counting houses being found under the same roof as living quarters. Apprentices and journeymen were encouraged to live with their own families, and servants and servants' quarters were increasingly separated from the family However, this was a slow process, only in its first stages before the 1870s.[56] The continued existence of 'household families' among small business groups meant that the separation of the nuclear family from servants and employees could not go far in this milieu. A study of such families in north-west English towns reveals that children of the blood family would often have had to share rooms, and probably beds, with these co-residents.[57] In the meantime, there were cultural forces encouraging the cult of domesticity among the middle classes. In a polemical battle with a supposedly violent, corrupt and debauched aristocracy, their representatives claimed a

---

[56] Davidoff and Hall, *Family Fortunes*, ch. 3; Guttormsson, 'Parent-Child-Relations', in Kertzer and Barbagli, *European Family*, vol. 2, p. 263.
[57] Hannah Barker and Jane Hamlett, 'Living above the Shop: Home, Business, and Family in the English "Industrial Revolution"', *Journal of Family History*, 35 (2010), 311–28 (321, 323–4).

moral authority from such virtues as intelligence, independence, and an orderly family life.[58] Moreover, they also rested their authority on their religious observance, most obviously in Germany and England. In the latter case, the Evangelical revival that invigorated all denominations during the late eighteenth and early nineteenth centuries was arguably central to middle-class culture, underpinning the argument that the home should provide a retreat in which the moral and religious life of the family could flourish.[59]

The bourgeois of towns also revealed a growing 'lust for consumption', as Simon Schama put it in the Dutch case.[60] This included buying consumer goods, such as curtains, mirrors, china and books, which would make the home more comfortable and hence a more desirable place to spend time with the family.[61] Although the lower orders in towns had some share in this type of consumption, there is evidence that it was merchants and shopkeepers who pioneered the 'consumer revolution'.[62] As far as children were concerned, a growing range of specialised furniture, such as baby-walkers, high chairs for infants at mealtimes, and little desks, helped them grow up as part of the family. They also benefited from the increasingly commercial society as parents put money into books, toys and games specially for them.[63]

Rich children, although presumably surrounded by expensive toys (a speciality of Nuremberg and the Groeden Valley in southern Germany), had nothing much to say about them in their reminiscences,

[58] David Blackbourn, 'The German Bourgeoisie: An Introduction', in D. Blackbourn and R. J. Evans (eds.), *The German Bourgeoisie: Essays on the Social History of the German Middle Class from the Late Eighteenth to the Early Twentieth Century* (London: Routledge, 1991), pp. 1–45 (pp. 12–13).

[59] This section relies on Catherine Hall, 'The Early Formation of Victorian Domestic Ideology', in Sandra Burman (ed.), *Fit Work for Women* (London: Croom Helm, 1979), pp. 15–32; Davidoff and Hall, *Family Fortunes*, pp. 155–79, and the rather different interpretation to be found in Dror Wahrman, '"Middle-Class" Domesticity Goes Public: Gender, Class, and Politics from Queen Caroline to Queen Victoria', *Journal of British Studies*, 32 (1993), 396–432 (401–2), and idem, *Imagining the Middle Class: The Political Representation of Class in Britain, c. 1780–1840* (Cambridge: Cambridge University Press, 1995), passim.

[60] Simon Schama, *The Embarrassment of Riches: An Interpretation of Dutch Culture in the Golden Age* (London: Collins, 1987), p. 304.

[61] Mark Overton et al., *Production and Consumption in English Households, 1600–1750* (London: Routledge, 2004); Sarah Maza, *Myth of the French Bourgeoisie: An Essay on the Social Imaginary, 1750–1785* (Cambridge MA: Harvard University Press, 2003), ch. 2.

[62] Cissie Fairchilds, 'Consumption in Early Modern Europe. A Review Article', *Comparative Studies in Society and History*, 35 (1993), 850–8 (852).

[63] Marta Ajmar-Wollheim, 'Geography and the Environment', in Cavallo and Evangelisti, *Early Modern Age*, pp. 75, 79–80. See also the pioneering article by J. H. Plumb, 'The New World of Children in Eighteenth-Century England', *Past and Present*, 67 (1975), 64–95; and Hamlin, *Toys in Germany*.

unless they were home-made.[64] They did however sometimes note the books they read. The middle classes of towns stood out by their willingness to spend money on literature to educate and entertain their children in the home. How then did the book trade respond to this demand for reading matter either written for children or considered suitable for them? Publishing material exclusively for children first emerged in north-west Europe during the mid-eighteenth century on a small-scale, part-time basis. From the middle of the nineteenth century onwards, children's publishing in Europe took on a whole new scale, in the context of technical progress on the production side, a developing economy that favoured the expansion of the urban middle classes, and the free flow of goods across borders.[65] No less importantly, religious revivals in both Protestant and Catholic countries encouraged publishing houses to produce suitably pious works for children on a massive scale,[66] the emergence of national education systems opened the way for patriotic textbooks, and rising literacy rates broadened the base of potential readers. Among the bestsellers, in England Hesba Stretton's *Jessica's First Prayer* (1867) sold no less than 1.8 million copies; in Italy, *Cuore: libro per iragazzi* (1886) by Edmondo De Amicis nearly a million by 1914.[67]

It is not difficult to trace the evolution of children's literature according to changing conceptions of childhood. Eighteenth-century works such as Thomas Day's *Sandford and Merton* (1783–9) or Bernardin de Saint Pierre's *Paul et Virginie* (1787) were clearly inspired by the child of nature in Rousseau's *Emile*. Evangelical writers of the early nineteenth century, such as Mary Martha Sherwood and Hannah More in England, assumed the innate sinfulness of children. The vogue for fairy tales, notable in nineteenth century France and Germany, rested on the

---

[64] Richard N. Coe, *When the Grass Was Taller: Autobiography and the Experience of Childhood* (Chicago, IL: UMI Books, 1996), p. 206–10; Gary Cross, 'Toys', in Fass, *Encyclopedia of Children;* Hamlin, *Toys in Germany*, p. 57.

[65] Penny Brown, *A Critical History of French Children's Literature* (2 vols., New York and London: Routledge, 2008), vol. 1, ch. 3, vol. 2, ch. 1; Matthew Grenby, *The Child Reader* (Cambridge: Cambridge University Press, 2011), pp. 4–5; David Finkelstein, 'The Globalization of the Book, 1800–1970', in Simon Eliot and Jonathan Rose (eds.), *A Companion to the History of the Book* (Oxford: Blackwell, 2007), pp. 329–40 (pp. 330–31).

[66] See Jan De Maeyer, 'The Concept of Religious Modernisation', in Jan De Maeyer et al. (eds.), *Religion, Children's Literature, and Modernity in Western Europe* (Leuven: Leuven University Press, 2006), pp. 41–50.

[67] Gillian Avery, *Childhood's Pattern: A Study of Heroes and Heroines of Children's Fiction* (London: Hodder and Stoughton, 1975), p. 115; Laura Kreyder, 'Italy', in Peter Hunt and Sheila Ray (eds.), *International Companion Encyclopedia of Children's Literature* (London: Routledge, 1996), pp. 757–60 (758).

idealisation of the child by the Romantics. There was also a response to the divergent tastes of boys and girls, perceived during the nineteenth century to require adventure stories for the former and domestic novels for the latter.

Literary critics have understandably highlighted the qualities of the exceptions: classic works, such as Lewis Carroll's *Alice's Adventures in Wonderland* (1865) and Collodi's *Pinocchio* (1881–3), which had a child as their protagonist and stimulated the imagination of the young reader. In the long term, it is generally agreed that children's books gradually moved from didacticism to freedom, leading to a 'golden age' during the second half of the nineteenth century. The temptation, of course, is to dismiss much of the eighteenth- and nineteenth-century literature as insipid and unappealing for children, especially the output of the numerous 'governess' authors: women writing to improve the morals of the young. Feminist scholars have rescued these women from general opprobrium.[68] A closer look reveals that early writers for children, both male and female, were acutely aware of the need to entertain as well as instruct children, and in addition proved themselves gifted writers. Mrs Sherwood (1775–1851), for example, may have a reputation as the fiercest of the Evangelical writers in England, but Gillian Avery notes the 'excellence' of her writing in the notoriously morbid novel *The Fairchild Family* (part 1, 1818), with the 'spectacle of these – on occasion – delightfully life-like children disporting themselves in a neo-Gothic stage set of graveyards and vaults and coffins'. In France, the works of the very Catholic and conservative Comtesse de Ségur (1799–1874) may be firmly associated with the impossibly pure and pious *'petite fille modèle'*. Yet Sophie Heywood draws attention to Ségur's efforts to make her language attractive for children, to her humour, and to her pacy narratives, concluding that 'She sugared her moral pill with prodigious skill'.[69] Evidently publishers had some success in encouraging young readers. If Charles Darwin's son George (b. 1845) was doubtless far from exceptional in saying 'I hate reading – I like drawing and money', a study of eighteenth-century English memoirs revealed that 'children

---

[68] Mitzi Myers, 'Impeccable Governesses, Rational Dames, and Moral Mothers: Mary Wollstonecraft and the Female Tradition in Georgian Children's Books', *Children's Literature*, 14 (1986), 31–58; Lynne Vallone, *Disciplines of Virtue: Girls' Culture in the Eighteenth and Nineteenth Centuries* (New Haven, CT: Yale University Press, 1995); Norma Clarke, '"The Cursed Barbauld Crew": Women Writers and Writing for Children in the Late Eighteenth Century', in Mary Hilton, Morag Styles and Victor Watson (eds.), *Opening the Nursery Door: Reading, Writing and Childhood 1600–1900* (London: Routledge, 1997), pp. 91–103.

[69] Avery, *Childhood's Pattern*, p. 99; Sophie Heywood, *Catholicism and Children's Literature in France: The Comtesse de Ségur, 1799–1874* (Manchester: Manchester University Press, 2011), chs. 2 and 5.

Figure 5.3 Alice trapped in a room. Illustration by Sir John Tenniel for *Alice in Wonderland*.
Getty Images, 171147862.

highly relished their reading'.[70] There was the growing variety of material available to them, with literary genres including moral and instructional works, fairy-tales, fantasies, nonsense verse, and school stories. There were the impressive illustrations and packaging used to make books and magazines more attractive. And there was the growing volume of sales over the two centuries in question (see Figure 5.3).[71]

It should be added that for all their willingness to spend money on their children, middle-class parents were wary of spoiling them.[72]

---

[70] Grenby, *Child Reader*, p. 267.

[71] Henri-Jean Martin, Roger Chartier and Jean-Pierre Vivet (eds.), *Histoire de l'édition française* (4 vols., Paris: Promodis 1982–6), vol. 3; Peter Hunt (ed.), *Children's Literature: An Illustrated History* (Oxford and New York: Oxford University Press, 1995); Martyn Lyons, 'New Readers in the Nineteenth Century: Women, Children, Workers', in Guglielmo Cavallo and Roger Chartier, *A History of Reading in the West* (Amherst: University of Massachusetts Press, 1999), pp. 324–31; Penny Brown, 'Capturing (and Captivating) Childhood: The Role of Illustrations in Eighteenth-Century Children's Books in Britain and France', *Journal for Eighteenth-Century Studies*, 31 (2008), 419–49.

[72] Ginger S. Frost, *Victorian Childhoods* (London: Praeger, 2009), pp. 23 and 26–7.

Devoted followers of Locke and Rousseau might impose a Spartan regime involving cold baths and light clothing in winter. Arrangements in the Victorian nursery had a disciplinary purpose behind them, with children expected to keep them tidy and put up with plain food.[73] In Germany, Carl Friedrich Pockels described his humiliating first memory at the age of two as a battle over table manners with his father, a parent 'determined never to pamper his children by complying with their wishes too promptly'.[74]

Education and Training

A fervent commitment to educating their young was a characteristic of the middle classes. Parents knew that their sons might have to make their way in a liberal profession or in business, with a call for 'careers open to talent' rather patronage. And daughters, in their view, needed to become good wives and mothers to fulfil themselves, requiring preparation of a different kind that was taken seriously in its own way. Education began on a mother's knee, for both boys and girls, as she taught the basics of religion and morality, and perhaps also of literacy. This was where the 'Angel of the House' could make her mark. For Jean-Noël Luc, from the late eighteenth century the child 'became interesting' for some adults between the ages of two and six, going through a 'second childhood' after infancy – one which lent itself to a precocious education.[75] Indeed, across Europe there was a general recognition that mothers had an important role to play in the creation of the virtuous citizen, influenced by Rousseau and his emphasis on the *mère éducatrice*.[76] Mothers in this milieu were by no means reluctant to resort to corporal punishment, or to threaten it from fathers, but they were in a position to resort to more subtle methods than intimidation by fear, exerting moral and emotional pressure on their charges. A disapproving glance from a loving mother might be sufficient.[77]

---

[73] Hamlett, *Material Relations*, p. 122–3.

[74] Jürgen Schlumbohm, 'Constructing Individuality: Childhood Memories in Late Eighteenth-century "Empirical Psychology" and Autobiography', *German History*, 16 (1998), 29–42 (36–7).

[75] Luc, *Invention*, pp. 147–52; see Chapter 4.

[76] Jennifer Poppiel, 'Making Mothers: The Advice Genre and the Domestic Ideal, 1760–1830', *Journal of Family History*, 29 (2004), 339–50; and eadem., *Rousseau's Daughters: Domesticity, Education, and Autonomy in Modern France* (Durham, NH: University of New Hampshire Press, 2008).

[77] On the changing emotional climate surrounding child rearing during the eighteenth and nineteenth centuries, see Peter N. Stearns, 'Childhood Emotions in Modern Western History', in Fass, *Childhood in the Western World*, pp. 158–73.

There was also a strong presumption in middle-class circles that girls were best educated in the home by their mothers since they were destined for a life of domesticity. They were invariably taught the quintessential feminine skills of sewing and needlework, and the importance of order and self-discipline. They sometimes had considerable scope for intellectual pursuits at home in the upper levels, taught by parents and tutors, sitting in on lessons for their brothers, or reading for themselves in library collections.[78] There was also much to be learned from watching or helping mothers and other women at work. Running the large household of a wealthy family with numerous servants and children, while perhaps also making contacts to advance the interests of a family business, helping to arrange suitable marriage partners for their offspring, supporting a husband's political career, or undertaking charitable work, was a considerable challenge. Alternatively, coping with the time-consuming tasks of housework and child rearing, with perhaps only one servant to assist and a tight budget, required another range of skills.

Over the course of the nineteenth century parents were increasingly inclined to send their daughters to school for part of their education. By the 1860s, perhaps a half of all middle-class girls in England and France were attending private schools. They would often start around the age of eight in France, remaining for a few years as a boarder before returning home.[79] Again, the aim was to prepare girls for marriage and motherhood rather than for intellectual development, though as an unintended consequence schooling might sometimes encourage a more active life outside the home.[80] A study of autobiographies written by middle-class German girls concluded that their education was 'unmethodical, often of poor quality, and not especially broad'. The emphasis was always on the humanities, with science, mathematics and classical languages, as studied by German males in higher education, entirely ignored.[81] Sarah Dendy in England was surely a credit to her school in claiming that her education 'made me a better mother to my children than any other

---

[78] Michèle Cohen, '"To Think, To Compare, To Combine, To Methodise": Girls' Education in Enlightenment Britain', in Barbara Taylor and Sarah Knott (eds.), *Women, Gender and Enlightenment* (Basingstoke: Palgrave Macmillan, 2005), pp. 224–42.

[79] Christina de Bellaigue, *Educating Women: Schooling and Identity in England and France, 1800–1867* (Oxford: Oxford University Press, 2007), pp. 139, 144, 154 and 162.

[80] Rebecca Rogers, *From the Salon to the Schoolroom: Educating Bourgeois Girls in Nineteenth-Century France* (University Park, PA: Pennsylvania State University Press, 2005), pp. 3–4, 74.

[81] Juliane Jacobi-Dittrich, 'Growing Up Female in the Nineteenth Century', in John C. Fout (ed.), *German Women in the Nineteenth Century* (New York, NY: Holmes and Meier, 1984), pp. 197–217 (p. 211).

training could have done.'[82] Discipline was strict, with a timetable meticulously planned for each day, and close supervision by adults at all times. The girls often complained of boredom and the feeling of being cooped up in a kind of prison. All the same, small, private schools for girls in England, usually day schools, were particularly successful in creating a homely atmosphere for their pupils, and allowing them some freedom outside the classroom. The boarding schools in France, by contrast felt more regimented, and the girls often struggled to adapt.[83] It is possible that underlying these differences was a Protestant as opposed to a Catholic conception of education. The suggestion is that the English adopted the former's concern with 'self government', giving girls responsibility early in life, while the French, along with the Spanish and Italians, continued the tradition of concentrating on the preservation of their innocence, modesty and virginity.[84] Such girls were to be sexually innocent *oies blanches* (white geese) before marriage.

Boys meanwhile were customarily the responsibility of fathers once breeched, starting on the long path to a career. They might learn from their father, or have a private tutor at home. The childhood diary of Otto van Eck (1780–98), son of a wealthy and influential father in the Dutch Republic, gives a hint of one such education. His was an enlightened version, influenced by Rousseau and in particular the more pragmatic approach of the German Philanthropinist movement. He spent much of his childhood on the family's country estate, weaving, painting and woodworking, but he also had a strict daily routine and he was encouraged to read works selected by his parents, notably J. B. Basedow's encyclopaedic *Manuel élémentaire*. His parents followed the principle of giving or withholding treats, such as buying pets at the market, to enforce discipline. The underlying aim was to develop his conscience, what his mother called 'the little man within'. One threat his father wielded when Otto behaved badly was to send him to a boarding school, though he never followed it through.[85]

Many other boys among the middle classes were not so fortunate, being sent off to a private boarding school from as early as the age of six. Supporters of an education at school as opposed to at home with a private tutor argued that it toughened boys up, encouraged emulation

[82] Bellaigue, *Educating Women*, p. 148.
[83] Bellaigue, *Educating Women*, pp. 144–9, 156–65.
[84] Gabrielle Houbre, 'Demoiselles catholiques et *misses* protestantes: deux modèles éducatifs antagonistes au XIXe siècle', *Bulletin de la société de l'histoire du Protestantisme Français*, 146 (2000), 49–68.
[85] Arianne Baggerman and Rudolf Dekker, *Child of the Enlightenment: Revolutionary Europe Reflected in a Boyhood Diary*, transl. Diane Webb (Leiden: Brill, 2009), ch. 1.

and prepared them for life in society.[86] However, one such supporter, Vicesimus Knox, spelled out in his *Liberal Education* (1781) that this required 'a strict, a long and laborious study of the grammar at a puerile age'. As Michèle Cohen tartly observes, 'Not surprisingly, ensuring that little boys complied with this relentless regime made corporal punishment "indispensably necessary"'.[87] Parents were aware that the jump from home to school was more of a shock for boys than girls, encouraging a harder edge to the formers' education while still at home. In the long and generally unedifying story of corporal punishment in boys' schools, the childhood reminiscences of Dimitri Ivanovich Rostislavov (1809–77) illustrate more starkly than most the notion that home is heaven, school is hell. The son of a village priest in Riazan Province, he began his own path into the Russian Orthodox Church at the age of ten by enrolling in the parish church school at Kasimov. There followed a nightmarish experience of tedious rote-learning combined with savage punishments, usually beatings of ten to fifteen strokes or more with a birch rod, made worse by the gloating of the other boys when it was not their turn to suffer, and the willingness of the more senior ones to set up the juniors for punishment.[88]

The Middle-Class Childhood

In so far as one can risk generalising about childhood in the middling ranks of society, it might be said that it had for centuries anticipated the modern, 'protected' form of childhood in various ways, including both its strengths and weaknesses. It avoided the extremes of poverty that blighted many lives among peasants and workers. It made efforts to create comfortable and in some cases even pious homes for the family. It also tended to exemplify Rousseau's call for parents to be humane, appealing to reason rather than the threat of the rod to correct bad behaviour in the home. And the willingness of the middle classes to support both informal and formal methods of education was never in doubt, not least because it was a cornerstone of their strategy for advancing their interests in society. Of course these were exacting demands, and custom or personal preferences meant that many families diverged from the enlightened ideals of the advice books. If in principle childhood was supposed to be a joyous and carefree period, in practice it was likely

---

[86] Cohen, 'Girls' Education', p. 226.   [87] Cohen, 'Girls' Education', pp. 232–3.
[88] Dimitri Ivanovich Rostislavov, in Alexander M. Martin (transl. and ed.), *Provincial Russia in the Age of Enlightenment: The Memoir of a Priest's Son* (De Kalb, IL: Northern Illinois University Press, 2002), pp. 145–50.

to be burdened with school work and household chores. We have noted the distant relations with mothers and especially fathers in some wealthier circles, the willingness to send daughters and especially sons to boarding schools at a tender age, and the varied approaches to discipline. In the German case, for David Hamlin, 'The *bürgerliche* family only loosely resembled the ideology that underpinned it'.[89]

Also on the downside, the close supervision and pressure to improve oneself could be burdensome for a child. Lloyd deMause, in his schema for the long-run evolution of parenting, has a point in labelling the eighteenth-century approach as the 'intrusive mode'. Parents, he suggested, attempted to conquer the child's mind, 'in order to control its insides, its anger, its needs, its masturbation, its very will'.[90] The devoted parent risked becoming something of a menace. Madame Roland (1754–93) was one such, who actively supported her husband's career, while managing to nurse her daughter Eudora and personally organise the girl's education by means of an idiosyncratic version of Rousseau's teachings. But teaching a little girl the alphabet at three, numbers at four, and music theory, the piano and botany at four-and-a-half, took its toll. Eudora was not up to this ambitious programme. When her daughter was six, Mme Roland wrote a *mea culpa*, a letter to her husband admitting that expecting a child to work in silence between the desks of her parents, without being allowed to sing or chat, was too much, and that it would soon be bored.[91] The young bourgeois could also be isolated from the world of adults, secluded in the parental garden: what the future historian Johann Friedrich Böhmer (1795–1863) in Frankfurt am Main described as a 'locked castle'.[92] Parents were inclined to dictate who their children could mix with, keeping them away from bad influences on the streets.[93] There is the image of the well-bred child looking out wistfully at the children outside playing on the street. Anatole France had the mother of the narrator 'Pierre', in his autobiographical novel *Le Livre de mon ami* (1885) spell out why he could not join the son of a laundress playing freely in the courtyard below: 'Alphonse is badly

---

[89] Hamlin, *Toys in Germany*, p. 27.
[90] Lloyd deMause, 'The Evolution of Childhood', in Lloyd deMause (ed.), *The History of Childhood: The Evolution of Parent-Child Relationships as a Factor in History* (London: Souvenir Press, 1976), pp. 1–73 (p. 52).
[91] Luc, *L'Invention du jeune enfant*, pp. 120–22; Douthwaite, *The Wild Girl*, pp. 141–5.
[92] Jürgen Schlumbohm, '"Traditional" Collectivity and "Modern" Individuality: Some Questions for the Historical Study of Socialization. The Examples of the German Lower and Upper Bourgeoisies around 1800', *Social History*, 5 (1980), 71–103 (91).
[93] Burnett, *Destiny Obscure*, p. 32.

brought up; it is not his fault, it is his misfortune; but well brought-up children should not associate with those who are not.'[94]

Conclusion

The climate of opinion in middle- and upper-class families during the eighteenth and nineteenth centuries was susceptible to the influence of enlightened thinkers. There were moves to discourage parents from trying beat the old Adam out of children in order to guarantee their eternal salvation. Instead, advice manuals adopted a more secular framework, advising that a loving parent would do better to work with the grain of a child deemed innocent and in need of gentle but firm guidance towards virtue. There were signs of this having an effect, with examples of mothers taking a close interest in the upbringing of their children, fathers departing from the role of strict patriarch, and gentler forms of discipline. However, it is likely that many families had taken a similar approach during earlier periods. It is also clear that the urban middle classes had a long history of domesticity, sheltering the family from the rest of society and showing concern for the education and cultural life of their offspring. Moreover, the forces of continuity were still much in evidence, with wealthy parents in particular often limiting contact with their children in the home, sending their sons away to school at an early age and relying on corporal punishment.

---

[94] Anatole France, *Le Livre de mon ami* (1885), as cited by Heywood, *Growing Up in France*, p. 203.

6   The 'Lower Depths'
Working-Class Children in the Early Industrial Town

The nineteenth-century town has an evil reputation. The image of Coketown lingers in the mind, vividly described by Charles Dickens as 'a town of unnatural red and black like the painted face of a savage', with its smoking chimneys, its 'rattling and trembling' factories, and its regimented inhabitants.[1] Historians have frequently drawn attention to the harm inflicted on the population of towns by early urbanisation in Europe. They note the rapid and haphazard expansion of the new industrial centres, and the protracted struggle to match it with the provision of basic services such as clean water, sanitation and housing for workers.[2] It was not all gloom and doom in towns, however. If those migrating to towns faced higher mortality rates than in villages, they were compensated by the better economic opportunities and wider range of amenities on offer. Besides the mushrooming manufacturing centres of the Industrial Revolution, there were capital cities, old-established centres of trade and manufacturing, ports and resort towns. Alongside the rough areas of a town, there were invariably the wealthy and the 'respectable' sections.[3] Following on from our study of the more affluent sections of the urban population, this chapter will look at those on the wrong side of the tracks. It will begin with the grim reality of high levels of infant mortality in towns and the conditions that lay behind it. It will move on to what we would now see as the last gasp of harmful customs for infants such as abandonment and wet-nursing, and examine family life among the working classes. Finally, it will consider the efforts of charities and the state to support (and control) the urban poor.

---

[1] Charles Dickens, *Hard Times* (London: Penguin, 1995 [1854]), p. 28.
[2] Eric Hobsbawm, *The Age of Revolution, 1789–1848* (New York: Mentor, 1962), p. 241.
[3] Andrew Lees and Lynn Hollen Lees, *Cities and the Making of Modern Europe, 1750–1914* (Cambridge: Cambridge University Press, 2007), pp. 2 and 4.

Infant and Child Health in Towns

Infant Mortality Rates

If peasant families struggled to keep their infants alive, their counterparts among workers in towns faced even more daunting odds. Infant mortality figures told their own tale, usually being higher in towns than in the countryside during the early industrialisation period. In the British case, a study of infant mortality by region has revealed that in 1861 the most disadvantaged were in the industrialising and increasingly urbanised counties in the midlands and the north of England, with a rate of over 150 per thousand live births. The most favoured were in the south and west of England, and parts of Scotland, with a rate under 120. Homing in on some of the municipal boroughs, one finds in 1871 very high rates of 269 per thousand in Liverpool, 241 in Leicester and 190 in Birmingham – though 165 in Bristol and 144 in Portsmouth.[4] In other parts of Europe, the pernicious influence of urban life on infants was even more in evidence. In Sweden, Stockholm had an evil reputation for its infant mortality rate, which hovered around 320 during the second quarter of the nineteenth century, as the city struggled with a stagnating economy. In France, Rouen was registering a rate of 300 as late as the period 1886–92, Reims 250 to 300.[5] An old saying in Germany, 'You really own your child only after its first year; before that it is only on loan', reflected the fatalistic attitude of people facing such losses.[6]

---

[4] C. H. Lee, 'Regional Inequalities in Infant Mortality in Britain, 1861–1971: Patterns and Hypotheses', *Population Studies*, 45 (1991), 55–65 (p. 56); Robert Woods, Naomi Williams and Chris Galley, 'Infant Mortality in England, 1550–1950: Problems in the Identification of Long-Term Trends and Geographical and Social Variations', in Carlo A. Corsini and Pier Paolo Viazzo, *The Decline of Infant Mortality in Europe, 1800–1950* (Florence: UNICEF, 1993), pp. 35–50 (pp. 41–4); Naomi Williams and Graham Mooney, 'Infant Mortality in an "Age of Great Cities": London and the English Provincial Cities Compared, c. 1840–1910', *Continuity and Change*, 9 (1994), 185–212 (191, table 1).

[5] Johan Söderberg, Ulf Jonsson and Christer Persson, *A Stagnating Metropolis: The Economy and Demography of Stockholm, 1750–1850* (Cambridge: Cambridge University Press, 1991), p. 161, figure 8.5; Catherine Rollet and Patrice Bourdelais, 'Infant Mortality in France, 1750–1950: Evaluation and Perspectives', in Corsini and Viazzo, *Decline of Infant Mortality*, pp. 51–70 (p. 63).

[6] Ute Frevert, 'The Civilizing Tendency of Hygiene: Working-Class Women under Medical Control in Imperial Germany, in John C. Fout (ed.), *German Women in the Nineteenth Century* (New York, NY: Holmes and Meier, 1984), pp. 320–44 (p. 334).

Endogenous and Exogenous Causes

Perhaps a quarter of infants died from 'endogenous' causes, such as complications during delivery and congenital illnesses. Most, however, succumbed to 'exogenous' causes, from the surrounding environment, leading to such diseases as pneumonia, bronchitis and above all gastroentric diseases.[7] Every summer, outbreaks of diarrhoea carried off vast numbers of infants in towns and cities across Europe. As Richard Meckel notes, the so-called cholera infantum was an awful sight for parents:

> With the onset of the disease, an infant would develop diarrhoea that persisted for eight to twelve days. Then it would begin vomiting and, though wracked with thirst, would be unable to retain any liquid. Almost overnight, the infant's body would become emaciated, its belly distended, and its eyes deeply sunk within their sockets. Its skin would lose its resilience and turn ashen and cold. Continuing to vomit and purge, the infant would cry without cessation until it went into convulsions, sank into a coma, and soon after died.[8]

Hot weather evidently brought out the worst in the urban environment, bearing down heavily on the weakest age groups in the population, and exposing towns with a poor record on public health measures. Contemporaries were inclined to blame mothers who went out to work when seeking explanations for high infant mortality, assuming that they could not breastfeed their babies or supervise them properly. Historians have proved less quick to condemn. They find the statistical evidence for such a case equivocal, and counter that poor families were often in desperate need of the income from wives and mothers.[9] The poor also had to face life in the darkest and dankest neighbourhoods, the most overcrowded housing and the worst sanitary arrangements. For as long as local authorities expected slum-dwellers to rely on wells rather than piped water, and midden privies rather than water closets, as was generally the case until mid-century at least, problems with 'filth diseases' would persist. Not surprisingly, then, the sparse data available, from France and Belgium, suggest that

---

[7] Michel Poulain and Dominique Tabutin, 'La Mortalité aux jeunes âges en Europe et en Amérique du Nord du XIXe à nos jours', in Paul-Marie Boulanger, Dominique Tabutin and Eduardo E. Arriaga (eds.), *La Mortalité des enfants dans l'histoire* (Liège: Ordina, 1980), pp. 119–57 (p. 129); Richard Meckel, 'Health and Science', in Colin Heywood (ed.) *A Cultural History of Childhood and Family in the Age of Empire* (Oxford: Berg, 2010), pp. 167–87 (p. 170).

[8] Meckel, 'Health and Science', p. 169.

[9] Carol Dyhouse, 'Working-Class Mothers and Infant Mortality in England, 1895–1914', *Journal of Social History*, 12 (1978), 248–67.

while endogenous infant mortality declined slowly during the nineteenth century, exogenous mortality remained high until the very end.[10]

Mortality, Morbidity and Short Stature during Childhood

Children in town and countryside who survived their infancy still risked a premature death. During the first half of the nineteenth century, they were as likely to die during the years 1–5 as during their first twelve months, according to evidence from the few countries where statistics are available. The result was that around a third of infants died before their fifth birthday. What they faced was a number of infectious childhood diseases, such as whooping cough, measles and diphtheria. Most deadly of all was scarlet fever, which increased in virulence during the nineteenth century to wreak havoc in towns and cities across the continent.[11] At least child mortality rates, as opposed to those during the first year if life, began to decline from around the 1860s.[12] More insidiously, slum-dwellers in towns who managed to grow up often continued to bear the mark of the harsh conditions they had faced early in life. A combination of a poor diet and struggles with disease during the first two or three years of life caused many to become puny children and to go through life well below the average height of their generational cohort.[13] The contrast between the heights of rich and poor children was all too obvious. In London, the impoverished boys supported by the Marine Society were very short indeed, with those born during the period 1753–80 averaging a height of 130.6 centimetres (51.4 inches) at the age of thirteen. Their results may be compared to those for the upper-class boys attending the Royal Military Academy at Sandhurst, revealing that nearly all of the Sandhurst boys were taller than almost all of the London boys. In Paris, the predominantly upper- and middle-class boys attending the elite Ecole Polytechnique were 'decidedly taller' than their fellow countrymen, by four centimetres compared to military conscripts in 1819–26. To quote Floud, Wachter and Gregory, 'It is only mildly flippant to assert that, in the early nineteenth century, the upper classes of France

[10] Poulain and Tabutin, 'La Mortalité', pp. 129–33.
[11] Meckel, 'Health and Science', pp. 170–5.
[12] Poulain and Tabutin, 'La Mortalité', pp. 125–9.
[13] John Komlos, 'Height and Social Status in Eighteenth-Century Germany, *Journal of Interdisciplinary History*, 20 (1990), 607–21; Roderick Floud, Kenneth Wachter and Annabel Gregory, *Height, Health and History: Nutritional Status in the United Kingdom, 1750–1980* (Cambridge: Cambridge University Press, 1990); Pamela Sharpe, 'Explaining the Short Stature of the Poor: Chronic Childhood Disease and Growth in Nineteenth-Century England', *Economic History Review*, 65 (2012), 1475–94.

and Britain could literally look down on the lower classes'. The same could be said of the Dutch, a sample of military conscripts from around 1860 in the town of Utrecht revealing that the offspring of elite families were nearly ten centimetres taller than those of unskilled workers.[14]

Newborn Child Murder and Child Abandonment

Infanticide

Being murdered or abandoned were two hazards faced by infants in towns as well as in the countryside.[15] Infanticide continued in towns during the nineteenth century, in a shadowy world that occasionally surfaced in the courts or in sensationalist newspaper accounts. In Paris, an average of forty-four women were prosecuted each year between 1866 and 1885. Typically the accused were very similar to their peasant counterparts: in the words of Rachel Fuchs, 'single domestic servants, in their early twenties, abandoned by their lovers, and afraid to dishonor themselves and their hardworking families'.[16] In London, there was an infanticide scare during the 1860s, with lurid accounts of 'infants found stuffed down privies, tossed into ornamental ponds of Regent's Park, or simply left in gutters'. As Josephine McDonagh puts it, material from journalists and professional men meant that 'the modern metropolis was haunted by child murder'.[17] The widely-reported trials of women involved in 'baby-farming', the term invented during this period for taking an unwanted (and often illegitimate) infant off its parents' hands, suggested a mercenary motive might often lie behind the murders. The prosecution in such trials alleged that the baby farmers were willing to dispose of infants they were supposed to be nursing in return for a lump sum. The defence countered that the unfortunate women struggled to keep their charges alive despite their best efforts. In the event, the

---

[14] Floud et al., *Height, Health*, pp. 3, 163–75, 196–200; Roderick Floud, 'Height, Health, and Mortality in Continental Europe, 1700–2100', in Roderick Floud et al. *The Changing Body: Health, Nutrition, and Human Development in the Western World since 1700* (Cambridge: Cambridge University Press, 2011), pp. 226–95 (pp. 229–31); John Komlos, 'The Nutritional Status of French Students', *Journal of Interdisciplinary History*, 24 (1994), 493–508 (495); Hans de Beer, 'Observations on the History of Dutch Physical Stature from the late-Middle Ages to the Present', *Economics and Human Biology*, 2 (2004), 45–55 (52).
[15] See above, 'Mortality, Morbidity and Short Stature during Childhood'.
[16] Rachel Fuchs, *Poor and Pregnant in Paris: Strategies for Survival in the Nineteenth Century* (New Brunswick, NJ: Rutgers University Press, 1992, pp. 201 and 205.
[17] Josephine McDonagh, *Child Murder and British Culture, 1720–1900* (Cambridge: Cambridge University Press, 2003), p. 124.

prosecution view generally prevailed, bringing popular support for doctors in England campaigning for the regulation of child care. A significant outcome, not least for the medical profession, was the Infant Protection Act of 1872.[18]

Towards the end of the nineteenth century, infanticide began to fade from view in public discourse across the continent. A general rise in real wages, the spread of contraception, and campaigns to promote infant welfare transformed the circumstances of young mothers and reduced the incidence of newborn child murder. Judges and juries began to treat offenders more sympathetically, considering them to be in need of help rather than punishment.[19] The English case revealed non-custodial sentences to be the norm for the mothers concerned from the 1920s onwards, as the law came to distinguish infanticide from murder. Nonetheless, there remained some unease among the population at large, as to whether these women were 'mad or bad'.[20]

Child Abandonment

While it seems that most infanticides escaped the attention of the police and the courts, and so have left few traces in the archives, abandonments of infants were meticulously recorded by the administrators of foundling homes across Europe. What stands out immediately is the sheer scale of abandonment in a number of cities. This was particularly in evidence during the nineteenth century, when the total in Europe is thought to have run to around 10 millions. In Milan alone, an outstanding centre for the practice, administrative records reveal that over a quarter of a million children were abandoned between 1659 and 1869. In such cities as Milan, Florence, Madrid, Paris and Vienna, rates of abandonment ran from the equivalent of one-fifth to over one-third of all births.[21] The

---

[18] Margaret L. Arnot, 'Infant Death, Child Care and the State: The Baby-Farming Scandal and the First Infant Life Protection Legislation of 1872', *Continuity and Change*, 9 (1994), 271–311; Ruth Ellen Homrighaus, 'Wolves in Women's Clothing: Baby-Farming and the *British Medical Journal*, 1860–1872', *Journal of Family History*, 26 (2001), 350–72.

[19] Daniel J. R. Grey, 'Parenting, Infanticide and the State in England and Wales, 1870–1950', in Hester Barron and Claudia Siebrecht, *Parenting and the State in Britain and Europe, c. 1870–1950* (Basingstoke: Palgrave Macmillan, 2017), pp. 73–92.

[20] Tony Ward, 'Legislating for Human Nature: Legal Responses to Infanticide, 1860–1938', and Julie Wheelwright, '"Nothing in Between": Modern Cases of Infanticide', in Mark Jackson (ed.), *Infanticide: Historical Perspectives on Child Murder, 1550–2000* (Farnham: Ashgate, 2002), pp. 249–69 and 270–85 respectively.

[21] Volker Hunecke, 'Intensità e fluttuazioni degli abbandoni dal XV al XIX secolo', in *Enfance abandonnée et société en Europe, XIVe-XXe siècle* (Rome: Ecole française de Rome, 1991), pp. 27–72; idem, 'The Abandonment of Legitimate Children in Nineteenth-

assumption among many contemporaries was that abandoned babies would (or should) all be illegitimate. However, in most cities a significant proportion was legitimate, sometimes with the approval of officials: a half or more of them in Madrid and Milan. In this case, hard-pressed parents were in effect trying to use the foundling home as a support service, hoping to retrieve their children once they had passed through infancy. Also, as a rule by the nineteenth century in Europe, in contrast to customs in other periods and places, among the illegitimate at least boys were as likely to be abandoned as girls.[22]

Foundling Homes

Much of the new research is concerned to show how the systems for dealing with abandoned children worked. Two salient points emerge for our purposes. Firstly, by the late eighteenth century there is a useful distinction to be made between the approach to abandoned children in the Protestant north and north-west of Europe on the one hand, and the Catholic south on the other. In northern countries such as Britain, Germany and the Netherlands, as well as those in Scandinavia, parents were expected to take responsibility for their children, even in difficult circumstances. In the case of illegitimate children, fathers were often harried to marry the mother or to contribute to the maintenance of the child.[23] There were experiments with specialised institutional care, in London with the Foundling Hospital, and in Moscow and St Petersburg with two huge foundling homes, but they never took hold on a broad front.[24] The debate in eighteenth-century Germany on whether to establish foundling homes was decisively won by opponents of these alleged

---

Century Milan and the European Context', in John Henderson and Richard Wall (eds.), *Poor Women and Children in the European Past* (London: Routledge, 1994), pp. 117–35 (p. 117); Louise A. Tilly et al., 'Child Abandonment in European History: A Symposium', *Journal of Family History*, 17 (1992), 1–23 (15); Anna-Maria Tapaninen, 'Motherhood through the Wheel: The Care of Foundlings in Late Nineteenth-Century Naples', in Perry Willson (ed.), *Gender, Family and Sexuality: The Private Sphere in Italy, 1860–1945* (Basingstoke: Palgrave Macmillan, 2004), pp. 51–70.

[22] Hunecke, 'Intensità e fluttuazioni', pp. 45–49.

[23] Patricia Crawford, *Parents of Poor Children in England, 1580–1800* (Oxford: Oxford University Press, 2010), ch. 2.

[24] Alysa Levene, *Childcare, Health and Mortality at the London Foundling Hospital, 1741–1800* (Manchester: Manchester University Press, 2007); eadem, *The Childhood of the Poor: Welfare in Eighteenth-Century London* (Basingstoke: Palgrave Macmillan, 2012), pp. 34–5; David L. Ransel, *Mothers of Misery: Child Abandonment in Russia* (Princeton, NJ: Princeton University Press, 1988).

'death camps for infants and morals'.[25] In the 'Latin' south, by contrast, notably in Italy, Spain, Portugal and parts of France and Belgium, mothers were encouraged or even forced to place illegitimate children in a foundling home. The system of 'wheels' or turning cradles on the outside walls of foundling homes, widely adopted in the wake of the Napoleonic invasions, allowed mothers to deposit such babies anonymously, hence preserving the honour of their families. Any attempt to establish paternity was prohibited by the Napoleonic Code, to protect the honour of the families involved, removing pressure on fathers to support their children. The merits of the system of wheels were widely debated, with critics arguing that it encouraged irresponsible behaviour by parents. In the event, the wheels were gradually closed from the mid-nineteenth century onwards as the sheer number of foundlings swamped the homes, and abandonment was made more difficult.[26] From the late nineteenth century, the various states moved to a policy of helping mothers look after their children instead of separating them.[27]

This leads to the second point: the persistent struggle of foundling home administrators to feed their charges and keep them alive. There was the unfortunate paradox of an institution designed to save newborns from infanticide becoming 'slaughter houses' for those it took in. As a contemporary in Madrid put it during the 1790s, 'They die of hunger one after another like waves on the ocean. They die of neglect, treated like a corpse while still alive'.[28] During the eighteenth century, mortality among the foundlings was often catastrophic. Most devastating was a smallpox epidemic in the Moscow home that wiped out almost the entire intake of infants for 1767. In Florence, at the Spedale degli Innocenti, the infant mortality rate (in this case, meaning deaths in the first year per thousand live infants deposited at the home) was 700–800 during the 1770s. In Rouen, at the end of the century, the rate was a grim 946; in Paris, 841; in Reims, a rather less disastrous 460.[29] The nineteenth

---

[25] Otto Ulbricht, 'The Debate about Foundling Hospitals in Enlightenment Germany: Infanticide, Illegitimacy, and Infant Mortality Rates', *Central European History*, 18 (1985), 211–56 (214).

[26] Ransel, *Mothers of Misery*, ch. 4; Hunecke, 'Abandonment of Legitimate Children', pp. 118–24; Jean-Pierre Bardet and Olivier Faron, 'Des enfants sans enfance: sur les abandonnés de l'époque moderne', in Egle Becchi and Dominique Julia (eds.), *Histoire de l'enfance en Occident*, (2 vols., Paris: Seuil, 1996), vol. 2, pp. 112–46 (pp. 115–17); Tapaninen, 'Motherhood through the Wheel'.

[27] See below, 'The Wet-Nursing Business'.

[28] Joan Sherwood, *Poverty in Eighteenth-Century Spain: The Women and Children of the Inclusa* (Toronto: University of Toronto Press, 1988), p. 125.

[29] Ransel, *Mothers of Misery*, p. 45; Pier Paolo Viazzo, Maria Bortolotto and Andrea Zanotto, 'Five Centuries of Foundling History in Florence: Changing Patterns of Abandonment, Care and Mortality', in Catherine Panter-Brick and Malcolm T. Smith

century brought some improvement in the rates, notably in Paris, but in Spain and Russia there was little sign of a decline until the turn of the twentieth century.[30]

The Life and Probable Death of a Foundling

Of all the paths taken by children in modern Europe, that of the abandoned child was by far the most hazardous – particularly if they were illegitimate.[31] The odds were against them from the very start, as they were generally born in poor health, the offspring of unmarried servants and others who were malnourished and saddled with heavy manual labour. The system of foundling homes had by the late eighteenth century largely eliminated the earlier custom of exposing babies in the streets, in a church or a doorway, making it possible for the midwife or the mother to take the infant directly into care. This worked satisfactorily when the baby was deposited locally, but in some cases it required a long and potentially lethal journey from the countryside to the home. During the 1770s, for example, the Hôpital des Enfants Trouvés in Paris drew in foundlings from a number of surrounding regions, some as far away as Brittany and Alsace.

Arrival at the home brought new dangers for the baby. The foundling homes were hotbeds of infection, and often obliged to fall back on artificial feeding methods. The Annunziata in Naples, for example, had no links to a maternity hospital and so struggled to find wet nurses, with disastrous consequences: four-fifths of its foundlings failed to survive their first year during the early nineteenth century.[32] Most homes made efforts to send the infants out to wet nurses in the countryside as quickly

---

(eds.), *Abandoned Children* (Cambridge: Cambridge University Press, 2000), pp. 70–91 (p. 84); Jean-Pierre Bardet, Corinne Dufour and Jacques Renard, 'The Death of Foundlings: A Tragedy in Two Acts', in Alain Bideau, Bertrand Desjardins and Hector Perez Brignoli (eds.), *Infant and Child Mortality in the Past* (Oxford: Clarendon Press, 1997), pp. 245–61 (p. 247, table 14.3); Antoinette Chamoux, 'L'Enfance abandonnée à Reims à la fin du XVIIIe siècle', *Annales de démographie historique* (1973), 263–85 (277).

[30] Rachel G. Fuchs, *Abandoned Children: Foundlings and Child Welfare in Nineteenth-Century France* (Albany, NY: State University of New York Press, 1984), p. 193; Pedro Trinidad Fernández, 'La infancia delincuente y abandonada', in José María Borrás Llop (ed.), *Historia de la infancia en la España contemporánea, 1834–1936* (Madrid: Ministerio de Trabajo y Asuntos Sociales, 1996), pp. 461–552 (pp. 506–7); Ransel, *Mothers of Misery*, p. 264, figure 12.3.

[31] For a focus on the route taken by foundlings, see Bardet and Faron, 'Enfants sans enfance', 131–35.

[32] David I. Kertzer, *Sacrificed for Honor: Italian Infant Abandonment and the Politics of Reproductive Control* (Boston, MA: Beacon Press, 1993), p. 91.

as possible. This required another journey, though one speeded up by transport improvements during the nineteenth century. Life for the infant settled down for a while once he or she was established in the home of the wet nurse. Mortality still remained exceptionally high, though, because the foundling homes had to compete for the services of the wet nurses with private clients, who always outbid them. The foundlings were therefore relegated to nurses from the most impoverished backgrounds, and those most distant from the city.

The Wet-Nursing Business

The eighteenth and nineteenth centuries witnessed a final flourish of wet-nursing in Europe, but also a growing revulsion at the custom among the educated elite. Campaigns to promote maternal breastfeeding were much in evidence during this period – though wet nurses did not finally disappear from Europe until well into the twentieth century.[33] In England, the physician William Cadogan published an *Essay Upon Nursing* in 1748, proclaiming that he was 'quite at a loss to account for the general practice of sending infants out of doors, to be suckled, or dry-nursed by another woman, who has not so much understanding, nor can have so much affection for it, as the parents'.[34] Best known now is the criticism in Jean-Jacques Rousseau's *Emile* (1762) of mothers who, 'despising their first duty, have no longer wanted to feed their children', handing them over to 'mercenary women'.[35]

There were signs that such sentiments had some influence, at the very least in encouraging parents who could afford it to insist that the wet nurse lived with the family and so could be closely supervised. In the Protestant countries of northern Europe, including Britain, Germany, Holland and Norway, wet-nursing went into decline during the nineteenth century. By contrast, in Catholic countries such as Italy, Spain and France, the extensive networks of wet nurses required by their foundling hospitals were still largely intact during the early twentieth century. Particularly in the case of France, the demand for private as well as charitable wet-nursing remained buoyant during the nineteenth century, involving large numbers of families from the 'popular classes', as well as those from among the aristocracy and the very wealthy.[36]

---

[33] Valerie Fildes, *Wet Nursing: A History from Antiquity to the Present* (Oxford: Basil Blackwell, 1988).

[34] As cited in Fildes, *Wet Nursing*, p. 114.   [35] Rousseau, *Emile*, pp. 44–6.

[36] George D. Sussman, *Selling Mother's Milk: The Wet-Nursing Business in France* (Urbana, IL: University of Illinois, 1982), ch. 2.

Numbers are hard to find before the 1890s, but an estimated 20 per cent of the babies born in Marseille went out to nurse in the countryside, 50 per cent in Paris, and 75 per cent in the Croix-Rousse area of Lyon.[37]

There was no shortage of horror stories about wet nurses skimping on feeds, substituting their own children when a nursling died, and leaving their charges stewing in their own excrement for hours while they worked in the fields. Why then did so many families persist with the practice? Wet-nursing was the safest alternative to artificial feeding methods for those physically unable to breastfeed until the Pasteurian revolution of the nineteenth century. There was also a widespread belief that peasant women were stronger than those in the cities. George Sussman suggests that looming large in the French case was the gradual pace of industrialisation, which hindered a rise in the standard of living and preserved large numbers of small businesses depending on a working wife. Weavers in the silk industry of Lyon, workers in the garment trade in Paris, and small shopkeepers everywhere would be obvious examples.[38] It was for these working women, as he puts it, 'probably a necessity, but not a very attractive one'.[39] Volker Hunecke argues along similar lines for the numerous mothers employed in the textile and clothing industries of Milan, unable to take time off for breast feeding even when working from home.[40]

Family Life among the 'Lower Ranks'

The 'lower ranks' in towns were those who, with little or no property to their name, depended on any skills they might possess, and principally on their manual labour, to support themselves. They formed the greater part of the urban population, in varying degrees. The increasing proletarianisation of labour associated with industrialisation, the numbers of unskilled workers swarming in from the countryside, and the recurrent crises that characterised the capitalist economy, made it difficult for many of them to make ends meet. The big cities in particular sucked in huge numbers of immigrants, seemingly oblivious to the flooding of the labour markets. In 1847, a little under half of the population of Berlin fell below an estimated poverty line of 180 thalers per year.[41] By the 1830s and 1840s, the 'social question' featured prominently in discussions

---

[37] Sussman, *Wet-Nursing Business*, ch. 5.   [38] Sussman, *Wet-Nursing Business*, pp. 8–11.
[39] George D. Sussman, 'Parisian Infants and Norman Wet Nurses in the Early Nineteenth Century: A Statistical Study', *Journal of Interdisciplinary History*, 7 (1977), 637–53 (652).
[40] Hunecke, 'Abandonment of Legitimate Children', pp. 126–8.
[41] Nicholas Bullock and James Read, *The Movement for Housing Reform in Germany and France 1840–1914* (Cambridge: Cambridge University Press, 1985), p. 23.

among the elites across Europe, with the breakdown of the working-class family a central issue for those on the left as well as the right of the political spectrum. Workers were accused of living in dissolute '*concubinage*' (common law unions) instead of stable marriage relationships and having children when they were too young to be able to afford them. There was the dismal image of fathers neglecting their families for time in the bars with their workmates, and of mothers in the slums preoccupied with their work outside the home, and incapable of the basics such as cooking and looking after a sick child.[42]

There was a grain of truth in all this, for there is no doubting the difficulties faced by workers trying to maintain a family life in the new manufacturing towns of the early nineteenth century. Yet social historians have generally sided with the 'lower ranks' rather than their illustrious critics such as Lord Shaftesbury or Dr Louis Villermé. They have rejected the older view that industrialisation destroyed a 'traditional' extended family, emphasising instead the capacity of the family to adapt to different situations.[43] Workers in towns generally lived in nuclear families, but like their rural counterparts, they responded to the difficulties they faced by relying heavily on kin and neighbours for support. In textile-producing regions such as Lancashire and the Nord Department in France, where women often continued to work in the mills after marriage, many couples lived near (rather than with) their parents; relatives and lodgers helped with child minding; and siblings, nieces, nephews and grandchildren sometimes lived with the nuclear family.[44]

Historians note the impossibly high standards of domesticity that middle-class critics expected of impoverished families crammed into one-room apartments without running water or enough beds to avoid sharing. They dispute the implied promiscuity associated with common law unions among workers, noting that such arrangements were often a prelude to marriage, or at least a stable relationship somewhere between casual cohabitation and regular marriage.[45] They also note the stern measures taken by working-class communities when cases of the sexual

---

[42] Katherine A. Lynch, *Family, Class, and Ideology in Early Industrial France: Social Policy and the Working-Class Family* (Madison, WI: University of Wisconsin Press, 1988); and Wally Seccombe, *Weathering the Storm: Working-Class Families from the Industrial Revolution to the Fertility Decline* (New York, NY: Verso, 1993).

[43] Martine Segalen, 'The Family in the Industrial Revolution', in André Burguière et al., *A History of the Family*, vol. 2, 'The Impact of Modernity' (Cambridge: Polity Press, 1996), pp. 377–415 (p. 378).

[44] The pioneering work here is Michael Anderson, *Family Structure in Nineteenth-Century Lancashire* (Cambridge: Cambridge University Press, 1971).

[45] See, for example, John R. Gillis, *For Better, For Worse: British Marriages, 1600 to the Present* (Oxford: Oxford University Press, 1985), ch. 7 (p. 206).

abuse of children came to light, including incest, with the men concerned being ostracised and possibly beaten up or reported to the police. Angry mothers often tracked down and brought to justice men they suspected of molesting their daughters; one such in London reported in 1870 that:

I went to ... [his] house, saw him and asked him how dare he take such a liberty with my child and he said 'You cow, I'll serve you the same' and I struck him and he hit me back and I hit him several times and I may have scratched his face. After that ... my husband met a policeman and told him.[46]

Above all, historians conclude that parents made every effort to maintain family life despite all the material obstacles they faced. Administrators from the Orphanage of the Prince Imperial in Paris, which subsidised the rearing of orphaned working-class boys by close relatives, were impressed by the deep emotional ties between family members. Visits to monitor these families during the 1850s and 1860s brought to light the sacrifices made to guarantee schooling and medical care for the children, and the willingness to indulge them in their favourite food and games.[47]

From the 1830s, workers pressed for their own vision of domesticity, based on a 'male breadwinner household'. This required a 'family wage' high enough for the husband to support his wife and children without them having to work. A few 'aristocrats' of labour were in a position to realise this ambition during the Industrial Revolution period: affecting perhaps 10–20 per cent of working-class women in late nineteenth-century Vienna.[48] Otherwise, the sheer weight of effort required to look after a young family meant that most working-class mothers gave up work as soon as their children could earn a wage. They then had to scratch around for casual jobs or part-time work in the home, such as taking in laundry or piece-work in the clothing industry, as well as being a wife and mother. In the long run, various influences, from organised labour, the state and employers, made it possible for other sections of the working class to follow, most obviously in Britain.[49]

---

[46] Anne-Marie Sohn, *Du Premier baiser à l'alcove: la sexualité des français au quotidian* (Paris: Aubier, 1996), pp. 57–65; Louise A. Jackson, *Child Sexual Abuse in Victorian England* (London: Routledge, 2000), ch. 2 (p. 33). Jackson suggests that the rare cases involving the sexual abuse of children that came to court must have been 'a very small tip of a very large iceberg' (p. 35).

[47] Lenard Berlanstein, 'Growing Up as Workers in Nineteenth-Century Paris: The Case of the Orphans of the Prince Imperial', *French Historical Studies*, 11 (1980), 551–76.

[48] Ute Frevert, *Women in German History: From Bourgeois Emancipation to Sexual Liberation* (Oxford: Berg, 1989), p. 89.

[49] Colin Creighton, 'The Rise of the Male Breadwinner Family: A Reappraisal', *Comparative Studies in Society and History*, 38 (1996), 310–37; idem, 'The Rise and Decline of the "Male Breadwinner Family" in Britain', *Cambridge Journal of Economics*, 23 (1999), 519–41; Sara Horrell and Jane Humphries, 'Women's Labour Force

Growing Up

Writers of autobiographies among urban workers often lingered in some detail on the difficult circumstances they faced early in life, ranging from ill-health to little or no schooling. They also conveyed a certain pride in coming to terms with such an unpromising start, not dissimilar to the pride of the self-made man among the middle classes.[50] Indeed, as many of those with the confidence to write about themselves were leaders in the labour or feminist movements, beginning with a childhood ravaged by capitalism was a convenient prelude to a life depicted as a struggle against injustice and exploitation.[51] Their reminiscences generally gave some hint of what it was like to be brought up in a home where the family budget was perilously tight. Adelheid Popp, born near Vienna in 1869 and later a prominent socialist, began her *Autobiography of a Working Woman* with observations on a 'gloomy and hard' childhood:

I knew nothing of what delights other children and causes them to shout for joy – dolls, playthings, fairy stories, sweetmeats, and Christmas trees. I only knew the great room in which we worked, slept, ate and quarrelled. I remember no tender words, no kisses, but only the anguish which I endured as I crept into a corner or under the bed when a domestic scene took place, when my father brought home too little money and my mother reproached him.[52]

As among the peasantry, working-class writers frequently noted the overcrowding and insanitary conditions of their accommodation, the sparse furnishings, the poor quality of their clothing, and the persistent feeling of not having enough to eat. Not surprisingly, as a study of childhood in Staffordshire observed, children were usually desperate to escape from their 'comfortless and overcrowded' homes so that they could play with their friends in the street.[53] Working-class children also often had a similarly ambivalent relationship with their parents,

Participation and the Transition to the Male-Breadwinner Family, 1790–1865', *Economic History review*, 48 (1995), 89–117.

[50] David Kelly, *The German Worker: Working-Class Autobiographies from the Age of Industrialization* (Berkeley, CA: University of California Press, 1987), p. 389; Robert J. Wegs, *Growing Up Working Class: Continuity and Change among Viennese Youth, 1890–1938* (University Park, PA: Pennsylvania State University Press, 1989), p. 66.

[51] Mary Jo Maynes, *Taking the Hard Road: Life Course in German and French Workers' Autobiographies in the Era of Industrialization* (Chapel Hill, NC: University of North Carolina Press, 1995), ch. 3.

[52] Adelheid Popp, *The Autobiography of a Working Woman*, transl. F. C. Harvey (London: T. Fisher Unwin, 1912), pp. 15–16.

[53] Pamela A. Sambrook, 'Childhood and Sudden Death in Staffordshire, 1851 and 1860', in Philip Morgan and A. D. M. Phillips (eds.), *Staffordshire Histories: Essays in Honour of Michael Greenslade, Staffordshire Historical Collections*, 19 (1999), 217–52 (238, 251).

particularly those in large families among the very poor.[54] On the one hand, they felt keenly the common reluctance among parents in their milieu to praise or kiss them. Alwin Ger (1857–1922) thought that mothers in her mining community in Saxony had been 'hardened to the point of cruelty' by poverty and their own joyless childhood.[55] On the other hand, many of them grasped, in retrospect at least, that under it all their fathers and mothers loved them. Looking forward to the 1890s, one might cite the hard-bitten assessment from Albert Goodwin in the Potteries of Staffordshire that his parents were 'the most obnoxious people I had ever seen' – though, with hindsight, he appreciated that were trying to prepare him for a world that was 'hard and harsh' to the children of the poor.[56] Mary Jo Maynes argues persuasively that there were emotional costs to be paid for surviving a childhood blighted by poverty, given that it was all too easy for children to blame parents rather than the social system for their predicament (see Figure 6.1).[57]

Historians have become wary of descending into melodrama by excessive resort to stereotypes of brutal, drunken fathers and mothers hardened by poverty and overwork. There is no disputing that working-class fathers tended to be authoritarian figures, insisting on obedience from their offspring, and expecting children to be seen not heard. Moreover, the drinking culture among male workers produced its crop of casualties. Lucy Luck (1848–1922), from Tring (Hertfordshire) stated forthrightly that her father was 'a drunkard and a brute', rather than the skilled bricklayer she had been led to believe. He reduced his family to poverty, and then deserted them.[58] Corporal punishment, or at least the threat of it, was common in working-class homes. However, evidence from British autobiographies indicates that abusive fathers were in a tiny minority.[59] Others earned the respect of their offspring as providers for the family. Jean-Baptiste Dumay, born in the company town of Le Creusot in 1841, revered the father who predeceased him trying to save fellow workers in a coal-mining accident, and acknowledged that his

---

[54] See Chapter 5.   [55] Maynes, *Taking the Hard Road*, p. 79.

[56] Albert Goodwin (b. 1890), 'Autobiography', in John Burnett (ed.), *Destiny Obscure: Autobiographies of Childhood, Education and Family from the 1820s to the 1920s* (London: Routledge, 1994), pp. 293–301 (p. 294).

[57] Maynes, *Taking the Hard Road*, p. 80.

[58] 'Lucy Luck, Straw-Plait Worker', in John Burnett (ed.), *Useful Toil: Autobiographies of Working People from the 1820s to the 1920s* (London: Allen Lane, 1974), pp. 67–77 (p. 68).

[59] Jane Humphries, *Childhood and Child Labour in the British Industrial Revolution* (Cambridge: Cambridge University Press, 2010), p. 135; she gives a figure of 3–5 per cent only.

Figure 6.1 Victorian London: Dudley Street, Seven dials, c. 1870.
Street children play in the road.
Getty Images, 182812178.

stepfather treated him as if he were his own son.[60] As for mothers, for all
the difficulties they faced, they generally inspired feelings of love and
affection among their offspring. Children sooner or later grasped the
sacrifices that were made for them and the fierce determination to
maintain respectability in the family. Ottilie Bader (1847–1925), the
daughter of sugar refinery workers in Frankfurt on the Oder, wrote that:

I only had a few carefree childhood years, and the images that flash before me of
those first seven years are loving and friendly. My mother was a hard-working
woman with a gentle face, and we children never heard a sharp word from her.

Mothers who held their family together when the father died or deserted
it inspired particular devotion. The mother of Adelheid Popp, for

---

[60] Jean-Baptiste Dumay, *Memoirs of a Militant Worker from Le Creusot, 1841–1905*, as cited
in Mark Traugott (ed.), *The French Worker: Autobiographies from the Early Industrial Era*
(Berkeley, CA: University of California Press, 1993), pp. 309–35 (pp. 311–12).

example, had to deploy her 'strength of will' and 'innate good sense' to support her five children when her husband died of cancer.[61] For all the praise for family and community, it is hard to avoid the conclusion that working-class children during the period of early industrialisation were 'taking the hard road'.[62]

Child Welfare during the Industrial Revolution

If, throughout the Industrial Revolution period, children who were orphaned or whose parents could not support them had to rely heavily on kin or neighbours to survive, this was because philanthropy and in particular the state did not provide much of a safety net for them.[63] During the late twentieth century, historians had to revise some of the accepted ideas on poor relief that influenced the generation that preceded them. The grand narrative of the modern period in which professionals employed by the state gradually (and by some inexorable logic) took over from well-meaning but amateurish philanthropists became unsustainable. This was in the context of a challenge to the general consensus in favour of the welfare state from free marketers during the 1980s, and renewed faith in voluntarism, increasingly perceived as innovative and cost effective.[64] There followed a re-evaluation of philanthropic activity in earlier periods, and a realisation that charities and state agencies often worked in tandem rather than in conflict with each other. It also became difficult to sustain the distinction between a backward Catholic south and a progressive Protestant north, given awareness of various initiatives taken by countries such as Italy and France from the Counter Reformation onwards.[65]

---

[61] 'Ottilie Baader, Seamstress', in Kelly, *The German Worker*, pp. 64–74 (pp. 65–6); Popp, *Working Woman*, passim.

[62] Borrowed from Maynes, *Taking the Hard Road*.

[63] Stuart Woolf, *The Poor in Western Europe in the Eighteenth and Nineteenth Centuries* (London: Methuen, 1986); Peter Mandler, 'Poverty and Charity in the Nineteenth-Century Metropolis: An Introduction', in Peter Mandler (ed.), *The Uses of Charity: The Poor on Relief in the Nineteenth-Century Metropolis* (Philadelphia, PA: University of Pennsylvania Press, 1990), pp. 1–37; Levene, *Childhood of the Poor*, ch. 8.

[64] Frank Prochaska, *The Voluntary Impulse: Philanthropy in Modern Britain* (London: Faber, 1988), pp. xiii–xiv, 1–3.

[65] Brian Pullen, 'Catholics and the Poor in Early Modern Europe', *Transactions of the Royal Historical Society*, Fifth Series, 26 (1976), 15–34; Marco H. D. van Leeuwen, 'Logic of Charity: Poor Relief in Preindustrial Europe', *Journal of Interdisciplinary History*, 24 (1994), 589–613; Colin Jones, 'Some Recent Trends in the History of Charity', in Martin Daunton (ed.), *Charity, Self-Interest and Welfare in the English Past* (London: UCL Press, 1996), pp. 51–63.

As far as children were concerned, they were affected by the long tradition in all parts of Europe of trying to distinguish the deserving from the undeserving poor. Among their ranks, orphans, abandoned children, and those labelled the *Pauvres Honteux* or *Verschämte Armen* ('shamefaced poor') whose parents struggled against the odds to support them, were firmly in the deserving camp. Vagrants, beggars and other delinquents were no less surely considered undeserving, and in need of a punitive regime. Alysa Levene notes that in London, by the late eighteenth century, having children in itself made the family more 'deserving'. She suggests that the new ideals of childhood at this period were filtering down to influence the image of the deserving poor in the city, and were being used to attract donors to charities.[66] Despite differences in approach to welfare among Catholic and Protestant countries during the early modern period, there was, as Joanna Innes demonstrates, a 'largely common European repertoire' in the forms of provision. This included workhouses, houses of correction, and, specifically for children, orphanages, cheap or free schools and boarding-out schemes for the very young.[67] The late eighteenth century saw some reaction against the earlier trend to enclose the poor in institutions, with various initiatives that gave relief to impoverished families in their homes.

As industrialisation and urbanisation gained momentum in western Europe during the early nineteenth century, the issue of 'pauperism' took a new turn. The more alarmist commentators depicted civilisation itself threatened by a huge wave of poor. What concerned them was the existence of a growing army of wage-earners with no property to support them in hard times, the rising costs of poor relief, and the threat to public order from hungry, desperate men and women. The response varied across the continent, with attitudes to poor relief in England diverging from those on the Continent, but there was a general reduction in expenditure by the state during this period.[68] Everywhere, though, poor relief was largely organised at the municipal or county level, with numerous public and private institutions operating side-by-side. Impoverished families, children included, had to learn how to exploit and manipulate these very limited resources to survive.

[66] Levene, *Childhood of the Poor*, p. 168.
[67] Joanna Innes, 'State, Church and Voluntarism in European Welfare, 1690–1850', in Hugh Cunningham and Joanna Innes (eds.), *Charity, Philanthropy and Reform: From the 1690s to 1850* (Basingstoke: Palgrave, 1998), pp. 15–65 (p. 23).
[68] Stuart Woolf, 'The Poor and How to Relieve Them: The Restoration Debate on Poverty in Italy and Europe', in John A. Davis and Paul Ginsborg (eds.), *Society and Politics in the Age of the Risorgimento* (Cambridge: Cambridge University Press, 1991), pp. 49–69 (p. 53).

The 'Deserving' Poor Child

In England and Wales, the strains and stresses created during the early nineteenth century by the pressure of numbers, and the 'not ungenerous' support on offer under the Old Poor Law, resulted in the Poor Law Amendment Act of 1834. The new law cut costs dramatically by clamping down on outdoor relief (though local resistance meant that it continued in many areas), and making indoor relief in a workhouse harsh enough to deter all but the most desperate. Parishes were encouraged to form Poor Law Unions and to build new workhouses. The principle of 'less eligibility' was enforced rigorously, to make sure that conditions for paupers were inferior to those of people in work. The workhouse was particularly hard on children, because of the policy of separating parents from children, and males from females. Charles Shaw recalled his first impressions of the workhouse in 1842, after his father was blacklisted for leading a strike. He was taken to a bare, prison-like cellar, where:

We youngsters were roughly disrobed, roughly and coldly washed, and roughly attired in rough clothes, our under garments being all covered up by a rough linen pinafore. Then we parted amid bitter cries, the young ones being taken one way and the parents (separated too) taken as well to different regions.[69]

Besides rough clothing, the children had to endure meagre food rations (think *Oliver Twist*; see Figure 6.2), harsh discipline and the stigma of the workhouse if they attended a local school, made obvious by their distinctive uniform and short or cropped hair. Conditions were even more frugal in Ireland, aggravated by the tendency of English officials to see the Irish poor as primitive and undisciplined, with ruthless cost-cutting imposed on food and clothing.[70] Charles Shaw recounted the awful ritual of a flogging, in front of all of the workhouse children, of a boy who tried to run away:

Thin red stripes were seen across the poor lad's back after the first stroke. They then increased in number and thickness as blow after blow fell on his back. Then there were seen tiny red tricklings following the course of the stripes, and ultimately his back was a red inflamed surface.[71]

---

[69] Charles Shaw, *When I Was a Child, by An Old Potter* (1903), pp. 97–8, as cited in Ginger S. Frost, *Victorian Childhoods* (London: Praeger, 2009), p. 128.

[70] Anna Clark, 'Irish Orphans and the Politics of Domestic Authority', in Lucy Delap, Ben Griffin and Abigail Wills (eds.), *The Politics of Domestic Authority in Britain since 1800* (Basingstoke: Palgrave Macmillan, 2009), pp. 61–83.

[71] Shaw, *When I Was a Child*, p. 112.

Figure 6.2 Oliver Twist asking for a second helping of porridge. The classic image of the workhouse child.
Getty Images, 92846658.

For all that, families sometimes made use of the workhouse for their own purposes, for example, depositing a child in the workhouse to tide them over a crisis. Improvements to the system were made from the 1840s and 1850s, including the construction of district or separate schools for the children in some Poor Law Unions, and more generous resources for workhouse schools in others, making elementary education comparable to that of poor children in general.[72] This may have helped the inmates to reintegrate into society later in life, but for much of the nineteenth century this remained difficult. The strict regimentation and daily grind when restricted to the bare necessities of life left many workhouse children 'permanently wounded', as Jane Humphries puts it. In particular, they struggled to find jobs, as they were apprenticed in overcrowded trades such as shoemaking and tailoring or, in the

---

[72] Francis Duke, 'Pauper Education', in Derek Fraser (ed.), *The New Poor Law in the Nineteenth Century* (London: Macmillan, 1976), pp. 67–86.

case of girls, were ill-adapted to domestic service in the unfamiliar environment of a middle-class home.[73]

Many observers on the Continent had little sympathy for what they saw as the heartlessness of the New Poor Law in England, not to mention the compulsory taxes involved. In France, liberals objected to the Poor Law on the grounds of its alleged expense and threat to individualism, while conservative Catholics emphasised its undermining of patron-client relations and the idea of voluntary charity.[74] There were some institutions similar to the workhouse in Germany, Denmark and Belgium during the nineteenth century. Other institutions inherited from the past, such as hospitals and orphanages, continued to operate everywhere, either run by religious charities, civil associations or combinations of public and private agencies.[75] All the same, there was more emphasis than in England on enhancing outdoor relief. Whether a municipal welfare bureau, or a charity inspired by Catholic or Protestant humanitarianism, this allowed local elites to reinforce their control of the populace, and at the same time enhance their own prospects of salvation beyond the grave.[76] There was even the aim in some cases of bringing a more 'scientific' approach to poor relief. The French philosopher and philanthropist Joseph-Marie de Gérando (1772–1842) was influential in his campaign to reform traditional Catholic charity.[77] He cited as an influence the system in Rome, reorganised during the Napoleonic occupation at the beginning of the century. It comprised *bureaux de charité*, a general census of the poor, frequent visits, detailed notes on the situation and needs of each family, and handouts in kind of bread, meat, linen, clothing, beds and medicines.[78] Innovations from voluntary societies included maternal societies, which provided funds to help poor mothers

[73] This paragraph relies on Humphries, *Childhood and Child Labour*, pp. 197–201, and eadem, 'Care and Cruelty in the Workhouse: Children's Experiences of Residential Poor Relief in Eighteenth- and Nineteenth-Century England', in Nigel Goose and Katrina Honeyman, *Childhood and Child Labour in Industrial England: Diversity and Agency, 1750–1914* (Farnham: Ashgate, 2013), pp. 115–34.
[74] Timothy B. Smith, 'The Ideology of Charity: the Image of the English Poor Law, and Debates over the Right to Assistance in France, 1830–1905', *Historical Journal*, 40 (1997), 997–1032.
[75] Rachel G. Fuchs, 'Charity and Welfare', in David I. Kertzer and Marzio Barbagli, *The History of the European Family* (New Haven, CT: Yale University Press, c. 2001–3), vol. 2, pp. 155–94 (p. 178).
[76] Jacques Donzelot, *The Policing of Families*, transl. Robert Hurley (London: Hutchinson, 1980), ch. 3; Smith, 'Ideology of Charity', 1005.
[77] Woolf, 'The Poor', pp. 57–62.
[78] Joseph-Marie de Gérando, *Les Visiteurs du pauvre* (Paris: J.-M. Place, 1990 [1824]). pp. 396–7; Woolf, 'The Poor', p. 53.

breastfeed their newborns, and crèches, which helped young children and released mothers for work.[79]

The 'Undeserving' Poor Child

The archetypal figure among so-called undeserving poor was an able-bodied man, assumed by most commentators to be able to look after himself by finding a job. Children took their place, on the periphery, when they turned to begging, petty theft or (for girls especially) prostitution. During the early modern period, begging for alms became unacceptable to municipal authorities, the sacred aura around the poor of the medieval period giving way to concerns over public order and the perceived waste of labour. A more repressive approach was much in evidence during the eighteenth and nineteenth centuries, notably with the *dépôts de mendicité* for locking up beggars that spread from France to neighbouring countries. As in the workhouse, conditions were deliberately made harsh to deter offenders.[80] Yet so desperate were the poor in Antwerp that they increasingly treated the *dépôt* (established in 1810) as a shelter rather than a disciplinary institution, despite a re-education programme based on 'intimidation and cruelty'. Children under fifteen formed a small group among the inmates, including those placed in the institution for a short period by their parents to keep the rest of the family together.[81]

Bands of child thieves, familiar in the countryside, were even more prominent in towns. All the same, the notion that there was a criminal 'underworld' exploiting children in the big cities is now thought to be much exaggerated, a product of lurid accounts in newspapers and novels. One is bound to point a finger at Charles Dickens (and Lionel Bart) for the striking image of Fagin, the Artful Dodger and their accomplices plying their trade from their den. Certainly there is evidence that shady characters among the adult population might recruit children for criminal pursuits, or fence stolen goods for them. An underworld of sorts certainly existed in London, lurking in a network of pubs, lodging houses

---

[79] Christine Adams, *Poverty, Charity, and Motherhood: Maternal Societies in Nineteenth-Century France* (Urbana, IL: University of Ilinois Press, 2010); Jean-Noël Luc, *L'Invention du jeune enfant au XIXe siècle: de la salle d'asile à l'école maternelle* (Paris: Belin, 1997).

[80] Catharina Lis and Hugo Soly, '"Total Institutions" and the Survival Strategies of the Labouring Poor in Antwerp, 1770–1860', in Mandler, *Uses of Charity*, pp. 38–67 (pp. 43 and 55).

[81] Lis and Soly, 'Survival Strategies', pp. 55–8.

and pawnshops.[82] However, most children had little or nothing to do with organised crime: their efforts were typically opportunistic, such as groups of boys going around their neighbourhood pilfering food from markets or picking pockets. Although contemporaries worried about a rising threat on the streets from youthful criminals, a close look at the evidence by historians reveals how unthreatening and 'trivial' most of their offences were. Detention records for the reformatories in Paris during the mid-nineteenth century showed that over half of the boys were locked up for vagrancy (being without a home or means of support) and begging, and most of the rest for some form of theft. Girls were far less likely to appear in court, and the general assumption among contemporaries everywhere was to associate boys with theft, girls with prostitution.[83]

The path of a child with a criminal record was a perilous one. Many of the boys had homes and guardians, and some experience of work, but less contact with the schools and apprenticeships than their peers: a third of those in Paris were completely illiterate (twice the rate for the Seine department). Those in London put their slide into criminality down to poverty, usually linked to insecure employment; the temptations in the city of leisure and entertainment; and the example of other children. There were the delights of easy money and joining others in gambling, drinking and mixing with girls, but also the high risk of getting caught, and years spent in a reformatory or transportation.[84]

The law in many countries gave children some protection, by distinguishing between those who committed a crime knowing right from wrong, and those unaware of the difference. In Britain, the common law doctrine of *Doli Incapax* ('incapable of evil') meant that children aged between seven and fourteen were presumed to be incapable of criminal intent, unless the prosecution could prove otherwise. In France, Belgium and Italy, following Napoleon's Penal Code of 1810, children under sixteen deemed to have acted '*sans discernement*' (without judgement), were to be acquitted. This was not a great help, however, as those not

---

[82] Heather Shore, 'Cross Coves, Buzzers and General Sorts of Prigs. Juvenile Crime and the Criminal "Underworld" in the Early Nineteenth Century', *British Journal of Criminology*, 39 (1999), 10–24.

[83] Lenard R. Berlanstein, 'Vagrants, Beggars, and Thieves: Delinquent Boys in Mid-Nineteenth Century Paris', *Journal of Social History*, 12 (1979), 531–52 (534–5).

[84] Berlanstein, 'Vagrants', 536–41; Patricia O'Brien, *The Promise of Punishment: Prisons in Nineteenth-Century France* (Princeton: Princeton University Press, 1982), pp. 112–13; Heather Shore, 'Home, Play and Street Life: Causes of, and Explanations for, Juvenile Crime in the Early Nineteenth Century', in Anthony Fletcher and Stephen Hussey (eds.), *Childhood in Question: Children, Parents and the State* (Manchester: Manchester University Press, 1999), pp. 96–114; eadem, *Artful Dodgers*, ch. 3.

returned to their parents were to be handed over to a house of correction for a period of confinement, left to the discretion of the court. (In the event, such houses did not start to appear until the 1830s.) Given that the only limit was reaching the age of majority, at twenty-one, this could involve a longer period of incarceration than if they had been found guilty.[85]

Interest in child criminals led to considerable efforts by philanthropists and the state to save them from an entire life of crime.[86] At the beginning of the nineteenth century, those children who ended up in prison were treated in the same way as adults, and exposed to theft, violence and corruption by hardened criminals. The first reformers therefore pressed for separate accommodation for minors. This took time to implement, having to await the 1870s and 1880s in Russia. In western Europe, there were experiments with special penitentiaries for boys during the 1830s, notably La Petite Roquette in Paris and Parkhurst on the Isle of Wight. Both of these latter soon failed. La Petite Roquette, constructed along the lines of Jeremy Bentham's Panopticon, began in 1836 with a collective life in the workshops, classrooms and refectories during the day, and isolation in the cells at night. Problems of indiscipline soon led to the adoption of the Philadelphia system, borrowed from the United States, which isolated the child from his peers more-or-less completely, requiring him to sleep, eat, work and study in his tiny cell. Education had been sacrificed to the maintenance of order: the resulting isolation, boredom and poor hygiene proved ruinous for the health of the inmates. La Petite Roquette erupted in a riot following a visit from the Empress Eugénie in 1865, and ceased operating as a prison for juveniles later that year.[87] Parkhurst Juvenile Penitentiary opened in 1838 in philanthropic mode, offering moral, religious and vocational training, followed by transportation to New Zealand as a 'free emigrant'. It followed a similar descent into brutality as La Roquette, eventually turning into a prison for young

---

[85] Margaret May, 'Innocence and Experience: The Evolution of the Concept of Juvenile Delinquency in the Mid-Nineteenth Century', *Victorian Studies*, 17 (1973), 7–29; Heather Shore (with Pamela Cox), 'Introduction: "Inventing" the Juvenile Delinquent in Britain and Europe 1650–1950', in Pamela Cox and Heather Shore (eds.), *Becoming Delinquent: British and European Youth, 1650–1950* (Aldershot: Ashgate, 2002), pp. 1–22 (pp. 7–11).

[86] Jean-Jacques Yvorel, 'L'"Invention" de la délinquence juvénile ou la naissance d'un nouveau problème social', in Ludivine Bantigny and Ivan Jablonka (eds.), *Jeunesse oblige: histoire des jeunes en France, XIXe-XXIe siècle* (Paris: PUF, 2009), pp. 83–94.

[87] Michelle Perrot, 'Les Enfants de la Petite Roquette', *L'Histoire*, 100 (1987), 30–38; Yves Roumajon, *Enfants perdus, enfants punis. Histoire de la jeunesse délinquante en France: huit siècles de controverses* (Paris: Robert Laffont, 1989), pp. 147–74.

convicts over the age of fourteen.[88] Reformers in England also attempted the alternative strategy of sending away delinquents or potential delinquents for a new start in the colonies. During the 1830s the Society for the Suppression of Juvenile Vagrancy co-operated with Poor Law authorities to dispatch children, for the most part adolescent boys, to the Cape Colony (in South Africa), and later to Western Australia and Canada. By the mid-1850s, this approach in its turn had proved far from ideal, as the Society (now known as the Children's Friend Society) was facing a problem that would blight all such schemes in the future: a lack of supervision in the colonies to ensure that the children were protected from abuse.[89] Delinquent girls meanwhile were sent to an assortment of penitentiary houses, refuges, asylums, and (for prostitutes) institutions such as magdalenes or Bons Pasteurs for a heavy dose of religious instruction and training in the skills of domestic service.[90]

Philanthropic initiatives throughout Europe had in fact produced a variety of refuges to care for rebellious children and adolescents of both sexes, attempting to reform them through education and moralisation.[91] Prominent during the 1830s and 1840s were agricultural colonies for delinquent boys and (eventually) girls, resting on the assumption that cultivating the soil was an effective way to cure poverty and crime. The Raue Haus, near Hamburg, was among the first, founded in 1833 by Emmanuel Wichern and his mother. It started with a cottage and some land for fourteen delinquent boys to farm, living as a family with the founders. In France, the young lawyer Auguste Demetz founded the agricultural colony for young offenders at Mettray (near Tours) in 1838, after visiting the Rauhe Haus and other such institutions. Mettray soon became famous throughout Europe and in its turn inspired imitators such as Redhill in Surrey. Mettray was large, with the capacity to take 1,000 boys (a source of difficulty later on), and enough land to employ them on its farms and workshops. It provided some elementary schooling, but generally aimed to produce honest citizens by encouraging practical morality and sociability. For this purpose it divided the boys into 'families'. For as long as the inspirational figure of Demetz was

---

[88] Shore, *Artful Dodgers*, p. 113.

[89] Shurlee Swain and Margot Hillel, *Child, Nation, Race and Empire: Child Rescue Discourse, England, Canada and Australia, 1850–1915* (Manchester: Manchester University Press, 2010), pp. 108–9.

[90] Linda Mahood, *Policing Gender, Class and Family: Britain, 1850–1940* (London: UCL Press, 1998), ch. 3.

[91] Carl Ipsen, *Italy in the Age of Pinocchio: Children and Danger in the Liberal Era* (New York, NY: Palgrave Macmillan, 2006), ch. 4; Shore and Cox, 'Juvenile Delinquent', pp. 11–14.

involved, Mettray was a success. Its disciplinary regime was moderate to begin with, relying on a short spell in the cells instead of corporal punishment, and rewards as well as punishments. Recidivism was in the order of 5–7 per cent. However, during the 1860s it ran into financial difficulties, and again the tension between the desire to educate and to maintain discipline eventually led to a regime marked by violence and bullying. The inmates' schooling dwindled to almost nothing, they were often cold and hungry, and their health suffered. Mettray survived until 1939, but like so many schemes to deal with juvenile delinquency, initial optimism eventually wilted when faced with the realities of daily administration.[92]

Conclusion

Even in the lower depths of towns, there was light as well as shade. Admittedly, as far as children were concerned, the murkier side does tend to stand out during the early phase of urbanisation and industrialisation. As some of the most vulnerable members of the population to the hazards of urban life, they died in droves, in some cases found themselves institutionalised in grim foundling homes, orphanages, workhouses, or reformatories, and faced daily the hard edge of poverty, notably the lack of warmth and good food. At the same time, there were signs of improvement, particularly during the second half of the nineteenth century. Child mortality began to decline, and there were various initiatives to give children in institutions a better chance of making something of their lives. No less importantly, it is worth reemphasising the resourcefulness of working-class families, in difficult circumstances. Many had moved in from villages determined to improve their lot, and the young as well as the old could benefit, in their case with better schooling and job prospects.

---

[92] Roumajon, *Enfants perdus*, pp. 184–287; O'Brien, *Promise of Punishment*, ch.4; Ivan Jablonka, 'Un Discours philanthropique dans la France du XIXe siècle: la réeducation des jeunes délinquantsdans les colonies agricoles pénitentiaires', *Revue d'histoire moderne et contemporaine*, 47 (2000), 131–47.

7   Work versus School during the Industrial Revolution

The 'Industrial Revolution', Child Labour and the Historians

It is tempting to think of a static, artisan economy preceding the Industrial Revolution, or, as Pierre Léon put it, to contrast 'industry', familiar down the ages, with 'industrialisation', a dynamic new phenomenon appearing during the late eighteenth and early nineteenth centuries.[1] However, since the 1970s, historians have generally moved away from the notion that the Industrial Revolution brought a radical break with the past in Europe, emphasising instead continuities with the past as well as discontinuities.[2] Change had been occurring on several fronts during the early modern period, with a huge expansion of manufacturing in the countryside, a flourishing craft economy in towns, and some moves to large 'manufactures'. Certainly the period 1780–1830 brought an impressive series of inventions and innovations, for the most part pioneered by the British. They pointed the way to new forms of production. The spectacular rise of the cotton industry among the early starters in western Europe, and the mobilisation of large numbers of women and children to work in its mills, are well documented. Yet studies of national accounts reveal a gradual pattern of economic growth across Europe, compared to what would come later. Even in Britain, the undisputed leader in the field, a new orthodoxy has now emerged, insisting on a modest rate of growth in the economy before 1830.[3] Moreover, the dualistic nature of the economies is much in evidence throughout the nineteenth

---

[1] Pierre Léon, 'L'Industrialisation en France en tant que facteur de croissance économique du début du XVIIIe siècle à nos jours', in *First International Conference of Economic History* (Stockholm, 1960).
[2] Angus Maddison, *The World Economy: A Millennial Perspective* (Paris: OECD, 2001), p. 49.
[3] Maxine Berg, *The Age of Manufactures, 1700–1820: Industry, Innovation and Work in Britain* (2nd edn., London: Routledge, 1994).

century. The new industrial centres, such as Manchester, Elberfeld and Brno, remained islands of modernity surrounded by large swathes of a traditional economy. On the one hand, there were a few 'modern' industries adopting capital-intensive methods of production and achieving impressive increases in productivity, such as cotton textiles, mining and basic metallurgy. On the other, there was a large 'traditional' sector, comprising agriculture, construction, domestic industry and many handicraft trades, which grew more slowly.[4]

It follows that a full account of child labour in industry needs to look beyond the factories. We have already considered developments in the cottage industries of villages and will mention only in passing the skilled artisan trades, given that their apprentices were normally youths rather than children.[5] This leaves numerous small-scale industries that were still labour-intensive, and reliant on women and children in their workforce. Historians began to pursue this agenda in the late twentieth century, bringing greater breadth as well as depth to their studies. They asked questions on issues such as the extent of child labour in the economy; the jobs children undertook; whether some industries were more exploitative of the young than others; the contribution made by children, including those in their twenties and thirties still living at home, to household budgets; the significance of child labour for industrialisation – and, finally, what young people themselves thought of their work.[6]

There is now an understanding of how important child labour was for some economies during the eighteenth and nineteenth centuries. Certainly, it was largely confined in its most intensive form to a few regions, as might be expected from the uneven pattern of industrialisation across each country. Hugh Cunningham usefully makes the point that the unemployment as well as the employment of children was a feature of the Industrial Revolution in England. During the 1830s, enquiries into the workings of the Poor Law revealed sharp contrasts in opportunities for employment, with plenty available for children in Lancashire, the West Riding, and the straw-plaiting and lace-making areas in counties such as Bedfordshire and Buckinghamshire – but few

---

[4] Joel Mokyr, 'Editor's Introduction: The New Economic History and the Industrial Revolution', in Joel Mokyr (ed.), *The British Industrial Revolution: An Economic Perspective* (Boulder, CO: Westview Press, 1999), pp. 1–127 (p. 12).

[5] For rural industry, see Chapter 3.

[6] For a comprehensive survey of child labour, see Hugh D. Hindman, *The World of Child Labor: An Historical and Regional Survey* (Armonk, NY: M. E. Sharpe, 2009).

in East Anglia, for example.[7] Overall, though, child labour was, to quote Jane Humphries, 'a kind of mastic holding the early industrial economy together'.[8]

Child Labour in the Factories

Work in the Cotton Mills

The textile industries featured prominently in the early stages of industrialisation in a number of European countries, including England, France, the Low Countries, Spain, Italy and Russia.[9] They also assembled substantial concentrations of female and juvenile labour in their factories, competing with, and in some cases complementing, workers in cottage industry and the handicraft trades. The linen, woollen and silk industries all had their mills, but cotton generally led the way as the most innovative and expansive branch.

Women and Children in the Mills

Precise information on the composition of the workforce in the early cotton mills is hard to come by. However, in England, Wales and Scotland, a survey by Patrick Colquhoun of 143 water-powered cotton mills in 1788 found that 'children' accounted for two-thirds of the workers on the machines. In 1818, a more comprehensive official enquiry indicated that 59 per cent of the cotton factory labour force in Britain consisted of children and adolescents under twenty. By 1833–4, their share in the cotton mills of Lancashire and Glasgow was down to a little over a third.[10] Meanwhile in France, Spain and the Low Countries the rapid (and illicit) transfer of technology across the Channel produced a similar pattern. A survey of mills in Alsace in 1822–3 found that

---

[7] Hugh Cunningham. 'The Employment and Unemployment of Children in England c. 1680–1851', *Past & Present*, 126 (1991), 115–50.

[8] Jane Humphries, *Childhood and Child Labour in the British Industrial Revolution* (Cambridge: Cambridge University Press, 2010), p. 8; eadem, 'Childhood and Child Labour in the British Industrial Revolution', *Economic History Review*, 66 (2013), 395–418.

[9] Marjatta Rahikainen, *Centuries of Child Labour: European Experiences from the Seventeenth to the Twentieth Century* (Aldershot: Ashgate, 2004), p. 133, table 4.1.

[10] Douglas A. Galbi, 'Child Labor and the Division of Labor in the Early English Cotton Mills', *Journal of Population Economics*, 10 (1997), 357–75 (358); Herman Freudenberger, Frances J. Mather, and Clark Nardinelli, 'A New Look at the Early Factory Labor Force', *Journal of Economic History*, 44 (1984), 1085–90 (1087, table 2); Carolyn Tuttle, 'A Revival of the Pessimist View: Child Labor and the Industrial Revolution', *Research in Economic History*, 18 (1998), 53–82 (p. 59, table 1).

children under sixteen comprised around a third of the personnel. In Ghent, children under seventeen were particularly numerous in the spinning mills, forming a quarter of the labour force, compared to 16 per cent in weaving and 12 per cent in textile printing. In Spain, where the textile industry was concentrated in Catalonia, the labour Census for the town of Sabadell suggests that in 1858 children made up around 25 per cent of labour in the cotton industry.[11]

Part of the explanation for the policy of recruiting women and children in the mills was the boost new machinery gave to their productivity. It is well known that some of the early textile machinery for carding and spinning cotton during the late eighteenth century was peculiarly suited to the young, perhaps even designed with them in mind. The first version of Hargreaves's spinning jenny (1767), with its horizontal wheel and treadle, was a case in point. According to a contemporary observer in Manchester, it was difficult for grown up people to operate, 'while they say, with a degree of surprize, children, from nine to twelve years of age, manage them with dexterity'. Arkwright's water frame (1769) was also awkward for an adult, insofar as its operation required frequent stooping, but it could be entrusted to the young.[12] A memorandum, written in 1784 by the future entrepreneurs of the large mill at Louviers, in Normandy, claimed that 'A child will do with the aid of a machine the work of twelve excellent male or female spinners.'[13] A later development of Arkwright's machine, the throstle, was generally associated with cheap, female labour. A report on the Douglas mill at Pendleton, near Manchester, mentioned that the youngest children were set to winding rovings and piecing. Once they were 'able dextrously to piece up the ends that break and keep their Bobbins in proper temper' they were competent to spin: 'They may be then about 14 or 16 years old.'[14]

---

[11] Colin Heywood, *Childhood in Nineteenth-Century France: Work, Health and Education among the Classes Populaires* (Cambridge: Cambridge University Press), 1988; René de Herdt, 'Child Labour in Belgium 1800–1914' and Enriqueta Camps, 'The Rise and Decline of Children's Labour Participation Levels during the Early Stages of Industrialization: Catalonia 1850–1925', in Kristoffel Lieten and Elise van Nederveen Meerkerk, *Child Labour's Global Past, 1650–2000* (Bern: Peter Lang, 2011), pp. 175–92 (p. 178, table 9.1) and pp. 241–56 (p. 244), respectively.

[12] Carolyn Tuttle, *Hard at Work in Factories and Mines: The Economics of Child Labor during the British Industrial Revolution* (Boulder, CO: Westview Press, 1999), pp. 113–15.

[13] Serge Chassagne, *Le Coton et ses patrons, France 1770–1840* (Paris: Editions de l'École des Hautes Études en Sciences Sociales, 1991), p. 195.

[14] Per Bolin-Hort, *Work, Family and the State: Child Labour and the Organization of the Production in the British Cotton Industry, 1780–1920* (Lund: Lund University Press, 1989), p. 117; Chris Aspin, *The Water-Spinners* (Helmshore: Helmshore Local History Society, 2003), p. 175.

Work as an Auxiliary

If some children operated machinery in the cotton mills, and thereby made redundant certain groups of adult workers, female as well as male, most continued with their traditional role as assistants to adults. Children undertook simple, repetitive tasks that required little in the way of skill or training. During the 1820s and 1830s, the large majority of children in the British cotton industry were employed in the mule-spinning departments. Most were 'piecers', who joined threads that broke during the spinning and removed cops from the spindles. Numerous variations were possible: in Alsace, for example, during the 1820s girls as well as boys could be piecers, while in Ghent the job was reserved for males. Whether the shift to the self-acting mule from the 1830s and 1840s increased or decreased the amount of piecing required remains a moot point among historians.[15] Other children worked as 'doffers' for throstle spinners or as assistants on the roving machines. By the 1880s, in Lancashire, children were more in evidence helping in the weaving shops, taking on such tasks as re-threading shuttles and cleaning the looms. Alice Foley (b. 1891) recalled starting work in her early teens at Moor Mill in Bolton: 'Here I was sent into the weaving shed "odding" about to get the feel of the place before settling down as a "tenter" to an older woman on four looms.'[16] Calico-printing was a further branch of the industry, particularly important in France, which employed large numbers of young people. Lists of employees in the famous Gros, Davillier and Roman Company's mills in Alsace during the 1820s included numerous *tireurs* and *tireuses* to help prepare the dyestuffs, as well as some youthful printers and engravers in their teens.[17]

Pauper Apprentices in the Mills

Finding workers willing to submit to the rigorous disciplinary regime of the factory system proved difficult for the first generation of cotton manufacturers. With their substantial investments in machinery and buildings, they needed a regular work routine from their employees to maximise their returns. Hence the notoriously long working hours, and such draconian measures as locking out anyone who turned up late in the morning. For artisans, accustomed to taking Mondays off ('Saint Monday') and wandering in and out of their workshops as they pleased,

---

[15] Tuttle, *Hard at Work*, pp. 115–18.
[16] Bolin-Hort, *Work, Family'*, pp. 119–24; Alice Foley, *A Bolton Childhood* (Manchester: Manchester University Extra-Mural Department, 1973), p. 51.
[17] The lists are in the Archives Départementales du Haut-Rhin, 9 M 22–3.

this was insupportable. Children and young women offered a possible solution, as male supervisors might hope to browbeat them more easily than older workers. This is not to ignore the problems to be faced with controlling large numbers of children, bored with their work and likely to tire easily.[18] The response was close attention from overlookers, and, although employers were loath to admit it in public, corporal punishment. John Hannam, for example, who had started work in a mill in 1797 at the age of ten, recalled for the Sadler's Committee in 1832 overlookers 'who beat the children shockingly'.[19] In general, though, corporal punishments on the shop floor were moderate: the aim after all was to keep the children going and maintain productivity.[20]

Recruitment problems in the early mills were often acute because many were located in isolated rural sites giving access to a fast-running stream or river for their water-wheels. One option, if free labour was in short supply, was to turn to the forced labour of pauper apprentices. This harnessed the long tradition in Europe of placing orphans and foundlings with families where they could learn a trade and become independent.[21] The rising cost of poor relief in England during the late eighteenth century meant that it was easy for manufacturers to strike a deal with Poor Law authorities to take batches of paupers as 'apprentices' on long-term contracts in their mill.[22] In France, the Revolutionary Wars precipitated a similar crisis during the 1790s, causing the state to invite bids from employers for *enfants assistés*. The conditions of employment were onerous for these latter children: they could be made to wear uniforms; their contracts lasted until they were twenty-one; their employers could reward and punish them as they saw fit; and they could be arrested if they ran away.[23] Some employers in Europe relied heavily on such labour, particularly for the thirty years or so during the late eighteenth and early nineteenth centuries. John Birch's Backbarrow mill, by the sea in the northwest of England, had 122 boys and 88 girls in its apprentice house in 1797, plus

---

[18] Sidney Pollard, 'Factory Discipline in the Industrial Revolution', *Economic History Review*, 16 (1963), 254–71 (259–60).

[19] Aspin, *Water-Spinners*, p. 52.

[20] Jane Humphries, 'Childhood and Violence in Working-Class England 1800–1870', in Laurence Brockliss and Heather Montgomery (eds.), *Childhood and Violence in the Western Tradition* (Oxford: Oxbow Books, 2010), pp. 135–40; Peter Kirby, *Child Workers and Industrial Health in Britain, 1780–1850* (Woodbridge: Boydell Press, 2013), ch. 4.

[21] See Chapter 6.

[22] Alysa Levene, 'Parish Apprenticeship and the Old Poor Law in London', *Economic History Review*, 63 (2010), 915–41; Mary B. Rose, 'Social Policy and Business: Parish Apprenticeship and the Early Factory System, 1750–1834', *Business History*, 31 (1989), 5–29; Katrina Honeyman, *Child Workers in England, 1780–1820; Parish Apprentices and the Making of the Early Industrial Labour Force* (Aldershot: Ashgate, 2007), ch. 5.

[23] Heywood, *Childhood in Nineteenth-Century France*, pp. 121–2.

about 100 local inhabitants. The children came from distant workhouses in Liverpool, Brighton and London, and were left isolated from the outside world in the self-contained community of the mill.[24]

Working and Living Conditions

Such conditions made the position of the paupers particularly vulnerable to abuse by employers and overlookers. They had no family to defend them, and supervision from the often-distant Poor Law institutions was difficult. In England, the famous *Memoir of Robert Blincoe* by the writer John Brown overshadows the reputation of the system. Blincoe (b. 1790) recalled the promises made to the orphans while they were in Saint Pancras workhouse by the parish officers 'that they would be fed on roast beef and plum-pudding – be allowed to ride their masters' horses, and have silver watches.' They soon realised the cruel deception, perhaps not difficult where a seven-year-old was concerned, as the reality in the mills was of poor food, squalid apprentice houses and fourteen-hour working days. Worst of all, at Litton Mill, in Derbyshire, his 'fierce and brutal' overlookers amused themselves with sadistic games that left him bruised and bleeding. Like many others, Blincoe tried running away, but the odds were stacked against him: he was soon caught, and while his captor received a five-shilling bounty, Blincoe was beaten.[25] Exaggerated or not, this surely gives a taste of the darker side to the mills and the predicament of parish apprentices in England.

An analysis of mills employing pauper apprentices by Katrina Honeyman concludes that 'parish children were, according to assessment at the time, rather more likely to have been bound to a neglectful or erratic master than to have been well supported.' She adds that the more responsible employers, such as the Gregs at the Quarry Bank Mill in Cheshire, and John Whitaker at the Burley-in-Wharfedale mill, were also the most successful. That is to say, their efforts to provide decent food and accommodation, a basic education and vocational training, paid off in the long term. In these circumstances, Honeyman argues, pauper apprentices might have been better off than their 'free' counterparts.[26] Eventually, a number of underlying developments reduced the appeal of

---

[24] Aspin, *Water-Spinners*, pp. 346–9.

[25] John Brown, *A Memoir of Robert Blincoe* (Firle: Caliban Books, 1977).

[26] Honeyman, *Child Workers*, p. 243; eadem, 'Compulsion, Compassion and Consent: Parish Apprenticeship in Early-Nineteenth-Century England', in Nigel Goose and Katrina Honeyman, *Childhood and Child Labour in Industrial England: Diversity and Agency, 1750–1914* (Farnham: Ashgate, 2013), pp. 71–95 (p. 76); Mary B. Rose, *The Gregs of Quarry Bank Mill: The Rise and Decline of a Family Firm, 1750–1914* (Cambridge: Cambridge University Press, 1986), passim.

the pauper apprentices and from around 1830 in Britain their numbers dwindled. Steam power meant that the mills could move to towns, where the labour supply was more abundant. The expense of feeding, lodging and housing the apprentices felt burdensome when employers began to question the value of often puny and troublesome workers. And the Poor Law authorities came under pressure to stop the practice of sending their charges to employers far away from their home towns.

Beyond the Mills: Coal Mines and Potteries

If textiles generally took the lion's share of child labour in Europe – an enquiry into the larger industrial enterprises in France during the period 1839–45 found that its mills and workshops accounted for almost three-quarters of all child workers under sixteen – there were other branches of modern industry that also relied on the young.[27] In the coal mines, for example, steam engines transformed the scale of production, with improved ventilation and drainage. Yet up at the coal face, men still worked with shovel and pick, and the large number of boys supporting them still dragged or pushed the coal back to the lift shaft using muscle-power alone.[28] These 'haulers', the most numerous group, had a particularly gruelling occupation where the coal seams were thin, as in parts of Lancashire and Yorkshire. This made it impossible to use wagons running on rails, forcing employers to rely on small children dragging the coal through in baskets or boxes. Other children opened and closed the trapdoors that formed part of the ventilation systems, to allow the coal tubs to pass through. This was easy work, but the young child had to spend hours alone in a pitch-black chamber. Overall, in 1842 over a quarter of workers in British coal mines were under nineteen years of age. Similar arrangements were to be found in the other countries that industrialised early, such as Belgium and France. The coal mines of Wallonia (Belgium) had as many as 10,000 children aged 10–12 in them in 1846, employed to push or pull coal (Figure 7.1).[29]

Pottery was another expanding industry, dominated by the factory system, which owed little to mechanisation well into the nineteenth century. The outstanding figure here was Josiah Wedgwood (1730–95). He pioneered the system from the 1760s with his Etruria Works, near

---

[27] Heywood, *Childhood in Nineteenth-Century France*, p. 104, table 4.2.

[28] Raphael Samuel, 'Workshop of the World: Steam Power and Hand Technology in Mid-Victorian Britain', *History Workshop*, 3 (1977), 6–72 (9–10, 21).

[29] Peter Kirby, 'History of Child Labor in Coal Mining in Britain', in Hindman, *World of Child Labor*, pp. 552–4; and de Herdt, 'Child Labour in Belgium', p. 177.

Figure 7.1 Child Labour. Children working in a coal mine shaft.
Getty Images, 696614912.

Stoke-on-Trent, by means of an extensive division of labour and the allocation of different processes to their own workshops. During the 1790s, all but 5 of the 278 men, women and children he employed had a specified post to indicate their particular task. Like the cotton mill owners, he was a fierce disciplinarian, insisting on punctuality, a steady pace of work, and meticulous attention to the quality of the products. Manufacturers of china and crockery everywhere employed women of various ages for the delicate task of painting patterns on the ware, and, together with children, for turning potter's wheels. Children were also deployed on numerous fetching and carrying tasks.[30]

Children and the Factory System

Child labour no longer appears a mere abuse by employers in the newly-emerging factory system that could be remedied by state intervention. Rather there is mounting evidence that it was deeply embedded in the early phase of development in Europe – sometimes known as the period of *industrialisation savage* or 'dirty industrialisation'. As we have seen, children played a key role in operating some of the machinery in the textile industries, and above all in acting as assistants to adults in the factories and the mines. They worked the same long hours as adults, and

[30] Neil McKendrick, 'Josiah Wedgwood and Factory Discipline', *Historical Journal*, 4 (1961), 30–55.

often filled the gaps left by the new technology as industry took its first steps on the path to mechanisation. 'It has been said that if the boys decided to go on strike, it would have stopped the whole factory', as a Danish observer put it. If we add the girls, and also the large numbers of adolescents of both sexes, often lost in the usual lumping together of 'women and children', the 'strategic role' of the work of the young in the factories stands out more clearly.[31] No less importantly, children allowed the early factory masters to cross the hurdle of recruiting workers among a population reluctant to enter the harsh new world of the factories. Without the forced labour of the pauper apprentices many of the first cotton mills would not have survived. Others managed with free child and adolescent labour, perhaps until that generation grew up, producing adults accustomed to factory work, and willing to trade its rigours for the higher wages they could earn.[32]

For working-class parents, securing a job for a child in a mill was a big step in securing the long-term viability of the household budget. Even in the early nineteenth century, families in Britain especially depended largely on the wages of the father, the 'male breadwinner'. Yet in the sample of around 600 working-class autobiographies assembled by Humphries, over one-third of the boys revealed that their father was either dead or missing. 'These poor and vulnerable families', she observes, 'were a major source of very young working.' In addition, a pause in the long-term increase in men's real wages in Britain during the period 1790 and the 1830s made life difficult even for families with a father present. Given the difficulty of combining motherhood and wage labour in towns, the pressure was for the wife to remain at home, and for children to replace her in the labour force. Detailed budget reconstructions during the 1830s and 1840s in France reveal a similarly precarious position among the working-classes.[33]

The children themselves must have had a fair idea of what they were in for when they started work: there were too many lame and sickly figures around the mill towns for them to have any illusions. The consensus among historians is that the factories brought an intensification of work

---

[31] Jeppe Toensberg, 'Child Labor in the Danish Textile Industry', in Hindman, *World of Child Labor*, pp. 584–88 (p. 587); Mary Jo Maynes, 'In Search of Arachne's Daughters: European Girls, Economic Development, and the Textile Trade, 1750–1880', in Mary Jo Maynes et al., *Secret Gardens, Satanic Mills: Placing Girls in European History, 1750–1960* (Bloomington, IN: Indiana University Press, 2005), pp. 38–53; Humphries, *Childhood and Child Labour*, p. 367.

[32] See Galbi, 'Early English Cotton Mills'; and Gregory Clark, 'Factory Discipline', *Journal of Economic History*, 54 (1994), 128–63.

[33] Humphries, *Childhood and Child Labour*, pp. 84–7, 96–102, 180–3, 368; Heywood, *Childhood in Nineteenth-Century France*, pp. 108–9.

for the young. Machinery, gas lighting and eventually steam power meant that the early spinning mills could work throughout the year, without the long winter 'dead' season on the farms. They could also make possible a long working day: twelve or even thirteen and a half hours of 'effective work'. This latter meant starting at five o'clock in the morning and continuing through till eight o'clock at night, with one and a half hours off for meal breaks. Overtime was also expected when orders were pressing, or in some mills alternating day and night shifts.[34] The whole system of rules and regulations, overlookers and threats of corporal punishment or exclusion reinforced the monotonous regularity of the machines. Children could try going on strike, though there is no evidence of much success, or in a town they could move around from factory to factory.[35]

Apologists for the factory system liked to argue that the machines took the strain out of manual labour. 'In an establishment for spinning or weaving cotton', according to Andrew Ure, 'all the hard work is performed by the steam engine, which leaves the attendant no hard labour at all'. He singled out children in the factories as a group that only worked intermittently: he thought that piecers employed on fine spinning had six hours of 'non-exertion' during their twelve-hour day. Reformers were more plausible in emphasising the arduous nature of piecing, since it required constant attention for broken threads and several miles of walking per day.[36] Perhaps only in the 'sweated' trades, such as metal working and eventually handloom weaving, were conditions for children more arduous than in the factories.[37] One can certainly find examples of good as well as bad employers in the factory system. There were model establishments where children were at least spared corporal punishment and given some schooling, to set beside the Litton mills of the system. The *tireurs* of the calico-printing works had shorter hours and lighter work than the piecers of the spineries. And some sources reveal a playful dimension to life in the mills. Norbert Truquin (b. 1833) presented his time in a woollen mill near Amiens in a favourable light – partly, it should be said, to heighten

---

[34] Heywood, *Childhood in Nineteenth-Century France*, p. 130.
[35] Marjatta Rahikainen, 'First Generation Factory Children: Child Labour in Textile Manufacturing in Nineteenth-Century Finland', *Scandinavian Economic History Review*, 50 (2002), 71–95 (90).
[36] Andrew Ure, *The Philosophy of Manufactures* (London: Charles Knight, 1835), pp. 301, 309–11; Marjorie Cruickshank, *Children and Industry: Child Health and Welfare in North-West Textile Towns during the Nineteenth Century* (Manchester: Manchester University Press, 1981), p. 49.
[37] See Chapter 3.

the contrast with his grim experiences in a domestic workshop. 'When the foreman was absent, workers would tell stories or recite plays. The jokers in the group would improvise a pulpit and amuse themselves by preaching. The time passed cheerfully.' In the first cotton mills in Finland, sometimes 'children behaved like children, with the youngest girls nursing dolls, and the boys climbing pillars, fighting and playing tricks.'[38]

No less importantly, conditions for child labour in the factories undoubtedly improved over the course of the nineteenth century. The horror stories recounted by reformers during the 1830s and 1840s were often dredged up from the first generation of mills earlier in the century. The claims by reformers that the factories ruined children's health also need to be treated with some scepticism. The long working hours, hot and dusty environment and the accidents involving machinery undoubtedly took their toll. But it is very difficult to disentangle the impact of these shopfloor conditions from that of the surrounding urban environment. It may also be the case that the factories took on many of the 'sickly' children mentioned above, who would have been unable to hold down a job as a skilled artisan or general labourer.[39]

Career Paths

There was some light at the end of the tunnel. The factories and mines had their skilled as well as their semi-skilled workers. As a general rule, skilled workers managed to keep their jobs within the family. Mule spinners in Lancashire, where they hired their own assistants, had two groups of piecers: their sons, on track to take over their own mules in time, and children from other families, who would be dismissed after a couple of years.[40] The former were thus able to work their way up the hierarchy of jobs from an early start as children. Besides piecers becoming mule spinners, tenters became weavers, and 'tear-boys' (*tireurs*) calico-printers. In this way they picked up the skills they needed, by watching the adults, moving from machine to machine, and learning trade secrets from experienced workers. The factory system in effect adapted the traditional apprenticeship system of the artisan trades to its

---

[38] Norbert Truquin, 'Memoirs and Adventures of a Proletarian in Times of Revolution', in Mark Traugott (ed.), *The French Worker: Autobiographies from the Early Industrial Era*, (Berkeley, CA: University of California Press, 1993), pp. 250–308 (p. 275); Rahikainen, 'Factory Children', 90.

[39] See Chapter 6. These points, associated with the 'optimists' in the British standard of living debate, are made in some detail in Kirby, *Industrial Health*, passim.

[40] Bolin-Hort, *Work, Family, and the State*, pp. 51–2.

own needs.[41] H. M. Boot observes that 'Most workers in cotton factories learned to complete tasks which might be described in a few words, but the dexterity needed to complete them quickly for many hours each day required considerable knowledge and experience of the behaviour of machines, and of the raw materials being worked'. He calculates that the skills acquired by a boy assisting the mule spinners in Lancashire during the 1830s would enable him to earn 70 per cent more over the course of his lifetime than a common labourer, and around 20 per cent more than a coal miner.[42] Overlookers, mechanics, calico-printers and modellers in the potteries, among others, could do even better. Girls too acquired skills in the factories, though they had fewer opportunities to exercise them when they matured, and struggled to have their jobs classified and paid as 'skilled'. In the mills, they were trained for the relatively low-wage jobs of carding and weaving, and were less likely than a male to continue working through their adult years.[43] They fared slightly better in Josiah Wedgwood's pottery, with extensive training in their particular specialisation leading to skilled work as an adult.[44]

Child Labour in 'Traditional' Industries

For all the attention paid to child labour in the cotton mills and mines during the Industrial Revolution, it is clear that most young people in Europe continued to work in more traditional settings well into the nineteenth century. It is easy to demonstrate from the 1851 census that in England and Wales, amongst males aged 10 to 14, agriculture was by far the largest employer, accounting for over a third (34.6 per cent) of child workers. Workshops and handicrafts came second, with 17.3 per cent, factories only third, with 15.5 per cent, and mines and quarries a distant fifth, with 8.8 per cent. On the female side, domestic service took the lead with 25.3 per cent, though it was closely followed by factories (24.1 per cent), workshops and handicrafts (23 per cent),

---

[41] Yves Lequin, 'Apprenticeship in Nineteenth-Century France: A Continuing Tradition or Break with the Past?', in *Work in France: Representations, Meaning, Organization, and Practice*, ed. Steven Kaplan and Cynthia J. Koepp (Ithaca, NY: Cornell University Press, 19860), pp. 457–74.

[42] H. M. Boot, 'How Skilled Were Lancashire Cotton Factory Workers in 1833?', *Economic History Review*, 48 (1995), 283–303 (288–90).

[43] Boot, 'How Skilled', 291–5.

[44] Deborah Simonton, 'Bringing Up Girls: Work in Preindustrial Europe', in Maynes et al., *Secret Gardens*, pp. 23–37 (pp. 34–5).

and agriculture (21.6 per cent).[45] This being the case in Britain, fast becoming the 'workshop of the world', one would expect the weight of the past to be even more in evidence among latecomers or those whose industrialisation proceeded more gradually. In the Netherlands, during the 1840s 70 per cent of children under twelve years of age registered as working were in agriculture and domestic service. In France, the census gives no aggregate data until late in the century, in 1896, but its 'unobtrusive' pattern of industrialisation is well known, with its large agricultural sector and preference for small-scale industrial enterprise.[46]

Steam Power and Hand Technologies

Raphael Samuel usefully makes the point that in mid-Victorian England 'there were few parts of the economy which steam power and machinery had left untouched, but fewer still where it ruled unchallenged.' Everywhere in Europe, hand technologies persisted, relying both on skilled workers and 'a plentiful supply of drudges' – with women and children of course featuring prominently among the latter.[47] This was particularly evident in the industries lying somewhere in the middle of the spectrum running from 'modern' to 'traditional' sectors. Those producing silk goods, paper, glass, bricks, tobacco and matches were conspicuous for their large numbers of juvenile workers. In these industries an extensive division of labour made it possible to employ the young on unskilled and relatively easy work.[48]

The silk industry, for example, provided early examples of large 'proto-factories' for its silk-reeling machines, but during the nineteenth century mechanisation remained very uneven across the various branches. As already noted, it was of major importance in northern Italy. Yet, in 1866, most of this area's 4,092 silk mills were still 'rather primitive'.[49] The young female workers in the mills beating and winding silk co-existed

---

[45] Peter Kirby, *Child Labour in Britain, 1750–1870* (Basingstoke: Palgrave Macmillan, 2003), p. 52, table 3.1.

[46] Elise van Nederveen Meerkerk, 'Child Labor in the Netherlands during Proto- and Early Industrialization', in Hindman, *Child Labor*, pp. 625–8 (626–7); Colin Heywood, 'Child Labour and Child Labour Reform in Nineteenth-Century France: An International Perspective', in Lieten and van Nederveen Meerkerk, *Child Labour's Global Past*, pp. 137–58.

[47] Raphael Samuel, 'Workshop of the World: Steam Power and Hand Technology in mid-Victorian Britain', *History Workshop Journal*, 3 (1977), 6–72 (46).

[48] Lars Olsson, 'Industrial Capitalism and Child Labour in Sweden, 1800–1930', in Lieten and van Nederveen Meerkerk, *Child Labour's Global Past*, pp. 303–30.

[49] Gianni Toniolo, *An Economic History of Liberal Italy*, transl. Maria Rees (London: Routledge, 1990), p. 67.

with those in the domestic workshops until late in the nineteenth century.[50] Glass and brick works were notorious for the heavy workloads they imposed on their younger employees. The glass works relied on the skilled labour of the glass blowers, but these men needed a team of younger males to support them. Eugène Saulnier (b. 1891) started at the age of twelve at a works in the Loir-et-Cher Department, opening and shutting moulds for the *souffleur*. He gradually worked his way up the hierarchy of jobs until he became a glass blower himself, under the watchful eye of the head of his team. At the age of thirteen, he remembered, he never had more than five or six hours of sleep, as he alternated between night and day shifts.[51] In the brickworks, there was less skill, but more hard graft. A former child worker recounted how during the early nineteenth century the work was beyond his strength at the age of eight, and aggravated by a vicious foreman later on. He and the other boys had to carry the bricks to him in their hands, two at a time over a distance thirty to fifty yards, but 'if he had to wait a single moment for the bricks, he would strike us with a clapper, nip our hands or bite our shoulders with his teeth.'

The Rise and Fall of Child Labour in Industry

An Upsurge in Child Labour

Measuring child participation rates in the labour force is difficult when relying on official sources, given that the state only took an interest in child labour at a relatively late stage, when protective legislation became an issue. Humphries gives a hint of what might have happened using her study of 600 male working-class autobiographies. She concludes that in Britain 'the classic era of industrialisation, 1790–1850, saw an upsurge in child labour.' It is particularly striking that many more of the boys were employed at a very young age than in the past, with a doubling of the proportion starting under ten during the late eighteenth and early nineteenth century.[52] This surge of child labour can partly be explained by the rapid growth in demand for its services from the textile mills and the coal mines. Yet it should also be clear by now that the farms, the small workshops and the service sector had given it momentum from an early

---

[50] See Chapter 3.
[51] Michel Chabot, *L'Escarbille: histoire d' Eugène Saulnier, ouvrier verrier* (Paris: Presses de la Renaissance, 1978), ch. 2.
[52] Humphries, *Childhood and Child Labour*, pp. 175–77, 366–7; and eadem., 'Childhood', passim.

stage during the 'industrious revolution'. In neighbouring countries, any such increase in the employment of children would have been less vigorous, and perhaps for that reason, more difficult to document.

The Start of a Decline

What is more in evidence is a long-term decline in the employment of children in the industrial sector.[53] The first stirrings in this direction can be traced during the middle of the nineteenth century in various parts of Europe, especially in front-runners such as Britain and France. The most obvious explanation would be that state intervention began to drive child labour out of the workshops. A mixed group of reformers, motivated by humanitarianism in some cases and more mercenary concerns in others, had some success in securing the passage of child labour legislation. Britain led the way, starting with a series of Acts during the early nineteenth century concerned mainly with the textile mills and coal mines. A few countries followed suit during the 1830s and 1840s, including Prussia and France, whilst other industrialising nations, notably Belgium, delayed action in the face of stiff resistance from employers. The laws invariably prohibited the employment of very young children: the Factory Act of 1833 in Britain set a minimum age of nine; the 1841 law in France, eight. Children below these ages were never very numerous on the shop floor, but it set an important precedent. For the most part, though, the laws aimed to restrict rather than abolish child labour in industry. With hindsight, one can see that this was a reasonable approach, given that adult wages were still so low that a complete ban on children's work would undoubtedly have reduced many families to destitution.[54] The laws generally followed a template that included grading the hours a child or adolescent could work according to their age; restricting children from night work and certain dangerous or unhealthy jobs; and stipulating a certain amount of schooling.[55]

Most of the early historians of child labour concentrated on reform campaigns and the child labour laws they fought to introduce, revealing the social and political backgrounds of the forces massing behind reformers and their opponents, and the arguments deployed by each side. However, there is some dispute over how effective these laws were in

---

[53] This paragraph is indebted to Hugh Cunningham, 'The Decline of Child labour: Labour Markets and Family Economies in Europe and North America since 1830,' *Economic History Review*, 53 (2000), 409–28.

[54] Patrick M. Emerson, 'The Economic View of Child Labor', in Hindman, *World of Child Labor*, pp. 3–9 (p. 4).

[55] Outline surveys include Hugh Hindman, 'Coming to Terms with Child Labor', in Hindman, *Child Labor*, pp. 45–8; and Rahikainen, *Centuries of Child Labour*, pp. 150–4.

curbing the practice. The consensus among historians is now that the decline in child labour set in before the passing and enforcement of such legislation, and that many children continued to work after that. Clark Nardinelli was influential in arguing that child labour was decreasing relative to adult labour in the British textile industry before inspectors began to enforce the 1833 Act, the first to have any serious effect.[56] The law merely acted as a 'tax' on the employment of children. Also, the laws that were put in proved difficult to apply, partly because everywhere governments were slow to provide sufficient resources for an inspection service, and partly because cheating by employers and employees alike was rife. Historians therefore now look beyond state intervention to consider the cultural and socio-economic contexts for the laws.

The reform campaigns indicated a growing revulsion against child labour on the grounds that it was simply wrong or contrary to Christian principles. In Britain the moral fervour that had driven reformers to call for the abolition of slavery in the United States and the West Indies carried over into the cause of factory children. In both cases, there was the claim that the issue was one of morality rather than profit and loss or party politics.[57] Supporters of the 1841 law on child labour in France frequently emphasised that it was a law of 'high morality'. As James Schmidt argues, the Romantic idea that the child was an innocent, vulnerable creature might have helped persuade governments to shift from their earlier stance of compelling the young to work to prohibiting them from doing so.[58] There were the workings of the labour market to consider also: movements in the willingness of working-class families to put their offspring to work, and of employers to hire children. There was a hint of these forces excluding children from key industries during the height of the Industrial Revolution period, as Nardinelli revealed. However, his critics have argued that he underestimated the persistence of child labour in Britain: according to the census, in 1851, 36.6 per cent of boys aged 10–14 had an occupation, and in 1871, still 32.1 per cent; the respective figures for girls were 19.9 and 20.5 per cent.[59] It is now clear

[56] Clark Nardinelli, *Child Labor and the Industrial Revolution* (Bloomington, IN: Indiana University Press, 1990), ch. 5–6.

[57] R. M. Hartwell, *The Industrial Revolution and Economic Growth* (London: Methuen, 1971), ch. 17, p. 406; David M. Pomfret, 'World Contexts', in Heywood, *Age of Empire*, pp. 189–211 (p. 193).

[58] James Schmidt, 'Children and the State', in Paula Fass (ed.), *The Routledge History of Childhood in the Western World* (Abingdon: Routledge, 2013), pp. 174–90 (pp. 176–7).

[59] Hugh Cunningham, 'Combating Child Labour: The British Experience', in Hugh Cunningham and Pier Paolo Viazzo (eds.), *Child Labour in Historical Perspective, 1800–1985: Case Studies from Europe, Japan and Colombia* (Florence: UNICEF, 1996), pp. 41–55 (p. 42, table 1).

that there was no substantial decline until the end of the century and influences that he considered important, especially a rise in real wages, had to wait until the 1850s at the earliest.[60]

Conclusion

Child labour reform campaigns generated a good deal of heat as well as light during the nineteenth century, and it remains an emotive issue today. Apologists for children's employment in the mills were barely credible when they dismissed the work as 'gymnastics', episodic or essential for the acquisition of skills. More convincing is careful documentation by inspectors, among others, of long working hours, unhealthy workshop environments, harsh discipline and limited opportunities for education and training. This is not to deny that reformers were equally capable of exaggerating the evils of the factory system, talking in terms of 'torture' or 'slavery'. There was considerable variation in the conditions faced by child workers, according to such influences as the nature of the industry, the location of the mill, and the character of the employer. Above all, there was the underlying reality of what a society in the early stages of industrialisation could afford to do for its labour force. Laying off all child workers and hoping that adult wages would increase enough to compensate, as pondered by Karl Marx, was probably unrealistic for most of the nineteenth century. Hence, legislators could be justified in their strategy of trying to safeguard the health and morality of workers by regulating rather than banning child labour. We may even agree with the economist Kaushik Basu when he asserts that 'there are worse things that can happen to children than having to work'.[61]

Religion and the Working Classes

During the nineteenth century the growing concentration of workers in towns, combined with widespread insecurity among ruling elites in the wake of the French Revolution, gave new impetus to the long-running 'civilising mission' of the churches and schools. As in the countryside, clergy and schoolteachers in towns faced an uphill struggle in the face of various material and cultural obstacles to their efforts.[62] Historians have generally taken it for granted that the clergy in particular struggled to

---

[60] See Chapter 11.

[61] Kaushik Basu, 'Child Labor: Cause, Consequence, and Cure, with Remarks on International Labor Standards,' *Journal of Economic Literature*, 37 (1999), 1083–1119 (1115).

[62] See Chapter 3.

maintain their influence over the working classes in towns. There is plenty of evidence of both Catholic and Protestant churches being unable to provide enough clergy and parish churches to keep up with the rapid expansion of the urban population. It may be that, unlike the peasantry, who were vulnerable to the uncontrollable forces of nature, workers were less likely to believe in the power of the supernatural. And the growing polarisation between capital and labour over the course of the century alienated workers from the established churches, which were generally seen as siding with the rich rather than the poor.

Yet of late some historians have challenged this orthodox view, emphasising the continuing importance of religion in people's lives, and the various initiatives taken in towns to respond to the challenges of industrialisation.[63] Hence the relationship between the churches and the workers now appears complex. One can safely assume that many working-class families were 'not so much hostile to the Church as simply untouched by it', as Ralph Gibson asserts in the case of the Catholic Church in France, given that the population of many urban parishes became impossibly large for their priests to manage. Historians have also established that towns were subject to regional influences on their rates of church attendance. Hence children in northern French towns, such as Roubaix and Tourcoing, were more likely to be brought up as good Catholics than their counterparts in Paris, in part because of the contrasting churchgoing habits in the surrounding rural populations. For the same reason, German Protestants brought up in towns of the south and west were generally more devoted to their churches than those in the north, above all in Berlin.[64]

More specific to the case of children, those from the poorest sections of urban society were discouraged from attending Sunday schools and church services because they could not afford the collection money and the appropriate clothing. Working practices in the new textile mills were also an obstacle, insofar as child workers were expected to help on Sundays with the cleaning and maintenance of machinery. Yet there were a number of factors that kept the young in touch with organised religion, albeit tenuously in many cases. Firstly, there was the 'feminisation' of religious practice widely observed across Europe, with adult males more likely to give up on the churches than females. Therefore it

---

[63] For more detail, see Hugh McLeod, *Religion and the People of Western Europe 1789–1989* (2nd edn., Oxford: Oxford University Press, 1997); and idem. (ed.), *European Religion in the Age of Great Cities 1830–1930* (London: Routledge, 1995).

[64] Ralph Gibson, *A Social History of French Catholicism, 1789–1914* (London: Routledge, 1989), p. 222; McLeod, *Age of Great Cities*, pp. 16–17.

seems likely that working-class children had some chance of being taught the basics of religious belief by their mothers – though the autobiographies have little to say on the matter. Secondly, most of the elementary schools in Europe included a fair dose of religious instruction in their curriculum, ranging from the systematic approach in church-run schools to the casual one in many private institutions. In Lyon, for example, famous for its silk manufacturing, most working-class children attended Catholic primary schools during the mid-nineteenth century. These schools were free, and dedicated to the religious regeneration of the population.[65] Thirdly, most people continued to observe the religious rites of passage throughout the nineteenth century. Children of workers no less than those of peasants usually prepared for their Confirmation or First Communion. However, workers' autobiographies usually went out of their way to deny any religious fervour at this stage in their lives. The authors often lingered on the problems caused by the expense of the special suit or dress required for the church service. The anonymous author of *Im Kampf ums Dasein* recorded her humiliation at being clothed for the occasion by a charity, meaning that 'We looked like outcasts in our shabby dresses, and many tears fell on them'. Georges Dumoulin revealed that his mother made him attend catechism classes during the 1880s in the Pas-de-Calais but added that she only sent him to mass when she anticipated a food voucher from the priest.[66]

Schooling and the Workers

The school systems of the early nineteenth century in their turn experienced serious disruption in regions affected by industrialisation. Like the churches, they struggled to meet the demand for new infrastructure with the rapid growth of population in many towns. They also found it difficult to reach out to the poorest section of urban society. Poor families could ill-afford the expense of schooling, and even less the forfeiting of income from a potential earner. Adelheid Popp described her mother being condemned to a humiliating twelve hours in prison for Adelheid's poor attendance record at school, 'But

---

[65] Laura S. Struminger, *Women and the Making of the Working Class: Lyon, 1830–1870* (St Alban's: Eden Press Women's Publications, 1979), ch. 5; Sarah A. Curtis, *Educating the Faithful: Religion, Schooling, and Society in Nineteenth-Century France* (Dekalb, IL: Northern Illinois University Press, 2000), ch. 4.

[66] Mary Jo Maynes, *Taking the Hard Road: Life Course in German and French Workers' Autobiographies in the Era of Industrialization* (Chapel Hill, NC: University of North Carolina Press, 1995), p. 108; Heywood, *Growing Up in France*, p. 134.

of what use was it to go to school when I had neither clothes nor food?'.[67] A survey of child workers employed in the textile mills of Mulhouse during the 1840s made it clear that parents often skimped on the education of their offspring. At the Charles Naegely mill, two-thirds of the children had spent less than a year in school.[68] Girls in particular often had to accept their education being sacrificed in the interest of their brothers, condemning them to the poorer schools, and to frequent interruptions when they had to help out their mothers at home.[69]

Although the decision to choose work over schooling appalled middle-class observers, it made some sense from a worker's perspective. The burdensome costs of schooling risked outweighing the benefits, given that there were few white-collar jobs available in towns until well into the nineteenth century. What most workers needed, for a bare minimum at least, was some instruction in basic literacy and religion, and then an apprenticeship or work experience to acquire manual skills. Certain occupations whose work needed some theoretical knowledge, such as stonemasons, carpenters and locksmiths, were conspicuous for their efforts to educate their children in the schools. They were rapidly outnumbered in the new manufacturing centres by semi-skilled workers in the domestic workshops and mills. The upshot was sometimes a 'catastrophic' impact of early industrialisation on literacy rates in towns. In Ashton-under-Lyne (Lancashire), for example, 40 per cent of marriage partners signed their name in 1803, but only 10 per cent in 1833. Overall in Britain there was little sign of a sustained rise in literacy rates until the second quarter of the nineteenth century. Similarly, in the Nord department of France, masses of illiterate textile workers and miners held back the spread of literacy in the industrialising areas.[70]

---

[67] Popp, *Autobiography*, pp. 28–9.
[68] Heywood, *Childhood in Nineteenth-Century France*, pp. 205–6.
[69] June Purvis, *Hard Lessons: The Lives and Education of Working-Class Women in Nineteenth-Century England* (Cambridge: Polity Press, 1989), ch. 4.
[70] Anne Digby and Peter Searby, *Children, School and Society in Nineteenth-Century England* (London: Macmillan, 1981), p. 5; W. B. Stephens, 'Illiteracy and Schooling in the Provincial Towns, 1640–1870: A Comparative Approach', in D. Reeder (ed.), *Urban Education in the Nineteenth Century* (London: Taylor and Francis, 1977), pp. 27–47 (p. 31); David Mitch, 'Education and Skill of the British Labour Force', in Roderick Floud and Paul Johnson, eds., *The Cambridge Economic History of Modern Britain* (3 vols., Cambridge: Cambridge University Press, 2004), vol. 1, pp. 332–56 (344–5); François Furet and Jacques Ozouf, *Reading and Writing: Literacy in France from Calvin to Jules Ferry* (Cambridge: Cambridge University Press, 1982), ch. 5.

Towards Mass Schooling

If industrialisation and urbanisation undermined school attendance in the short term, in the long run they were very favourable to it in a way that was by no means evident for organised religion. The concentration of population in towns made it easier to provide access to schools. The larger numbers of pupils available also made it possible to adopt the two main teaching innovations of the early nineteenth century: the Bell and Lancaster method of the monitorial schools, and the 'simultaneous' method favoured by church schools. The former began in 1798, and flourished during the first half of the nineteenth century. It involved a system of 'mutual instruction', whereby a schoolteacher trained some of the older or cleverer pupils to be monitors, and they in turn taught basic literacy to the other pupils. The obvious advantage was the low cost of the method, as one teacher could preside over a school of up to a thousand pupils. Monitorial schools first appeared in England, and soon spread to countries such as France, Denmark and Russia. The drawback to the mutual method for the churches was its cursory treatment of religious instruction – evidently beyond the capacity of a hastily-trained youth. The Protestant, Catholic and Orthodox churches therefore preferred the 'simultaneous' method. Here the teacher addressed the whole class at once, replacing the 'individual' method, in which each pupil took it in turn to spend a few minutes going over their work with the teacher.[71] Otherwise, the central supervision by the teacher could ideally impose a silent working atmosphere, reminiscent of traditional monastic teaching. In practice, teachers struggled to keep large classes silent and well behaved. Xavier Lejeune recalled that during his time at a Catholic school during the 1850s, prayers were recited 'in a manner so discordant, that I understood nothing of it and I stopped up my ears in order not to be deafened by such nonsense'.[72]

Children were also caught up in the nation-building efforts of various governments during the nineteenth century.[73] The Prussians led the way, stung by the humiliating defeat at the hands of the French army in 1806 at Jena. This led to an intense period of reform, including compulsory education at the elementary level in a *Volksschule*. States among the Scandinavian countries also took the initiative in constructing a national educational system, including compulsion in Denmark in 1814 and in

[71] James Bowen, *A History of Western Education* (London: Methuen, 1981), vol. 3, ch. 9.
[72] *Calicot* (1984), as cited by Curtis, *Educating the Faithful*, p. 99.
[73] Andy Green, *Education and State Formation: The Rise of Education Systems in England, France and the USA* (Basingstoke: Macmillan, 1990), ch. 1.

Sweden in 1842. Others at least legislated for a national system, as in Spain, Portugal and Italy, even if they lacked the means to enforce it. Finally, countries such as France, the Netherlands and above all Britain preferred to maintain a balance between the public funding and regulation of education on the one hand, and the expansion of schooling by private enterprise and various religious organisations on the other.[74] In England and Wales, during the middle decades of the nineteenth century, working-class children might attend a dame school, a Sunday school, a workhouse school, a factory school, a Roman Catholic school, or a school run by either the Church of England's National Society or the Nonconformists' British and Foreign Society.[75] Even where elementary education was not compulsory, let alone free, rising numbers attending school indicated that working-class and peasant families were increasingly prepared to make sacrifices for their children in this area. In France, for example, by the 1880s, when the Ferry Laws finally established a state system, the evidence suggests that nearly all children were receiving some schooling.[76]

The urban environment was generally more favourable to schooling than the rural one, with the written word much in evidence, the 'respectability' of the educated elites on hand to emulate, and heightened political awareness among sections of the population. Yet autobiographical evidence suggests that children from the working-class neighbourhoods of towns looked back on their time in class with as much bitterness as their peasant counterparts. Many of the authors claimed to have been good scholars and emphasised the wrench they felt when the need to support the family economy took priority over their education. All the same, there were the familiar complaints from many quarters of poor-quality teaching and a ready resort to corporal punishments as boys in particular grew older. No less than in the workplace, children without a family to protect them were particularly vulnerable to abuse: in England the workhouse schools were notoriously free with their use of the cane. Some of the religious orders also

---

[74] For more detail, see Mary Jo Maynes, *Schooling in Western Europe: A Social History* (Albany, NY: State University of New York, 1985), ch. 3; Yasemin Nuhoglu Soysal and David Strang, 'Construction of the First Mass Education Systems in Nineteenth-Century Europe', *Sociology of Education*, 62 (1989), 277–88; Green, *State Formation;* Bengt Sandin, 'Education', in Heywood, *Age of Empire*, pp. 91–110 (pp. 92–3).

[75] Purvis, *Hard Lessons*, pp. 72–3.

[76] Raymond Grew and Patrick J. Harrigan, *School, State, and Society: The Growth of Elementary Schooling in Nineteenth-Century France – A Quantitative Analysis* (Ann Arbor, MI: University of Michigan Press, 1991), passim.

Figure 7.2 Boy being birched by his school master. Illustration by
George Cruickshank, 1838.
Getty Images, 504135622.

had an unenviable reputation for violence, as in the case of the Christian
Brothers Schools. Teachers and children alike suffered from the campaigns in early industrial society to start educating the masses as
cheaply as possible. Teachers in towns found themselves confronted
with large classes of up to a hundred pupils with few incentives to take
their studies seriously: working-class children had very little chance of
moving on from an elementary to a secondary school, and any boosts to
their career prospects were both uncertain and a long way off. Hence
the heavy reliance on canes, straps, rulers and other instruments to
maintain some sort of order in class. Children for their part were often
bewildered by the punishments meted out to them, for mistakes in their
work as well as for bad behaviour. Most resigned themselves to the idea
that this was how one learned in school (Figure 7.2).[77]

---

[77] David Vincent, *Bread, Knowledge and Freedom: A Study of Nineteenth-Century Working
Class Autobiography* (London: Europa, 1981). ch. 5; John Burnett (ed.), *Destiny Obscure:
Autobiographies of Childhood, Education and Family from the 1820s to the 1920s* (London:
Routledge, 1994), part 2; Humphries, *Childhood and Child Labour*, ch. 10; Jean-Claude
Caron, *A l'Ecole de la violence: châtiments et sévices dans l'institution scolaire au XIXe siècle*
(Paris: Aubier, 1999), passim.

Conclusion

Work loomed large in the experience of children during the early stages of industrialisation. The emphasis in the recent historical literature is on the importance of child labour for the launching of the Industrial Revolution in Europe, and its significant contribution to household budgets in manufacturing areas. To the stock figures of the Industrial Revolution, notably the little mill hands and the tiny figures working underground, one should add others such as the young silk reelers, lace makers, glass and metal workers who have come into view. There were also the large numbers of children employed in the family workshops of the protoindustrial sector. For those children who went on through the stages of being an apprentice, a journeyman and possibly an independent workshop master, there was the reward of a certain status and security. Humphries found that, among her sample of male working-class autobiographies, boys who had served an apprenticeship fared slightly better later in life than those who had not, and were less vulnerable to spells of unemployment.[78] Otherwise, there was considerable diversity in the nature of work performed by children, with the most gruelling probably found in the domestic workshops largely located in the countryside. Finally, the school was starting to be accepted as the right place for a child to be, taking over in some ways from the traditional apprenticeship system. There were, however, various obstacles to this transition during the nineteenth century. Governments in most countries either lacked the will or the means to enforce attendance at school. Families in sections of the working-class families were also still wary of the schools, being hard-pushed to afford a lengthy period in class for their children, or doubting that it had much to offer them.

[78] Humphries, *Childhood and Child Labour*, pp. 263–8.

Part III

Childhood in an Industrial and Urban Society, c. 1870–2000

'By the 1970s', according to Gerold Ambrosius and William Hubbard, 'all European societies approached total urbanisation, at least in socio-economic functional terms, if not in actual residential patterns'.[1] The agricultural society of earlier centuries finally lost its prominent position, as industry and the services came to employ most of the working population. Western Europe led the way, with agriculture employing only 6 per cent of the working population in 1980, industry 39 per cent and the services 55 per cent. The economies of southern and particularly eastern Europe developed more slowly, with the latter still having 24 per cent of their workforce employed in agriculture, 42 per cent in industry, and only 34 per cent in the services at this point. The large-scale movement of population from rural to urban areas that accompanied this shift meant that in all countries, except Albania, over half of the population lived in an urban settlement by the 1980s. In countries such as Belgium, Britain and the Netherlands, at least three-quarters of the population did so.[2] No less importantly, modern communications encouraged the spread of urban values across each nation.[3] The upshot was a general convergence in the experience of childhood across Europe in important respects, with such developments as a movement towards small nuclear families, mass consumerism and the decline of religious observance.

The pace of life certainly accelerated with the shift towards an urban and industrial society, given its inbuilt tendency to encourage innovation on a broad front. This was evident in numerous areas affecting the young, including medicine, education, penal reform and the leisure industry. Hugh Cunningham argues that the twentieth century brought a 'most rapid change in the conceptualisation and experience of

---

[1] Gerold Ambrosius and William H. Hubbard, *A Social and Economic History of Twentieth-Century Europe* (Cambridge, MA: Harvard University Press, 1989), p. 43.
[2] Statistics on urbanisation, it should be noted, are bedevilled by the varying definitions of an urban settlement across the continent.
[3] Ambrosius and Hubbard, *Twentieth-Century Europe*, pp. 37–41, 56–62.

childhood' in the West.[4] It is hard to disagree. Change was particularly evident after 1945, with an unprecedented period of economic growth lasting until the early 1970s, followed by a slowing of this growth and the emergence of a so-called post-modern society. This latter included exhilarating but also disturbing changes such as the collapse of the traditional family, challenges to established forms of authority, and unprecedented access to films and television programmes through various mass media. The twentieth century also brought a greater exposure of young people in Europe to influences from other continents. The 'scramble for colonies' in Africa and Asia that began during the 1870s had repercussions for education, in preparing young males for military conquest and the colonial administration, not to mention more generally promoting racist ideologies. The rise of the United States as a world power led to cultural influences on childhood that were in some ways welcomed, in the field of child psychology for example, but also resented in others, with obvious hostility to American comics and marketing methods at certain periods. No less importantly, from the 1950s onwards such influences as mass migrations from former colonies and other Third World nations, more time in school, and the growing influence of television, fostered a greater awareness of events in the wider world.

---

[4] Hugh Cunningham, *Children and Childhood in the West since 1500* (2nd edn., Harlow: Pearson Longman, 2005), p. 202.

In this chapter we return for the third and final time to the conceptual-isation of childhood in Europe, in terms of its boundaries, nature and significance. During the late nineteenth and twentieth centuries, the boundaries have increasingly been set in an institutional framework, by clinics, kindergartens, sports clubs and above all by schools, as well as by a new understanding of differences between childhood and adolescence.[1] As for the nature of childhood the Child Study Movement of the late nineteenth and early twentieth centuries brought the first concerted effort to apply scientific methods to the study of children, in a bid to understand the laws of normal child development. This was in the context of concerns such as the supposed 'degeneration of the race' in industrial societies and the feeling that education was based on academic tradition rather than on the needs of children.[2] From this early venture there evolved the academic study of child development by psychologists, which continues down to the present. Finally, the influence of Sigmund Freud in particular meant that earlier assertions of the significance of childhood experiences for the future of the individual were reempha-sised. Children's rights also became a serious issue, beginning in 1924 with a declaration from the League of Nations.

Boundaries in the Age of Mass Schooling

The School System and Childhood

By the late twentieth century, growing up in Europe almost invariably involved making one's way through an age-graded school system.

---

[1] Chris Jenks, *Childhood* (2nd edn., London: Routledge,2005), p. 5.
[2] Hans Pols, 'Child Study', in Paula Fass, *Encyclopedia of Children and Childhood in History and Society* (3 vols., New York, NY: Thomson Gale, 2003); Adrian Woolridge, *Measuring the Mind: Education and Psychology in England, c. 1860–c. 1990* (Cambridge: Cambridge University Press, 1994), p. 19; Daniel Pick, *Faces of Degeneration: A European Disorder, c. 1848–c. 1918* (Cambridge: Cambridge University Press, 1989), passim.

Childhood became associated with schooling more closely than ever before, so that the ages of starting and leaving school, and of moving from the primary to the secondary level, came to be seen as major turning points in any child's life. As noted above, a contemporary scholarly convention is to associate 'children' with primary schools and 'young people' with the secondary level. By the year 2000, right across the continent, nearly everyone in the official age group for their country was attending a primary or secondary school.[3] Typically a school career could last thirteen, fourteen or fifteen years, through childhood and much of adolescence.[4]

By this point, the starting age for full-time schooling had become five, six or seven, depending on the national context. This replaced the earlier 'age of reason' at seven, or its equivalent in villages, as the beginning of a new phase in childhood. Younger children were gradually excluded from the primary schools, as age-grading took effect from the start. Infants below school age remained at home or attended a crèche or nursery school from varying ages, which had the effect of emphasising their distinctiveness as an age group. Memories of the first day at school as a significant turning-point in life in earlier decades sometimes appear in autobiographies. They are particularly vivid when they concern children from peasant or working-class backgrounds. Antoine Sylvère (b. 1888), from a village in the Auvergne, lingered in detail on his bitter feelings that day. There was the sense of foreboding when, most unusually, his mother washed him thoroughly. He feared that his parents were trying to dispose of him, like the calves that went to market and never returned. He feared the unfamiliar environment of the town, and above all the shock and the pain when the nun introducing him to his letters caned his hand when he made a mistake, 'more painful than all known punishments', causing him to wet himself. There was also the risk of being teased or roughed up as a newcomer by the other children, as happened to Spiridon Kozlov in Russia during the 1890s, and to William Woodruff in Blackburn (Lancashire) during the 1920s.[5]

---

[3] These figures are for the net primary and secondary school enrolment rates, the former, for example, defined as the 'ratio of children of primary school age who are enrolled in primary school to the total population of primary school age'; data from the World Bank website, data.worldbank.org/indicator/, accessed 26 March 2015.

[4] *Education at a Glance 2014: OECD Indicators;* UNESCO Institute for Statistics, www.uis.unesco.org/Education; accessed 26 March 2015.

[5] Antoine Sylvère, *Toinou: le cri d'un enfant auvergnat* (Paris: Plon, 1980), pp. 29–35; Catriona Kelly, *Children's World: Growing Up in Russia, 1890–1981* (New Haven, CT: Yale University Press, 2007), p. 519; William Woodruff, *The Road to Nab End: An Extraordinary Northern Childhood* (London: Abacus, 2002), pp. 123–4.

At the other end of their school careers, at least until the post-1945 period, most children still went straight into the labour market at a relatively early age after a very basic education. In 1938, no less than 88 per cent of children in England attended elementary schools within the maintained system, and the 'great bulk' of them left at the age of fourteen to start paid work.[6] The secondary schools in Europe, the grammar schools, *lycées* and *Gymnasien* inherited from earlier periods, for long remained almost exclusively the preserve of the middle classes. It was only in the 1930s and 1940s that governments began to take steps to extend secondary schooling beyond a small elite.[7] By the time of the millennium, education had become compulsory well into the teen years, with school-leaving ages in the range of fifteen to eighteen.

From Childhood to Adolescence

The end of childhood was also redefined at the beginning of the twentieth century with the so-called discovery of adolescence by the American G. Stanley Hall (1846–1924). In truth, ideas on adolescence as a stage in life had a long gestation period during the eighteenth and nineteenth centuries. What Hall did was to systematise existing ideas, as one might gather from the title of his weighty two-volume work, *Adolescence: Its Psychology and Its Relations to Physiology, Anthropology, Sociology, Sex, Crime, Religion, and Education* (1904). He brought a veneer of scientific respectability to the subject, incorporating ideas from the Darwinian theory of evolution and the then fashionable law of recapitulation. He also produced a shorter version of the work for parents and teachers, which helped to ensure a wide readership, particularly in the United States and Britain.[8] His timing in the early 1900s was impeccable, capitalising on anxieties over the young during this period, notably about their health in an increasingly urbanised society, their ability to defend European empires, and their temptation into criminal activity.

Hall followed earlier thinkers, notably Jean-Jacques Rousseau, in thinking that growing up involved moving through a series of stages. In his case, he linked it to recapitulation theory by asserting that the growth of the individual retraces the development of the human race from its animal origins to modern civilisation. He linked infancy with an animal

---

[6] Brian Simon, *Education and the Social Order, 1940–1990*, (London: Lawrence and Wishart, 1991), p. 26.
[7] James Bowen, *A History of Western Education* (London: Methuen, 1981), vol. 3, chs. 13–14.
[8] Olsen, *Juvenile Nation*, p. 156.

stage of existence, childhood between the ages of eight and thirteen with savagery, and adolescence between fourteen and twenty-four with the first stages of civilisation. Hence the child, revelling in its savagery, had 'tribal, predatory, hunting, fishing, fighting, roving, idle, playing proclivities'.[9] Adolescence he characterised as an extended period of 'storm and stress', full of numerous contradictions, between selfishness and altruism, enthusiasm and lethargy, euphoria and gloom, and so forth. Hall also revealed the influence of Rousseau in depicting puberty as a 'second birth', which launched this period of emotional turbulence. The idea travelled widely, appearing in textbooks across the continent, with Pierre Mendousse in France referring to *La seconde naissance*, Eduard Spranger in Germany to *Von der Ewigen Renaissance* (the eternal renaissance).[10] Hall had his critics from the start, and later research by psychologists has found little evidence to support some of his key points. It refutes the idea that the physical changes associated with puberty can be linked to emotional disturbance. It doubts that conflictual relations with parents are typical of adolescent behaviour. And it looks sympathetically at female adolescence.[11] Yet the image of the moody adolescent, in contrast to the more biddable child, remains firmly rooted in the popular imagination.

Finally, we should note that during the twentieth century the experience of adolescence in its modern sense has broadened to nearly all of the population in Europe. During the eighteenth and nineteenth centuries, it was restricted to a small group of middle- and upper-class males. This was because of their near-monopoly of secondary school places. Distinguishable by their extended period of dependence on their parents, they generally accounted for around 2 to 3 per cent of their age group during the decades leading up to World War I.[12] Finally, during the second

---

[9]   G. Stanley Hall, *Adolescence: Its Psychology and Its Relations to Physiology, Anthropology, Sociology, Sex, Crime, Religion, and Education* (2 vols., New York, NY: D. Appleton, 1904), vol. 1, p. x.

[10]   Rolf E. Muuss, *Theories of Adolescence* (3rd edn., New York, NY: Random House, 1975), pp. 33–6; John Springhall, *Coming of Age: Adolescence in Britain 1860–1960* (Dublin: Gill and Macmillan, 1986), pp. 28–34; Willem Koops and Michael Zuckerman, 'Introduction: A Historical Developmental Approach to Adolescence', in *The History of the Family*, 8 (2003), special issue on 'The History of Adolescence', 345–54 (347); Jeffrey Jensen Arnett, 'G. Stanley Hall's *Adolescence*: Brilliance and Nonsense', *History of Psychology*, 9 (2006), 186–97.

[11]   Willem Koops and Michael Zuckerman, 'Historical Developmental Approach', in Willem Koops and Michael Zuckerman (eds.), *Beyond the Century of the Child: Cultural History and Developmental Psychology* (Philadelphia, PA: University of Pennsylvania Press, 2003), 349–51; Judith Semon Dubas, Kristelle Miller and Anne C. Petersen, 'The Study of Adolescence during the 20th Century', *The History of the Family*, 8 (2003), 375–97.

[12]   Hartmut Kaelbe, 'Educational Opportunities and Government Policies in Europe in the Period of Industrialization', in Peter Flora and Arnold J. Heidenheimer (eds.), *The*

half of the twentieth century, the masses were steadily drawn into secondary schools by free places and eventually compulsion, with the raising of the school-leaving age. In this way they began to experience a protected adolescence, even if a relatively short one, in contrast to the broader conception of 'youth' characteristic of the early modern period.[13]

In sum, as in earlier periods, precise boundaries for childhood remained elusive throughout the twentieth century. Indeed, there is a widespread feeling among scholars that from the 1970s onwards there has been a blurring of the lines between childhood and adulthood in a 'post-modern' world. The various dimensions to childhood, including the spheres of work, education, physical growth and the law, have all tended to provide different answers on where childhood begins and ends. A number of authorities have defined childhood by setting age limits, such as the standard demographic classification of zero to fourteen, the birth to fifteen adopted by UNICEF, or the upper limit of eighteen proclaimed by the United Nations Convention on the Rights of the Child (UNCRC) in 1989. On the legal side, the traditional age of majority was twenty-one in most parts of Europe, though there has been a general move to reduce it to eighteen in the late twentieth century. Biologists and child psychologists have provided detailed evidence of stages of growth during the early years. From the perspective of a biologist, Barry Bogin identifies five stages, which he suggests are perceived on a pan-human scale. These are: infancy, up until weaning; childhood, still dependent on adults for feeding and protection, until the age of six or seven; a juvenile stage running until puberty, around ten for girls and twelve for boys, in which humans have some ability to look after themselves; adolescence, notable for an acceleration of growth; and finally, when this growth spurt ends and reproductive maturity is achieved, adulthood.[14] There are other scholarly definitions of adolescence. Rolf E. Muuss, for example, describes it as the transitional period between a dependent childhood and a self-sufficient adulthood, running from around twelve or thirteen to the early twenties – though 'with wide individual and cultural variations'.[15]

Development of Welfare States in Europe and America (New Brunswick, NJ: Transaction Books, 1984), pp. 239–68 (p. 245).

[13] See Chapter 4.

[14] Barry Bogin, 'Evolutionary and Biological Aspects of Childhood', in Catherine Panter-Brick (ed.), *Biosocial Perspectives on Children* (Cambridge: Cambridge University Press, 1998), pp. 11–44 (pp. 21–3).

[15] Muuss, *Theories of Adolescence*, p. 4.

More meaningful for most people are the ages for starting and finishing primary and secondary schooling in each country, as the child has increasingly come to be seen as the schoolchild. These now vary slightly in Europe within the range of five to seven, to eleven to fourteen for primary schooling, and the leaving ages of fifteen to eighteen for the secondary level. For much of the twentieth century, the leaving age of fourteen or thereabouts for an elementary school and the start of work has been an obvious end to childhood for the mass of the population. (In the Netherlands, 'twelve years' was the stock phrase in pre–World War II working-class autobiographies separating school from work.[16]) By the 1970s, sixteen was a more common boundary, with the raising of the school-leaving age: to take the British example, 60 per cent of those aged sixteen still went from school to work at this point. There were complications, such as the introduction of middle schools between primary and secondary schools, and the importation from the United States during the 1940s of the 'teenager'. By the millennium, the association of children with the primary school and young people with the secondary schools, but also referring to both as children in a generic sense, probably made the most sense in Europe.[17]

The Nature of the Child in a Scientific (and Digital) Age

Although the twentieth century saw scientists and social scientists steadily asserting their authority as experts on the nature of childhood, this did not mean that the ideas of the poets and philosophers of the past were entirely discarded. The Romantic view of the child as a pure, innocent creature continued to exert considerable influence, notably in underpinning the 'protected childhood' associated with the welfare state. This latter notion held sway in most of Europe among the population at large, as an ideal at least, during the first half of the twentieth century.[18] However, from the 1980s onwards, there have been concerns that in western societies supposedly dominated by the mass media and rampant consumerism, children are losing their innocence. There has also been an awareness that being thought of as innocents abroad has its

[16] Ali de Regt, 'Children in the Twentieth-Century Family Economy: From Co-Providers to Consumers', *The History of the Family*,9 (2004), 371–84 (373).
[17] This follows Carol Smart, Bren Neale and Amanda Wade, *The Changing Experience of Childhood: Families and Divorce* (Cambridge: Polity, 2001), p. 187, n. 1.
[18] See, for example, Jenny Hockey and Allison James, *Growing Up and Growing Old: Ageing and Dependency in the Life Course* (London: Sage, 1993), pp. 66–8; Dennis Thompson, John D. Hogan and Philip M. Clark, *Developmental Psychology in Historical Perspective* (Oxford: Wiley-Blackwell, 2012), p. 3.

drawbacks. In campaigns against the sexual abuse of children, for example, it has helped mobilise public support for action, but risked stigmatising the precocious, 'sexually knowing child'. Also, abused children who have lost their aura of innocence might be dismissed as 'damaged goods'.[19] At the same time, developmental psychology has proceeded with its core mission 'to understand the processes of change, with age, in the psychological functioning of individuals', which has produced various ideas on the nature of the child along the way. It began as a small and fractured branch of its discipline, but rose to prominence from the late1940s. As a science, it has always had a tendency to seek universally applicable laws of human development for 'the child'. Nonetheless, significantly for historians and social scientists, developmental psychologists now tend to pay some attention to the social, cultural and historical context in which the individual is immersed.[20]

The Child Study Movement

The Child Study Movement began in the United States, and soon inspired imitators in Europe, 'from St Petersburg to London', during the period 1890–1914.[21] Thus James Sully's *Studies of Childhood* (1895), an early work in the field, was translated into Russian in 1909, and had a considerable influence on the literature on childhood in Russia. The movement rejected the older tradition of studying childhood by introspection as an adult, preferring what G. Stanley Hall called the 'far more laborious method of observation, description, and induction'.[22] In its bid to discover the laws of natural development it therefore adopted a variety of methods, including questionnaires (favoured by Hall), observations of children's behaviour, and measurements of height and weight. There were certain precedents in Europe here, especially the detailed records that a number of scholars had kept of their own children's development.

[19] Jenny Kitzinger, 'Who Are You Kidding? Children, Power and the Struggle against Sexual Abuse', in Allison James and Alan Prout (eds.), *Constructing and Reconstructuring Childhood: Contemporary Issues in the Sociological Study of Childhood* (Washington, DC: Falmer Press, 1997), pp. 165–89 (pp. 168–9).

[20] Thompson et al., *Developmental Psychology*, p. vii.

[21] Marc Depaepe, 'Social and Personal Factors in the Inception of Experimental Research in Education (1890–1914): An Exploratory Study', *History of Education*, 16 (1987), 275–98 (275). See also Gerrit Breeuwsma, 'The Nephew of an Experimentalist: Ambivalence in Developmental Thinking', in Koops and Zuckerman, *Beyond the Century of the Child*, pp. 183–203 (pp. 186–90); and Sally Shuttleworth, *The Mind of the Child: Child Development in Literature, Science, and Medicine, 1840–1900* (Oxford: Oxford University Press, 2010), ch. 14.

[22] See Chapter 5; Hall, *Adolescence*, p. vii.

These included observations made by Dietrich Tiedemann during the 1780s, Charles Darwin in 1840–41, and Wilhelm Preyer during the early 1880s.[23] At the outset, child study involved people interested above all in the reform of education, including teachers and parents (especially mothers) as well as scientists. It also drew on a range of disciplines, including in its ranks physicians, anthropologists and criminologists as well as psychologists and educators. It was not long before the scientists began to chafe at the amateurism of many in the movement, often in the form of condescending remarks by males about female participants, and so they excluded the 'practical' as opposed to the 'scientific' forms of child study. In western Europe, they often adopted the banner of paidology (the 'science of the child'), suggesting that they were a more rigorous form of child study, leaving behind the romanticism of pioneers such as Hall.

These early researchers made a significant contribution to thinking in Europe about the nature of the child during the twentieth century. Particularly prominent was the intelligence test, and a scientifically-based notion of the 'normal child'. The French psychologist Alfred Binet (1857–1911) came to prominence in this field with a request from the Ministry of Public Instruction in Paris for a method to identify mentally handicapped children who would benefit from admission to special schools. The Binet-Simon scale, which first appeared in 1905, involved thirty psychological tests, in such areas as vocabulary, memory and 'judgement'. It rested on the finding that mentally handicapped children closely resembled normal children who were a number of years younger. Hence there was the possibility of comparing the mental age of a child with its chronological age. This paved the way for what became known as the IQ (intelligence quotient) test, and the multiplicity of ways in which it has been used. Simon considered the concept of the IQ a 'betrayal' of his and Binet's original intention, as it moved from a means to diagnose and support 'backward' children to one for ranking everyone according to their performance in an intelligence test.[24] It remains deeply rooted in

[23] Jonn Cleverley and D. C. Phillips, *From Locke to Spock: Influential Models of the Child in Modern Western Thought* (Melbourne: Melbourne University Press, 1976), pp. 71–4; Denise Riley, *War in the Nursery* (London: Virago, 1983), pp. 43–59.
[24] Robert B. Cairns, 'The Emergence of Developmental Psychology', in P. H. Musson (ed.), *Handbook of Child Psychology*, vol. 1, 'History, Theory and Methods' (New York, NY: Wiley, 1983), pp. 41–102 (pp. 46–51); Nikolas Rose, *Governing the Soul: The Shaping of the Private Self* (2nd edn., London: Free Association Books, 1999), ch. 11; Peter K. Smith et al., *Understanding Children's Development* (6th edn., Chichester: Wiley, 2015), pp. 580–3.

our thinking about the nature of the child – and the way the 'normal' can be distinguished by clinicians from the 'abnormal'.[25]

The pioneering psychologists of the late nineteenth and early twentieth century also bequeathed to later generations the notion of development during childhood. This was of course not the only possible perspective on the child. All the same, the influence of evolutionary theory cast the child in a new light, notably the changes inherent in recapitulation theory. Moving on from the observation of their own children, psychologists took advantage of the unprecedented concentrations of young children in clinics and nurseries to assemble a huge amount of data on such variables as height, weight and speech to chart 'landmarks of development'. Once again, as Nikolas Rose observes, there was a process of normalisation at work that had a major impact on society at large. Developmental scales of the type associated with the work of Arnold Gesell (1880–1961) at Yale University 'provided new ways of thinking about childhood, new ways of seeing children that rapidly spread to teachers, health workers and parents through the scientific and popular literature.'[26]

Thirdly, around 1900 scientists and psychologists led a challenge to the prevailing assumption that children are by nature innocent, asexual beings. Instead, these revisionists proposed that children have a sexual drive, and if some considered any sexual activity before puberty as pathological, others saw it as part of normal development. Sigmund Freud (1856–1939) was the most influential among these authorities, though he was by no means on his own: the discovery of childhood sexuality was very much 'in the air' in Europe and the United States during this period.[27] Freud argued in his *Three Essays on the Sexuality of Childhood* (1905) that 'germs of sexual impulses are already present in the new-born child', and that they continue to develop over time, so that 'the sexual life of children usually emerges in a form accessible to observation round about the third or fourth year of life.'[28] He also asserted that repression of the child's sexuality by adults risked storing up problems later in life. Such ideas were widely contested, and continued to be so

[25] Erica Burman, *Deconstructing Developmental Psychology* (London: Routledge, 2008), p. 22.
[26] Rose, *Governing the Soul*, pp. 144–54 (p. 153); André Turmel, *A Historical Sociology of Childhood: Developmental Thinking, Categorization and Graphic Visualization* (Cambridge: Cambridge University Press, 2008), passim.
[27] Stephen Kern, 'Freud and the Discovery of Childhood Sexuality', *History of Childhood Quarterly*, 1 (1973), 117–41 (117).
[28] Sigmund Freud, 'Infantile Sexuality', in Angela Richards (ed.), *On Sexuality: Three Essays on the Theory of Sexuality* (1905) (Harmondsworth: Penguin, 1977), pp. 88–125 (p. 92).

throughout the twentieth century, notably his emphasis on infantile sexuality and his interpretation of many actions by the child as sexual in nature. All the same, they spared new generations anxiety over the alleged physical dangers of the 'abominable practice' of masturbation,[29] and the inclination to treat any sexual activity by supposedly 'innocent' children as pathological. Rather, following Dr Spock and numerous others during the twentieth century, the emphasis was on avoiding the repression of childhood sexuality and the fostering of guilt in this area.[30]

Developmental Psychology and the Child

During the inter-war period, a number of 'grand theories' came to be formulated in developmental psychology. With their own particular aims, issues and methods, the various theorists went their separate ways rather than engaging in debate with one another.[31] The influence of earlier generations of philosophers and educators, as well as of psychologists, on their assumptions about the nature of the child is not hard to find. Thus the American John Watson and his fellow behaviourists argued that children developed in response to rewards and punishments from adults, reviving John Locke's idea of the child as a blank slate. Freudians arguably gave a hint of the traditional line that children were essentially evil, in asserting that they were born with an id, dedicated to the pleasure principle (also known as the 'lust principle').[32] And a number of theorists, including Gesell, Sigmund Freud, Jean Piaget and Lev Vygotsky breathed new life into the long tradition of depicting children as developing in stages. Piaget, for example, identified four stages of intellectual development: the sensorimotor stage, from birth to (approximately) two years of age; the preoperational stage, from two to seven; the concrete operational stage, from seven to twelve; and the formal operational stage from twelve to adulthood. Rousseau in *Emile* (1762) had identified five stages, with slightly different boundaries, but made the same assumption

[29] *Onania* (1718), as cited by Thomas Laqueur, *Solitary Sex: A Cultural History of Masturbation* (New York, NY: Zone Books, 2003), p. 25.
[30] Sterling Fishman, 'The History of Childhood Sexuality', *Journal of Contemporary History*, 17 (1982), 269–83; Heather Montgomery, *An Introduction to Childhood: Anthropological Perspectives on Children's Lives* (Chichester, Wiley-Blackwell, 2009), ch.7; Lutz Sauerteig, 'Loss of Innocence: Albert Moll, Sigmund Freud and the Invention of Childhood Sexuality around 1900', *Medical History*, 56 (2012), 156–83.
[31] Cairns, 'Emergence', 82.
[32] From the beginning, psychologists and doctors were willing to argue that chidren were malicious creatures; see Katharine H. Norris, 'Mentir à l'âge de l'innocence: enfance, science et anxiété culturelle dans la France fin-de-siècle', *Sociétés et représentations*, 38 (2014), 171–202.

that all children pass through a set sequence of stages. Rousseau also focused on the maturation process, 'the natural unfolding of the organism', an emphasis on biological influences which was particularly important for Gesell.[33]

From the late 1940s, developmental psychology began to gain in prestige and coherence in the West. To begin with, the behaviourist influence was in the ascendant, though far more in the United States than in Europe. There was a particular interest in childrearing, with the emphasis on children as learners from those around them: from this perspective, behaviours 'did not develop, they were acquired'. During the 1960s, such social learning theories lost ground to the very different cognitive-developmental theory associated with the Swiss-born Jean Piaget (1896–1980).[34] The 'cognitive revolution' of this period gave the child an active role in its development, as it interacted with its environment to move through its various stages of growth. In other words, Piaget combined two traditions, depicting the child in biological terms, with the 'endogenous' factors that propelled its growth, and also, as its cognitive abilities increased, as a learner, actively seeking knowledge from the world around it to reach the equilibrium of a new stage.[35]

During the late twentieth century, sociologists picked up on some of the dissenting voices from the main stream of developmental psychologists, and in effect launched the sociology of childhood as a reaction to the approach of the latter. For sociologists, 'developmentalism' was the cardinal sin committed by psychologists during the twentieth century: treating children as 'human becomings' rather than 'human beings'.[36] To be more specific, recently Diane Hogan has highlighted a number of key issues in their critique, including 'the search for "universal" laws of child development, the assumption that child development is "natural" (biologically based), a view of children as passive, and a focus on age-related competency/deficits rather than on subjective experience'.[37] As a developmental psychologist herself, Hogan concedes that there is some substance to this, particularly the latter point, during the twenty-first century. At the same time, she draws attention to the way the relentlessly

---

[33] Cleverley and Phillips, *From Locke to Spock*, passim; Neil J. Salkind, *An Introduction to Theories of Human Development* (Thousand Oaks, CA: Sage, 2004), passim; Hogan et al., *Developmental Psychology*, ch. 6.

[34] Cairns, 'Emergence', 86–90.

[35] Salkind, *Human Development*, ch. 9; Hogan et al., *Developmental Psychology*, pp. 112–16.

[36] See Introduction chapter in this volume.

[37] Diane Hogan, 'Researching "the Child" in Developmental Psychology', in Sheila Greene and Diane Hogan (eds.), *Researching Children's Experience: Approaches and Methods* (London: Sage, 2005), pp. 22–41 (p. 23).

negative accounts by sociologists underestimate the variety and complexity of approaches in psychology throughout the twentieth century. Thus if the maturational approach tends to see the child in biological terms, the 'sociocultural theory' of Lev Vygotsky (1896–1934) placed even more weight than Piaget did on the role of social interaction in the development of cognition. Working in the Soviet Union during the 1920s and 1930s, Vygotsky had little choice but to remain within the framework of Marxist orthodoxy in starting with social, cultural and historical conditions before moving to the individual.[38] (The *Manifesto of the Communist Party* asserted that 'man's ideas, views and conceptions, in one word, man's consciousness, changes with every change in the conditions of his material existence, in his social relations and in his social life.'[39]) In France and the francophone world, Henri Wallon (1879–1962) was the main rival to Piaget. Also a Marxist, he considered the child as a social being, and placed less weight than Piaget on 'within the child' development from stage to stage, and more on environmental events and interaction with people.[40] During the late twentieth century, neuroimaging techniques and corresponding advances in neuroscience transformed developmental psychology. *Developmental cognitive neuroscience* became an important branch of the discipline. Any notion of the child as a blank slate became difficult to sustain, as developmental theories moved towards a complex interaction of genes, the brain and the environment.[41] Overall, then, the image of the 'naturally developing child' that was influential, though far from all-conquering, up until the late twentieth century, has yielded ground to theories taking some account of the environment for growth – evidently more congenial to historians and social scientists.

The 'Death of Childhood' Thesis

There would be a pleasing symmetry to a book on childhood in modern Europe that began with the emergence of the idea of childhood during the sixteenth and seventeenth centuries and ended with its disappearance during the late twentieth century. This was precisely what Neil Postman

---

[38] Salkind, *Human Development*, ch. 10.
[39] Karl Marx and Frederick Engels, 'Manifesto of the Communist Party', in David Fernbach (ed.), Karl Marx, *The Revolutions of 1848* (Harmondsworth: Penguin, 1973), pp. 67–98 (p. 85).
[40] Beverly Birns and Gilbert Voyat, 'Wallon and Piaget', *Enfance*, 32 (1979), 321–33 (325–8).
[41] Steven Pinker, *The Blank Slate: The Modern Denial of Human Nature* (London: Penguin, 2002), ch. 3; Smith et al., *Children's Development*, ch. 2.

argued in *The Disappearance of Childhood* during the 1980s.[42] He linked the appearance of the idea of childhood to the invention of the printing press, on the grounds that it allowed adults to keep secrets, and particularly sexual secrets, from children. Before that, in an oral as opposed to a literate culture, and with children mixing freely with adults, he suggested that there was little in the culture that could be kept hidden. With the spread of literacy and the school system, adults were able to control the symbolic environment of the young.[43]

For Postman, this separation of the child's world from that of the adult began to unravel with the coming of television, perceived as an essentially visual medium that was readily accessible to both adults and children. The result, according to him, was the disappearance of both adulthood and childhood. The former was reduced to the level of an 'adult-child', a grown-up whose intellectual and emotional development had been stymied by years of watching television.[44] The latter was barely distinguishable from the adult-child, since the young could discover for themselves all the old secrets of adult life. With children now aware of murky areas such as incest, violent crime and the sexual exploits of politicians, their innocence was a thing of the past, and the idea of childhood was fast disappearing. A number of other authors made similar claims for a blurring of the boundaries between childhood and adulthood in modern society. Again, the corrupting influence of television on childhood innocence featured prominently in these accounts.[45] Most were based on the American experience, though the Dutch psychiatrist J. H. van den Berg made an early contribution to the argument. His *The Changing Nature of Man* (1956) proposed that the child before the mid-eighteenth century and Rousseau's *Emile* (1762) was different from children after this time. 'The child had become a child', separated from an increasingly complicated adult life. Later, in the 1970s, van den Berg concluded that during the twentieth century children had rejoined the adult world, in the context of a general infantilisation of the population.[46]

As it happens, few historians would now accept that an awareness of childhood in Europe had to await the sixteenth century. And the sensational claim that it is now disappearing is open to criticism on a number

---

[42] Neil Postman, *The Disappearance of Childhood* (New York, NY: Vintage Books, 1994 [1982]).

[43] Postman, *Disappearance*, p. 45.   [44] Postman, *Disappearance*, p. 45.

[45] Marie Winn, *Children without Childhood: Growing Up Too Fast in the World of Sex and Drugs* (New York, NY: Penguin, 1984); and Joshua Meyrowitz, *No Sense of Place: The Impact of Media on Social Behaviour* (Oxford: Oxford University Press, 1985), ch. 13.

[46] Van den Berg, *Changing Nature*, ch. 2; Willem Koops, 'Imaging Childhood', in Koops and Zuckerman, *Beyond the Century of the Child*, pp. 1–18 (p. 10).

of grounds. It invariably makes sweeping generalisations about children and adults without reference to distinctions such as class and gender. It makes no attempt to discover what children themselves think. It proposes a determining influence on human behaviour of technology, in the form of the printing press and electronic media, ignoring the social context. It particularly points the finger at American commercial television, which was different from its European counterparts: an enquiry into the impact of British television during the late 1950s concluded that the majority of children 'were not drastically affected'.[47] And it takes a reactionary stance in the face of change in such areas as sexuality, knowledge of current affairs and clothing.[48] Other commentators during the 1970s and 1980s, it might be noted, welcomed the new developments and called for more radical change, such as allowing children to vote and to choose their own form of education.[49] Yet it may be that those arguing for the end of childhood were on to something. Historians in particular are bound to acknowledge Postman's long-term perspective, and his perception that an extended period that was particularly successful in keeping children apart from adults in their own social world (Postman suggests 1850 to 1950) was coming to an end.

The digital revolution, with its personal computers, the Internet, video games, DVDs, and all that this has entailed for the availability to children of 'adult' material, has given a boost to this type of debate since the 1980s. On the one side, it allegedly accelerated the erosion of boundaries between childhood and adulthood. In particular, it followed a well-beaten path laid down by earlier electronic media, in the form of films and radio as well as television, in undermining the construction of the child as an original innocent.[50] On the other, more plausibly in our view, it may have increased the distance between the generations, as children embraced the new forms of communication with far more enthusiasm than adults.[51] Rather than the end of childhood, it would surely be better

---

[47] Hilde T. Himmelweit et al., *Television and the Child: An Empirical Study of the Effect of Television on the Young* (London: Oxford University Press, 1958), pp. 40–2.

[48] Tommi Hoikkala et al., 'Wait a Minute, Mr Postman! – Some Critical Remarks on Neil Postman's Childhood Theory', *Acta Sociologica*, 30 (1987), 87–99; and David Buckingham, *After the Death of Childhood: Growing Up in the Age of Electronic Media* (Cambridge: Polity, 2000), ch. 2.

[49] Notably, from the United States, Richard Farson, *Birthrights* (Harmondsworth: Penguin, 1974) and John Holt, *Escape from Childhood: The Needs and Rights of Children* (Harmondsworth: Penguin, 1974); and, from England, Martin Hoyles, *The Politics of Childhood* (London: Journeyman Press, 1989).

[50] Chas Crichter, 'Making Waves: Historical Aspects of Public Debates about Children and Mass Media', in Kirsten Drotner and Sonia Livingstone (eds.), *International Handbook of Children, Media and Culture* (Los Angeles: Sage, 2008), pp. 91–104.

[51] Buckingham, *Death of Childhood*, p. 5.

to see it evolving in the face of social change. The earlier ideal of divorcing children entirely from the world of work has now come to be seen as undesirable. The young may have found themselves exposed to sex and violence in advertisements, films and television programmes, but there remained the countervailing influences of parents and friends – and they have emerged better informed about world affairs than earlier generations. No less importantly, with more disposable income than previous generations, they have become a force to be reckoned with as consumers.[52] How far all this has gone varies according to such influences as age, social class and ethnic background. All the same, the 'knowing child' or the 'competent child' is surely taking over from the supposedly innocent one – with attendant advantages as well as disadvantages.[53]

The Significance of Childhood during the 'Century of the Child'

In 1900 the Swedish feminist Ellen Key published the *Century of the Child*, and rather surprisingly found herself with an international bestseller on her hands. The work was after all hostile to Christianity, opposed to the existing system of education in the schools, and at odds with the modern capitalist world. She even included a quotation from the eugenicist Francis Galton favouring 'strict rules, to hinder inferior specimens of humanity from transmitting their vices or diseases, their intellectual or physical weaknesses'. At the same time, Key's strand of feminism envisaged mothers devoting themselves to providing a loving home for their offspring. She had a rather daunting vision of a new breed of mothers, fit, trained and dedicated to their task. She also followed Rousseau in his desire to preserve for as long as possible a 'natural' childhood. Her new education would therefore unobtrusively allow nature to help itself. Current systems of education, she complained, maintained a belief in human depravity, and attempted to suppress rather than change it. She was under no illusion that this type of childhood was going to establish itself universally in the new century, given the widespread poverty in society.[54] Yet the enthusiastic reception of Key's message in Europe and

---

[52] See Chapter 10.
[53] Anne Higonnet, *Pictures of Innocence: The History and Crisis of Ideal Childhood* (London: Thames and Hudson, 1998), p. 12; Bengt Sandin, 'Children and the Swedish Welfare State: From Different to Similar', in Paula S. Fass and Michael Grossberg (eds.), *Reinventing Childhood after World War II* (Philadelphia, PA: Pennsylvania State University Press, 2012), pp. 110–38 (p. 129).
[54] Micha de Winter, 'On Infantilization and Participation: Pedagogical Lessons from the Century of the Child', and Michael Zuckerman, 'The Millenium of Childhood That

North America gives a hint that preserving childhood from the pressures of adult society for as long as possible had a ready constituency.

For much of the twentieth century, psychologists also emphasised in various ways the differences between children and adults, as well as the importance of what happened during the early years for later development. In Europe, Freudianism was again notably influential, with its emphasis on the hazardous business of leading an infant through three of its 'psychosexual stages' (the oral, anal and phallic stages) during the first five or six years of its life. The danger was that if a child became fixated on a particular stage it would have serious repercussions for the later adult personality.[55] Attachment theory, first proposed by the English clinician John Bowlby during the 1950s, in its turn highlighted the period between the ages of six months and four as crucial for personality development. Bowlby explained how a study of mental health among homeless children led him to conclude in 1951 that 'What is believed to be essential for mental health is that the infant and young child should experience a warm, intimate and continuous relationship with his mother (or permanent mother-substitute) in which both find satisfaction and enjoyment.'[56] Any young child experiencing a prolonged period deprived of maternal care, he alleged, faced threats to his or her future life. But this focus on the mother-child relationship, popularised through the media in Britain and the United States in particular, proved difficult to put into practice in the real world. The often isolated nuclear family, notably among working-class families in high-rise flats, left young mothers deprived of the support and sociability earlier generations had enjoyed, and hence made difficult the warm relationships at the heart of 'Bowlbyism'.[57] Feminists also bristled at the suggestion that mothers needed to devote themselves full-time to child care, and indeed later versions of the theory insisted that a network of attachment figures, including fathers, grandparents, care workers and teachers, was an alternative to Bowlby's hierarchy headed by the mother.[58] In addition, later research did not fully support Bowlby's dire prediction that maternal deprivation could

Stretches Before Us', in Koops and Zuckerman, *Beyond the Century of the Child*, pp. 159–82 (pp. 162–4) and pp. 225–42 (pp. 227–8), respectively.
[55] Salkind, *Theories of Development*, ch. 5.
[56] John Bowlby, *Attachment and Loss*, vol.1, 'Attachment' (London: Hogarth Press, 1970), p. xi.
[57] Mathew Thomson, *Lost Freedom: The Landscape of the Child and the British Post-War Settlement* (Oxford: Oxford University Press, 2013), ch. 3.
[58] Jeremy Holmes, *John Bowlby and Attachment Theory* (Hove: Brunner-Routledge, 1993), ch. 3; Carollee Howes, 'Attachment Relationships in the Context of Multiple Caregivers' and Marinus H. Van Ijzendoorn and Abraham Sagi, 'Cross-Cultural Patterns of Attachment: Universal and Contextual Dimensions', in Jude Cassidy and Phillip R.

lead to physical, intellectual, behavioural and emotional damage. Yet his theory remains the starting point in the literature on the effects of early parent–child relationships.[59]

Children's Rights

Thomas Hobbes wrote in his *Leviathan* (1651) that 'Like the imbecile, the crazed and the beasts, over … children … there is no law'.[60] Children were in effect considered to be the property of their parents, with fathers having the power of life and death over them. Without rights, children, like other minorities, were powerless to pursue their interests, having to 'grovel, plead or beg' for what they felt they deserved.[61] Moreover, in contrast to women or racial minorities, they had to rely on others to campaign for them, and, to begin with, the demand was for them to be excluded from rather than included in the polity, to be deemed 'helpless and dependent'.[62] The origin of children's rights lay in the social legislation of the nineteenth century, particularly the period 1870 to 1914. Gradually, the European states introduced legislation that separated the young from the adult world, banning them from the factories, for example, and compelling them to attend school.

Increasingly during the twentieth century, reformers talked the language of children's rights to promote their cause.[63] This first step on the international stage was the Geneva Declaration of the Rights of the Child, issued by the League of Nations in 1924.[64] Its five points were above all a response to the wretched condition of many children in the aftermath of World War I. Hence its second paragraph declared

Shaver (eds.), *Handbook of Attachment: Theory, Research, and Clinical Applications* (London: Guildford Press, 1999), pp. 671–734 and 713–34, respectively.

[59] Holmes, *Bowlby*, pp. 49–50; Jude Cassidy and Phillip R. Shaver, 'Preface', *Handbook of Attachment*, pp. x–xiv; Peter Fonagy, *Attachment Theory and Psychoanalysis* (New York, NY: Other Press, 2001), ch. 1.

[60] Hobbes, *Leviathan*, as cited in M. D. A. Freeman, *The Rights and Wrongs of Children* (Dover, NH: Frances Pinter, 1983), p. 53.

[61] Freeman, *Rights*, p. 32.

[62] James Schmidt, 'Children and the State', in Paula D. Fass, *The Routledge History of Childhood in the Western World* (Abingdon: Routledge, 2013), pp. 174–90 (pp. 174, 184–5).

[63] This section is indebted to Freeman, *Rights and Wrongs*, chs. 1 and 2; idem, 'Children's Rights as Human Rights: Reading the UNCRC', in Jens Qvortrup et al. (eds.), *The Palgrave Handbook of Childhood Studies* (Basingstoke: Palgrave Macmillan, 2009), pp. 377–93; David Archard, *Children: Rights and Childhood* (2nd edn., London: Routledge, 2004), ch. 4; and Paula S. Fass, 'A Historical Context for the United Nations Convention on the Rights of the Child', *Annals of the American Academy of Political and Social Science*, 633 (2011), 17–29.

[64] www.un-documents.net/gdrc1924.html, consulted 15 July 2015.

that 'The child that is hungry must be fed; the child that is sick must be nursed; the child that is backward must be helped; the delinquent child must be reclaimed; and the orphan and the waif must be sheltered and succored.' This was hard to deny, but it was not clear whose duty it was, among the 'men and women of all nations' mentioned in the prologue, to take action. The next step, the United Nations Declaration of the Rights of the Child, from 1959, again followed a devastating world war for children, and was similarly vague and not obviously enforceable. Among its ten principles, the 'right to understanding and love by parents and society' was a case in point.

An important step forward was the 1989 UNCRC, also from the United Nations.[65] Citing the Universal Declaration of Human Rights, it stated emphatically that 'childhood was entitled to special care and assistance', bearing in mind its physical and mental immaturity. Unlike its predecessors, it made clear at the outset what it meant by a child ('every human being below the age of eighteen'). It ventured beyond the realm of 'protective rights' to the more ambitious 'participatory rights'. As before, many of its fifty-four articles were designed to protect children's health and education, expecting adults to act in 'the best interests of the child'. But there was also the granting of rights encouraging more autonomy for children, and more of a role in adult life. Article 12.1, a vital part of the Convention, required States Parties to 'assure the child who is capable of forming his or her own views the right to express those views freely in all matters affecting the child', with the important rider that the weight to be given to these views would take account of the age and maturity of the child. No less importantly, Article 12.2 stated that children were to be given the opportunity to be heard in judicial or administrative proceedings that affected them. Other articles granted children freedom of expression, freedom of association, and 'freedom of thought, conscience and religion'. Finally, states were required to 'respect and ensure' the rights within their jurisdiction, and 190 out of the 192 members agreed to do so. Needless to say, many states neglected to fulfil their obligations, and without an international court to enforce the Convention, it has remained in part a statement of aspirations.

The Convention can with some justification be seen as an effort by western nations to impose their vision of childhood on African and Asian nations. Yet some European nations themselves stand accused of failing to meet all of its (admittedly exacting) obligations: the appropriate

---

[65] Texts of the 1959 Declaration and the UNCRC are available at www.unicef.org.

protection of refugee children (Article 22) comes to mind, as do an adequate standard of living (Article 27), or treatment as a prisoner with humanity and 'in a manner which takes into account the needs of persons of his or her age (Article 37). There were noticeable leads and lags on children's rights among the nations during the twentieth century.[66] Russia proved remarkably progressive during the first flush of idealism after the Revolution. The Code on Marriage and the Family of 1926 undermined the traditional subordination of children to parents by stipulating that 'parental rights are to be enacted entirely in the interests of children', and allowing the courts to deprive parents of these rights if they failed to do so. There were also calls for 'self-government' in children's institutions, with children involved in the running of schools, for example – a principle more honoured in the breach than the observance.[67]

Later in the century, the Nordic countries were outstanding in their support for children's rights in their 'welfare societies'. There was the familiar emphasis on childhood as a period of vulnerability, and hence in need of protection. An official enquiry into childcare in Sweden during the 1970s talked in terms of a 'long, helpless childhood'. From the 1960s this view was partially supplanted by a new conception of childhood, giving it an autonomous, adult-like character. In the words of Bengt Sandin, 'the competent child was discovered, constructed and romanticised, as a partner in collaboration with the professionals.' This in turn required a new approach to children's rights, anticipating much that was in the UNCRC (indeed, Swedish representatives were prominent in campaigning for it). During the late 1970s, respect for the physical and mental integrity of children led to the Swedes banning corporal punishment and the mental abuse of children in families. The competent child needed a lighter touch from parents, and like adults, opportunities to participate in sports and the arts. Giving a voice to children revealed widespread feelings of stress and anxiety, which led to a certain reaction in favour of dependency, but the participatory approach remained influential.[68] A survey of child well-being in rich countries by UNICEF in 2007 revealed the Netherlands and the Nordic countries ranking highly in the six indicators adopted, partly inspired by the UNCRC, while Austria, Hungary and the United Kingdom more often appeared in the bottom third.[69]

[66] Schmidt, 'Children', pp. 185–6.   [67] Kelly, *Children's World*, pp. 62–5.
[68] Sandin, 'Swedish Welfare State', pp. 118, 129–31 and 136.
[69] UNICEF, 'Child Poverty in Perspective: An Overview of Child Well-Being in Rich Countries', *Innocenti Report Card 7*, UNICEF Innocenti Research Centre, Florence.

Conclusion

For the philosopher David Archard, taking a leaf from Philippe Ariès, 'the most important feature of the way in which in the modern world age conceives of children is as meriting separation from the world of adults.'[70] The increasing association of childhood with schooling during the twentieth century made this particularly obvious. In addition, children were no longer supposed to join adults at work, on the grounds that it was bad for their health and morals. They had their own games and sports leagues. And they were considered too immature to vote in elections and hold public office. The developmental model in psychology conceived of childhood as a stage on the way to adulthood, a 'becoming' rather than a 'being'. Around the turn of the twenty-first century, there were signs of some blurring of these lines between childhood and adulthood, as children began to encroach on the adult world, and adults often struggled to settle down into a secure job and family. The tendency of children's rights movements to give children a greater say in the running of their own lives than in the past was symptomatic of the change. For most people, the boundaries between childhood, adolescence and adulthood remain as fuzzy and uncertain as ever.

[70] Archard, *Children*, p. 37.

9   Growing Up during the Twentieth Century, Part 1

In the Family or on the Margins of Society

The domestic ideology remained influential in Europe well into the twentieth century, idealising the type of family where the father was the main provider and the mother devoted to the upbringing of her children. This ideal was not without its critics, as a 'bourgeois' institution for those on the extreme left, for example, and many more struggled to put it into practice. None the less, the majority of people in Europe long aspired to something like it. Organisations responsible for children in need of care and protection, ranging from orphans to delinquents, also attempted to reproduce it for their charges, gradually moving away from large, barrack-like institutions. However, providing the love and affection on which the young thrive was no easy matter, at all levels of society. This chapter will consider first the history of the family during the twentieth century, as it evolved from a modern to a postmodern form, and the long struggle to find satisfactory solutions to the continuing problems faced by the numerous 'marginal and excluded' children

The Demographic Context

The proportion of children in the population declined markedly during the twentieth century. At the end of the nineteenth century, children aged 0–14 accounted for around a third of the total population in all countries (except France, where it was closer to a quarter), a figure that had probably changed little since the eighteenth century. The 'demographic transition' that sooner or later affected all countries in Europe during the nineteenth and twentieth centuries, involving a dramatic shift from high to low birth and death rates, brought the proportion to less than a fifth in nearly all cases. The corollary was an 'ageing' of the population, as the proportion aged 65 and over increased, with all the cost implications that had for pension systems and health services.

More advantageous to children were the smaller families that emerged with the decline in marital fertility. In England and Wales, for example, where this decline began relatively early, Michael Anderson notes that

'Those [married women] born in the 1880s had only half as many children to care for, entertain, clothe and feed as their parents had had; their own children had only two-thirds as many as they did.' Here, in the short space of two generations, the average number of children born to a married woman fell from approximately six to slightly above two.[1] The large families still common in much of Europe during the nineteenth century became quite rare, with the decline starting in the west, and spreading to the south and east after 1945. Along with this, the complex families, characteristic of certain parts of southern and eastern Europe in particular, gradually gave way to the nuclear family. By 2010, in the European Union, households that had four or more children accounted for a mere 2.5 per cent of all households with children. Two children per family had become the norm across the social spectrum, with larger families generally confined to the two extremes of the very well off and the very poor. Attempts by governments to maintain a relatively high birth rate by discouraging contraception and providing incentives for parents to have big families in certain countries, notably by the Fascists in Italy and the National Socialists in Germany during the interwar period, made little headway in the long term (Figure 9.1).[2]

No less importantly, towards the end of the twentieth century, the traditional pattern of marriage and the family began to unravel. Marriages often came to an end more quickly than earlier in the century, and, with married women increasingly likely to be working outside the home, there was a challenge to the established division of labour between the sexes. Divorce rates rose steeply from the 1960s onwards, especially in western and eastern Europe. In 1970, divorce was already quite common in the Baltic states, Denmark and Sweden, but, at the other extreme, very difficult in Portugal and illegal in Spain and Ireland. By 2008, divorce rates had risen in most European countries. They now ranged from over 3 per 1000 population in Belgium and Lithuania to under 1 per thousand in Italy and Ireland. In England and Wales, marriages in the late twentieth century were being disrupted by divorce on the same scale as they had been by death in the 1820s. There was also an increase in cohabitation across Europe, revealing a widespread rejection of legal marriage. Births out of wedlock were rare in the 1960s, forming less than 10 per cent of the total in 1970 in most countries. Forty years later there was a very

[1] Michael Anderson, 'The Social Implications of Demographic Change', in F. M. L. Thompson (ed.) *Cambridge Social History of Britain, 1750–1950*, (Cambridge: Cambridge University Press, 1990), vol. 2, pp. 1–70 (p. 39).
[2] Gerold Ambrosius and William H. Hubbard, *A Social and Economic History of Twentieth-Century Europe* (Cambridge, MA: Harvard University Press, 1989), pp. 17–24; EU survey of income and living conditions, Eurostat.

Figure 9.1 A late nineteenth-century mother with her children, from *Our Own Magazine*, 1893. This large family is typical of the nineteenth rather than the twentieth century.
Getty Images, 653561378.

different picture, with around half of all births taking place outside marriage in a number of countries, including Denmark, Estonia, France, Slovenia and Sweden.[3] To keep all this in perspective, it is worth emphasising that in 2007 the majority of children were still living in a household with both of their parents. Around two-thirds of those aged 0–14 were doing so in Belgium and the United Kingdom; over 90 per cent in Finland, Greece, Italy and Spain.[4]

Advice to Parents: The Reign of Physicians and Psychologists

Over the long run, according to Jay Mechling, the source of expertise on child-rearing 'has moved from family to religious leaders to physicians

---

[3] Ambrosius and Hubbard, *Twentieth-Century Europe*, pp. 25–7; www.oecd.org/social/family/database, Chart SF3.1.E: The increase in crude divorce rates from 1970 to 2008, accessed 27 July 2015; Anderson, 'Demographic Change', p. 30; EU Marriage and divorce statistics, Eurostat.

[4] OECD Family database, table SF1.3.A: Distribution of children aged 0–14 by living arrangements, 2007; www.oecd.org/els/social/family/database, accessed 1 September 2015.

and psychologists'.[5] It is easy to exaggerate the influence of the latter: new parents during the twentieth century still turned to family and friends for advice, trusting in their experience of the myriad details of bringing up a child. A study of working-class families in East London during the 1950s, for example, emphasised the gains for young mothers from the willingness of their own mothers to share 'the mysteries as well as the tribulations, the burdens as well as the satisfactions' of childbirth and motherhood.[6] Even among the advice manuals, the two best-sellers in twentieth-century France were written by women claiming authority solely from having raised children themselves.[7] And if the trend inherited from the Enlightenment of adopting a purely secular approach to child-rearing advice continued apace, the religious influence still lingered on in certain quarters.[8] All the same, the new knowledge accumulating from the late nineteenth century onwards concerning the physical and mental health of children gave professionals with a training in medicine or developmental psychology a formidable authority. Many of them produced advice books to complement the activities of clinics, health visitors and primary schools in spreading their vision of modern child-rearing methods. Mechling also asserts that the general drift of advice literature during the modern period has been towards a permissive form of child-rearing, with feeding on demand and a relaxed approach to toilet training, interrupted by an occasional reversion to more regimented approaches. The twentieth century certainly exhibits an ongoing tension between advocates of these two contrasting models.

The early manuals gave eminently practical advice on such matters as diet and personal hygiene, which played their part in reducing infant mortality. But they also included what would now appear as excessively restrictive routines for mothers and infants, and disapproval of displays of emotion that might overexcite what was considered the delicate nervous system of an infant. Among German paediatricians around the turn of

---

[5] Jay Mechling, 'Child-Rearing Advice Literature', in Paula D. Fass, *Encyclopedia of Children and Childhood in History and Society* (3 vols., New York, NY: Thomson Gale, 2003).

[6] Michael Young and Peter Willmott, *Family and Kinship in East London* (London: Routledge and Kegan Paul, 1957), p. 159.

[7] Geneviève Delaisi de Parseval and Suzanne Lallemand, *L'Art d'accommoder les bébés: 100 ans de recettes françaises de puériculture* (Paris: Editions du Seuil, 1980), pp. 20–1.

[8] Julia Grant, 'Parent-Child Relations in Western Europe and North America,1500-Present', in Fass, *Childhood in the Western World*, pp. 103–22. On the influence of Protestantism in Germany during the 1900s, see Carolyn Kay, 'How Should We Raise Our Son Benjamin? Advice Literature for Mothers in Early Twentieth-Century Germany', in Dirk Schumann, *Raising Citizens in the Century of the Child: The United States and German Central Europe in Comparative Perspective* (New York, NY: Berghahn, 2010), pp. 106–21 (p. 116).

the twentieth century, the watchwords were 'functionality, extreme cleanliness, punctuality, regularity, order, obedience and subordination'. They insisted on a regular timetable for feeding and an early start to toilet training, with strict enforcement of the rules to accustom the infant to obeying authority. Cuddling a baby to stop it crying was to spoil it: these paediatricians had no time for 'doting mothers' and their 'cuddling mania'. In Soviet Russia during the 1920s and 1930s, no less than in western Europe, there was this same emphasis on strict regimes for feeding, sleeping and potty training. In the English case, historians recount with relish how Dr Frederick Truby King (1858–1938) had the bright idea of applying his experience with intensive cattle-rearing in his native New Zealand to the business of child-rearing. On a visit to England he established a Mothercraft School, which promoted breastfeeding and personal hygiene, but also strict adherence to four-hourly feeds and a refusal to feed a baby at night.[9] Whether middle-class parents, the group most likely to read these manuals, took much notice of such an austere regime is difficult to determine. The frequent warnings against 'spoiling' children in Stalinist propaganda suggest that many Russian parents were reluctant to follow the advice.[10]

A reaction to this regimentation of infants set in during the mid-twentieth century. The outstanding influence on the global stage was the American Dr Spock and his *Common Sense Book of Baby and Child* (1946), evident in Soviet Russia as well as western Europe. Spock urged mothers to trust in their own 'maternal instincts', and enjoy a warm, affectionate relationship with their infants. Influenced by Freud and Piaget, he also typified the post-war concern with mind rather than the body, as the emotional and intellectual development of the child came to the fore.[11] Europe produced its own, home-grown experts preaching a similar message. In England, for example, John Bowlby and David Winnicott were consistent in their simple message: 'Being a loving parent and trusting to one's instincts was all that was needed.'[12] From the

---

[9] Reinhard Spree, 'Shaping the Child's Personality: Medical Advice on Child-Rearing from the Late Eighteenth to the Early Twentieth Century in Germany', *Social History of Medicine*, 5 (1992), 317–35; Kay, 'Advice Literature'; Catriona Kelly, *Children's World: Growing Up in Russia, 1890–1981* (New Haven, CT: Yale University Press, 2007), pp. 324–32; Christina Hardyment, *Dream Babies: Childcare Advice from John Locke to Gina Ford* (London: Frances Lincoln, 2007), pp. 167–72.

[10] Mathew Thomson, *Psychological Subjects: Identity, Culture, and Health in Twentieth-Century Britain* (Oxford: Oxford University Press, 2006), pp. 137–8; Kelly, *Children's World*, p. 380.

[11] Hardyment, *Dream Babies*, pp. 266–8, 308.

[12] Mathew Thomson, *Lost Freedom: The Landscape of the Child and the British Post-War Settlement* (Oxford: Oxford University Press, 2013), p. 88.

1970s, advice books began to take seriously the options for day-care that would allow women to combine motherhood and paid work. In this, they belatedly followed countries such as Sweden, which, resistant to 'Bowlbyism' and its insistence that infants needed the constant attention of a full-time mother, had always been more inclined to place children in nurseries and other institutions as the solution to such problems.[13] There was also a clear reaction against child-centred parenting and the 'permissive society' it allegedly produced during the 1960s, leading to a renewed emphasis on discipline and set routines for infants. In Russia there was always an undercurrent inherited from Stalin that continued to emphasise 'discipline', imposed from an early age. In England, the maternity nurse Gina Ford established herself as the best-selling author in her field with the *Contented Little Baby* (1999) and *Contented Little Child* (2000) books, which revolved around the establishment of regular routines for feeding and sleeping.[14] In retrospect, given the ebb and flow of fashion, it is hard to disagree with the observation from Delaisi de Parseval and Lallemand that there was a yawning gap between the conviction of the authors of the advice books and the ephemeral usage of their recommendations.[15]

'Haven in a Heartless World': Family Life in the Twentieth Century

The post-war years after 1945 brought to fruition a number of favourable developments for children in Europe. With small families the norm, and growing affluence, mothers could spend more time with each child than ever before. Even mothers in the upper ranks of society were now heavily involved with child rearing, as the domestic servants on whom they had relied in the past became more difficult to recruit. There was also a continuation of the general drift towards more affectionate relations between parents and children. The patriarchal family gave way to a democratic one; corporal punishment maintained its slow (very slow) retreat from the home; children were even supposed to be happy. 'Thank You Dear Comrade Stalin for a Happy Childhood' was a constant refrain

---

[13] Hardyment, *Dream Babies*, p. 266; Bengt Sandin, 'Children and the Swedish Welfare State: From Different to Similar', in Paula S. Fass and Michael Grossberg (eds.), *Reinventing Childhood after World War II* (Philadelphia, PA: Pennsylvania State University Press, 2012), pp. 110–38 (pp. 118–19).

[14] Kelly, *Children's World*, p. 387; Hardyment, *Dream Babies*, pp. 292–5; Angela Davis, *Modern Motherhood: Women and Family in England, 1945–2000* (Manchester: Manchester University Press, 2012), ch. 5.

[15] Delaisi de Parseval and Lallemand, *L'Art d'accommoder les bébés*, p.16.

in Stalinist propaganda in the Soviet Union.[16] A study of childcare among 700 families in Nottingham during the 1960s provided a rare, systematic account of parental practice. It found that only 5 per cent of mothers with four-year-old children were working full time, though 23 per cent worked a few hours part time. The parents no longer expected unquestioning obedience from their children, and the investigators noted among all social classes particularly warm relations between mother and son, and father and daughter. Mild corporal punishment, though, was still common: 75 per cent of mothers with four-year-olds admitted smacking them at least once a week, 41 per cent of those with seven-year-olds. Boys were more at risk than girls, and those in the middle of the class structure more than those at the very top and bottom.[17]

This state of affairs emerged from a number of underlying influences that originated during the nineteenth century.[18] The 'separate spheres' for men and women were more and more in evidence after 1870, as the rise of big corporations in industry and commerce, and of middle-class suburbs, reinforced the separation of work from home for many families. An increasing number of working-class families also realised their ideal of having the wife released from the need to work. The state and philanthropic organisations gradually intervened in various countries to deal with abusive or negligent parents. During the 1880s and 1890s, for example, governments in Britain, France and Germany passed laws that allowed the authorities to remove children 'in moral danger' from their families and place them with what was considered a suitable alternative, such as relatives, foster care or a workhouse.[19] Moreover, in an urban-industrial society, institutions such as schools, hospitals and care homes encroached on many of the family's earlier functions.

---

[16] Kelly, *Children's World*, p. 107.

[17] John Newson and Elizabeth Newson, *Four Years Old in an Urban Community* (London: George Allen and Unwin, 1968), pp. 43 and 402; and idem, *Seven Years Old in the Home Environment* (London: George Allen and Unwin, 1976), chs. 8–9; See also Deborah Thom, '"Beating Children Is Wrong": Domestic Life, Psychological Thinking and the Permissive Turn', in Lucy Delap, Ben Griffin and Abigail Wills, *The Politics of Domestic Authority in Britain since 1800* (Basingstoke: Palgrave Macmillan, 2009), pp. 261–83 (p. 276).

[18] A useful introduction to this section is Antoine Prost and Gérard Vincent (eds.), *A History of Private Life*, vol. 5, 'Riddles of Identity in Modern Times', transl. Arthur Goldhammer (Cambridge, MA: Harvard University Press, 1991).

[19] Rachel Fuchs, 'The State', in Colin Heywood (ed.), *A Cultural History of Childhood and Family in the Age of Empire*, Oxford: Berg, 2010, pp. 129–47 (p. 143).

Its main role was to provide an emotional refuge for its members: a 'haven in a heartless world'.[20]

We should not lose sight of the drawbacks to this so-called traditional (or 'normal') family of the mid-twentieth century. Its emphasis on the father as provider meant that, despite the encouragement of stronger emotional bonds and of play with his offspring, his involvement in child rearing remained limited.[21] Even with 'new fathers', and an 'intensification' of fathering as well as mothering later in the century, everywhere in Europe most of the work involved in running a house and raising children still fell to the mother.[22] Smaller families meant fewer siblings for children to play with around the home. Leonora Davidoff suggests that the close attention paid by parents to a small number of children produced a claustrophobic atmosphere in the middle-class home during the late nineteenth and early twentieth centuries. Some commentators, notably Ellen Key, were critical of the usurping of mothers' function of educating young children by the school system. And of course from the 1960s an increasing number of mothers resented relegation to a life revolving around *Kirche-Küche-Kinder* (church-kitchen-children).[23]

It should be added that during the 1980s and 1990s researchers became aware that the sexual abuse of children by adults was less a matter of assaults by strangers (the dreaded 'paedophiles') outside the home, and more one of incestuous relationships within the family, perpetrated largely by fathers, boyfriends of mothers, uncles and grandfathers. A number of survivors of such abuse produced harrowing accounts of their childhood, partly to help them come to terms with their problems. The family home (and by extension, it soon emerged, the institutional home for children in care) was thereby emerging as potentially anything but a haven for the young. In fact, spending time cooped

---

[20] Christopher Lasch, *Haven in a Heartless World: The Family Beseiged* (New York, NY: Basic Books, 1977); we should note here that Lasch's book challenges the assumption that the 1950s saw the heyday of the 'traditional family', countering that it has been 'slowly coming apart for more than 100 years' (p. xiv).

[21] See above, 'The Demographic Context'.

[22] David I. Kertzer and Marzio Barbagli, 'Introduction', in David I. Kertzer and Marzio Barbagli (eds.), *The History of the European Family* (New Haven, CT: Yale University Press, c. 2001–3), vol. 3, pp. xi–xliv (pp. xxi–xxiii); Laura King, 'Hidden Fathers? The Significance of Fatherhood in Mid-Twentieth-Century Britain', *Contemporaray British History*, 26 (2012), 25–46 (28).

[23] Martine Segalen, *Historical Anthropology of the Family*, transl. J. C. Whitehouse and Sarah Matthews (Cambridge: Cambridge University Press, 1986), pp. 87–9; Leonore Davidoff, 'The Family in Britain', in Thompson, *Cambridge Social History*, vol. 2, pp. 71–129 (p. 102); Ingeborg Weber-Kellermann, 'The German Family between Private Life and Politics', in Prost and Vincent, *History of Private Life*, vol. 5, pp. 503–37 (p. 505).

up in the home at the expense of contacts with the wider world was taken as a sign of abuse.[24]

Historians have cast doubt on the widespread assumption among contemporaries that such abuse had only recently come to light, and was more widespread than in the past. They have found it well-nigh impossible to trace change over time in a blanket term covering a wide diversity of crimes, including rape, buggery, gross indecency and indecent exposure. However, they have shown that the sexual abuse of children was far from being ignored by earlier generations, even if there were few convictions in the courts.[25] The child-savers of the late nineteenth and early twentieth centuries campaigned to protect children from abusive parents, and from the (much exaggerated) dangers of prostitution and 'white slavery'. During the 1920s, an official report in Britain highlighted the trauma for a child of having to give repeated accounts of their ordeal, and to be confronted in open court by their abuser. Yet reformers faced 'delay and procrastination': procedures in Britain in this area were unchanged until the 1990s.[26] Child abuse remained a difficult problem for all concerned to solve. There was the challenge of balancing the desire to increase the number of convictions with the importance of justice for the accused. And removing children from their families risked doing more harm than good. Witness the public humiliation of paediatricians and social workers in the north-east of England during the 'Cleveland Affair' of 1987, after they placed 121 children in care on the basis of a new and controversial 'anal dilation' technique for detecting the sexual abuse of children.[27]

Besides the drawbacks to the traditional family, we should not ignore the divergences from this path, and the long struggle down the decades to put it into practice. Not all families consisted of a working father,

---

[24] Thomson, *Lost Freedom*, p. 179.

[25] George Rousseau, editorial Introduction to *Children and Sexuality: From the Greeks to the Great War* (Basingstoke: Palgrave Macmillan, 2012), p. 17; Adrian Bingham, Lucy Delap, Louise Jackson and Louise Settle, 'Historical Child Sexual Abuse in England and Wales: The Role of Historians', *History of Education*, 45 (2016), 411–29.

[26] George K. Behlmer, *Child Abuse and Moral Reform in England, 1870–1908* (Stanford, CT: Stanford University Press, 1982), pp. 224–7; Judith R. Walkowitz, *City of Dreadful Delight: Narratives of Sexual Danger in Late-Victorian London* (London: Virago Press, 1992), p. 83; Harry Ferguson, 'Cleveland in History: The Abused Child and Child Protection, 1880–1914', in Roger Cooter (ed.), *In the Name of the Child: Health and Welfare, 1880–1914* (London: Routledge, 1992), pp. 146–73; Carol Smart, 'Reconsidering the Recent History of Child Sexual Abuse, 1910–1960', *Journal of Social Policy*, 29 (2000), 55–71; Carl Ipsen, *Italy in the Age of Pinocchio: Children and Danger in the Liberal Era* (New York, NY: Palgrave Macmillan, 2006), pp. 70–5.

[27] Larry Wolff, 'Sexual Abuse', in Fass, *Encyclopedia of Children*; Ian Hacking, 'The Making and Molding of Child Abuse', *Critical Inquiry*, 17 (1991), 253–88 (256).

housewife mother, and two or three dependent children: indeed, by the early 1980s, only 40 per cent of households did so.[28] Neighbours or relatives in working-class areas often took in children when parents were in difficulties; single parents had to manage on their own; and remarriage after the death of a spouse, or increasingly separation and divorce, produced composite families with step- and half-siblings.[29] Affection for children was often missing in exceptionally large families, and the older children generally had a tougher time than the younger ones. The erosion of class and regional differences in parenting, in the face of such influences as rising real wages and a national press, was a very gradual process. At the beginning of the twentieth century, Siân Pooley reveals evidence of striking divergences in this sphere at the regional level in England. Families in Bromley, a market town near London with a substantial middle-class presence, were already close to the 'normal' model, with few working mothers and a relatively low fertility rate. The cotton weaving town of Burnley, by contrast, had around a quarter of mothers in employment, and a higher fertility rate, close to the national average.[30] Above all, the persistence of poverty in town and countryside throughout the twentieth century meant that, as in the past, many parents had too much on their hands to pay much attention to their offspring. Mothers might be nurturing or affectionate, but, as Ellen Ross emphasises, their main focus had to be on their work.[31] This was particularly the case for single mothers among the poor. René Michaud, brought up in a working-class neighbourhood in Paris during the early twentieth century, revealed a child's perspective on a particularly impoverished background. He remembered the toll taken on his widowed mother by the long hours she spent ironing the fine clothes of the rich: constantly harassed by some pressing task, she hid her feelings for him (which he never doubted) behind an abrupt manner.[32] Similarly, children of fathers with low-paid and physically-exhausting jobs, such as coal-mining or farm labouring, gradually came to appreciate the affection for them that was involved in these efforts to provide for the family, even

---

[28] Theo Engelen, 'A Transition Prolonged: Demographic Aspects of the European Family', in Kertzer and Barbagli, *European Family*, vol. 3, pp. 273–308 (p. 299).

[29] Davidoff, 'Family in Britain', p. 126; Anna Davin, *Growing Up Poor: Home, School and Street in London 1870–1914*, London: Rivers Oram Press, 1996, pp. 40–3.

[30] Laura King, *Family Men: Fatherhood and Masculinity in Britain, c. 1914–1960* (Oxford: Oxford University Press, 2015), passim; Siân Pooley, 'Parenthood, Child-Rearing and Fertility in England, 1850–1914', *History of the Family*, 18 (2013), 83–106.

[31] Ellen Ross, *Love and Toil: Motherhood in Outcast London* (New York: Oxford University Press, 1993, pp. 128–9.

[32] Colin Heywood, *Growing Up in France: From the Ancien Régime to the Third Republic* (Cambridge: Cambridge University Press, 2007), p. 127.

if the fathers rarely showed it. As Julie-Marie Strange shows from a sample of British autobiographies, this was often a matter of male authors writing during the 1920s and 1930s, with their own experience of work, and shorter working hours, finally able to grasp the predicament of fathers in earlier generations.[33]

Besides, children in working-class neighbourhoods had little inclination to hang around their mother in their home. They preferred to play outside on the streets whenever possible, as they had done in the past. Middle-class parents often refused to allow their offspring to join poorer children playing outside, confining them to their homes, gardens and walks in the park. Toni Sender, born to a middle-class family in Frankfurt-am-Main, recalled that she was forbidden to play with 'less well-off children', even though she would have liked to do so.[34] Working-class mothers, by contrast, whether by choice or by force of circumstances, did not usually share this vision of domesticity. They were pleased to let their brood play outside, confident until well into the twentieth century that there was little danger from traffic, and that there were neighbours around to keep half an eye on them. As a Viennese worker put it, looking back to the turn of the twentieth century: 'We were all street kids. In those days everyone was just a street kid. We grew up in the alley, the street...' A man brought up in the working-class district of Favoriten in the city recalled that in the open spaces one could 'dig holes in the meadows, play Indians and trappers, shoot birds, play soccer, steal vegetables from the surrounding gardens'.[35] In London during this period children took advantage of the paving stones or asphalt to play marbles or hopscotch, used the walls for ball games, skipped or made swings if they had a rope and marked out football or cricket pitches on the road surface. There were also numerous diversions for them, such as street musicians, road works or perhaps on a Saturday night a fight between local drunks.[36] This was the children's part of the working-class communities that crystallised in urban areas during the late nineteenth century, providing an alternative path through childhood to the middle-class one. Louis Heren (b. 1919) described his slum parish in the

---

[33] Julie-Marie Strange, 'Fatherhood, Providing, and Attachment in Late Victorian and Edwardian Working-Class Families', *The Historical Journal*, 55 (2012), 1007–27.

[34] Marion A. Kaplan, *The Making of the Jewish Middle Class: Women, Family, and Identity in Imperial Germany* (Oxford: Oxford University Press, 1991), p. 60.

[35] Reinhard Sieder, '"Vata, derf i aufstehn?: Childhood Experiences in Viennese Working-Class Families around 1900', *Continuity and Change*, 1 (1986), 53–88 (62); J. Robert Wegs, *Growing Up Working Class: Continuity and Change among Viennese Youth, 1890–1938* (University Park, PA: Pennsylvania State University Press, 1989), p. 73.

[36] Davin, *Growing Up Poor*, pp. 63–68.

East End of London as a friendly place, where he could play on the streets in complete safety: 'Life was nearly always absorbing and often exciting. I never felt poor or deprived.'[37] Boys in particular enjoyed the freedom of the streets; girls were invariably expected to spend more time helping their mothers with housework or minding younger siblings. There were moves afoot from the 1860s onwards to provide playgrounds for city children, as a safer and more easily supervised space for them to play in, with some success. All the same, children generally preferred to stay out on the streets for as long as they were perceived to be safe.[38]

How children fared during the late twentieth century, with women's liberation, 'new fathers', and more fluid family forms much in evidence, is open to question. Some historians emphasise the disadvantages for children of the 'narcissistic parents of today, who often put their own happiness before that of their children', of the relative instability of relationships among cohabiting couples, of being left by working parents to fend for themselves for hours after school. There were also the disruptive effects of divorce for children to contend with: the 'custody battles, long-running emotional tug of wars and step-parents' now on a larger scale than earlier in the century.[39] Other observers welcome the increased opportunities for children to mix with others of their own age in nurseries, and to enjoy greater autonomy within the family. They also note that families increasingly expected both parents and children to have a right to self-fulfilment: in the words of François de Singly, children were neither kings nor martyrs.[40] A survey by sociologists of childhood in contemporary Europe noted the broad spectrum of experience emerging from recent changes in family life. At one end were wealthy families in which both parents continued to pursue a career, but were willing to devote considerable energy and resources to their children, including additional child care. The children become self-reliant as they 'learn to deal with (over)occupied parents and negotiate their own interests'. At

---

[37] Louis Heren, *Growing Up Poor in London* (London: Hamish Hamilton, 1973), pp. 9–10.

[38] Ning de Coninck-Smith, 'Geography and Environment', in Heywood, *Age of Empire*, pp. 73–90 (p. 82).

[39] David Gaunt and Louise Nyström, 'The Scandinavian Model', and Martine Segalen, 'The Industrial Revolution: From Proletariat to Bourgeoisie', in André Burguière et al. (eds.), *A History of the Family* (2 vols., Cambridge: Polity Press, 1996), vol. 2, pp. 476–501 (p. 501) and pp. 377–415 (p. 409), respectively; Joe L. Kincheloe, 'The Advent of a Postmodern Childhood', in Shirley R. Steinberg and Joe L. Kincheloe (eds.), *Kinderculture: The Corporate Construction of Childhood* (Boulder, CO: Westview Press, 1997), pp. 31–52 (pp. 31–3); Steve Humphries et al., *A Century of Childhood* (London: Sidgwick and Jackson, 1988), p. 58.

[40] François de Singly and Vincenzo Cicchelli, 'Contemporary Families: Social Reproduction and Personal Fulfillment', in Kertzer and Barbagli, *European Family*, vol. 3, pp. 311–49 (p. 340).

the other end, single mothers and other poor families were often struggling to make ends meet and lacked a worthwhile social life. Their children were vulnerable to emotional as well material deprivation, and their future prospects in life were not good.[41] Doubtless, for all the striking changes in family life, the forces of inertia remained strong. To take one important indicator, the study of child well-being in rich countries, from 2007, revealed that everywhere in Europe at least two-thirds of children in a sample of fifteen-year-olds usually ate meals with their parents. Italy and France stood out in the continuation of this tradition.[42] Given the evidence that a loving relationship with the family is the key to children's happiness, the dire warnings of widespread misery among children in the early twenty-first century may be exaggerated, although not entirely without foundation.

Marginal and Excluded Children

A mixed group of children existed on the margins of society, pitied but also feared (and even loathed) by the majority, especially when confronted by dirty, foul-mouthed specimens on the streets. The Italian magistrate Giuseppe Cesare Pola proclaimed to a congress in 1912 that 'It is time that our beautiful 100 cities be freed of those bands of insolent, disruptive, ragged guttersnipes who infest our streets, perennial insult to the proud triumphs of modern civilization.'[43] The orphaned, the abandoned, the destitute, the homeless and the delinquent were all at risk of neglect in the twentieth century as in the past. The 1933 Children's Act in Britain had good grounds for playing down the distinctions and referring instead to all those 'in need of care and protection'.[44] Under it all, these were the children of the very poor, 'often stunted in body and mind' by their early experiences.

The composition of the group changed somewhat during the twentieth century. The classic abandonment of newborn babies, so common during earlier periods in Catholic Europe, soon disappeared, as the whole apparatus of turning-wheels, foundling homes and wet nurses fell

---

[41] Manuela du Bois-Reymond, Heinz Sünker, and Heinz-Hermann Krüger, 'Childhood Research, the Politics of Childhood, and Children's Lives in Europe: An Introduction', in Manuela du Bois-Reymond et al., *Childhood in Europe: Approaches – Trends – Findings* (New York, NY: Peter Lang, 2001), pp. 1–12 (pp. 2–3).
[42] UNICEF, 'Child Poverty', pp. 23–4, figures 4.2a and 4.2b.
[43] As cited in Ipsen, *Italy in the Age of Pinocchio*, p. 166.
[44] Harry Hendrick, *Child Welfare: Historical Dimensions, Contemporary Debate* (Bristol: Policy Press, 2003), p. 118.

into disrepute with the infant welfare movement.[45] The ranks of street children were soon thinned out in north-western Europe by laws on street trading, compulsory education and the efforts of school attendance officers, though this happened much later in the south and east. And the number of orphans declined in the long run, as parents came to live longer, with interruptions from very obvious spikes during the two world wars. This still left large contingents of children 'morally abandoned' by negligent or abusive parents, stranded in families too poor to support them, or sentenced to some form of correction by the criminal justice system. There were also the huge numbers of children displaced during the twentieth century by government action, including exchanges of population between states, evacuations, deportations and expulsion on the basis of ethnicity.[46]

The general drift of welfare policy in both western Europe and in the Communist countries was to treat children on the margins of society more sympathetically than in the past, considering them as victims of their circumstances rather than simply as a threat to good order. Witness the appearance early in the twentieth century of special juvenile courts (or child welfare boards in the Nordic countries); the spread of child guidance clinics from the 1920s; the general desire to remove children from large, impersonal institutions; the reining back on corporal punishment; the aim to rehabilitate, educate and train juvenile delinquents rather than punish them; and a strategy of supporting children within their families instead of attempting to cut all links with a supposedly corrupting environment. What Jacques Donzelot described as '*le social*' (the social sector), the judges, doctors, psychiatrists, teachers and social workers responsible for child welfare, grew in numbers and influence in France in particular, but also everywhere else in Europe.[47] The forces of inertia were strong, however, and there was always a countercurrent in favour of coercive measures to deal with children seen as vagabonds or criminals. 'Therapeutic models' to treat young offenders did not always meet expectations: thus even in Sweden there was a crisis concerning them during the 1950s and 1960s following a steep increase in crime rates.[48] The thefts which children were associated with made

---

[45] See Chapter 6.

[46] Nick Baron, 'Placing the Child in Twentieth Century History: Contexts and Framework', in Nick Baron (ed.), *Displaced Children in Russia and Eastern Europe, 1915–1953: Ideologies, Identities, Experiences* (Leiden: Brill, 2017), pp. 1–39.

[47] Jacques Donzelot, *The Policing of Families: Welfare versus the State*, transl. Robert Hurley (London: Hutchison, 1979), pp. 88–9.

[48] Matti Joutson, 'Treatment, Punishment, Control: Juvenile Delinquency in Scandinavia', in Albert G. Hess and Priscilla F. Clement (eds.), *History of Juvenile Delinquency: A Collection of Essays on Crime Committed by Young Offenders in History* (2 vols., Aalen: Scientia Verlag, 1993), vol. 1, pp. 599–623 (p. 609).

delinquents unpopular with the general public. Hence moves to emphasise rehabilitation were met by calls in Soviet Russia during the 1930s to
stop 'pussyfooting around', and in Britain from the Prime Minister
(Margaret Thatcher) during the 1980s to 'condemn a little more and
understand a little less'.[49] As in the nineteenth century, voluntary organisations continued to play a prominent role, at least in the non-
Communist world. In the Federal Republic of Germany, in 1959,
73 per cent of all welfare services were delivered by charities.[50]

Street Children

Most visible for the population at large, to begin with at least, were the
street children of the big cities. It was possible to admire them for their
independence and sense of humour. However, 'respectable' members of
society, who were often jostled, importuned or robbed by these youngsters, generally viewed them with a jaundiced eye. They were after all a
challenge to the conventional childhood of the middle classes, centred on
the home and the school. The language used to describe them, with
names such as street arabs, vermin, young apaches and savages, showed
the widespread contempt for their way of life. Of particular concern to
philanthropists, and eventually the state, was the predicament of the
homeless. The story is well known of how Dr Barnardo first became
aware of their plight in London when one of their number, Jim Jarvis,
led him to a group sleeping rough on a cold night during the winter of
1869/70.[51] Homelessness on a far larger scale erupted later in Russia, as
children fell victim to hurried evacuations during World War I, the
1917 revolutions, civil war and the Volga famine. By the early 1920s,
at least seven million of them had been made homeless. Nearly all of
these *besprizorniki* had a peasant or working-class background, and were
either orphans or semi-orphans. They were generally aged between ten
and fifteen, and a little over half were male. Some were inveterate
travellers, criss-crossing the country in search of better conditions or a
change of scenery. They concealed themselves on ships and trains to
avoid paying: one lad who hid under the locomotive described how 'It
was like a bath-house there, but I didn't climb out [at stops]. You can't

---

[49] Kelly, *Children's World*, p. 230; Hendrick, *Child Welfare*, p. 190.
[50] Dickinson, *German Child Welfare*, p. 278.
[51] Gillian Wagner, *Barnardo* (London: Weidenfeld and Nicolson, 1979), pp. 27–34; Hugh
Cunningham, *The Children of the Poor: Representations of Childhood since the Seventeenth
Century* (Oxford: Blackwell, 1991), ch. 5.

do this because you may return too late and find new passengers in your place.'[52] Like street children elsewhere in Europe, the *besprizorniki* often formed into groups to improve their chances of survival, with a strict and even brutal hierarchical order, and their own hideouts and jargon. A contemporary described groups of children in Russia roaming the streets 'with gnomelike, filthy faces, childish eyes, shaggy hair, men's long overcoats, trousers pinned up or cut and ragged'. They congregated in particular areas of the big cities, notably central squares, railway stations and markets, with the latter providing plenty of food to pilfer and customers laden with cash, bags and bundles of goods.[53] Sadly, a further spike in homelessness and neglect occurred in the Soviet Union during World War II, when over one million children ended up on the streets.[54]

Children in Care

How to care for destitute children, whether orphaned, abandoned, or beyond the means of their family, proved particularly contentious in England during the second half of the nineteenth century. The country's heavy reliance on the workhouse system under the New Poor Law led to a fierce debate between, on the one hand, officials favouring huge training schools for hundreds of pauper children and, on the other, reformers countering with a 'family system'. The former insisted on the benefits of creating special institutions for children, to separate them from the corrupting influence of adult paupers, and laying on a programme orientated towards vocational training and moral discipline. A handful of large District Schools duly appeared on this model by mid-century, mainly in the big cities. Their critics argued that these 'barrack schools' imposed deadly dull routines on their inmates, and smothered any sense of individuality in their bid for economies of scale. An influential report by Jane Senior, commissioned in 1873 by the Local Government Board, argued these points forcefully, and supported the 'family system' in the form of 'cottage homes'. In the event, it was private charities that first adopted the 'family system' most wholeheartedly.

---

[52] Allan M. Ball, *And Now My Soul Is Hardened: Abandoned Children in Soviet Russia, 1918–1930* (Berkeley, CA: University of California Press, 1994), pp. 25–8.

[53] Jennie A. Stevens, 'Children of the Revolution: Soviet Russia's Homeless Children (*Besprizorniki*) in the 1920s', *Russian History*, 9 (1982), 242–64; Margaret K. Stolee, 'Homeless Children in the USSR, 1917–1957', *Soviet Studies*, 40 (1988), 64–83; Ball, *Abandoned Children in Russia*, passim; Kelly, *Children's World*, p. 201.

[54] Olga Kucherenko, *Soviet Street Children and the Second World War: Welfare and Social Control under Stalin* (London: Bloomsbury, 2016).

Dr Barnardo (1854–1905), for instance, tried to recreate a family atmosphere for the girls in his care by setting up a series of cottages with 16–20 inmates, supervised by a 'Mother'. Poor Law officials took a number of initiatives along these lines. They set up cottage homes either in special villages, or scattered across whole communities (to avoid isolation) in the 'Sheffield System'. By 1908, around a third of pauper children were living in these homes, and a further 18 per cent were boarded out with families. At this point, the local authorities were providing a standard of care that the philanthropic societies could rarely match, based on the professionalism of their staff as opposed to the charisma of the founders of successful charities such as Dr Barnardo or Benjamin Waugh (1839–1908).[55] There were also schemes from the philanthropists and Poor Law Guardians to send destitute children to new homes in the colonies of the British Empire, especially to farming families in Australia, New Zealand, South Africa and above all Canada. The assumption was the familiar one that the rural way of life was superior to the urban one, and hence that the children would have a better chance of becoming useful citizens if removed from the corrupting influence of the slums and their pauperised families. Between 1868 and 1925, no less than 80,000 boys and girls emigrated to Canada under these conditions, to work as indentured agricultural labourers or domestic servants. Most of these 'home children' were under 14 years of age, and only around a third were orphans; the rest were nonetheless unaccompanied by parents, a small minority even going without parental consent, following the notorious 'philanthropic abductions' by Dr Barnardo and others.[56]

Everywhere in Europe the established custom of boarding out children in need of care continued, subject to the constraint of finding suitable host families. The Scottish Parochial Board, the central body responsible for poor relief in Scotland, stood out for its commitment to this approach. Unlike its English counterpart, it only placed children in a poorhouse if it could not find them a home: by 1910, 90 per cent of

---

[55] Felix Driver, *Power and Pauperism: The Workhouse System, 1834–1884* (Cambridge: Cambridge University Press, 1993), pp. 94–105; Lydia Murdoch, *Imagined Orphans: Poor Families, Child Welfare, and Contested Citizenship in London* (New Brunswick, NJ: Rutgers University Press, 2006), ch. 2; Shurlee Swain and Margot Hillel, *Child, Nation, Race and Empire: Child Rescue Discourse, England, Canada and Australia, 1850–1915* (Manchester and New York: Manchester University Press, 2010), ch. 7; Nicola Sheldon, '"Something in the Place of Home": Children in Institutional Care 1850–1918', in Nigel Goose and Katrina Honeyman, *Childhood and Child Labour in Industrial England: Diversity and Agency, 1750–1914*, Farnham: Ashgate, 2013, pp. 255–76.

[56] Joy Parr, *Labouring Children: British Immigrant Apprentices to Canada, 1869–1924* (London: Croom Helm, 1980), ch. 2; Swain and Hillel, *Child, Nation, Race*, ch. 6.

pauper children in its care had been placed with a foster family. Its policy of placing children from the big cities with farmers and crofters in rural areas, including ones as distant as the Highlands and the Outer Hebrides, was not without its abuses. But it now looks enlightened by the standards of the day (as well as being cost effective), and was admired in countries as far afield as Russia.[57]

The upshot across Europe during the first half of the twentieth century was a variety of institutions caring for children, including orphanages, refuges from the streets, workhouses and industrial schools, in addition to foster families. Shortages of resources and therefore of places was a common and persistent theme. There were also mixed results for the children concerned, ranging from a fresh start in life to serious abuse. Fostering, and later adoption, provided a family environment most successfully, though it could go badly wrong if the new parents were unsuited to their task. The children sent out from Britain to the colonies faced the most daunting conditions of all. Experience on the farms of southern Ontario and western Quebec soon shattered any illusions that they would settle in comfortably as members of their host families. The relationship with the household was a contractual one, and, predictably enough, an enquiry in 1875 by a Canadian official revealed widespread overwork and abuse. The children were shown to be poorly supervised by the authorities and ill-prepared for their jobs.[58] Wrenched from their families, and accustomed to the hustle and bustle of their institutions in Britain, they struggled with feelings of loneliness and boredom on the farms, not to mention hostility from the local population to the foreign (and possibly criminal) paupers. Most of the emigrants who wrote about their childhood put on a brave face for the public, but did not hide the ups and downs of their existence. Michael Driscoll left England in 1913 at the age of eight and went to work for a farmer in Ontario. He was given to understand that 'an orphan was the lowest type of person on earth just about' and was treated as such with frequent kickings and beatings. Fortunately for him his next employer was 'a very nice family', with the wife a schoolteacher who helped him with his reading and writing.[59]

---

[57] Wagner, *Barnardo*, ch. 5; Hendrick, *Child Welfare*, pp. 40–9; Lynn Abrams, *The Orphan Country: Children of Scotland's Broken Homes from 1845 to the Present* (Edinburgh: John Donald, 1998), ch. 2; Kelly, *Children's World*, p. 177.

[58] Parr, *Labouring Children*, pp. 51–2.

[59] Parr, *Labouring Children*, passim; Swain and Hillel, *Child, Nation, Race*, chs. 6 and 8; Phyllis Harrison (ed.), *The Home Children: Their Personal Stories* (Winnipeg, Manitoba: Watson and Dwyer Publishing, 1979), pp. 160–2.

TRANSFORMATION SCENES IN REAL LIFE
EFFECTS OF THE EAST END JUVENILE MISSION

"PLEASE 'M, DO YOU TAKE IN POOR LITTLE GIRLS?"   AN INDUSTRIOUS LITTLE MAID
A GIRL BEFORE AND AFTER RECLAMATION

Figure 9.2 Victorian child poverty. Depiction of a poor girl begging on the street and as a maid after being saved from poverty. Getty Images, 471194563.

At the outset, most institutions in Europe attempted some form of vocational training, usually in menial trades such as carpentry and tailoring for boys, and textile work or domestic service for girls. No less importantly, they set out to instil the appropriate attitudes for a subservient workforce, requiring a regimented and highly disciplined existence. There was always the risk that street children would desert such schemes and return to the more exciting life in their old haunts. The desire to provide a training for the inmates often came up against the need to maximise the income from their work. Moreover, securing jobs for children when they left the various institutions was not always easy. Evidence from London reveals that the training children in care received was often of poor quality and based on a vision of a harmonious pre-industrial society that was fast disappearing around 1900. The institutions involved therefore soon concentrated on the schooling of those in their care until they reached adolescence (Figure 9.2).[60]

---

[60] Murdoch, *Imagined Orphans*, ch. 5.

In England, Harry Hendrick concludes that little change occurred in the care of institutionalised children between the late nineteenth century and the 1940s, the regimes being characterised by 'neglect, insensitivity and violence'. Charlie Chaplin (1889–1977) recalled in his autobiography his time in the Hanwell Schools for Orphans and Destitute Children, stating that he was well looked after, yet 'it was a forlorn existence'. Besides the regimentation, monotony and impersonal care of such institutions, the Poor Law children (as opposed to those cared for by voluntary societies) were subject to harsh discipline. Chaplin described the grim ritual every Friday morning at Hanwell of canings and birchings of those who broke the rules, witnessed in the gym by all of the pupils.[61] Despite such conditions, the poor in London persisted in seeking out places for their children in workhouses or charitable institutions as a desperate measure to hold their families together in the long term, when help from family and friends had been exhausted. Indeed, despite Dr Barnardo's emphasis on his forays during the night to rescue orphans from the streets, in most cases it was parents (or even some of the older children themselves) who made the first approach for a place.[62]

In Russia, the main problem was the sheer weight of numbers of children in need of help during recurrent periods of war and famine. During the late nineteenth and early twentieth centuries the response came largely from philanthropic initiatives, as in the West, aiming to improve both the health and the morals of such children. After the Revolution in 1917 'bourgeois philanthropy' was out of favour, and after a short period of 'revolutionary utopianism and elemental chaos' during the difficult period 1917 to 1922, the state began to force the homeless into closed institutions, imposing a more regimented existence on those in its care. The Soviet state itself exacerbated the problems, with such policies as the collectivisation of agriculture and the campaign against the *kulaks* (the allegedly wealthier peasants). The harsh conditions in the labour camps to which many of the *kulak* families were sent meant that their children 'died in droves'.[63]

---

[61] Hendrick, *Child Welfare*, p. 123; Linda Mahood, *Policing Gender, Class and Family: Britain, 1850–1940* (London: UCL Press, 1995), pp. 121–2; Charles Chaplin, *My Autobiography* (New York, NY: Simon and Schuster, 1964), pp. 29–30.

[62] Murdoch, *Imagined Orphans*, ch. 3.

[63] Stevens, 'Children of the Revolution', passim; Kelly, *Children's World*, chs. 5–6; Kaznelson and Baron, 'Memories of Displacement', pp. 97–130.

Delinquent Children

Children who fell foul of the law, or were considered in danger of doing so, were particularly exposed to harsh treatment. By the late nineteenth century, the flaws inherent in 'correctional education', removing delinquent children from their families for treatment in agricultural colonies and other reformatories, were much in evidence. Above all there was the contradiction between punishment and education, with the long hours of work, limited leisure time, and strict regimentation all too often provoking discipline problems, including riots, and a brutal response from hard-pressed and ill-trained staff. Yet it continued to be widely used, with a huge expansion in Prussia, for example, during the early twentieth century.[64] Worse was to come under the Nazis: at Breitenau, a reformatory of last resort in northern Hesse, an established strategy of breaking the will of its inmates through 'work and short rations' was pushed to the limits under the pressure of cost cutting, all too often proving fatal. Meanwhile, in Soviet Russia experiments with labour camps to reform delinquents in their early teens met with stiff resistance from the inmates, leading to the end of all attempts to rehabilitate under the Stalinist regime.[65]

After World War II there was a general movement across Europe to abandon correctional education, supporting the younger children within their families as far as possible, or at least finding foster homes for them, attempting rehabilitation through child guidance clinics, and leaving custodial sentences as a last resort. Finally, it seems, the ruling elites recognised that most crimes committed by children were relatively insignificant, and their involvement in criminal activity episodic. Instead of 'delinquents', the professionals involved talked of 'antisocial behaviour' and 'maladjustment'; a moralistic discourse gave way to medical and psychological diagnoses.[66] In the Federal Republic of Germany, a reaction against the repressive approach of the Nazis was much in

---

[64] Dietrich Oberwittler, 'The Decline of Correctional Education, ca. 1900–1920. England and Germany Compared', *European Journal of Crime, Criminal Law and Criminal Justice*, 7 (1999), 22–40.

[65] Nick Stargardt, *Witnesses of War: Children's Lives under the Nazis* (London: Jonathan Cape, 2005), pp. 59–68; Peter H. Juviler, 'Contradictions of Revolution: Juvenile Crime and Rehabilitation', in Abbott Gleason, Peter Kenez and Richard Stites (eds.), *Bolshevik Culture* (Bloomington, IN: Indiana University Press, 1985), pp. 261–78.

[66] Frieder Dünkel, 'Legal Differences in Juvenile Criminal Criminology in Europe', in Tim Booth (ed.), *Juvenile Justice in the New Europe* (Sheffield: Social Services Monographs: Research in Practice, 1991), pp. 1–29; Kaisa Vehhkalahti, 'Notions of Parenting and the Home in the Institutional Care of Delinquent Girls in Finland, 1920s–1940s', in Hester Barron and Claudia Siebrecht (eds.) *Parenting and the State in Britain and Europe, c. 1870–1950* (Basingstoke: Palgrave Macmillan, 2017), pp. 161–82 (pp. 173 and 176).

evidence from the 1950s onwards. There was a shift to preventive methods, especially the counselling of families and children by psycho-therapists, known in Germany as 'educational counselling'. Reformatories moved towards 'free' methods, with smaller, better-staffed 'homes', organised on a 'family like' basis, replacing large, impersonal institutions.[67] In France, a law passed in 1945 stated that the 'Children's Court will pronounce measures of protection, assistance, supervision, education, or reform that it deems appropriate to each case.' In a number of French 'public institutions for supervised education', the inmates learned a trade or prepared for exams, enjoyed various leisure facilities and in return for good behaviour were allowed out to go to the cinema or a dance. Unfortunately, there was the familiar decline into a more repressive atmosphere as the initial crusading zeal wore off. Many female offenders in France during the 1940s and early 1950s continued to languish in oppressive conditions. This was especially the case if they were confined in a state-run 'public preservation school', with drab uniforms, hair cut short in 'Joan of Arc' style, and long hours of work. Eventually, the French followed the general trend in Europe to 'deinstitutionalise', with only around 1 per cent of minors sent to institutions by 1982.[68]

Rehabilitating young offenders was still no easy matter, with high rates of recidivism and populist calls for a 'boot camp' approach difficult to overcome. European countries generally remained committed to the therapeutic rather than the coercive end of the spectrum, despite various scandals during the 1990s, such as the murder of the toddler Jamie Bulger by two ten-year-old boys in England, and concerns over the threats to public order from a new 'underclass' of socially-excluded youth. Moreover, legislation introduced by a Conservative government in 1994 planned new prisons for twelve- to fourteen-year-olds, in flagrant disregard of the United Nations 1989 Convention on the Rights of the Child (UNCRC). And New Labour, eager to prove that it was 'tough on crime, tough on the causes of crime', continued the drift towards retribution and punishment for juveniles. Its 1998 Crime and Disorder Act abolished the old-established defence of *Doli Incapax* for ten- to thirteen-year-olds, and, more seriously, further encouraged the locking up of children over the age of twelve.[69]

---

[67] Dickinson, *German Child Welfare*, pp. 254–61.

[68] Sarah Fishman, *The Battle for Children: World War II, Youth Crime, and Juvenile Justice in Twentieth-Century France* (Cambridge, MA: Harvard University Press, 2002), ch. 6; Ivan Jablonka, *Les Enfants de la République: l'intégration des jeunes de 1789 à nos jours* (Paris: Seuil, 2010), ch. 10.

[69] Hendrick, *Child Welfare*, pp. 189–92, 226–34.

Conclusion

A number of scholars have noted the scandal, evident in this chapter, of children in need of care and protection suffering from appalling ill-treatment in institutions that were supposed to rescue and rehabilitate them. As Harry Ferguson puts it, one might expect that children who had been abused or neglected would be treated with care and compassion, yet in the case of the Irish industrial schools that he studied, they were often 'routinely starved, beaten, humiliated, sexually abused, deprived of education ... and their emotional needs were often totally neglected'.[70] The underlying problem was the way such unfortunates were seen in a society where the prevailing view was that the child was born innocent. If all went well, the 'normal' family and the school would provide an environment to preserve such innocence, with the physical, moral and intellectual welfare of their charges the main concern. However, if the child grew up in the corrupting environment of an abusive or negligent family, and acquired knowledge of supposedly adult matters such as thieving (for boys especially) and sexuality (for girls), then they themselves became contaminated and hence a danger to the others around them. On the one side then, there was the ideal of the protected child in the family, on the other, the demonisation of the street arab, the 'fallen' or 'vicious' girl, the pauper in the workhouse. For the latter, judged as morally deficient rather than in need of therapy, the way to restore their innocence was knock the Old Adam out of them by means of a harsh regime. Hence the counter-intuitive argument that children in institutions such as the industrial schools were treated harshly *because* they were victims of cruelty.[71]

---

[70] Harry Ferguson, 'Abused and Looked After Children as "Moral Dirt": Child Abuse and Institutional Care in Historical Perspective', *Journal of Social Policy*, 36 (2007), 123–39 (124 and 130).

[71] Ferguson, 'Child Abuse', 130. See also Louise A. Jackson, *Child Sexual Abuse in Victorian England* (London: Routledge, 2000), pp. 6–7; Swain and Hillel, *Child, Nation, Race*, passim.

10 Growing Up during the Twentieth Century, Part 2
Light and Shade in an Affluent Society

By the 1950s and 1960s, it could be said with some justification, that children in Europe, no less than adults, had never had it so good. Over the previous century, the young had nearly all given up full-time work for school, were generally better fed, clothed and housed than in the past, and had improved mortality rates. It was widely assumed that child poverty would soon be a thing of the past, eradicated by further economic growth and spending on welfare. But from the perspective of the early twenty-first century, one can see that this latter vision was only partially realised. Joseph Hawes and Ray Hiner note the 'tragic failures' that need to be weighed against the progress that was made: 'Wars, economic depression, exploitation, commodification, abuse and ethnic, racial, gender and class discrimination all damaged the lives of children and families in the twentieth century.'[1] The powerful surge of growth in the economy in the wake of World War II faltered from the 1970s onwards. Welfare states proved to be very expensive, and the problem of balancing security for unemployed families with the work incentive difficult to resolve. And, most important of all, persistent social inequality in some countries led to fears of an under-class denied the opportunity to succeed in school and in a career. Meanwhile the Communist system in eastern Europe gradually collapsed, depriving families of the modicum of security it provided, and forcing them to make a difficult adaptation to a market economy. Childhood in the twentieth century was clearly a matter of contrasting light and shade. In this chapter, we examine the record on children's health and mortality, which was generally positive, their experiences in an age of mass consumption, where there were some concerns over their welfare, and the impact of two world wars, which was disastrous for many of them.

---

[1] Joseph M. Hawes and N. Ray Hiner, (eds.) *Introduction to a Cultural History of Childhood and Family in the Modern Age* (Oxford: Berg, 2010), pp. 1–20 (p. 1).

The Economic and Social Context

The twentieth century brought unprecedented rates of economic growth to Europe, lifting per capita incomes in all parts of the continent. The process started with a period of relatively modest but sustained growth before World War I. The years 1913–1950 were marred by a series of setbacks caused by wars and depression, leading to low rates of growth overall. By contrast, the period 1950 to 1973 was one of unprecedented expansion. Paul Bairoch calculates that during the 28 years between 1947 and 1975, per capita incomes made more progress than in the previous 175 years.[2] After what the French call the *'trentes glorieuses'* ('the thirty glorious years') that followed World War II, growth once again slowed from the 1970s. From an annual average growth rate of 4.05 per cent a year in 1950–73, western Europe decelerated to 1.88 per cent in 1973–2001. The decline was even sharper in eastern Europe and the former USSR, as their political and economic systems began to collapse. During the post-1945 golden age they had more-or-less kept up with growth rates in the west, but after that there was an actual decline in the former USSR economy.[3]

In long-term perspective, children undoubtedly benefitted from the higher standard of living characteristic of the second half of the twentieth century. Those living in the West in particular had a better chance of, among other things, a more nourishing diet, a room of their own, and access to educational resources in the form of computers and school textbooks. The associated decline in mortality also meant that it became normal for them to grow up with grandparents, uncles, aunts and cousins still alive: kin remained important at all social levels.[4] At the same time, a series of UNICEF reports on child poverty in rich countries after the year 2000 revealed that no country in Europe could rest complacent in this sphere. They noted that the industrialised nations had come to recognise

---

[2] Paul Bairoch, 'Europe's Gross National Product: 1800–1975', *Journal of European Economic History*, 5 (1976), 273–340; Gerold Ambrosius and William H. Hubbard, *A Social and Economic History of Twentieth-Century Europe* (Cambridge, MA: Harvard University Press, 1989), pp. 135–47.

[3] Angus Maddison, *The World Economy: A Millennial Perspective* (Paris: OECD, 2001), pp. 33–49, 125–160; idem, *The World Economy: Historical Statistics* (Paris: OECD, 2003), p. 263, table 8b.

[4] Angélique Janssens, 'Economic Transformation, Women's Work, and Family Life', in David I. Kertzer and Marzio Barbagli, *The History of the European Family* (New Haven, CT: Yale University Press, c. 2001–3), vol. 3, pp. 55–110 (p. 66).

the complexities of poverty.[5] Hence, besides income, the reports investigated health, housing, family relationships, experience of violence, educational achievements and children's overall satisfaction with themselves and their lives.[6] By the end of the twentieth century, the 'rich' countries of Europe had developed sufficiently to make relative rather than absolute child poverty their main concern. The exceptions were three countries still struggling with their communist inheritance: Poland, Hungary and the Czech Republic. Poverty as a relative state involved living in a household where in the UNICEF study the equivalent income was taken as less than 50 per cent of the national median.[7] In this case, Italy and the United Kingdom came near the bottom of the table in 2000, with over 15 per cent of their children in relative poverty. Both were wealthy countries, but the latter in particular stood out for its commitment to free markets during the 1980s and 1990s, trading equality for growth. (As the Report wryly observed, ministries of finance set targets for growth, leaving ministries of social affairs to pick up the pieces.) The problem with a high level of relative poverty is its impact on equality of opportunity, considered important in an industrialised economy. At the other end of the spectrum, the Nordic countries of Denmark, Sweden, Norway and Finland had a consistently good record, with less than 5 per cent of their children in relative poverty.[8] The obvious conclusion, given the strongly welfarist tendencies of these countries, was that 'Higher government spending on family and social benefits is associated with lower child poverty rates.'[9]

Finally, there was the predicament of ethnic and racial minorities in Europe to take into account. The second half of the twentieth century brought a significant modification to the composition of the population, caused by large waves of immigration. These gained impetus in the wake of World War II, when various countries welcomed supplies of cheap labour to help reconstruct their economies. Some relied on their Imperial heritage, with Britain turning above all to the West Indies, India and Pakistan for its immigrants, the Netherlands to Indonesia, the former Dutch East Indies, and Surinam. Others looked to their neighbours, as Germany relied on Turkey and Yugoslavia, Sweden on Finland, and later Yugoslavia, Greece and Turkey. Naturally, some

---

[5] UNICEF Innocenti Research Centre, Florence, Italy, 'Child Poverty in Perspective: An Overview of Child Well-Being in Rich Countries', Innocenti Report Card no. 1, June 2000, 'A league table of child poverty in rich nations', pp. 5–6.
[6] UNICEF Innocenti Research Centre, 'Child Poverty', p. 9.
[7] A more common figure is 60 per cent.
[8] UNICEF Innocenti Research Centre, 'Child Poverty', pp. 4–11.
[9] UNICEF Innocenti Research Centre, 'Child Poverty, 2005', p. 2.

workers brought their families with them; others produced children after they had arrived. By the late 1970s, there were 820,000 Algerians in France, including 130,000 children under 16 years of age. To begin with, the child migrants attracted little attention, as it was widely assumed that they and their parents would soon return home. However, this assumption soon proved to be wrong, and the immigrants had to face widespread hostility from the local populations. During the 1970s, the easy entry of the post-war years ended, and attention shifted from the adult workers among the immigrants to their children. A sociological study of the young in the infamous *banlieues* around Paris and Lyon during the 1980s concluded that the common experience of the young immigrant was to be pushed out to the periphery of the big cities, to live in poverty and to struggle with boredom and feelings of being trapped in a despised underclass. Those with an Algerian background had a reputation for being particularly hard to assimilate, right through to the end of the century. As far as the authorities were concerned, they were likely to turn out badly, as delinquents, drug dealers or rioters.[10] With the benefit of hindsight, one can see that the experience of immigrants from, say, Turkey, Algeria, Nigeria, India and China, not to mention those moving from other European countries such as Portugal and Greece, varied in the host countries, both within and between such groups. Nonetheless, there is no doubting the struggles of many children among the minorities in important areas such as housing, education and leisure.

Health and Mortality

The Decline of Infant and Child Mortality

Among the improvements in the material welfare of children during the late-nineteenth and twentieth centuries, better health was of particular importance. The rapid decline in infant mortality from the years 1895–1905 onwards was one important indicator of this development. To begin with, infant mortality rates were in the range of around 100 to 250 per thousand live births in the various European countries.[11] By the early twenty-first century, the rates had fallen to below five per thousand in many of them. Nonetheless, there were a few outliers in eastern Europe, notably Romania with a rate of 21.6 and the Russian Federation

---

[10] Robin Cohen, 'East-West and European Migration in a Global Context', *New Community*, 18 (1991), 9–26 (15–16); Ivan Jablonka, *Les Enfants de la République: l'intégration des jeunes de 1789 à nos jours* (Paris: Editions du Seuil, 2010), ch. 11.
[11] See Chapter 6.

with a rate of 117.7 in 2002.[12] Child mortality also declined, starting in this case during the second half of the nineteenth century. Statistics in this area are difficult to assemble during the early period, but it appears that during the first half of the nineteenth century approximately one child in three never reached the age of five.[13] By 2003, this under-five mortality rate (deaths per thousand live births) had fallen to single figures in most European countries.[14]

Towards a Multi-Causal Explanation

Finding explanations for this rapid decline in mortality, and corresponding improvement in child health, has proved challenging. Thomas McKeown convincingly overthrew an established orthodoxy in this area during the 1960s and 1970s, demonstrating that advances in medical science were not responsible for the long-term decline in overall mortality during the eighteenth and nineteenth centuries. Effective immunisation and therapy to cope with diseases that took a heavy toll on infant life such as tuberculosis, whooping cough and intestinal infections, all historians would now agree, were simply unavailable until the mid-twentieth century. In any case, medical services during this period were generally pitched at adults rather than children.[15] McKeown's alternative explanation for the decline, the 'invisible hand' of a rise in the standard of living and the improved nutrition that went with it, has found few takers. It appears particularly unsuited to the case of infant mortality, given its sudden decline at a late stage after 1900.[16] Historians have now generally moved on from the type of monocausal explanation proposed by

[12] Michel Poulain and Dominique Tabutin, 'La Mortalité aux jeunes âges en Europe et en Amérique du Nord du XIXe siècle à nos jours', in Paul-Marie Boulanger, Dominique Tabutin and Eduardo E. Arriaga (eds.), *La Mortalité des enfants dans le monde et dans l'histoire* (Liège: Ordina, 1980), pp. 119–157; Carlo A. Corsini and Pier Paolo Viazzo, 'The Historical Decline of Infant Mortality', in Corsini and Viazzo *Decline of Infant Mortality*, pp. 9–17; Catherine Rollet, 'The Fight against Infant Mortality in the Past: An International Comparison', in Alain Bideau, Bertrand Desjardins and Hector Pérez Brignoli (eds.), *Infant and Child Mortality in the Past* (Oxford: Clarendon Press, 1997), pp. 38–60; www.data.worldbank.org/indicator/SP.DYN.IMRT.IN, accessed 25 August 2015.
[13] Poulain and Tabutin, 'La Mortalité aux jeunes âges', p. 125.
[14] World Health Organization [WHO], The European Health Report 2005. Public Health Action for Healthier Children and Populations, p. 50, figure 5.
[15] Siân Pooley, '"All We Parents Want Is that Our Children's Health and Lives Should Be Regarded": Child Health and Parental Concern, c. 1860–1910', *Social History of Medicine*, 23 (2010), 528–48 (543–4).
[16] Thomas McKeown, *The Modern Rise of Population* (London: Edward Arnold, 1976); Simon Szreter, 'The Importance of Social Intervention in Britain's Mortality Decline c. 1850–1914: A Re-Interpretation of the Role of Public Health', *Social History of*

McKeown. A detailed study of infant mortality in England and Wales for the period 1861–1921, for example, highlighted a number of factors: a decline in fertility from the 1870s; long-term improvements in the level of women's education; the 'health of towns' movement; campaigns to improve the milk supply and food quality; the availability of more qualified midwives; and the establishment of antenatal care and a health visitor service.[17]

The influence on infant and child mortality of public health measures in towns during the late nineteenth and early twentieth centuries is hard to dispute. It is now generally agreed that in most countries industrialisation brought higher wages for workers, but also crowded living conditions that were disastrous for their health.[18] What was needed was a direct response to tackle such problems as slum housing, adulterated food and inadequate sanitation. Britain led the way during the middle of the nineteenth century with various pioneering efforts, as might be expected from its precocious urbanisation. But real progress there had to await the 1870s, with, for example, legislation that made local authorities responsible for pure water supplies and established inspectors and public analysts to monitor the quality of the food supply. Other nations followed suit: in Germany, for example, there was a spate of building centralised water systems in the larger German towns during the 1870s and 1880s, and, later, networks of sewers.[19] These public health measures were particularly effective in curbing water- and food-borne diseases that afflicted children, such as cholera and typhoid.

The Infant Welfare Movement

Yet during the last third of the nineteenth century, infant mortality remained stubbornly high. Ruling elites across Europe became concerned about this heavy loss of young lives, motivated more by the implications for the political, economic and military strength of their countries than by any humanitarianism. The general inclination to blame supposedly feckless mothers in the poorer sections of society for this running sore continued from earlier in the century, with accusations that

    Medicine, 1 (1988), 1–37; Catherine Rollet-Echalier, *La Politique à l'égard de la petite enfance sous la IIIe République* (2 vols., Paris: INED/PUF, 1990), vol. 1, p. 6.

[17] R. I. Woods, P. A. Watterson and J. H. Woodward, 'The Causes of Rapid Infant Mortality Decline in England and Wales, 1861–1921. Part II', *Population Studies*, 43 (1989), 113–32 (130).

[18] See Chapter 6.

[19] Szreter, '"Social Intervention', 21–5; Jorg P. Vögele, 'Urban Infant Mortality in Imperial Germany', *Social History of Medicine*, 7 (1994), 401–25 (415).

they were woefully ignorant of basic personal hygiene and neglected their offspring by working outside the home. Doctors, supported by health officials and politicians, demanded measures targeting this type of mortality, such as encouraging breastfeeding, educating mothers in childcare and personal hygiene, and allowing maternity leave. Societies to support mothers and babies appeared across the continent during the early twentieth century as the movement gained momentum. Women's organisations took a prominent role in these campaigns, with many early feminists seeing the way forward for female emancipation in promoting respect for motherhood.[20]

French governments were particularly vexed by the widespread fear of 'depopulation', given that their country had the lowest birth rate in the world by this period. They were also spurred on by the desire to avenge the humiliating loss of Alsace and Lorraine in the Franco-Prussian War of 1870. Together with numerous charities, governments of the Third Republic (1870–1940) were conspicuous in developing a reasonably coherent programme to protect mothers and babies. This included charities giving material support and advice to poor mothers; the Roussel Law of 1874 regulating 'mercenary' wet-nurses; and help for unwed mothers, whose infants were particularly at risk of a premature death. In 1913, legislation brought in two months of paid maternity leave; family allowances, initially for civil servants, were later extended to all employees in the private sector during the 1930s. From the 1890s, a series of private initiatives in towns led to the famous *Goutte de lait* centres. They served a triple purpose of checking the weight of the infants, laying on consultations with doctors for mothers, and supplying safe, sterilised milk for those who needed it. In 1907, there were approximately 500 such medical consultation centres in France, and by the 1930s over 4,000, financed by a combination of private and public funds.[21] Germany was the other country that was outstanding in its efforts to curb infant and child mortality. German leaders were as concerned as their French counterparts with the flow of recruits for their army and industries, and in their case they faced an exceptionally high infant mortality rate (at 278 per thousand during the early 1870s). Hence the familiar combination of private and public initiatives to fund sterile

---

[20] Rachel G. Fuchs, 'The State', in Colin Heywood (ed.), *A Cultural History of Childhood and Family in the Age of Empire* (Oxford: Berg, 2010), pp. 129–47; Seth Koven and Sonya Michel, 'Womanly Duties: Maternalist Politics and the Origins of Welfare States in France, Germany, Great Britain, and the United States, 1880–1920', *American Historical Review*, 95 (1990), 1076–1108.

[21] Rollet-Echalier, *La Politique*, passim.

milk distribution centres, infant day-care centres, infant welfare stations and social insurance for mothers.[22]

However, in all parts of Europe, schemes for infant welfare faced some harsh realities on the ground during the early twentieth century. Supplying the population with clean milk was an uphill struggle, given the continuing risk of contamination at all stages: on the farms; during transport to towns; from adulteration by farmers, wholesalers and retailers; and in working-class houses poorly adapted to storing food. P. J. Atkins argues that in England numerous deaths from 'infantile diarrhoea' can be attributed to artificial feeding with infected milk. In Germany a decline in breastfeeding was a concern, with 55 per cent of mothers in Berlin feeding their babies with breast milk in 1883, but only 33 per cent in 1910. Yet before World War I, municipal milk supplies always fell far short of what was needed.[23] There was also some initial resistance among working-class families to the advice dispensed by doctors, nurses and philanthropic women, so that old habits such as not washing hands or cleaning bottles died hard. The low priority given to educating women in many circles took its toll here. No less importantly, the doleful influence of poverty lingered on to make life difficult for many parents: something that the advice manuals rarely took into account.[24] Increases in wages generally brought improvements in infant mortality rates, even if this involved mothers working outside the home: the additional income more than compensated for the time lost for breastfeeding.[25] Overall, though, the level of infant mortality in towns began to fall below that in the countryside. By the mid-1920s, the rate was 90.1 in Berlin, compared to 103.8 in Prussia as a whole.[26]

---

[22] Vögele, 'Urban Infant Mortality', 414–20; Edward Ross Dickinson, *The Politics of German Child Welfare from the Empire to the Federal Republic* (Cambridge, MA: Harvard University Press, 1996), ch. 3.

[23] P. J. Atkins, "White Poison"? The Social Consequences of Milk Consumption, 1850–1930', *Social History of Medicine*, 5 (1992), 207–27; Jörg Peter Vögele, Wolfgang Woelk and Silke Fehlemann, 'Decline of the Urban Penalty: Milk Supply and Infant Welfare Centres in Germany, 1890s to 1920s', in Sally Sheard and Helen Power (eds.), *Body and City: Histories of Urban Public Health* (Aldershot: Ashgate, 2000), pp. 194–213; Katja Haustein, 'The "Breastfeeding Crisis": Parenting, Welfare Policies, and Ideology in Imperial Germany, 1871–1914', in Hester Barron and Claudia Siebrecht, *Parenting and the State in Britain and Europe, c. 1870–1950* (Basingstoke: Palgrave Macmillan, 2017), pp. 49–71 (p. 62).

[24] Siân Pooley, 'Child Care and Neglect: A Comparative Local Study of Late Nineteenth-Century Parental Authority', in Lucy Delap, Ben Griffin and Abigail Wills (eds.), *The Politics of Domestic Authority in Britain since 1800* (Basingstoke: Palgrave Macmillan, 2009), pp. 223–42 (p. 226).

[25] Vögele, 'Urban Infant Mortality', 421.   [26] Vögele, 'Urban Infant Mortality', 406.

Infant and Child Health in the Late Twentieth Century

A major breakthrough came during the 1940s and 1950s, with the use of antibiotics and vaccines to combat diseases that had once killed off large numbers of the young, including diphtheria, scarlet fever and whooping cough. With modern medicine, and better nutrition, such sad sights as children with bandy legs from the deficiency disease rickets, or the paralysing effects of polio, gradually disappeared. Various less serious afflictions, including skin complaints, eye and ear infections, and rotting teeth were also under control. Richard Meckel is on firm ground in arguing that 'among the many changes that have transformed childhood in the West over the past two centuries, perhaps the most significant has been a dramatic decrease in the probability of disease, physical incapacitation, or death during the first decade of life.'[27] And yet in 2005 a World Health Organization survey warned that the overall improvement in the European region masked significant differences in children's health, with the poor particularly hard hit. In the poorest countries of eastern Europe, children were still suffering from the respiratory and infectious diseases that had ravaged the lives of their counterparts in the west during the nineteenth century. In the more developed countries, by contrast, children were generally in better health, but many struggled with non-communicable diseases such as asthma, diabetes, obesity and neuropsychiatric disorders. In the United Kingdom, for example, short stature still afflicted children of the poor, and around 10 per cent of children aged 5–15 had a mental health disorder.[28]

The Material World of Children in an Age of Affluence

Whereas at the turn of the twentieth century in Europe there were still struggles over children as producers, by the turn of the twenty-first century there was more concern over children as consumers.[29] This reflected the general rise in living standards of the period, and a shift from material deprivation to relative abundance for most of the population. Old scourges such as hunger, cold and overcrowding were gradually receding during the twentieth century, accompanied by some convergence in the standards of rich and poor. Yet, such was the success of the

---

[27] Richard Meckel, 'Health and Science', in Heywood, *Age of Empire*, pp. 167–87 (pp. 167–8).
[28] WHO, European Health Report, pp. ix, 46–56.
[29] Viviana Zelitzer, 'A Grown-Up Priceless Child', in Anna Sparrman et al., *Situating Child Consumption: Rethinking Values and Notions of Children, Childhood and Consumption* (Lund: Nordic Academic Press, 2012), pp. 71–9 (p. 71).

developed economies in generating material wealth that by the end of the century there were warnings in some quarters about childhood being corrupted by rampant consumerism.

Basic Necessities: Food and Housing

On the eve of World War I, a working-class child like Robert Roberts (1905–74) in industrial Salford could still worry above all else about food and warmth. Meanwhile, among the aristocracy in Paris, from the age of seven Pauline de Broglie (1888–1972) was joining her family at midday and evening meals where seven or eight dishes were routinely served, including huge amounts of meat, rich sauces, and a variety of *entremets* (desserts).[30] Such ostentatious forms of *haute cuisine* barely survived World War I. And it was around the late nineteenth and early twentieth century that the more affluent countries in Europe were reaching an acceptable level of calories in the diet of their population as a whole. A more varied food supply was also becoming available from overseas in the wake of improved transport facilities and free trade treaties. The long-term shift over the course of the twentieth century was away from the preponderance of bread, cereals and dairy products in the diet, towards meat, fruit and vegetables.

All the same, behind the averages lurked a persistence of low nutritional standards among the poor, and not least their children. Where the breadwinner was in a manual occupation, there was still the need to ensure that he had enough energy to hold down his job, obliging mothers and young children to skimp on their food to support him. Children among the labouring classes suffered from a lack of milk, lean meat, and fresh fruit and vegetables. Medical inspections of school children in England during the 1930s revealed that 11–12 per cent were undernourished. Less than 6 per cent were affected in a well-off area such as London, compared to 22.5 per cent at the other end of the scale in county Durham, as its workers struggled with high levels of unemployment during the depression. In Soviet Russia, typical of much of southern and eastern Europe, most families outside a small elite struggled to provide enough food for their children. After World War II, and the period of austerity that followed, general affluence in Europe meant that nearly everyone could afford a diet with sufficient calories, vitamins and minerals. The sting in the tail for the young was the emergence during

---

[30] Robert Roberts, *A Ragged Schooling* (London: Flamingo, 1984), pp. 67–8; Comtesse Jean de Pange, *Comment j'ai vu 1900* (Paris: Bernard Grasset, 1962), pp. 27–8.

the late twentieth century of problems of affluence, notably tooth decay and obesity.[31]

As for housing, families on low incomes often struggled to pay the rent, and as Thomas Morgan (b.1892) remembered about his upbringing in London, were regularly thrown on to the streets with their furniture. 'Course nearly everybody only had one room', he added; 'If you'd two rooms you thought you had a mansion'.[32] Improving the housing stock of the nineteenth-century towns in Europe, as they struggled to cope with waves of migrants from the countryside, had proved very challenging for the authorities. Modest interventions by governments and philanthropic societies before World War I had a limited impact. After 1918, governments in Europe took the initiative in supporting social housing for those on low incomes, though the extent of their commitment, and the way it was organised and funded, varied considerably. In the Soviet Union and later its eastern European satellites, it was considered a universal right, with the result that there was provision for around half of the population – though standards were very basic. In Soviet Russia, for example, communal apartments were not large enough to allow children to have their own room, or even their own corner.[33] In Western Europe, the right was more limited, though Britain stood out during the interwar period by the extent of its commitment to council housing. In the aftermath of World War II, France and Germany in particular embarked on a huge programme of house building, with the emphasis on quantity rather than quality. By the 1960s, the worst of the shortages were over. Governments began to withdraw from the housing market, owner-occupancy increased, and the drive to improve standards continued. There were benefits from improved accommodation for children's health, and for their chances of having their own room in which to study or relax.

Unfortunately, from the 1970s problems in the management of high-rise flats became apparent, and social housing in general became associated with the most disadvantaged in society, including large numbers of families among ethnic minorities. Those children living in 'sink estates' or *banlieues* were isolated from the rest of society, and in their 'ghettos of

---

[31] Ambrosius and Hubbard, *Twentieth-Century Europe*, pp. 243–8; D. J. Oddy, 'Food, Drink and Nutrition', in F. M. L. Thompson (ed.), *The Cambridge Social History of Britain 1750–1950* (3 vols., Cambridge: Cambridge University Press, 1990), vol. 2, pp. 251–78; Catriona Kelly, *Children's World: Growing Up in Russia, 1890–1981* (New Haven, CT: Yale University Press, 2007), pp. 374–5.

[32] Anna Davin, *Growing Up Poor: Home, School and Street in London 1870–1914* (London: Rivers Oram Press, 1996), pp. 32 and 35.

[33] Kelly, *Children's World*, p. 375.

poverty' were particularly at risk of under-achievement at school, drug abuse, alcoholism, ill-health and crime. There were concerns that children of pre-school age and their mothers in high-rise flats were being cooped up for hours without any other human contact. Older children, short of play areas, amused themselves in the lifts or played tricks on their neighbours, to the annoyance of older residents. Gangs of children roamed the estates, following earlier generations in fighting to defend their territory. And contemporaries lumped together problems with the estates, immigration and juvenile delinquency, producing a toxic mix for social cohesion. A report from Marseille in 1977 emphasised the 'aggressiveness' of immigrants aged 7–10, the thefts committed by little gangs of immigrants aged 10–14, and the more serious delinquency of those between 14 and 17, 'especially immigrants'. In France, families from North Africa were particularly discriminated against by landlords and, surreptitiously, by local politicians. The French state supported a number of measures to improve the infrastructure, and to turn the denizens of the estates into good citizens. These included the familiar strategy of packing large numbers off to the countryside during the summer, laying on outdoor activities to channel their aggression in the right direction. Unfortunately, such initiatives largely failed – and squalid housing conditions continued to plague the lives of a minority of children in Europe at the end of the twentieth century.[34]

Children as Consumers

If the eighteenth century saw a start to identifying children as consumers, the late-nineteenth and twentieth centuries brought a huge expansion in this area, with the emergence of a truly mass market. To begin with, it involved spending on children by parents and other adults; eventually, it also included spending by children themselves (amounting to £3 billion per year by the millennium for those under sixteen in Britain).[35] By 1900, according to David Hamlin, the 'bulk of the population' was

---

[34] Colin Ward, *The Child and the City* (London: Bedford Square Press, 1990), pp. 33–42, 87; Véronique de Rudder, 'Immigrant Housing and Integration in French Cities', in Donald L. Horowitz and Gérard Noiriel (eds.), *Immigrants in Two Democracies: French and American Experience* (New York, NY: New York University Press, 1992), pp. 247–67; Anne Power, *Hovels to High Rise: State Housing in Europe since 1850* (London: Routledge, 1993); Denise Lawrence-Zúñiga, 'Material Conditions of Family Life', in Kertzer and Barbagli, *European Family*, vol. 3, pp. 3–54; Jablonka, *Enfants de la République*, ch. 12; Mathew Thomson, *Lost Freedom: The Landscape of the Child and the British Post-War Settlement* (Oxford: Oxford University Press, 2013), pp. 43–5.

[35] Richard Layard and Judy Dunn, *A Good Childhood: Searching for Values in a Competitive Age* (London: Penguin, 2009), p. 57.

buying toys in Germany, with a segmented market that produced increasingly elaborate and expensive toys for the upper classes, and cheap ones that workers could at the very least buy at Christmas time.[36] It was also a highly gendered market, with toys thought of as in some way educational, preparing girls and boys for very different paths later in life. Dolls would supposedly help prepare girls for motherhood. Toys following military, technical and imperial themes, allowed boys to recreate battles, keep up with new technology such as aircraft and electrical goods, and to admire the exploits of famous explorers.[37] This mass market provoked criticism from a number of quarters, including academic pedagogues, middle-class reformers and artists, anticipating arguments that would reappear during the late twentieth century. They suggested that commercial toys, 'colorful, inartistic trash', stifled creativity and discouraged imaginative play. The market responded with simple wooden toys and realistic 'character dolls', which enjoyed some success, but the mainstream in the department stores continued to flourish none the less.[38]

Later, during the middle of the twentieth century, the Europeans were slow to exploit the tie-ins with radio programmes and films, such as dolls and games, so deftly exploited by Walt Disney in the United States from the 1930s onwards. During the interwar period, and again after 1945, European manufacturers persisted with well-established lines such as Meccano sets in England and the simple wooden trains and animals produced by Brio in Sweden. These toys had a strong educational underpinning, and remained gendered in character, with construction toys pitched at boys and dolls at girls. They also served the interests of middle-class parents very well, keeping their children off the streets. Eventually the American invasion could be staved off no longer, and European companies had to adapt or go under. Lines Brothers in Britain produced Sindy, an obvious imitation of Matell's Barbie (itself very popular across the continent); Brio for a time distributed Matell and Hasbro toys. The arrival of video games during the 1980s transformed the market, led by Nintendo, narrowing the differences between the North American and European pattern of consumption.[39] By the late twentieth century, children from a wide swathe of the population in the

[36] David Hamlin, *Work and Play: The Production and Consumption of Toys in Germany, 1870–1914* (Ann Arbor, MI: University of Michigan Press, 2007), pp. 57–9.
[37] Hamlin, *Work and Play*, ch. 1; Bryan Ganaway, *Toys, Consumption, and Middle-Class Childhood in Imperial Germany, 1871–1918* (Oxford: Peter Lang, 2009), chs. 4–5.
[38] Hamlin, *Work and Play*, ch. 4.
[39] Gary Cross, 'Toys,' in Paula Fass (ed.) *Encyclopedia of Children and Childhood in History and Society* (New York, NY: Thomson Gale, 2003); Daniel Thomas Cook, 'Children As

West had their own consumer goods on a scale unimaginable in the past, including toys, clothes, music systems and televisions. Like adults, they had to make choices between famous brands, heavily advertised and associated with issues of status and identity. Even very young children were involved, with their 'pester power' allegedly wielded to force parents to buy goods they had seen in advertisements on television.

These developments led to a fierce debate between those emphasising the vulnerability of children to the marketing strategies of big corporations, and those asserting that the young were perfectly capable of appropriating consumer culture for their own ends. Among the former, and most pessimistic, Sue Palmer depicted children living in an electronic world of mass communications and entertainment, exposed to the insidious influence of advertising, saddled with toys that failed to stimulate the imagination, and still nudged towards traditional gender differences even as parents were trying to escape them. The developed world, she asserted in 2006, was sowing an 'imagination-rotting, creativity-dumbing whirlwind'.[40] (Various countries in fact took measures to restrict advertising directed at children, including total bans in Norway and Sweden during the 1990s.) In the other camp, marketers countered that children were hard to please as consumers, and 'empowered' by their products. A third position avoided any such polarisation. Daniel Cook pointed out that one side took the moral position that children were sacred beings, in need of protection from corporate influences, the other that they were knowing, choosing persons, capable of resisting or enjoying what the commercial world had to offer.[41] Neither is entirely convincing for Cook. The impact of advertising is easily exaggerated: a study of 557 children aged 9–13 in the United Kingdom, carried out in 2006, found that the majority did not like advertisements on television, and 70 per cent did not think they told the truth.[42] For David Buckingham, 'Consumers are not simply "slaves to the brand", but nor are they joyfully creating their own meanings'. He suggests locating children in a network of social relations, with parents and peers coming into play. Thus in the contemporary world, the greater spending power granted

Consumers: History and Historiography', in Paula Fass, *The Routledge History of Childhood in the Western World*, Abingdon: Routledge, 2013, pp. 283–95.

[40] Sue Palmer, *Toxic Childhood: How the Modern World Is Damaging Our Children and What We Can Do About It* (London: Orion, 2007), pp. 227–8.

[41] Daniel Thomas Cook, 'Beyond Either/Or', in *Journal of Consumer Culture*, 4 (2004), 147–52.

[42] Agnes Nairn and Jo Ormrod, with Paul Bottomley, *Watching, Wanting and Well-Being: Exploring the Links. A Study of 9–13-year-olds* (London: National Consumer Council, 2007).

to children by parents gives them considerable autonomy – and he sees no reason to denigrate their consumption pattern. But inequality in a market-oriented society such as Britain left poorer families struggling to meet their children's demands, and pressured to buy expensive brands to mask their poverty.[43]

Publishing for Children

A 'golden age' for children's literature during the second half of the nineteenth century brought a huge increase in both the quantity and the quality of the books on offer.[44] It also saw a segmentation of the market, with high-minded works from such familiar authors as Carlo Collodi, Johanna Spryi, Jules Verne and Rudyard Kipling, aimed at the middle and upper classes, and more lurid, commercially-oriented works, notably the 'penny dreadfuls' in Britain, pitched at the working classes. The early twentieth century saw a more static market, but the 1950s and 1960s launched another massive increase in the output of books for children as well as for adults. There was also a concentration of firms in the publishing industry, eventually integrating them into the large corporate sector of business, with profit maximisation in a mass market the principal objective. A study of the French publisher Hachette during the 1950s revealed that to produce cheap, illustrated children's books for its Bibliothèque Rose and Bibliothèque Verte collections, books that would tap into the wider readership produced by near-universal literacy, it had to achieve substantial economies of scale. Print runs of at least 30,000 were the norm, and sales of books from the two collections ran to somewhere between seven and nine millions per year during the 1960s.[45] Across Europe, publishers came to distinguish more clearly various age groups among the young when marketing their works, ranging from the simple readers for young children, for example Dr Seuss's *The Cat in the Hat* (1957), to the increasingly sophisticated books for adolescents, an early starter being J. D. Salinger's *The Catcher in the Rye* (1951). Besides individual works, they produced series books, with the same set of characters (such as the Famous Five) running through them. They took

---

[43] David Buckingham, *The Material Child: Growing Up in Consumer Culture* (Cambridge: Polity, 2011), pp. 19–22, 163, 225–30.

[44] See Chapter 9.

[45] David Finkelstein, 'The Globalization of the Book, 1800–1970', in Simon Eliot and Jonathan Rose (eds.), *A Companion to the History of the Book* (Oxford: Blackwell, 2007), pp. 329–40; Sophie Heywood, 'Adapting Jules Verne for the Baby-Boom Generation: Hachette and the Bibliothèque Verte, c. 1956–1966', *Modern and Contemporary France*, 21(2013), 55–71 (58 and 68).

advantage of advances in colour printing to include in their lists picture books: the French excelled at these, with distinguished pioneers such as Jean de Brunhoff and his Babar series during the 1930s leading on to more affordable works reaching a mass market from the 1950s onwards, notably the Astérix albums created by René Goscinny and Albert Udozo in 1959.[46] And, towards the end of the century, belatedly following the Americans, they linked books to film and television programmes.[47]

The various genres can be conveniently grouped under the two headings of the imaginative/fantasy genre and the realist genre – though in practice the two are far from mutually exclusive, and, from the late twentieth century, all such divisions were arguably disappearing.[48] The fortunes of the two genres in fact ebbed and flowed over the decades. In Russia, for example, during the period of experimentation during the 1920s and 1930s when its children's books led the field, there was a struggle between those in favour of 'socialist realism', with themes such as the collectivisation of farming and preparation for war, and an increasingly influential movement in favour of the 'poetic-fantastic narrative' of the *skazka* form.[49] Also much in evidence was a transition beginning during the 1960s and 1970s that reflected changing conceptions of childhood in society at large. The emancipated and competent child replaced the innocent one of the nineteenth century; the adult perspective gave way to that of the child. Leading authors abandoned the didactic, preachy approach of so many of their predecessors and instead explored themes relevant to a child in contemporary society, such as divorce, alcoholism, drug addiction and racism. They generally moved on from the third person narrator, and resorted to more complex structures to explore the mind of a child or adolescent.[50]

If educators across Europe wanted children to read 'quality' books from the 'high' culture, they were generally disappointed, as children

---

[46] Penny Brown, *A Critical History of French Children's Literature* (2 vols., New York and London: Routledge, 2008), vol. 2, ch. 6.

[47] Jan Susina, 'Children's Literature', in Fass, *Encyclopedia of Children*.

[48] Ganna Ottevaere-Van Praag, *Histoire du récit pour la jeunesse au XIXᵉ siècle 1929–2000* (Brussels: P. I. E.-Peter Lang, 1999), p. 348; Maria Nikolajeva, 'Children's Literature', in Fass, *Childhood in the Western World*, pp. 313–27 (p. 319); M. O. Grenby, *Children's Literature* (Edinburgh: Edinburgh University Press, 2008), ch. 6.

[49] Ben Hellman, 'Russia', in Peter Hunt (ed.), *International Companion Encyclopedia of Children's Literature* (London and New York: Routledge, 1996), pp. 765–73 (769–71); Kelly, *Children's World*, pp. 73–5, 88–92, 97–101.

[50] Hans-Heino Ewers, 'La Littérature moderne pour enfants: son evolution historique à travers l'exemple allemand du XVIIIe siècle', in Egle Becchi and Dominique Julia (eds.), *Histoire de l'enfance en Occident* (2 vols., Paris: Editions du Seuil, 1996), vol. 2, pp. 434–60; Ottevaere-Van Praag, *Histoire du récit*, pp. 6–8 and 335–49; Nikolajeva, 'Children's Literature', pp. 324–5.

themselves often chose to read the cheap, melodramatic magazines and comics of the 'low' culture.[51] Scholars have tended to describe campaigns to clean up Victorian 'penny dreadfuls' and their successors as 'moral panics', or more specifically 'media panics'. In other words, they dismiss them as overreactions, fuelled by the mass media, with the ulterior motive of propping up existing social and generational inequalities.[52] An alternative approach is to take seriously the concerns of people in the past, trying to understand the historical context for their polemics.[53]

Witness the barrage of criticism levelled at the 'penny dreadfuls' in Britain during the 1870s and 1880s. These were weekly periodicals, read mostly by working-class and lower middle-class boys, whose staple fare was stories about notorious criminals. They certainly provoked an emotional reaction from numerous Victorian worthies. The satirical magazine *Punch* weighed in with the line that 'It is scarcely possible to exaggerate the nauseous quality of the trash that is prepared [for the young] in the shape of penny numbers.' It asserted that immature youths were being led into crime themselves by the romanticised depiction of highwaymen and murderers (an accusation not supported by a study of court records).[54] Yet, as Patrick Dunae makes clear, what gave the debate a particular intensity were the peculiar circumstances of the period. There was the heightened concern with the moral and material welfare of the young evident in the child-saving legislation, and, among the socially conservative, worries that mass education would produce young people who had been taught to read, but not how to discriminate between good and bad literature (see Figure 10.1).[55]

Similarly, campaigns evident across much of Europe during the 1940s and 1950s against comics imported from the United States should be seen in the context of a post-war desire among intellectuals to encourage peace and friendship. In 1953, for example, Jella Lepman in Zurich

---

[51] For example, Helle S. Jensen, 'Nobody Panicked! The Fifties' Debate on Children's Comics Consumption', in Sparrman et al., *Situating Child Consumption*, pp. 253–72 (pp. 258–60).

[52] Kirsten Drotner, 'Dangerous Media? Panic Discourses and Dilemmas of Modernity', *Pedagogica Historica*, 35 (1999), 593–619; and John Springhall, *Youth, Popular Culture and Moral Panics: Penny Gaffs to Gangsta-Rap, 1830–1996* (Basingstoke: Macmillan, 1998).

[53] David Buckingham and Helle S. Jensen, 'Beyond Media Panics', *Journal of Children and Media*, 6 (2012), 413–29.

[54] *Punch*, 20 February 1886, as cited by Patrick A. Dunae, 'Penny Dreadfuls: Late Nineteenth-Century Boys' Literature and Crime', *Victorian Studies*, 22 (1979), 133–50 (138); Springhall, *Youth, Popular Culture*, ch. 3.

[55] Dunae, 'Penny Dreadfuls', 134–6.

Figure 10.1 Engraving of a Victorian boy reading a comic, 1870.
Getty Images, 686370968.

founded the International Board on Books for Young People, whose
aims included promoting international understanding through children's
books.[56] In Scandinavia, Helle Strandgaard Jensen asserts the logic of
the campaigners' hostility to comics, in the light of the strong commitment to democracy and the welfare state in the countries concerned.
American superheroes such as Superman and Batman were criticised for
resorting to violence as a way of achieving their aims, contrary to the
principles of democratisation being taught in the schools.[57] In France, an
'uneasy alliance' including the Communist Party and the Catholic social
democrats of the Mouvement Républicaine Populaire took on the
comics, leading to a 1949 law regulating publications for the young.
For Richard Jobs, this formed part of a struggle to forge a new national
identity following the humiliations of World War II. Hence the Commission set up by the law to oversee and control publications for children
opposed all violent and erotic content. But it also revealed peculiarly
French concerns in its desire to rejuvenate the country, such as

---

[56] See the IBBY website www.ibby.org/about.o.html, consulted 26 September 2016.
[57] Jensen, 'Beyond Panic'; eadem, *From Superman to Social Realism: Children's Media and
Scandinavian Childhood* (Amsterdam: John Benjamins Publishing, 2017), ch. 3.

Figure 10.2 Flying classic retro superhero smiling and throwing a punch.
Getty Images, 477780403.

encouraging optimism and promoting the values of community and social solidarity.[58] Likewise, in the Federal Republic of Germany, a 1951 law on 'smutty and trashy literature' followed close on a catastrophic defeat and critiques of the spiritual poverty of the mass society emerging from the ruins (Figure 10.2).[59]

Children in Two World Wars

Warfare in the twentieth century took a heavy toll on civilians, their children included. Civilian casualties amounted to an estimated 10 per cent of the total in World War I and 45 per cent in the Second. The young fell victim to such scourges as strategic bombing, starvation during sieges and blockades, epidemics in overcrowded orphanages and genocidal campaigns against Armenians, Slavs and above all Jews. An estimated 1.5 million Jewish children and youths died as a result of the Holocaust, over 90 per cent of the total alive in Europe in 1940. Children also had to endure uprooting on a massive scale, with evacuations from the cities, the flight of refugees from war zones, expulsions of ethnic groups and exchanges of population after the wars. Added to this was the common experience of the disruption of family life, with fathers and brothers away for long spells in the armed forces, and, if they came back alive, struggling to settle back into their old routines. Yet children were not simply the victims of modern warfare. They pursued their studies in school, sometimes in difficult circumstances. They maintained links with relatives in the front line by writing letters to them, and helped with their country's war effort. Their activities included making collections of scrap metal, working on the harvests, helping around hospitals and clearing up after bombing raids. Some even joined regular armies or resistance movements in occupied territories. Children were generally well

---

[58] Richard Ivan Jobs, 'Tarzan under Attack: Youth, Comics, and Cultural Reconstruction in Postwar France', *French Historical Studies*, 26 (2003), 687–725 (703–4).
[59] Dickinson, *German Child Welfare*, pp. 267–8.

prepared for war in schools and youth movements, and indeed many relished the excitement of it all.[60]

Preparing Children for War

Before both world wars, there were public and private initiatives in the major European powers to try to toughen up the bodies of the young for fighting and breeding, and to instil martial values in all social classes. These included promoting 'racial motherhood', insisting on drill as the main form of physical exercise in schools, founding gymnastics and sports clubs, laying on activities among organised youth movements to prepare boys for war, glorifying the homeland and setting up famous soldiers and sailors as masculine role models. In England, from the 1880s, teachers in the elementary schools which taught boys and girls of the working and lower middle classes were encouraged to provide stirring accounts of great battles in the past and romanticised views of military heroes such as Lord Nelson and General Gordon. Across the Channel in France, the desire for revenge after defeat in the Franco-Prussian War spurred on similar moves in the schools of the early Third Republic. After watching the military on display at a Bastille Day parade in Paris in 1913, the writer André Chamson recalled thinking that 'I was French, and, what I saw, was the French army, the army of the leading country in the world, an army which nobody could beat!' Schools in Imperial Germany, according to Andrew Donson, were more muted in their militarist and nationalist tone, though they soon caught up with the rest in 1914 and 1915 with a fervent *Kriegspädagogik* (war pedagogy). War crept into the teaching of all subjects, for both boys and girls: arithmetic lessons, for example, might involve calculating the weight of ammunition needed to wipe out a French division.[61] There were

---

[60] Jim Marten, 'Children and War', in Fass, *Childhood in the West*, pp. 142–57; Monika Janfelt, 'War in the Twentieth Century', in Fass, *Encyclopedia of Children*; Nick Stargardt, *Witnesses of War: Children's Lives under the Nazis* (London: Jonathan Cape, 2005); Berry Mayall and Virginia Morrow, *You Can Help Your Country: English Children's Work during the Second World War* (London: Institute of Education, 2011); Rosie Kennedy, *The Children's War: Britain, 1914–1918* (Basingstoke: Palgrave Macmillan, 2014).

[61] Stephen Heathorn, 'Representations of War and Martial Heroes in English Elementary School Reading and Rituals, 1885–1914', in Marten, *Children and War*, pp. 103–15; Kennedy, *Children's War*, ch. 5; Stéphane Audoin-Rouzeau, 'Children and Primary Schools of France, 1914–1918', and Andrea Fava, 'War, "National Education" and the Italian Primary School, 1915–1918', in John Horne (ed.), *State, Society and Mobilization in Europe during the First World War* (Cambridge: Cambridge University Press, 1997), pp. 39–52 and 53–69 respectively; Heywood, *Growing Up*, pp. 254–5; Andrew Donson, 'From Reform Pedagogy to War Pedagogy: Education Reform before 1914 and the Mobilization for War in Germany', in Schumann, *Raising Citizens*, pp. 68–84; and idem, *Youth in the Fatherless Land: War Pedagogy, Nationalism, and*

in all countries some dissenting voices, but they remained a minority. Stephanie Olsen notes the influence in Britain of informal educational channels, such as the periodical press, which ran alongside the schools, and sought to disseminate Christian values. Their main aim was to persuade the nation's boys to become 'manly domesticated men and good fathers'. In 1914, she argues, some men took this as a reason to fight for their families, and so volunteered for military service; others concluded that their duty was to stay at home, and avoid risking their life in battle, and so held back.[62]

The indoctrination of the young increased in intensity under the Communist and Nazi regimes of the interwar period. During the 1930s, Communist Party leaders in Russia decided that Marxist-Leninist principles were failing to mobilise the masses, and so they turned to patriotism. The young proved more eager than most to rally around the Soviet Motherland and the Party, with their combination of 'enthusiasm, idealism and credulity', as Olga Kucherenko puts it. During the period of 'militarised socialism' between 1939 and 1941, the leadership exhorted artists, schoolteachers, and the Young Pioneers (a youth league for those aged ten to fifteen) to prepare children for the 'unavoidable war' ahead. In the schools, the military usefulness of subjects was emphasised once again, such as learning from chemistry survival techniques in case of poison gas attacks, and from history the Russian martial tradition. The Pioneers meanwhile encouraged physical fitness and the vision of leading the world proletariat. In Nazi Germany, the junior branches of the Hitler Youth for ten- to fourteen year-olds, the *Jungvolk* and *Jungmädel*, preached a more pernicious doctrine of racial superiority. Like the Pioneers, they had managed to sign up nearly all of their age group by the outbreak of hostilities, and concentrated on pre-conscription training, with sporting activities, war games and drill.[63] Calls for devotion to the cause, self-sacrifice and heroic deaths on the battlefield were much in evidence everywhere.

Child Soldiers

In this atmosphere, it is hardly surprising that some children became frontline soldiers or members of the Resistance movements, though it must be emphasised that child soldiers played only a minor role in

Authority in Germany, 1914–18 (Cambridge, Massachusetts, and London: Harvard University Press, 2010), chs. 2–3.

[62] Olsen, *Juvenile Nation*, pp. 166–7.

[63] Olga Kucherenko, *Little Soldiers: How Soviet Children Went to War, 1941–1945* (Oxford: Oxford University Press, 2011), ch. 2; Guido Knopp, *Hitler's Children*, transl. Angus McGeoch (Stroud: Sutton Publishing, 2002), ch. 1.

military operations in the two world wars. Official policy in Soviet Russia was actively to discourage children under the call-up age of eighteen from joining the armed forces, though sixteen- and seventeen-year-olds could sometimes persuade conscription officers to bend the rules. However, once German forces had invaded in 1941, many below these ages (including a minority of girls) went to the front line and tried to join army units or partisan groups. They were motivated in part by a desire to defend their homeland, in part by desperation to escape harrowing conditions in their towns and villages, notably a shortage of food. They were often not welcomed by the Red Army, but if they had useful skills in, say, foreign languages or nursing, they might be. Thus twelve-year-old Sasha Eichmann, from a family of Volga Germans, was taken on because of his fluency in German and also his accordion-playing. Children could make themselves useful to both regular troops and partisans as messengers, local guides, spies infiltrating enemy positions – and as reminders of home life to cheer up the adults. If the worst came to the worst, they might also join in the fighting. The numbers involved are difficult to estimate, but children probably accounted for less than 1 per cent of troops in the Red Army.[64]

In Nazi Germany, there was the same unwillingness to conscript children: in the early campaigns, the youngest soldiers were nineteen or twenty years of age. However, in August 1944 members of the Hitler Youth aged fifteen and sixteen were encouraged to volunteer for the regular army, and in October that year a 'final levy' saw this cohort conscripted into the *Volkssturm*, to help defend the country against invaders from the east and the west. Many younger children joined in during the final, desperate months, even as it became increasingly obvious that the cause was lost. The elderly men and boys of the *Volkssturm* were poorly armed and poorly trained. Yet many of its child soldiers, like their Russian counterparts, proved themselves brave and resourceful in combat, to the point of recklessness. One observer described how '*Hitlerjungen*, just kids, were literally jumping at tanks with their grenade launchers. My God, how they were mown down...' They were also likely to reveal their brittleness under pressure. When captured, in the perception of the Americans, they were transformed into 'completely overwrought children, shaking, bleeding, and weeping "hysterically"'.[65]

---

[64] Kucherenko, *Little Soldiers*, passim.
[65] Stargardt, *Witnesses of War*, ch. 10; Knopp, *Hitler's Children*, ch. 5.

Displaced Children

Less dangerous than joining armies, but far more widespread, was the displacement and re-placement of hundreds of thousands of children before, during and immediately after the wars. During the 1930s, thousands of Jewish children fled Hitler's empire, either with their families or on their own. Among the latter, the Youth-Aliyah organisation took 3,200 unaccompanied children from Germany to safety in Palestine; the famous Kindertransports brought around 10,000 from central Europe to the United Kingdom.[66] This brought safety but risked anguish for those separated from their families. Vera Schaufeld, aged nine when she left Prague on a Kindertransport, recalled that when letters from her parents stopped coming in 1940, 'I imagined that my parents must have forgotten me or that I must have done something really terrible to deserve to be in England … I used to go through all the things that I'd ever done wrong as a child, and said that it was because I'd done these things that I didn't deserve to be with my parents.'[67] One of the first instances of mass displacement during World War II was the evacuation of children from the big cities and their relocation to safer rural areas. In France, this was relatively easy to achieve. The gradual pace of economic development there meant that most of the families concerned still had relatives in the countryside who could look after their children with a minimum of upheaval. The government merely had to invite parents to make their own arrangements, and offer to help the residual group that was unable to do so.[68] In Soviet Russia, by contrast, the process was generally chaotic. The rapid progress made by the invading German forces saw many 'safe' areas at risk of being overrun, and while some evacuees were well looked after in their reception areas, others found themselves in sparse, poorly-heated accommodation.[69] The Nazi regime in Germany, haunted by fears of a collapse in civilian morale, refused to countenance talk of evacuation, disguising its scheme as a holiday programme. Indeed, the huge infrastructure of transport links, staff offices and accommodation, inherited from the pre-war organisation for giving working-class children a holiday in the countryside, was a critical factor in its success. It allowed the government to arrange the evacuation of at

---

[66] Tara Zahra, *The Lost Children: Reconstructing Europe's Families after World War II* (Cambridge, MA: Harvard University Press, 2011), p. 66.

[67] Interview in Rebekka Göpfert, *Der jüdische Kindertransport von Deutschland nach England 1938/9* (Frankfurt/Main: Campus Verlag, 1999), as cited in Zahra, *Lost Children*, p. 69

[68] Laura Lee Downs, 'Enfance en guerre: les évacuations d'enfants en France et en Grande Bretagne (1939–1940), *Annales HSS*, 66 (2011), 413–48.

[69] Kucherenko, *Little Soldiers*, p. 156.

least 800,000 children from Berlin over the short space of two weeks in October 1940. Before that, the regime had made no plans for evacuation, encouraging the German population to believe that the war would only be fought on foreign soil. The first British bombing raid on Berlin in September 1940 destroyed any such illusions. A further wave of evacuations occurred in 1943, as the Allied bombing campaign intensified. As in France, many families made private arrangement to send their offspring to safety with friends and relatives. Some children returned home after suffering from abuse or homesickness; most managed to adapt to new families and the rural way of life.[70]

This left the British case, where the evacuation by the government of almost 1.5 million children and adults in three days on the eve of the war created numerous problems (and a substantial historiography). The Government had carefully planned Operation Pied Piper over several years, and, from a logistical perspective, it was a success. However, in London 40 per cent of those expected to leave never showed up, and during the initial 'Phoney War' period, many evacuees returned home. The authorities soon found themselves fielding numerous complaints from the children, their parents and the host families. The 'cattle auctions' that took place on arrival, when the host families were allowed to choose the evacuees they would shelter, was a miserable experience for some. A former evacuee recalled that 'The ones that went first were the twelve- and thirteen-year-olds because they could work or earn their keep'; others risked humiliation. There were tensions between the country folk and what they called 'dirty evacuees' (though most of them were clean and healthy). And at worst, there were cases of child abuse, made possible by the limited supervision of families. The administration learned some lessons from this experience during two further waves of evacuation in September 1940 and 1944. Overall, most children adapted to their new environment, learning from the villagers, attending the schools arranged for them, and helping on the farms. The older notion that the evacuations made country folk aware for the first time of the dire predicament of many urban workers, and so paved the way for the welfare state after 1945, is now widely contested. Numerous enquiries since the mid-nineteenth century had exposed the plight of slum dwellers. An alternative approach is to conclude that the evacuation was a failure. In Britain, as in Germany, many children remained in the cities during the bombing. The leadership in both countries failed to

---

[70] Niko Gärtner, *Operation Pied Piper: The Wartime Evacuation of Schoolchildren from London and Berlin 1938–1946* (Charlotte, NC: Information Age Publishing, 2012), passim; Stargardt, *Witnesses of War*, pp. 51–2, 55–60.

grasp the resistance of working-class parents in particular to accept separation from their children. At least British politicians made some concessions to pressure from below, re-opening schools in the cities for example, and, unlike their counterparts in the Nazi regime, resisting the temptation to make evacuation compulsory.[71]

Other mass movements of the young included those who joined the flight from Latvia to Russia following the German invasion of their country in 1915, the *Kindertransports* of 10,000 Jewish children (without their families) from Nazi Germany to England in 1938–9, the estimated 50,000 children 'stolen' from occupied territories in the East for 'Germanisation' with foster families in Germany and Austria during World War II, and the expulsion by the Czech government of 3 million Germans after 1945. Children always risked being orphaned, abandoned or lost during desperate attempts to escape from invading armies. Even well-meaning schemes had their casualties: some of the Jewish children sent to England to escape a near-certain death in the concentration camps failed to settle in with their host families; not all of the 'stolen' Slav children wanted to part from their German foster parents after the war.[72]

Conclusion

The gradual shift to affluence over the course of the twentieth century encouraged a certain convergence in the experience of growing up in Europe, whether looked at in comparing countries or the paths taken by various socio-occupational groups. There was most obviously the general decline to very low levels in infant and child mortality, all-round improvements in diet and housing, and the rise of mass communications. Everywhere, national and local governments intervened to promote child welfare, either directly or indirectly, including such measures as encouraging infant day-care centres, providing free school meals, banning unsuitable reading material and investing in clean water systems. The darker side to development also began to spread widely, notably in the

[71] Martin Parsons and Penny Starns, *The Evacuation: The True Story* (Peterborough: DSM, 1999); John Welshman, *Churchill's Children: The Evacuee Experience in Wartime Britain* (Oxford: Oxford University Press, 2010); Gärtner, *Operation Pied Piper*.

[72] Aldis Purs, 'Orphaned Testimonies: The Place of Displaced Children in Independent Latvia, 1918–26', in Baron, *Displaced Children*, pp. 40–69; Eric J. Sterling, 'Rescue and Trauma: Jewish Children and the Kindertransports during the Holocaust', in Marten, *Children and War*, pp. 63–74; Tara Zahra, *Kidnapped Souls: National Indifference and the Battle for Children in the Bohemian Lands, 1900–1948* (Ithaca, NY: Cornell University Press, 2008).

form of two world wars, concerns over the corrupting influence of consumerism, and even childhood obesity. Yet it is equally obvious that the case for convergence is easily overstated. As Kertzer and Barbagli point out, there were deep-seated influences from the past still at work in contemporary Europe during the late twentieth century. It is clear that Nordic countries had a long-standing commitment to welfare legislation for children, enabling married women to work and shifting burdens of childcare from the family to the state. At the opposite pole, Mediterranean countries retained a strong commitment to the traditional family, with fewer working mothers than in the north and west, and less generous benefits towards institutions such as day-care centres.[73] The differences between social classes also persisted, even if more in the form of relative rather than absolute poverty.

---

[73] This section is indebted to the 'Introduction' to Kertzer and Barbagli, *European Family*, vol. 3, pp. xi–xliv (pp. xxxvii–xliv).

11 Work and School in an Urban-Industrial Society

It is now widely taken for granted that the practice of child labour disappeared from Europe years ago. Certainly, the sight of small children working on machines in the textile mills or going down coal mines has long gone from practically every part of the continent. Gradually, all strata of society have been persuaded that school is the proper place for children, not least by nineteenth-century legislation that made it compulsory. The twentieth century has brought a 'long' childhood for nearly everyone, in the sense that the norm is now to remain in education of some form, and dependent on parents or guardians, until well into one's teens or early twenties. Yet the 'rediscovery' of child labour in the advanced economies during the 1970s revealed that it never really went away, though it no longer took the form conventionally associated with the Industrial Revolution period. While it disappeared from textile mills and other key industries, it continued on the margins of the economy, in combination with time in school, especially on family farms, in small businesses and in numerous outlets in the service sector. By the end of the twentieth century, a little work experience was widely considered to be useful for the young, in the middle-classes as well as the working classes. All the same, questions remain over whether it still undermines the health and education of many children from poor families.

Children's Work in Transition, 1870–1914

The Decline of Child Labour in Industry after 1870

The retreat of child workers from industry, especially large-scale industry, was already under way during the middle of the nineteenth century in the more advanced economies, and it gained momentum after 1870.[1] Countries that had followed Britain in pioneering child labour legislation

---

[1] See Chapter 7.

earlier in the century became more ambitious in this sphere from the 1860s and 1870s onwards. New laws included clauses extending coverage beyond the factories and mines to small workshops, raising the minimum working age, insisting on shorter working hours and more time in school, and, most importantly, putting more resources into the inspection system. In France, the 1874 law on child labour applied to all 'factories, mills, works, mines, yards and shops'; it raised the minimum working age from eight to ten or twelve (depending on the industry); and it replaced the unpaid local commissions of the 1841 law with fifteen divisional inspectors, recruited and paid for by the state. In Germany, a Worker Protection Law of 1891 set a minimum working age of thirteen and extended coverage from factories to 'enterprises that cannot be characterised as factories with ten or more workers'; a further law in 1903 included children in smaller workshops.[2] Other countries that had resisted state intervention, or were relatively late to industrialise, in their turn passed child labour laws on similar lines during this period. Russia's first child labour law, passed in 1882, covered all private industrial establishments with more than sixteen workers, barred the employment of children under twelve, and led to the organisation of nine 'industrial districts' for the purpose of inspection. By 1886 legislators in Italy were complaining that theirs was almost the only 'civilised' country without a child labour law: they duly passed one later that year. The Belgians followed suit in 1889, outstandingly late for a major industrial power.[3]

How effective such state intervention was in discouraging employers from hiring children remains a matter of some dispute among historians, for the late as well as the early nineteenth century.[4] What does stand out is that, with a viable inspection service at this stage, it was a relatively straightforward matter to enforce the laws in factories and other

[2] Lee Shai Weissbach, *Child Labor Reform in Nineteenth-Century France: Assuring the Future Harvest*, (Baton Rouge, LA: Louisiana State University Press, 1989), pp. 198–202; Gunnilla Budde, 'From the "Zwergschule" (One-Room Schoolhouse) to the Comprehensive School: German Elementary Schools in Imperial Germany and the Weimar Republic, 1870–1930', in Laurence Brockliss and Nicola Sheldon (eds.), *Mass Education and the Limits of State Building, c. 1870–1930* (Basingstoke: Palgrave Macmillan, 2012), pp. 95–116 (p. 95).

[3] Boris B. Gorshkov, *Russia's Factory Children: State, Society, and Law, 1800–1917* (Pittsburgh, PA: University of Pittsburgh Press, 2009), ch. 4; Carl Ipsen, *Italy in the Age of Pinocchio: Children and Danger in the Liberal Era* (New York, NY: Palgrave Macmillan, 2006), ch. 3; René de Herdt, 'Child Labour in Belgium 1800–1914', in Kristoffel Lieten and Elise van Nederveen Meerkerk (eds.), *Child Labour's Global Past, 1650–2000* (Bern: Peter Lang, 2011), pp. 175–92. See also Marjatta Rahikainen, *Centuries of Child Labour: European Experiences from the Seventeenth to the Twentieth Century* (Aldershot: Ashgate, 2004), ch. 4.

[4] See Chapter 7.

establishments with large concentrations of workers. Conversely, it was very difficult in the myriads of small workshops dispersed across towns and countryside. This led to the perverse outcome of the relocation of under-age or illiterate child workers from the former to the latter, from regulated establishments to workshops in unregulated, often 'sweated' trades. In eastern France, for example, a divisional inspector reported in 1895 that rope makers, dyers, finishers, launderers and stonemasons were the most common employers of fugitives from the factories.[5] It is unfortunately impossible to measure the scale of any such movement, given the clandestine nature of much of the work concerned.

None the less, the workings of the labour market continued to encourage the removal of child workers from many industries. On the supply side, the general rise in real wages in the developed economies during the second half of the nineteenth century encouraged parents to delay the entry of their children into the workforce and allow more time (and money) for schooling. This was by no means a straightforward mechanism. As Emma Griffin shows from her study of working-class autobiographies in Britain, the very poor did not invariably send their children out to work at a young age. At the same time, relatively well-off cotton workers in Lancashire regularly clashed with leaders of the labour movement during the early twentieth century as they resolutely held on to children working as half-timers in mule-spinning and power loom weaving.[6] There was also the influence of a decline in fertility and the size of families in the background to limit the supply of child workers, though it was unevenly spread across the various occupational groups among workers. On the other side of the labour market, the onward march of mechanisation and an 'intensive' rather than 'extensive' use of labour, in the interests of productivity, caused many employers to become disenchanted with child labour. The context here was heightened international competition during the late nineteenth century as new industrial powers such as Germany and the United States challenged the early starters. Some of the simple tasks performed by children, including turning wheels, winding yarn on to bobbins, and fetching and carrying, were mechanised or taken over by older workers. And a general increase in the size and speed of machinery rendered much of it unsuitable for operation by the young. In the silk industry of Lombardy,

[5] Colin Heywood, *Childhood in Nineteenth-Century France: Work, Health and Education among the Classes Populaires* (Cambridge: Cambridge University Press, 1988), p. 316.
[6] Emma Griffin, *Liberty's Dawn: A People's History of the Industrial Revolution* (New Haven, CT: Yale University Press, 2013), pp. 60–2; Per Bolin-Hort, *Work, Family and the State: Child Labour and the Organization of the Production in the British Cotton Industry, 1780–1920* (Lund: Lund University Press,1989), ch. 10.

for example, the number of children employed under the age of fourteen dropped by a half between 1876 and 1891, following the spread of steam power, and technical advances that allowed such developments as the mechanisation of the drawing and twisting of the silk.[7]

The general climate of opinion also continued to move against child labour. There was the growing demand from organised labour that the 'male breadwinner' should earn a high enough wage to spare his wife and children the need to work. This ideal of a 'family wage' was far from being realised, but it was relatively successful where child labour was concerned.[8] Following the line taken by Myron Weiner in his survey of advanced industrial economies, the gradual acceptance by workers as well as employers that at least some education was essential for everyone proved to be one of the most important influences on the decline of child labour in industry. Moreover, it was easier to secure compliance with child labour laws once elementary education had been made compulsory.[9]

This is not to lose sight of a fierce rear-guard action to defend the presence of children in the industrial workshops by many employers and working-class families. The story of child labour reform is peppered with examples of resistance, persistent violations and cheating by employers. In the French case, in the wake of the 1874 law, they often hid children when an inspector called, encouraged those that remained to lie about their ages and working hours, complied with the law only on the inspection day, and obstinately protested to the authorities that they could not possibly survive without their youngest employees.[10] There was the familiar line from textile manufacturers that they depended on the small stature and nimble fingers of their child workers, or from glassmakers that an early start was necessary to learn a trade. Labour shortages were another common reason for opposition to the law: spinning mills, glassworks and paperworks located in the countryside frequently made a case for exemption along these lines. Inspectors were generally lenient in such circumstances, and governments were sometimes willing to make concessions to manufacturing interests. In 1890, the Russian government

---

[7] Antonia Pasi, 'Children in Lombard Industrialization, 1876–1911', in Lieten and van Nederveen Meerkerk, *Child Labour's Global Past*, pp. 209–40 (pp. 220–1).

[8] Michael Lavalette, 'The Changing Form of Child Labour circa 1880–1918: The Growth of "Out of School Work"', in Michael Lavalette, *A Thing of the Past? Child Labour in Britain in the Nineteenth and Twentieth Centuries* (Liverpool: Liverpool University Press, 1999), pp. 118–38 (p. 127).

[9] Myron Weiner, *The Child and the State in India: Child Labor and Education Policy in Comparative Perspective* (Princeton: Princeton University Press, 1991), ch. 6.

[10] Heywood, *Childhood in Nineteenth-Century France*, ch. 10.

agreed to relax the ban on children working on Sundays and imperial holidays, under pressure from employers struggling to recruit labour during a period of recovery from a crisis. The Italian government soon backtracked after a new, more stringent child labour law introduced in 1902 proved unenforceable, replacing it with a milder version in 1907.[11] Parents for their part often connived in the cheating by employers, claiming that denying their children the opportunity to work or reducing their hours and wages would leave the family budget in desperate straits. In some cases they may have had a point, given the tendency of factories to recruit among the poor, especially those with large families. Inspectors sometimes had to confront the realities of extreme poverty: witness the French divisional inspector who in 1879 yielded to the pleas from a tearful widow in the Ardèche department to allow one of her five children to work extra hours illegally.[12]

Nonetheless, the somewhat patchy evidence suggests a slow but ultimately inexorable decline in the employment of children, though by no means its elimination. The census for England and Wales gave an exceptionally informative indication of what was happening during the late nineteenth and early twentieth centuries. By 1871, children under 10 years of age had almost disappeared from the labour force, with a mere 0.8 per cent of boys and 0.7 per cent of girls aged 5 to 9 recorded as working. From 1881, it was no longer considered worthwhile giving information on this group. Working children aged 10 to 14 experienced a slow and slightly uneven decline at this point: the upshot was that between 1871 and 1911 the percentage of the age group in work dropped from 32.1 per cent to 18.3 per cent for boys, and from 20.5 to 10.4 per cent for girls. By the latter date most of these would have been thirteen or fourteen years of age.[13] One can assume that these figures were underestimates, particularly for girls, but the direction of change was clear.

Children's Work in the Service Sector

What the censuses could not fully convey was that the market for child workers was also undergoing a period of transition, especially in northwestern Europe, as the young were edged out of strategic industries to a

[11] Gorshkov, *Russia's Factory Children*, pp. 137–8; Ipsen, *Italy in the Age of Pinocchio*, pp. 85, 118–21.

[12] Heywood, *Childhood in Nineteenth-Century France*, pp. 279–80.

[13] Hugh Cunningham and Shelton Stromquist, 'Child Labor and the Rights of Children: Historical Patterns of Decline and Persistence', in Burns H. Weston (ed.), *Child Labor and Human Rights: Making Children Matter* (Boulder, CO: Lynne Rienner Publishers, 2005), pp. 55–83 (pp. 62–3).

position on the periphery of the labour force. On the one side, if they were not playing truant and working illegally, most children were from now on only available for work on a part-time or casual basis, slotting in the hours when free from their compulsory schooling. On the other side, meanwhile, demand for child and adolescent workers was shifting from industry to various niches in the service sector. The 'half-timers' in the Lancashire cotton industry, dividing their days between earning on the shop floor and studying in class, were by the 1900s a vestige of the old type of child labour in the factories. (They disappeared with the passing of the 1918 Education Act.) The children most likely to be employed in manufacturing were to be found in small workshops, which, as we have seen, were either beyond the scope of the law or given a degree of immunity from it by their sheer number. Also numerous were the young boys and girls helping their parents in family workshops, without pay, in occupations such as handloom weaving, framework knitting, lace making and metalworking.[14] Governments had a tendency to shy away from intervention in this type of enterprise, being unwilling to breach the family's right to privacy.[15]

For the most part, though, children ended up in numerous jobs that were opening up or expanding in the service sector in the more mature economies of Europe. The younger children, say from around the age of seven, were mostly to be found helping their family with domestic chores, such as baby minding, cooking, cleaning and washing. A study in the Netherlands in 1913 noted that much of the heavy work in the household fell to girls, leaving them less time than boys for earning a wage or for play.[16] This readily mutated later into paid work as a domestic servant: the usual job for young females in many parts of Europe. The example of London shows that there were plenty of jobs for girls, when they had sufficient strength, in shops, pubs, lodging houses and eating houses. This was arduous and poorly paid work which often fell to those brought up in institutions such as orphanages or workhouses. There were also numerous child-servants, known aptly enough in London as 'slaveys', burdened with the most menial tasks in and around the scullery.[17] Boys

---

[14] Heywood, *Childhood in Nineteenth-Century France*, pp. 314–15.

[15] Ning de Coninck-Smith, 'The Struggle for the Child's Time – At All Times. School and Children's Work in Town and Country in Denmark from 1900 to the 1960s', in Ning de Coninck-Smith et al., *Industrious Children: Work and Childhood in the Nordic Countries 1850–1990*, Odense: Odense University Press, 1997, pp. 129–59 (p. 134); Heywood, *Childhood in Nineteenth-Century France*, p. 315, n.101.

[16] Ali de Regt, 'Children in the 20th-Century Family Economy: From Co-Providers to Consumers', *The History of the Family*, 9 (2004), 371–84 (374).

[17] Anna Davin, *Growing Up Poor: Home, School and Street in London 1870–1914*, London: Rivers Oram Press, 1996, ch. 9.

meanwhile had the opportunity to work outdoors selling newspapers, delivering milk or running errands. The children generally took the initiative themselves to secure such jobs, eager for the extra money and experience. Parents also approved such 'out of school work'. An enquiry in Kristiana (Oslo) in 1912 revealed that around a fifth of schoolchildren had a part-time job: half of the girls concerned worked as domestic servants, three-quarters of the boys were running errands. The school-teachers organising the enquiry did not think that the work affected children's studies, even though some of their pupils started at the age of seven. They felt that it encouraged the virtues of order, obedience and punctuality. Moreover, those with a job were not necessarily poor, and included some of their best pupils.[18] In Copenhagen, by contrast, the work of boys delivering milk provoked considerable opposition. Here the milk carts went out early every morning with a milkman and five or six 'milk boys' to help him. The work brought status and a wage, but it was hard in winter, tired the boys out for school, and risked beatings from teachers hostile to the arrangement.[19]

Children's Work in an Affluent Society, c. 1914–2000

During the inter-war period, children's work remained entrenched in a largely invisible form across much of Europe. In the British case, Stephen Cunningham argues that civil servants in the Home Office consistently favoured employers' interests over those of the children, convinced that part-time work was character-forming for the young and useful in com-bating juvenile delinquency. Consequently, they downplayed any prob-lems, and resisted regulation as far as possible: the 1933 Children and Young Persons Act followed earlier legislation from 1918 in leaving the minimum working age at twelve and allowing children to work from six o'clock in the morning on school days.[20] (It lasted with minor modifica-tions until 1998.) At the same time, in southern Europe, the relatively slow development of the economies meant that children were drawn into industrial employment in much the same way as they had been further north during the early stages of industrialisation. In Portugal, at mid-century, most children were still employed in agriculture and domestic service, but a minority were drawn into 'cruel' working conditions in

---

[18] Ellen Schrumpf, 'From Full-Time to Part-Time: Working Children in Norway from the Nineteenth to the Twentieth Century', in de Coninck-Smith et al., *Industrious Children*, pp. 47–78 (60–3).

[19] de Coninck-Smith, 'The Struggle for the Child's Time', pp. 138–43.

[20] Stephen Cunningham, 'The Problem That Doesn't Exist? Child Labour in Britain, 1918–1970', in Lavalette, *A Thing of the Past?* pp. 146–55.

industry. Girls tended to be employed in tobacco, shoes, clothing and textiles, boys in construction, metalworking and furniture.[21]

The two World Wars did bring a reversion to earlier practices, as the desperate need to maintain production while mobilising millions of men for military service meant that on all sides child welfare was low on the authorities' agenda. In 1917, the Chief Medical Officer of the Board of Education in Britain, Sir George Newman, warned that 'Munitions work of various kinds, a great variety of industrial occupations in the urban districts, and agricultural labour in the rural districts are extremely common for both boys and girls down to the age of 8 and 9 years.' With working hours uncontrolled, he warned, there was a 'grave risk' to the health and physique of the population. The 'lessons of 1918' were not learned by 1939. Children once again streamed out of their classrooms during the Second World War, to the chagrin of trade unionists as well as educators, providing farmers especially with a cheap and flexible supply of labour.[22]

The period of full employment, increasing real wages and improved welfare measures after 1945 transformed once more the experience of working as a child. The long-established link between poverty and child labour was finally broken in much of Europe. Most children now made it clear that they were working because they wanted to and not because they felt under pressure to contribute to the family budget. They sought jobs where they might have some fun and sociability, and had no hesitation in spending their earnings on themselves, bringing a measure of independence and enhanced self-esteem. Girls caught up with boys in taking on a job, though gender differences in the type of work done and average wages persisted. Also, middle-class children as well as those from the working class now took up part-time work while they were still at school, reducing further the stigma attached to such employment. The upshot by the 1970s was a general feeling that child labour had become 'a thing of the past', transformed into a little part-time work in harmless 'children's occupations' such as babysitting or delivering newspapers, and tightly regulated by law.[23] However, towards the end of the twentieth century, investigators across Europe sought to raise awareness of a more complex, and in some ways more disturbing

---

[21] Pedro Goulart, 'History of Child Labor in Portugal', in Hugh Hindman (ed.), *The World of Child Labor: An Historical and Regional Survey* (Armonk, NY: M. E. Sharpe, 2009), pp. 644–8 (pp. 644–5).

[22] Cunningham, 'Child Labour in Britain', pp. 141–5, 155–8.

[23] Cunningham, 'Child Labour in Britain', pp. 164–71; Phil Mizen, 'Child Labor in the Developed Nations Today', in Hugh D. Hindman, *The World of Child Labor: An Historical and Regional Survey* (Armonk, NY: M. E. Sharpe, 2009), pp. 62–6.

picture. They faced various problems associated with defining 'work' and measuring its impact on children's welfare, but a number of important points emerged.

In the first place, they revealed that in some countries the majority of children had taken up some form of paid employment before the minimum school-leaving age (generally fifteen or sixteen). A number of studies indicated that, during the 1980s and 1990s, this was the case for somewhere between 63 and 77 per cent of children in Britain, and around 80 per cent in the Federal Republic of Germany.[24] Younger children worked informally for friends and neighbours, or to help around family farms and businesses. In the latter, as in the past, the distinction between domestic 'duties' and 'work' was not easy to make. Later, some of the young would move into the formal sector of the economy with regular hours and wages. Secondly, working illegally as a child was by no means uncommon. This ranged from taking a job without the required permit in Britain, to the association with criminal gangs in big cities such as Moscow and Lisbon, which in the latter cases meant begging on the streets, acting as a drugs courier, or (more rarely) becoming a child prostitute. Researchers found ample evidence across the continent of weak controls on the minimum working age (the ILO set a benchmark of thirteen for 'light work' which many countries adopted), on children working early in the morning or during the evening, and on jobs deemed unsuitable for them such as bar and factory work.

Thirdly, most jobs undertaken by children were poorly paid and unskilled. Heinz Ingenhorst argues from the German case that child labour rarely prepared the ground for a future career, or even had any educational value. As against this, the 'developmental model', mainly based on research in the United States, proposes that work experience can form part of the character-building of an individual. It is certainly a widespread (and common-sense) notion that it brings skills and attitudes useful later in life, including a sense of responsibility and self-reliance.[25] The danger remains of idealising children's work in a developed economy, given the persisting threat to the health and education of children trying to combine work with schooling: our fourth point. Besides

---

[24] Sandy Hobbs and Jim McKechnie, *Child Employment in Britain: A Social and Psychological Study* (Edinburgh: The Stationary Office; Scotland, 1997), ch. 2; and Heinz Ingenhorst, 'Child Labour in the Federal Republic of Germany', in Phillip Mizen et al., *Hidden Hands: International Perspectives on Children's Work and Labour* (London: Routledge/Falmer, 2001), pp. 139–48 (p. 140).

[25] Ingenhorst, 'Child Labour', 146; Hobbs and McKechnie, *Child Employment in Britain*, ch. 6.

newspaper delivery and babysitting, children took on a number of 'adult' jobs in domestic service (for girls especially), in a family business or in the numerous cafes, restaurants, hotels and shops of the service sector. In most cases, the benefits doubtless outweighed the costs. Children themselves almost invariably viewed their work in a positive light, relishing the opportunity to earn a little extra cash, without feeling that they were compromising their futures. The most pessimistic line would be to suggest that they felt compelled to work to satisfy their 'need' for consumer goods such as clothes, compact discs and magazines in an affluent society.

And yet there was a 'hard core' of child workers, mainly from poor families, that put in exceptionally long hours, took on the heavier work (such as lifting potatoes on Scottish farms), and were most likely to be caught up in criminal activity. Given that children had to spend around thirty hours a week in school, anything over ten hours a week was likely to prove burdensome, particularly as domestic chores might lift their exposure to a sixty-hour week. These children were the ones most likely to fall asleep in class, or even give up on schooling altogether with few qualifications.[26] More serious was the persistence of child labour in industry in parts of Mediterranean Europe.[27] Typically, in Italy many among the poor dropped out of elementary school or secondary school before the age of fourteen, presumably to work with their families or illegally in the formal sector of the economy. In Portugal, according to Eaton and Goulart, child labour was still an 'enduring, difficult, and damaging issue' during the early twenty-first century, with a small minority of children underpinning certain regional economies. This was in the context of persistent pockets of poverty, and demand for child workers from employers in rural and industrialising areas of the country. Although the general picture in Portugal was one of decline, abuses such as the exploitation of a legal loophole allowing the employment of children on piecework in a private home persisted.[28]

---

[26] Madeleine Leonard, 'Child Work in the UK, 1970–1998', in Lavalette, *A Thing of the Past?*, pp. 177–92; Phillip Mizen, Christopher Pole and Angela Bolton, 'Why Be a School Age Worker?', and Valery Mansurov, 'Child Labour in Russia', in Mizen et al., *Hidden Hands*, pp. 37–54 and pp. 149–66 respectively; Ingenhorst, 'Child Labour', passim.

[27] Council of Europe, *Children and Work in Europe* (Strasbourg: Council of Europe Publishing, 1996), pp. 24–9.

[28] Martin Eaton and Pedro Goulart, 'Child Labor in Portugal Today', in Hindman, *World of Child Labor*, pp. 649–51.

Schooling in the Late Nineteenth and Twentieth Centuries

'Are children still useful today?'[29] The obvious reply would be that they are not. After all, in most cases what work they do, paid or unpaid, does little to help support their family. Rather, parents across Europe now have to devote considerable resources to raising their offspring, to make possible the extended period taken up by compulsory education, without having any claims on them as producers. Time in class appears to have more to do with socialisation than anything constructive. But for the sociologist Jens Qvortrup, this line of reasoning ignores the part that children's school work plays in human capital formation. As modern economies move from manual work to jobs that require abstract reasoning and competence in handling symbols (such as letters, numbers and digits), he argues, so the need for school work during childhood increases. The state has in effect expropriated children's labour and allocated it to school work in the long-term interests of the economy. In this way, the twentieth century merely brought one more chapter in the history of children's adaptation to the requirements of the prevailing economic system. 'In hunting societies children hunt; in fishing societies they fish; in agricultural societies they undertake farm work; in embryonic industrial society they work in factories; and in developed industrial society children do school work.'[30] In this context, it is readily understandable why schooling for all children is almost universally accepted in contemporary Europe. What needs to be understood here is the long struggle to bring about this state of affairs, involving influences of class, religion and gender in the school systems as well as economic considerations.

'All to School' and 'A School for All', c. 1870–1940

The late nineteenth and early twentieth centuries brought a wave of utopian and progressive thought in the West, with the aim of launching a new era in education. In the first place, it sought a concerted effort to ensure that all children went to school, both for their own personal development and for the benefit of an urban-industrial, democratic society. In the second place, there was a desire to transform the school itself, replacing the grim regimentation of the past with a more creative

---

[29] This paragraph is based on Jans Qvortrup, 'School-Work, Paid Work and the Changing Obligations of Childhood', in Mizen et al., *Hidden Hands*, pp. 91–107.
[30] Qvortrup, 'School-Work', p. 97.

and cooperative atmosphere.[31] Circumstances at the time were by no means unfavourable. By the end of the nineteenth century, state intervention in the education system was increasingly in evidence across Europe, including legislation to make elementary schooling both free and compulsory. Also, by this period progressive, child-centred education had a respectable pedigree, with contributions from such renowned figures as Jean-Jacques Rousseau (1712–78), Johann Heinrich Pestalozzi (1746–1827), and Friedrich Froebel (1782–1852). Developments in psychology gave a new impetus to such theories of teaching.[32] Yet the ideal of *'tous à l'école'* and *'une école pour tous'*, summing up the aims of Jules Ferry and his Republican associates in France from the 1880s, made only limited headway across Europe. Not all children were attending school regularly before the 1940s, nor was there a unique school for everyone, as a two-track system continued to keep the middle classes and 'the people' apart.[33]

Following the legislation on compulsory schooling, and the considerable build-up of numbers already attending at the elementary level, what was required from the 1870s and 1880s onwards were measures such as enforcing regular attendance, raising the school-leaving age and providing more schools and trained teachers. Yet dragooning every last child into the school system was no easy matter. A study in this area reveals the 'uneven, tentative, and varied' path to primary school expansion during the period 1870 to1940, in contrast to the rapid growth in supply and demand during the years following World War II.[34] The late nineteenth century brought a considerable boost to enrolments in Europe; this stalled during the early twentieth century, only picking up again during the inter-war period. There was also a huge initial lag in parts of southern and eastern Europe to overcome. Around 1870, whereas certain countries in northern Europe had already achieved high levels of primary schooling, with Switzerland and Germany outstanding, others in the south and east, such as Italy, Portugal and Russia, remained well behind.[35] England and Wales stood out for their relatively modest achievement compared to their neighbours, indicating the need for

---

[31] James Bowen, *A History of Western Education*, (London: Methuen, 1981), vol. 3, p. 440.
[32] See Chapter 9.
[33] Maurice Crubellier, *L'Enfance et la jeunesse dans la société française, 1800–1950* (Paris: Armand Colin, 1979), p. 228.
[34] Aaron Benavot and Phyllis Riddle, 'The Expansion of Primary Education, 1870–1940: Trends and Issues', *Sociology of Education*, 61 (1988), 191–210 (204).
[35] Benavot and Riddle, 'Expansion of Primary Education', (200–1, and 205, appendix). This article gives an unadjusted enrolment rate, dividing enrolments at the various levels by the population of a constant school age category for all countries (5–14 for primary education).

caution in linking the rise of mass schooling to industrialisation and urbanisation. The prevailing liberal ideology in Britain, as in France, discouraged governments from spending public money on education, and delayed legislation to make primary schooling free and compulsory until relatively late in the nineteenth century.

Progressive educational methods made some inroads into the school systems of Europe before World War II.[36] They were most in evidence in a few celebrated 'free' schools that adopted them wholeheartedly, such as Bedales (founded in 1893) and Summerhill (1921) in Britain. This 'English model' spread to other European countries including Holland, Belgium and Switzerland. Their 'holistic' approach was a head-on challenge to existing secondary schools, with its emphasis on individualised learning and practical activities such as handicrafts, acting and dancing. More pervasive in its influence during the inter-war period was the method devised by Maria Montessori (1870–1952). Following on from Rousseau and his heirs in a twentieth-century context, she encouraged children to learn, under the supervision of a teacher, with a range of stimulating toys, books and other apparatus in the classroom. Some of this type of thinking found its way into other nursery and primary schools. With watchwords such as 'child-centred education' and 'active learning' much in evidence, there were moves to introduce activities including art, educational walks and games.

Beyond the schools, organisations such as the churches and the Scout movement revealed this same desire to develop in harmonious fashion the mind, body and soul of the children in their care. In France, for example, the *colonies de vacances* began in the 1880s with the aim of improving the health of working-class children in the cities by giving them six to eight weeks of holiday in the countryside. However, as public health became less of an issue, the educational opportunities offered by these institutions gradually came to the fore. During the 1930s, over 400,00 children from the working and lower-middle classes spent their summers in the camps, and although Catholic, Socialist and Communist organisations all had different objectives, they adopted the same strategy of giving children doses of fresh country air, wholesome food and activities to harness their creative energies in singing, folk dancing, acting and playing games.[37]

---

[36] Bowen, *Western Education*, vol. 3, ch. 11.
[37] Laura Lee Downs, *Childhood in the Promised Land: Working-Class Movements and the Colonies de Vacances in France, 1880–1960* (Durham, NC: Duke University Press, 2002), passim.

The vast majority of children, however, were firmly under the thumb of their teachers in the schools, with their subordination rather than their liberation the main objective. The 'Herbartian system', seized upon by the education authorities late in the nineteenth century, with its detailed curriculum and individual lesson plans, appeared far more attuned to the needs of an urban-industrial society – certainly for the ruling elites. Their main aim after all was the conservative one of creating a disciplined work-force and an electorate immune to the siren calls for revolution.[38] The obvious exception here was Soviet Russia, which for a decade or so following the Bolshevik Revolution attempted a radical departure from the system inherited from the Tsarist regime.[39] In 1918, the Commissariat of Enlightenment (Narkompros) attempted nothing less than the creation of a new, classless society through education. The plan was for a United Labour School, open to all, with uninterrupted progression from primary to secondary school. Traditional disciplines were to be abandoned in favour of a concentration on the themes of work, nature and society. A regime that banned all marks, examinations, homework and punishment, together with allowing pupils representation on a school's administration, seriously undermined the authority of teachers. As might be anticipated, such an ambitious scheme fell far short of achieving its aims. Illiteracy rates increased during the 1920s, the old religious and 'bourgeois' values continued among the young, and it was children of the elite rather than workers and peasants who progressed through the system. The dire circumstances of civil war and famine were hardly propitious at the start, but most importantly, the visionaries at Narkompros failed to carry parents, local officials and teachers with them. From 1928 onwards, as Stalin tightened his grip on what was now the Soviet Union, the government insisted on a reversion to more traditional methods.

Obstacles to Early Reform Movements

Any visions for a new era in education before World War II had to face various obstacles, deeply embedded in the culture of the peoples, besides the obvious shortage of resources in the poorer countries. In the first place, the elites across Europe were still generally wedded to a two-track system, with secondary schools based on the classical humanities reserved for a tiny

---

[38] Bowen, *Western Education*, vol. 3, pp. 232–41, 375–6.
[39] Bowen, *Western Education*, vol. 3, ch. 14; Larry Holmes, *The Kremlin and the Schoolhouse: Reforming Education in Soviet Russia, 1917–1931* (Bloomington, IN: Indiana University Press, 1991); Ben Eklof, 'Russia and the Soviet Union: Schooling, Citizenship and the Reach of the State, 1870–1945', in Brockliss and Sheldon, *Mass Education*, pp. 140–66.

minority of the wealthy (around 2 to 3 per cent of the age group around 1900), and elementary schools, offering only a very basic, utilitarian education, that was considered sufficient for the masses. The notorious 'Cook's Circular' issued in 1887 by the Tsarist Minister of Education made this explicit, seeking to 'free the *gymnasiums* from children of coachmen, menials, cooks, washerwomen, small shopkeepers, and the like'.[40] The secondary schools ran their own preparatory classes or recruited from exclusive preparatory schools, so that their pupils could avoid contact with the plebs. On the other side of the coin, the 'people's schools' were a dead-end for most, with their leaving-certificates worth very little on the job market.[41] There were always various initiatives to prolong the schooling of the working classes, involving intermediary (or 'quasi-secondary') institutions such as 'complementary courses', 'higher' or 'senior' primary schools, and 'middle schools'. In England, after 1902, Local Education Authorities were allowed to set up secondary schools – though they did not teach Latin, which was essential for access to the professional and administrative elite. There were also a small number of scholarships in the grammar schools awarded to outstanding pupils from humble backgrounds. The upshot of all this was that the vast majority of children across Europe were excluded from secondary education (Figure 11.1).

Impatience with time spent in class proved deeply ingrained in peasant and working-class culture, leading to widespread compliance with the limited educational opportunities on offer to most children. Robert Roberts (1905–74) remembered what happened when he opened a debate at his elementary school in Salford with an impassioned plea for the motion that 'Children should go to school until they are fifteen.' His opponent, Lily Weeton, replied with the simple assertion that 'we should gerrout to work at fourteen and fetch some money for us parents'. This brought the house down, and the humiliating result of two votes for him, and forty-eight for her. In addition, the dire circumstances in which some families found themselves left little choice in the matter. Adelheid Popp started work at ten to support her widowed mother, noting that her withdrawal from the eight-year programme required by the law in Austria went unnoticed. In any case, she asserted defiantly, 'I did not consider myself a child – I was a working woman'.[42]

---

[40] Holmes, *Reforming Education*, p. 97.
[41] Budde, 'German Elementary Schools', p. 101.
[42] Robert Roberts, *A Ragged Schooling: Growing Up in the Classic Slum* (London: Flamingo, 1978), pp. 150–2; Adelheid Popp, *The Autobiography of a Working Woman*, transl. F. C. Harvey (London: T. Fisher Unwin, 1912), pp. 31–2.

Figure 11.1 Photograph of a group of schoolboys playing rugby during the late nineteenth- or twentieth-century periods.
Getty Images, 172515802.

Historians have generally suggested that schooling was an unpleasant experience for working-class children, with rote learning, religious or political indoctrination, and in some countries excessive reliance on corporal punishment continuing from the past. As in earlier decades, it is not difficult to find testimony from disgruntled adults remembering boredom or harsh treatment in class.[43] A sample of working-class people from Vienna interviewed by Robert Wegs had little to say about their time in school during the first four decades of the twentieth century, least of all anything positive.[44] There was also the occasional school strike to suggest simmering discontent beneath the surface, such as the wave that swept Britain in 1911.[45] Yet Jonathan Rose argues that although the education provided by elementary schools in England around the turn of the twentieth century now appears most unsatisfactory, evidence from working-class memoirs and an oral history project indicates that the

---

[43] See Chapter 10.
[44] J. Robert Wegs, *Growing Up Working Class: Continuity and Change among Viennese Youth, 1890–1938*, (University Park, PA: Pennsylvania State University Press, 1989), p. 86.
[45] Martin Hoyles, *The Politics of Childhood* (London: Journeyman, 1989), ch. 7.

majority were satisfied with it. The impression given was that teachers kept control of their classes, 'albeit via the cane', and gave a good grounding in literacy and numeracy, plus a little extra in the form of history, geography and even a foreign language.[46] Similarly, during the inter-war period the higher primary schools in France proved quite popular with families of modest means: they required a shorter period of study than the *lycées*, and if the jobs available at the end were of lower status, they were at least plentiful in commerce, industry and administration.[47]

The second major obstacle to a transformation of education was the persisting belief that males and females should have a different education to prepare them for differing roles in adulthood. At the elementary school level, the two sexes tended to study the same subjects, essentially the 3 Rs plus some needlework for girls, but a 'hidden curriculum' pushed them in different directions. Reading material everywhere depicted men going out to work, while women remained at home as mothers.[48] Moreover, particularly obvious in the English case, as more optional subjects became available, so girls and boys took different subjects. For girls, there were courses in domestic economy, and the more practically-orientated cookery, laundry work and housewifery; for boys, there was a choice of mechanics, algebra and eventually manual work. School authorities were more tolerant of girls missing school than boys, assuming that they were helping their mothers at home. Separate schools or classes for the two sexes were still considered important, especially by the churches, despite moves to promote co-education in progressive circles.

When it came to secondary schooling, the 'separate spheres' ideology held back girls even more if they sought an academic education to match that of their brothers. The custom continued, in the upper ranks of society, of sending boys to prestigious private or state-run secondary schools, while educating girls at home and in small schools dedicated to producing cultured, marriageable young women rather than classical scholars. The French Camille Sée law of 1880 is a case in point. For the first time, it enabled girls to attend a *lycée* or *college*, and to follow a reasonably progressive curriculum including studies of the classics (in translation), French, modern languages and the history of civilisation.

---

[46] Jonathan Rose, *The Intellectual Life of the British Working Classes* (New Haven, CT: Yale University Press, 2002), ch. 5.
[47] Antoine Prost, *Education, société et politiques: une histoire de l'enseignement en France, de 1945 à nos jours* (Paris: Seuil, 1992), p. 72.
[48] Linda L. Clark, *Schooling the Daughters of Marianne: Textbooks and the Socialization of Girls in Modern French Primary Schools* (Albany, NY: State University of New York, 1984), p. 57.

But it also included courses in domestic science and hygiene, and, most importantly, it did not lead to the *baccalauréat* examination and entry into a career. At least in 1924 parental pressure and feminist critiques made it possible for girls to follow the boys' curriculum and sit the *baccalauréat*. One can readily understand how an ambitious young woman like Simone de Beauvoir (1908–1986), set on a career as a teacher, envied the education of her cousin Jacques at an exclusive Parisian *collège*.[49] Across the Channel, the second half of the nineteenth century brought a flurry of initiatives to establish new secondary schools for girls, ranging from posh public schools such as Rodean (founded in 1885) to high schools modelled on the North London Collegiate School (1850). Again, though, as Carol Dyhouse emphasises, they could only hope to recruit pupils by remaining within the conventional framework of family life among the professional middle classes, turning out 'refined ladies of leisure'.[50] During the 1930s and 1940s, the Nazi regime made a flagrant attempt to turn the clock back in this sphere, by steering girls away from intellectual prowess and towards domesticity. While boys continued to attend the established secondary schools, girls went to special schools concentrating on preparation for life as a wife and mother. Most in evidence were very practical lessons on such subjects as nutrition and cooking, hygiene, baby care and needlework.[51]

Finally, opposition to reform from the established churches proved difficult to overcome in certain circumstances. For centuries, official Catholic, Orthodox and Protestant churches had dominated the schools in Europe, until in the wake of the French Revolution of 1789 the state in various countries began to challenge their influence.[52] A series of struggles began during the nineteenth century, between states feeling their way towards a national system of education, and churches determined to defend their traditional role as teachers and spiritual guides. Historians of education have tended to side with the secular authorities, and there is no shortage of evidence to buttress their case. To take a Protestant example, in England during the 1920s and 1930s the Anglican Church proved incapable of managing its numerous publicly-funded elementary schools efficiently. It failed to reorganise its 'all-age' schools to make specialised teaching possible and allowed many of its buildings

---

[49] Colin Heywood, *Growing Up in France: From the Ancien Régime to the Third Republic* (Cambridge: Cambridge University Press, 2007), pp. 246–51.

[50] Carol Dyhouse, *Girls Growing Up in Late Victorian and Edwardian England* (London: Routledge & Kegan Paul, 1981), pp. 55–9.

[51] Lisa Pine, *Education in Nazi Germany* (Oxford: Berg, 2010), pp. 60–1.

[52] This is the argument underlying Hugh McLeod, *Religion and the People of Western Europe 1789–1989* (Oxford: Oxford University Press, 1997).

to fall into disrepair.[53] However, it is usually the Catholic Church that emerges as the villain of the piece, especially where it supported right-wing, authoritarian regimes. In Spain, short-lived Republican governments beginning in 1873 and 1931 attempted to bolster state schools and exclude religious congregations from teaching. More importantly, though, restored monarchist regimes and the military dictatorship of General Franco, left the Catholic Church in a commanding position. The result was a resistance to modern ideas in the classroom, hindering mass literacy and support for girls' education. Spanish schools in the 1950s, according to Frances Lannon, were little different from those of the 1920s. Education in Portugal also suffered from an alliance between anti-democratic royalists and Ultramontane Catholics (looking to Rome), and after 1926 from the corporatist regime of Antonio Salazar. Portugal was arguably the 'least educated nation in Europe'.[54]

The 'Democratisation' of Education after 1945

During the years that followed World War II, the 'democratisation' of education, frequently mooted in earlier decades, finally gained momentum. In the first place, the practice of corralling the vast majority of workers into elementary schools, and reserving secondary schooling for the middle class, was gradually abandoned. Henceforth all children routinely progressed from primary to secondary education, either by moving to a different institution or by progressing through a common school. Participation rates at the secondary level increased rapidly: in France, for example, less than half (43 per cent) of sixteen-year-olds were attending school in 1958–9, but 87.4 per cent were doing so in 1985–6.[55] By the millennium, as we have already shown, nearly everyone in Europe was attending secondary school until at least the minimum school-leaving age of around fifteen or sixteen.[56] Underpinning this change was a growing appetite for education among the working classes, made possible by growing affluence and the realistic prospect of upward social mobility, and consciousness in government circles of the need for more scientific and technical training. In the second place, there were moves, by no means universal, to replace the established hierarchies with a 'school for all' of some sort. This might involve merging elementary

---

[53] Brian Simon, *Education and the Social Order, 1940–1990* (London: Lawrence & Wishart, 1991), pp. 51–4.

[54] Frances Lannon, *Privilege, Persecution, and Prophecy: The Catholic Church in Spain, 1875–1975* (Clarendon Press: Oxford, 1987), pp. 18, 73–88; Bowen, *Western Education*, vol. 3, pp. 465–9.

[55] Prost, *Education, société et politique*, p. 143, tableau 8.   [56] See Chapter 10.

and grammar schools into a common school, such as the Danish *Folks-kole*, which all children attended from the age of seven for nine years (with an optional tenth year), or in East Germany the Soviet-style Poly-technic Secondary School, covering all children aged six to sixteen (with an optional move to a *Gymnasium* afterwards). Elsewhere, governments reorganised secondary schools along the lines of the American high school, as in England and Wales, where the comprehensive school took over from most of the grammar schools and secondary moderns. Thirdly, the more blatant forms of inequality in the education of girls and boys were removed. Co-education increasingly became the norm, and the assumption that the two sexes would for the most part follow a common curriculum. Finally, the dwindling influence of organised religion in Europe from the 1960s onwards, with most of the churches in western Europe in crisis, was accompanied by a retreat from some of the more reactionary approaches to education in its schools.[57] In Spain, during the 1960s and 1970s, the Catholic Church made determined efforts to diversify the social background of the pupils in its secondary schools by relying on state subsidies as well as fees, and to tone down the right-wing political ideologies that had pervaded its teaching.[58]

Such changes allowed children across Europe to spend more time in school and to study a broader range of subjects. Other reforms further enhanced the quality of education. Small, rural schools, such as those with two teachers and two classes, and 'all-age schools' were gradually closed to allow for finer age-grading and more specialised teaching. Corporal punishment, already banned in schools by many countries during the nineteenth and early-twentieth centuries, finally went out of favour everywhere. Special needs schools were established for the approximately 3 per cent of children with learning disabilities – though there was a counter-view that integration into ordinary schools was a better solution. There was also an expansion of nursery schooling, to support mothers wishing to return to work. Some of these emphasised play, as in Sweden, others, notably the *écoles maternelles* in France, started teaching the 3 Rs and even a foreign language (Figure 11.2).

However, dissatisfaction with the school system remained widespread across Europe. Much was expected of it, including high standards in reading, mathematics and the sciences; improved opportunities for all children to make the most of their abilities; better health and child care; and responsible citizens for the (Communist or democratic) future. In practice, this was always going to be difficult, and by the 1960s and early

---

[57] McLeod, *Religion and the People of Western Europe*, ch. 8.
[58] Lannon, *Catholic Church in Spain*, pp. 85–6.

Figure 11.2 Schoolchildren in an open-air school, Tunbridge Wells, Kent.
Getty Images, JB3702–001.

1970s there was growing disillusionment with the results from huge outlays of public money on education. The most radical reaction came from the 'deschooling' movement, which called for lifelong learning via an informal network of specialised tutors in place of a school system.[59] The rigidity of the school as an institution in the midst of a rapidly changing society was one prominent theme. Suzanne Mollo, investigating readers for boys and girls in French primary schools during the mid-1960s, discovered that they were still rooted in a rural world of peasants and artisans. Contrasting the joys of working the land with the martyring of industrial workers by the machine was, as she notes, 'not very encouraging for a society in the throes of rapid industrialisation!'[60] Everywhere it proved difficult to reconcile the interests of the various stakeholders in

---

[59] Bowen, *Western Education*, vol. 3, pp. 543–5; Ivan Illich, *Deschooling Society* (London: Calder and Boyars, 1971).

[60] Suzanne Mollo, *L'Ecole dans la société: psychosociologie des modèles éducatifs* (Paris: Dunod, 1969), p. 94.

the schools: politicians of various hues, civil servants, experts such as psychologists and pedagogues, schoolteachers, parents – and children. Governments in the various states of the Federal Republic of Germany followed in the reformist footsteps of the Weimar Republic during the 1950s and restricted or banned outright the use of corporal punishment in the schools, but faced determined opposition from teachers, and, especially in rural areas, from parents.[61] Attempts to merge institutions to produce a single school led to conflict between primary and secondary school teachers, as in Sweden and France. Schoolchildren or their parents complained of the anxiety produced by examinations such as the 11+ in England, or the pressure to achieve good marks to get into a *lycée* in France. It also proved difficult to shake off the stereotyping of sex roles in the schools, particularly as in the aftermath of the World War II there was a widespread feeling that married women should become homemakers. Studies from the 1970s showing that, in England, while girls were 'successful' pupils in primary schools, it was still boys who became the academic 'high-flyers' in the secondary schools.[62] From the 1990s, various attempts to make international comparisons revealed girls in all countries to be outperforming boys in reading, but it was the other way round in the sciences. A report on the study of maths and science (TIMMS) in 1995 noted the superiority of boys at the eighth grade, above all in physics, chemistry and earth science.[63] A newer concern was the performance of children from some of the ethnic minorities, including Turkish migrants in Germany, North Africans in France and Afro-Caribbean's in England. The OECD's Programme for International Student Assessment (PISA) revealed in 2003 that students whose parents were immigrants were still well behind native students in the study of mathematics in all countries, and particularly in Germany. For those who were born abroad themselves the gap was even larger, as they struggled with an unfamiliar educational system and often also with language difficulties.[64] However, the socio-professional background of parents was always an important influence on children's success or

---

[61] Dirk Schumann, 'Asserting Their "Natural Right": Parents and Public Schooling in Post-1945 Germany', in Dirk Schumann (ed.), *Raising Citizens in the Century of the Child: The United States and German Central Europe in Comparative Perspective* (New York, NY: Berghahn, 2010), pp. 206–25 (pp. 214–15).

[62] Clark, *Schooling the Daughters*, ch. 7; Glenys Lobban, 'The Influence of the School on Sex-Role Stereotyping', in Jane Chetwynd and Oonagh Hartnett (eds.), *The Sex-Role System: Psychological and Sociological Perspectives* (London: Routledge & Kegan Paul, 1978), pp. 50–61; Sara Delamont, *Sex Roles and the School* (London: Methuen, 1980), p. 44.

[63] TIMMS 1995, http://timms.bc.edu/timss1995i/HiLightB.html, accessed 16 August 2016.

[64] OECD, *Learning for Tomorrow's World: First Results from* PISA 2003 (Paris: OECD Publishing, 2004), pp. 167–730.

failure at school: evidence from France during the 1970s and 1980s made it clear that school results were identical for foreign students and their French classmates when they had similar social backgrounds. The school system was simply unable to overcome existing social inequality.[65] Moreover, more recent data from the twenty-first century does not show children of these immigrants disadvantaged in the same way.

To Select or Not to Select

A particularly contentious issue for each country was how to cope with the substantial difference between the highest and lowest performing pupils. Some chose to group together those of similar ability, on the basis of a selection process, assuming that 'differing kinds of mind needed different environments'.[66] In practice, this usually meant differentiating schools into a number of streams that catered for a general, a technical or a vocational type of education. Other countries opted for a 'school for all', that did not select or screen its pupils in any way, offered them all the same learning opportunities, and made it possible for each school to handle all levels of pupils' performance. This meant very large comprehensive schools, and mixed ability teaching often preferred to streaming. (Some combination of the two approaches was also possible.)[67] In the background were passionate debates on priorities: maintaining academic standards versus promoting equality, for example, or concentrating resources on educating an intellectual elite versus spreading them more widely over the ability range.

The Federal Republic of Germany remained generally committed to a tracking system, resisting pressure from its American occupiers during the 1940s to adopt their high-school model. This meant that nearly all children first attended a state primary school (the *Grundschule*) between the ages of six and ten, and then on the basis of teachers' reports and consultation with parents, moved on to a secondary school deemed appropriate for their talents. The *Gymnasium* creamed a small elite for a highly academic education, potentially leading on to university. The

---

[65] Danielle Boyzon-Fradet, 'The French Education System: Springboard or Obstacle to Integration? in Donald L. Horowitz and Gérard Noiriel (eds.), *Immigrants in Two Democracies: French and American Experience* (New York, NY: New York University Press, 1992), pp. 148–66 (pp. 152–5).

[66] Roy Lowe, *Education in the Post-War Years: A Social History* (London: Routledge, 1988), p. 7.

[67] OECD/UNESCO, Institute for Statistics, *Literacy Skills for the World of Tomorrow: Further Results from PISA 2000* (Paris: OECD Publishing, 2003), p. 188.

Realschule took around 40 per cent of young people from a broad range of ability, destined for a white-collar job. The third-tier *Haupschule* catered for those destined for a trade or blue-collar job, though it was outstanding for the quality of its vocational education. There were moves towards comprehensive schooling in a few of the *Länder* (states) with a *Gesamtschule*, but this merely added a new strand to the system without fundamentally changing it. Like the Austrians and the Swiss, the Germans remained committed to their highly selective system, satisfied with the results it produced.[68]

In England and Wales, the implementation of the 1944 Education Act also led to a tripartite system of education in the maintained sector. In this case, no more than 25 to 30 per cent of pupils were to go to a grammar school, after passing their 11+ exam; another group would attend a technical school (though over the following years this strand never really got off the ground); and the rest, deemed not to need much education to prepare them for their destiny in a manual occupations, would end up in a secondary modern school.[69] It was not long before the new system attracted criticism from various quarters. Psychologists cast doubts on the validity of the selection process, and especially the assumption that each individual had a relatively fixed level of intelligence that could be assessed accurately by an examination at the age of eleven. Around 10 per cent of the exam results were thought to be erroneous, and the system made no allowance for the 'educability' of children, with the possibility of an improvement in performance. Sociologists suggested that the social mobility the grammar schools were supposed to deliver, giving bright working-class children the opportunity to attend university and pursue a high-status career, was not materialising. They provided evidence that the grammar schools continued to recruit mainly from the middle classes, with children of manual workers hardly better served than in the past. Finally, many parents seethed at the implacable verdict of the 11+ exam, and the consigning of their children to what was in effect a continuation of the old elementary school. The fact that wealthy parents could continue to send their sons and daughters to the high-status 'public' (meaning private or 'independent') schools did not help. The upshot was that Local Education Authorities increasingly went over to a comprehensive school system, with a small minority retaining the old tracking system – and a determined rear-guard action

---

[68] www.german-way.com/history-and-culture/education/the-german-school-system, accessed 15 August 2016.
[69] Simon, *Education and the Social Order*, chs. 1–2.

from conservatives defending the grammar schools and presenting a dismal picture of education in the comprehensives.[70]

In contrast to the tracking system, the Nordic model adopted by Denmark, Sweden, Norway, Finland and Iceland was based on a more egalitarian approach. At its heart was a common school 'for all pupils regardless of social class, abilities, gender or ethnicity'. In Sweden, for example, in 1962 the traditional grammar and elementary schools gave way to a *Grundskolan* for children aged nine to sixteen, with mixed ability teaching after 1988, and following that the option of a *gymnasieskolan* for young people aged sixteen to eighteen. As elsewhere, this Nordic model faced criticism from neo-liberals that it was failing to produce the knowledge and skills necessary to compete on the global market.[71] We might note here that France finally had its 'school for all' during the 1960s and 1970s, as the *collège* gradually turned into a middle school for twelve- to sixteen-year-olds, with time for negotiations between parents, teachers and pupils over whether the pupil would move on to an academic or technical *lycée*.[72]

How then, as the acid test, did these various school systems fare when exposed to international comparisons? Certainly, there were a few shocks when the first PISA report appeared for the year 2000: the much-vaunted German system fared relatively poorly, while Finnish schools emerged from the shadows to dominate the rankings. This followed evidence from other sources that various Asian countries were outperforming their European counterparts in the teaching of mathematics and science. Such findings were not without controversy, the PISA scheme being described by critics as 'useless', and its attempt to rank diverse educational systems across the globe meaningless.[73] All the same, such exercises were influential in government circles and the best available at the time. What is of interest here is the way both PISA 2000, which concentrated on the reading literacy of fifteen-year-olds, and PISA 2003, focussed more on mathematics, noted the interaction between schools and the socio-economic background of their students.

Firstly, there was the evidence, all too predictable, that the family background of pupils had a significant influence on their performance in class. The PISA results showed found that children with parents who

---

[70] Roy Lowe, *Education in the Post-War Years*; idem, *Schooling and Social Change, 1964–1990* (London: Routledge, 1997); Simon, *Education and the Social Order*.

[71] Ulf Blossing, Gunn Imsen and Lejf Moos (eds.), *The Nordic Education Model: A 'School for All' Encounters Neo-Liberal Policy* (Dordrecht: Springer, 2014).

[72] Prost, *Education, société, et politiques*, passim.

[73] William Stewart, 'Is Pisa Fundamentally Flawed?', *Times Higher Educational Supplement*, 26 July 2013.

had high-status occupations, an advanced education, and 'possessions related to the classical culture' (such as literature and works of art) performed better in reading and mathematics than their less advantaged peers.[74] In 2000, among the Europeans the disparity in reading scores by parents' occupation was least in evidence in Iceland and Finland, and most marked in Switzerland and Germany.[75]

Secondly, it followed that some school systems were better at compensating for the influence of family background on student performance than others. The two Pisa reports noted that in a number of countries much of the variation in student performance could be attributed to differences between schools, rather than within schools, hence the characteristics of the school may have had an important impact. This was the case above all in Belgium and in German-speaking and East European countries, notably Germany, Hungary, Austria and Poland. The 2000 report also pointed out that these were countries that selected children from the early age of ten to twelve for different streams of education – and 'While the intention is generally to create academically rather than socially homogenous groups, selection at early grade levels as well as selection primarily based on parental choice may lead to a predominance of socio-economic criteria.'[76] The German system provides a clear example, with nearly half of the students from professional and clerical occupations attending a *Gymnasium*, compared to around one tenth from families of workers.[77]

Thirdly, the PISA data did not support the common assumption that streaming students into homogenous groups would maximise overall results. Quite the opposite, in fact: the reports concluded that 'intended or unintended differentiation between schools tends to be negatively associated with overall student performance levels.'[78] There was certainly a tendency for Germany and the eastern European countries to produce a relatively large variation in student performance combined with a low level of overall performance. At the other end of the spectrum were to be found some (though not all) of the Nordic and western European countries. To take the obvious examples once again, in 2000 both Switzerland and Germany were close to the OECD average in the proportion of their students at the highest level of reading

---

[74] OECD, PISA 2003, Executive Summary, p. 20.
[75] OECD/UNESCO, PISA 2000, Executive Summary, p. 18.
[76] OECD/UNESCO, PISA 2000, pp. 188–91, 220–21.
[77] *PISA 2000. Overview of the Study: Design, Method and Results* (Berlin: Max Planck Institute for Human Development, 2002), p. 10, at www.mpib-berlin.mpg.de/Pisa/PISA-2000_overview.pdf, accessed 15 August 2016.
[78] OECD/UNESCO, PISA 2000, pp. 189–90.

proficiency, with a little under a tenth in this category, but around a fifth of their students were either in the lowest level, or even unable to reach that. By contrast, in Finland, 23.6 per cent of students were in the highest category, and a mere 7.0 per cent performing poorly. This led to a relatively modest overall score in the literacy scale of 494 for Switzerland and 484 for Germany, compared to 546 in Finland. A similar though less striking pattern emerges when comparing Hungary with Sweden and the United Kingdom.[79] Finally, to put all this into perspective, the PISA 2000 report concludes that a successful performance for countries and schools cannot be pinned down to a single influence, rather to a variety of factors, including the resources available to schools, policies adopted by the schools, and classroom practice.

Conclusion

The late-nineteenth and twentieth centuries brought a decisive shift in the balance between work and school for the children of the masses in Europe. Henceforth work would have to fit in with the demands of the school, rather than the other way round. The deployment of large numbers of children in the factories and mines gradually came to an end, as the various economies across the continent matured from the early stages of industrialisation, and as families at all levels of society came to accept that childhood and at least part of adolescence was best set aside for education and vocational training. This was by no means a clean break, since there was always a strong current of opinion, among the elite as well as workers, that work experience from an early age was highly desirable. All the same, such experience was only acceptable if it did not interfere with the students' studies.

Yet, for all the 'democratisation' of the school systems after 1945, childhood in Europe around the year 2000 still retained its diversity according to the classic dimensions of class, gender and ethnicity. A number of countries tried to minimise the advantages inherited from parents enjoyed by those from well-off or cultured backgrounds, and maximise the opportunities for all on the job market, with a common school compulsory for several years before the inevitable separation into streams. This would occur during the late teens, for those who had not already left school, with streaming for general or a more technical education. Others were reluctant to close down elite institutions, such as the venerable *Gymnasium*, the *lycée* or the public school, with their winning

---

[79] OECD/UNESCO, PISA 2000, p. 335, table 6.1a.

combination of high academic standards and a strong social cachet. This generally meant more continuity with the past, streaming children from as early as the age of ten, and tripartite systems such as the English grammar, technical and secondary modern schools. Historians of education have tended to depict the former in a more favourable light, and to bemoan the backlash against progressive educational methods at the end of the twentieth century. Yet if the weaknesses of the very traditional German system were exposed in the year 2000, we should bear in mind that the progressive Swedish system slipped down the international rankings over the following years.

Conclusion

In the past, the experience of childhood in Europe was neither as bad as some suggest, nor as good as many others would like to believe. It is important to avoid the extremes of *misérabilisme* on the one hand and nostalgia for a world we have lost on the other. The past three centuries have brought significant changes for the young, associated with such developments as the Enlightenment, scientific advances, industrialisation and the coming of the welfare state. These could be two-edged in their impact. They undoubtedly brought a number of benefits for children, including a long-run improvement in health, indicated by a spectacular decline in infant and child mortality; a rise in living standards, evidenced by a population that was better fed, clothed and housed; serious investment in education, leading to near-universal literacy; and a greater sensitivity to children's rights, culminating in the 1989 UNCCR. Other advantages must remain more speculative, and more contestable. It is likely that in comparison with the past children were more valued by adults, enjoyed closer relationships with their parents in smaller families, and were better informed about the world around them. At the same time, there is plenty of evidence that the emergence and consolidation of an urban-industrial society took its toll on some of its youngest members. The early stages of industrialisation imposed considerable hardship on working-class families, including a heavy reliance on child labour in industry and unhealthy living conditions. Social legislation from philanthropic reformers had its advantages, but it could deprive poor children of income from work, separate them from their families for long periods of time in an institution, or seek to impose highly regimented child-rearing practices. Unparalleled affluence after 1945 was also a very positive influence, but not without its drawbacks, substituting obesity for hunger and mental disturbance for physical ailments as major sources of concern. The 'modern' childhood, largely separated from the adult world and its responsibilities in schools and the family home, had its roots deep in the past among the urban middle classes. It gradually took shape for the masses from the late nineteenth century onwards. However, it was never as sheltered from the realities of work and sexuality as the ideal suggested, nor was it even desirable for its critics.

This was the context for the great diversity of childhoods evident in modern Europe. As the continent moved further and further away from its agrarian origins during the eighteenth and nineteenth centuries, so it became an increasingly pluralistic society. The most obvious divergence, emphasised throughout this work, was between socio-occupational groups. At one extreme, there were the highly privileged children of the aristocracy and the upper reaches of the middle classes, and at the other, the offspring of the rural and urban poor. The former did not necessarily have an easy life either at home or at school, but they were spared material hardship and their high status in society was assured. The latter faced a far more hazardous path through childhood, assuming they survived their early months, with the risk of abandonment, poor health and an early start to work. Lacking property and skills, their most likely fate was a lifetime of low wages and general insecurity. In between rich and poor, (or 'bourgeoisie' and workers), there lay a considerable variety of conditions for children according to their background, ranging from the relative affluence of substantial farmers and traders, through the more modest position of clerical staff and skilled workers, to the more marginal groups of small peasant farmers and proto-industrial workers. Of course, social background only provided a framework for individuals, and some were more successful than others at making the most of the opportunities available. Children from families that were neither conspicuously rich nor poor took advantage of a combination of some schooling, vocational training, acquaintance with the values of a trade, and perhaps the prospect of inheriting some property. If all went well, it was possible for these groups to negotiate a path through childhood and youth leading to a degree of security and respectability.

Cutting across class was the pervasive influence of gender. Girls were likely to spend more time than their brothers helping with household chores, and they were long denied access to the school system and to vocational training on the same terms as boys, on the assumption that it was more important for them to prepare for motherhood and domesticity later in life. Again, there was scope for negotiating a way through such expectations for the ambitious: many girls, in the middle classes especially, were eager to acquire as much tutoring and schooling as possible, encouraged by moves afoot during the nineteenth century to raise academic standards in schools for them, with a view to activities outside the home. There were various other influences to further diversify childhoods. The schools, and the print culture that went with them, were slower to make headway in rural than in urban areas: the stock figure of the village yokel continued as a source of amusement for townsfolk well into the twentieth century. A Catholic upbringing, in Spain or France for example, was very different from a secular, republican one; a 'happy childhood' under Stalin was distinct from the ideal in a liberal democracy; and preparations for war tended to exaggerate national differences among the young.

By the late twentieth century, the various paths through childhood were largely channelled through the education system. Of course, as Maurice Crubellier warned, the influence of the schools on children was limited, insofar as they spawned time for leisure during the holidays as well as work during term time.[1] All the same, the school system played a major role in preparing the young for their future careers, in principle according to their ability, in practice also according to their gender, social background, immigrant status and so forth also. This was most in evidence where there was a tracking system, funnelling pupils from an early age (nine or ten even) into academic, technical or vocational schools. Some countries, notably the Nordic ones, proved better able to minimise the influence of parental background, rejecting selection and delaying decisions on specialisation until the mid-teen years. The very wealthy or highly educated professional groups in society were adept at placing their sons and daughters in prestigious schools that gave a huge advantage in accessing top jobs, such as a few exclusive *lycées* in France and some of the old 'public schools' such as Eton and Harrow in Britain. Under the Soviet system in Russia, it was high party officials who successfully manipulated the school system. At the other end of the social scale, children with a disadvantaged background risked ending up in a school or a stream headed for a similar manual occupation to their parents, having 'failed' in the selection or sorting process. Even in 2016, the OECD official in charge of PISA tests comparing educational performance across the world stated that in most European countries 'Schools are very, very good at selecting students by their social background, and they're not very good at selecting students by their academic potential. And the earlier you select, the worst [sic] that relationship is.'[2] Modern Europe is more diverse than in the past, but moving to a fair society through the education system continues to prove difficult.

---

[1] Maurice Crubellier, *L'Enfance et la jeunesse dans la société française, 1800–1950* (Paris: Armand Colin, 1979), pp. 301–7.

[2] Sally Weale, 'Children of immigrants more likely than others to achieve a degree', citing Andreas Schleicher, OECD director for education and skills, *The Guardian*, 16 September 2016.

Finally, reacting against the earlier tendency to leave children out of the historical record almost entirely, historians now try to give due recognition to their roles in society. In the first place, children embody the future of any country or movement. Hence there was concern in government circles for their health and education, to ensure the military strength, economic prospects and political stability of the country. This propelled politicians across Europe to support reforms in areas such as infant welfare and mass education. The young are also generally considered to be more receptive to change than adults, encouraging groups ranging from Protestant evangelists to Catholic priests, and from Communist to Fascist regimes, to target them for indoctrination. In the second place, children made an impact on the material world, supplying workers in some of the key industries for early industrialisers, and taking up a niche as consumers in an increasingly affluent society. How far they were actors in their own right is not so obvious, despite historians' efforts to depict them in this role. They were (and remain) one of the least powerful groups in European society, obliged to negotiate from a position of weakness with adults. Some of their actions were typical of the underdog, such as running away from home, fending for themselves on the streets of the big cities, playing truant or pilfering food. At the same time, they have taken the initiative in, say, organising gangs with others of a similar age, finding part-time work and spending their own money. This high profile for children's issues persists into contemporary Europe. Witness the regular feed of stories in the media on child abuse cases in the courts, child labour at home and abroad, and child poverty in the midst of plenty, child soldiers in civil wars, child obesity, child geniuses, child actors, and child crime: everything from a toxic to a happy childhood.

Select Bibliography

Abrams, Lynn. *The Orphan Country: Children of Scotland's Broken Homes from 1845 to the Present*, Edinburgh: John Donald, 1998.

Baggerman, Arianne and Dekker, Rudolf. *Child of the Enlightenment: Revolutionary Europe Reflected in a Boyhood Diary*, transl. Diane Webb, Leiden: Brill, 2009.

Bailey, Joanne. *Parenting in England, 1760–1830*, Oxford: Oxford University Press, 2012.

Ball, Alan M. *And Now My Soul Is Hardened: Abandoned Children in Soviet Russia, 1918–1930*, Berkeley, CA: University of California Press, 1994.

Barron, Hester and Siebrecht, Claudia, eds. *Parenting and the State in Britain and Europe, c. 1870–1950*, Basingstoke: Palgrave Macmillan, 2017.

Bowen, James. *A History of Western Education*, 3 vols., London: Methuen, 1981.

Brockliss, Laurence and Sheldon, Nicola. *Mass Education and the Limits of State Building, c. 1870–1930*, Basingstoke: Palgrave Macmillan, 2012.

Brown, Marilyn, ed. *Picturing Children: Constructions of Childhood between Rousseau and Freud*, Aldershot: Ashgate, 2002.

Bunge, Marcia, ed. *The Child in Christian Thought*, Grand Rapids, MI: William B. Erdmans, 2001.

Burnett, John, ed. *Destiny Obscure: Autobiographies of Childhood, Education and Family from the 1820s to the 1920s*, London: Routledge, 1994.

Corsini, Carlo and Viazzo, Pier Paolo, eds. *The Decline of Infant Mortality in Europe, 1800–1950*, Florence: UNICEF, 1993.

Cunningham, Hugh. *Children and Childhood in the West since 1500*, 2nd edn., Harlow: Pearson Longman, 2005.

Davin, Anna. *Growing Up Poor: Home, School and Street in London 1870–1914*, London: Rivers Oram Press, 1996.

de Coninck-Smith, Ning, Sandin, Bengt, and Schrumpf, Ellen. *Industrious Children: Work and Childhood in the Nordic Countries 1850–1990*, Odense: Odense University Press, 1997.

Dekker, Rudolf. *Childhood, Memory and Autobiography in Holland: From the Golden Age to Romanticism*, Basingstoke: Macmillan, 2000.

Dickinson, Edward Ross. *The Politics of German Child Welfare from the Empire to the Federal Republic*, Cambridge, MA: Harvard University Press, 1996.

Dyhouse, Carol. *Girls Growing Up in Late Victorian and Edwardian England*, London: Routledge & Kegan Paul, 1981.

Fass, Paula, ed. *Encyclopedia of Children and Childhood in History and Society*, 3 vols., New York, NY: Thomson Gale, 2003.

Fass, Paula, ed. *The Routledge History of Childhood in the Western World*, Abingdon: Routledge, 2013.

Fletcher, Anthony. *Growing Up in England: The Experience of Childhood, 1600–1914*, New Haven, CT: Yale University Press, 2008.

Foyster, Elizabeth and Marten, James, eds. *A Cultural History of Childhood and Family in the Age of Enlightenment*, Oxford: Berg, 2010.

Frost, Ginger S. *Victorian Childhoods*, London: Praeger, 2009.

Goose and Honeyman, Katrina (eds.). *Childhood and Child Labour in Industrial England: Diversity and Agency, 1750–1914*, Farnham: Ashgate, 2013.

Gorshkov, Boris B. *Russia's Factory Children: State, Society, and Law, 1800–1917*, Pittsburgh, PA: University of Pittsburgh Press, 2009.

Hawes, Joseph M. and Hiner, N. Ray, eds. *A Cultural History of Childhood and Family in the Modern Age*, Oxford: Berg, 2010.

Heywood, Colin. *Childhood in Nineteenth-Century France: Work, Health and Education among the Classes Populaires*, Cambridge: Cambridge University Press, 1988.

Heywood, Colin, ed. *A Cultural History of Childhood and Family in the Age of Empire*, Oxford: Berg, 2010.

Heywood, Colin. *Growing Up in France: From the Ancien Régime to the Third Republic*, Cambridge: Cambridge University Press, 2007.

Heywood, Colin. *A History of Childhood: Children and Childhood in the West from Medieval to Modern Times*, Cambridge: Polity, 2001.

Higonnet, Anne. *Pictures of Innocence: The History and Crisis of Ideal Childhood*, London: Thames and Hudson, 1998.

Hindman, Hugh D. (ed.). *The World of Child Labor: An Historical and Regional Survey*, Armonk, NY: M. E. Sharpe, 2009.

Honeyman, Katrina. *Child Workers in England, 1780–1820; Parish Apprentices and the Making of the Early Industrial Labour Force*, Aldershot: Ashgate, 2007.

Horn, Pamela. *The Victorian Country Child*, Stroud: Sutton Publishing, 1997.

Horrell, Sara and Humphries, Jane. '"The Exploitation of Little Children": Child Labor and the Family Economy in the Industrial Revolution', *Explorations in Economic History*, **32** (1995), 485–516.

Humphries, Jane. *Childhood and Child Labour in the British Industrial Revolution*, Cambridge: Cambridge University Press, 2010.

Immel, Andrea and Witmore, Michael, eds. *Childhood and Children's Books in Early Modern Europe, 1550–1800*, London: Routledge, 2006.

Ipsen, Carl. *Italy in the Age of Pinocchio: Children and Danger in the Liberal Era*, New York, NY: Palgrave Macmillan, 2006.

Jackson, Louise A. *Child Sexual Abuse in Victorian England*, London: Routledge, 2000.

Kelly, Catriona. *Children's World: Growing Up in Russia, 1890–1981*, New Haven, CT: Yale University Press, 2007.

Kelly, David, ed. *The German Worker: Working-Class Autobiographies from the Age of Industrialization*, Berkeley, CA: University of California Press, 1987.

Kertzer, David I. and Barbagli, Marzio, eds. *The History of the European Family*, 3 vols., New Haven, CT: Yale University Press, c. 2001–3.

Koops, Willem and Zuckerman, Michael, eds. *Beyond the Century of the Child: Cultural History and Developmental Psychology*, Philadelphia, PA: University of Pennsylvania Press, 2003.

Lavalette, Michael. *A Thing of the Past? Child Labour in Britain in the Nineteenth and Twentieth Centuries*, Liverpool: Liverpool University Press, 1999.

Levene, Alysa. *The Childhood of the Poor: Welfare in Eighteenth-Century London*, Basingstoke: Palgrave Macmillan, 2012.

Lieten, Kristoffel, and van Nederveen Meerkerk, Elise, eds. *Child Labour's Global Past, 1650–2000*, Bern: Peter Lang, 2011.

Magnússon, Sigurður Gylfi. 'From Children's Point of View: Childhood in Nineteenth-Century Iceland', *Journal of Social History*, **29** (1995), 295–323.

Martinson, Floyd M. *Growing Up in Norway, 800 to 1990*. Carbondale, IL: Southern Illinois University Press, 1992.

Maynes, Mary Jo. *Schooling for the People: Comparative Local Studies of Schooling History in France and Germany, 1750–1850*, London: Holmes & Meier, 1985.

Maynes, Mary Jo. *Schooling in Western Europe: A Social History*, Albany, NY: State University of New York, 1985.

Maynes, Mary Jo. *Taking the Hard Road: Life Course in German and French Workers' Autobiographies in the Era of Industrialization*, Chapel Hill, NC: University of North Carolina Press, 1995.

Maynes, Mary Jo, Søland Birgitte and Benninghaus, Christina, eds. *Secret Gardens, Satanic Mills: Placing Girls in European History, 1750–1960*, Bloomington, IN: Indiana University Press, 2005.

Mitterauer, Michael. *A History of Youth*, Oxford: Blackwell, 1992.

Mizen, Phillip, Pole, Christopher, and Bolton, Angela. *Hidden Hands: International Perspectives on Children's Work and Labour*, London: Routledge/ Falmer, 2001.

Olsen, Stephanie. *Juvenile Nation: Youth, Emotions and the Making of the Modern British Citizen, 1880–1914*, London: Bloomsbury, 2014.

Pollock, Linda. *Forgotten Children: Parent-Child Relations from 1500 to 1900*, Cambridge: Cambridge University Press, 1983.

Rahikainen, Marjatta. *Centuries of Child Labour: European Experiences from the Seventeenth to the Twentieth Century*, Aldershot: Ashgate, 2004.

Shore, Heather. *Artful Dodgers: Youth and Crime in Early Nineteenth-Century London*, Woodbridge: Boydell Press, 1999.

Schumann, Dirk, ed. *Raising Citizens in the Century of the Child: The United States and German Central Europe in Comparative Perspective*, New York, NY: Berghahn, 2010.

Simon, Brian. *Education and the Social Order, 1940–1990*, London: Lawrence and Wishart, 1991.

Sparrman, Anna, Sandin, Bengt and Sjöberg, Johanna. *Situating Child Consumption: Rethinking Values and Notions of Children, Childhood and Consumption*, Lund: Nordic Academic Press, 2012.

Stargardt, Nick. *Witnesses of War: Children's Lives under the Nazis*, London: Jonathan Cape, 2005.

Stearns, Peter N. *Childhood in World History*, New York, NY: Routledge, 2016.

Thomson, Mathew. *Lost Freedom: The Landscape of the Child and the British Post-War Settlement*, Oxford: Oxford University Press, 2013.

Vincent, David, *The Rise of Mass Literacy: Reading and Writing in Modern Europe*, Cambridge: Polity, 2000.

Wegs, J. Robert. *Growing Up Working Class: Continuity and Change among Viennese Youth, 1890–1938*, University Park, PA: Pennsylvania State University Press, 1989.

Weissbach, Lee Shai. *Child Labor Reform in Nineteenth-Century France: Assuring the Future Harvest*, Baton Rouge, LA: Louisiana State University Press, 1989.

Index